ACTING FOR FREEDOM

May 19, 2015
Navnit Kaur

MARIAN BOTSFORD FRASER

WITH SUKANYA PILLAY AND KENT ROACH

ACTING *for* FREEDOM

FIFTY YEARS OF CIVIL LIBERTIES IN CANADA

Second Story Press

Library and Archives Canada Cataloguing in Publication

Fraser, Marian Botsford, 1947-, author
Acting for freedom : fifty years of civil liberties in Canada /
by Marian Botsford Fraser with Sukanya Pillay and Kent Roach.

Includes index.
Published in conjunction with the Canadian Civil Liberties Association.

Issued in print and electronic formats.
ISBN 978-1-927583-49-4 (pbk.).—ISBN 978-1-927583-50-0 (epub)

1. Canadian Civil Liberties Association—History. 2. Civil rights—Canada—History. I. Roach, Kent, 1961-, author II. Pillay, Sukanya, 1966-, author III. Canadian Civil Liberties Association IV. Title.

JC599.C3F73 2014 323.0971 C2014-903519-5

C2014-903520-9

Editor: Kathryn White
Copyeditor: Kelly Jones
Managing editor: Kathryn Cole
Photo research: Allie Chenoweth
Index: Kelly Jones
Design: Melissa Kaita
Cover photo: Steve Russell/GetStock.com

Printed and bound in Canada

Second Story Press gratefully acknowledges the support of the Ontario Arts Council and the Canada Council for the Arts for our publishing program. We acknowledge the financial support of the Government of Canada through the Canada Book Fund.

ONTARIO ARTS COUNCIL
CONSEIL DES ARTS DE L'ONTARIO
50 YEARS OF ONTARIO GOVERNMENT SUPPORT OF THE ARTS
50 ANS DE SOUTIEN DU GOUVERNEMENT DE L'ONTARIO AUX ARTS

Canada Council for the Arts
Conseil des Arts du Canada

FSC www.fsc.org
MIX
Paper from responsible sources
FSC® C004071

Published by
Second Story Press
20 Maud Street, Suite 401
Toronto, ON M5V 2M5
www.secondstorypress.ca

CONTENTS

FOREWORD

Joseph Boyden

I don't think I'll ever forget a certain surprise call that came while sitting out in my backyard one afternoon a number of years ago. I didn't recognize the voice, but I certainly recognized the name of the caller when he announced it.

"Hello," he said. "This is Alan Borovoy of the Canadian Civil Liberties Association. Is this Joseph Boyden?"

"Uh, yes," I answered hesitantly, racking my brain for whose civil liberties I might have trampled lately. I'd recently told my teenage son he needed to find a part-time job. Might he have ratted me out? My wife was doing the majority of the cooking and cleaning lately as I worked hard to finish a novel. Had she finally been pushed too far? Nothing much else came to mind.

All joking aside, I certainly knew who Alan Borovoy is. He'd been leading one of our nation's most important institutions for many, many years, had been acting as general counsel for an organization that not just enriched but strengthened the fabric of our country

We talked about our work and our families and even briefly about the state of the nation before Alan got to the point of his call. "I'd like you to join the board of the CCLA," he said.

I remember my head spinning, the giddy rush of being asked to join such an amazing and special group, how overwhelmed I was by the offer. But that was only for a few moments, before the true weight of this honour began to rest upon my shoulders. Did I deserve such a thing? Would my every action, both publicly and privately, be under the microscope if I accepted board membership? What did becoming a board member even entail? I pictured being cross-examined by fellow board member Eddie Greenspan while board member Katherine Govier took judicious notes and board member David Cronenberg filmed the proceedings. But just as quickly as these fears and worries clouded my afternoon, the sun literally broke through as I stood in my backyard speaking to Alan, and I thought of my deceased father, a physician and war hero. What would he have done if offered this chance? The answer was simple: of course he would accept it.

"Of course I will accept," I blurted to Alan. "I don't know what to say except thank you for thinking of me," I offered, or something equally lame-sounding. And that was that. I was officially a board member of the Canadian Civil Liberties Association.

That's when my own work began. I knew quite a lot about CCLA already. After all, CCLA had challenged Pierre Trudeau's 1970 invocation of the *War Measures Act* during the FLQ Crisis. CCLA questioned the Canadian government's post-9/11 anti-terror measures. CCLA had always campaigned against laws on hate speech and obscenity, and had rallied against the restoration of capital punishment. Clearly, this was an organization that wasn't afraid to lose popularity contests because of the understanding that civil rights don't just apply at certain times or only to certain people but apply always and to all.

I'll admit that for a while I looked upon this new role of mine as something to be secretly cherished, to be worn as an invisible badge, but that didn't last long either. When I received my first correspondence from CCLA in the mail, I immediately noticed a quotation at the bottom of the letterhead: *The freedom of no one is safe unless the freedom of everyone is safe*. It was simple. It was straightforward, and yet it was one of the most profound sentences

I'd ever read. That was it in a gorgeous little nutshell. This wasn't about me at all. This is about all of us.

I'll admit that as a board member, I'm not very good at those pesky things called board meetings. I prefer to think of myself as a behind-the-scenes kind of operator. What I've come to accept as my responsibility is being a spokesperson for CCLA whenever the opportunity presents itself, being a conduit of sorts. I want to fight for the equal rights of my people, the First Nations of this country, as much as I want to fight for my people, the immigrants of this country.

The Canadian Civil Liberties Association turns fifty in 2014. The big 5-0. And I believe this institution has never been more necessary or more needed. With the amazing Sukanya Pillay now at the helm, our ship's course is set. And at a time when it often feels like the rights of corporations blatantly trample individual and community rights, when our LGBT communities continue to fight for equality, when our environment is under siege, when our prisons continue to overflow with non-violent offenders, and when police and government feel it is simply a part of the new order when they overreach their authority, it is up to CCLA and all of its members to not just remind the powers that be of this but to go that big step farther and work to defend the rights of the individual. After all, the freedom of no one is safe unless the freedom of everyone is safe. It's this one phrase that grounds me in these turbulent—and fascinating—times.

And so let's all join Sukanya Pillay and the rest of CCLA in celebrating the many, many accomplishments we've managed in these first fifty years as we gather together to prepare for fifty more. No doubt that the world is quickly changing. But the one constant I try to always remember is that Canada can and should always remain the global light that truly represents what a great democracy is and can be. Yes, we've indeed stumbled at times, and we will continue to sometimes stumble, but it's the members of the Canadian Civil Liberties Association who are always there, reaching out a hand as they help to pick us up and brush us off and get us back into the race again.

As a member of the Canadian Civil Liberties Association, I want to say happy fiftieth, CCLA. I've never been more proud to belong to such an important and amazing organization.

Joseph Boyden
Ahmic Lake, ON
July 2014

PREFACE

John D. McCamus

50TH ANNIVERSARY OF CCLA

Publication of this volume marks the 50th anniversary of the founding of the Canadian Civil Liberties Association in 1964. The book celebrates five decades of effective advocacy and activism in protecting the civil liberties of Canadians.

The historical context in which the establishment of the association was provoked is well described within by the volume's principal author, Marian Botsford Fraser. The precipitating event was the introduction by the government of Ontario of the notorious Bill 99, often referred to as the Ontario Police Bill, in March of 1964. Bill 99 was intended by the province as a response to the alleged threat of an increase in organized crime within the province and it proposed to confer upon the Ontario Police Commission a wide-ranging and highly provocative set of police powers that would set aside the normal constraints on the investigation of crime and the detention of suspects traditionally imposed within common law jurisdictions. The remarkable extent of these powers and the political crisis it provoked are described in greater detail by the author. Among other reactions, it inspired a Toronto lawyer, Irving Himel, who had headed the then moribund Association for Civil Liberties, together with a number of similarly progressive spirits, to form the Canadian Civil Liberties Association later that year. The founding president of the association was J. Keiller MacKay, a distinguished lawyer and judge and, indeed, a former lieutenant governor of the province of Ontario. The founders included a number of eminent or soon-to-be eminent lawyers, law professors, journalists, and clerics. Among others were three law professors from the University of Toronto Law School (Bora Laskin, eventually to become the chief justice of Canada, Mark McGuigan, a future law school dean and member of the federal cabinet, and Edward McWhinney, also an eventual federal member of provincial Parliament), Professor Harry Arthurs of Osgoode Hall Law School, later to become its dean and then president of York University, to which Osgoode Hall eventually became affiliated; journalists and writers Pierre Berton, June Callwood, and Ron Haggart; lawyers Sidney Midanik and Glen Howe, the latter well-known for his vigorous defence of the rights of Jehovah's Witnesses; the Reverend Donald Gillies, a United Church minister; and Rabbi Abraham Feinberg. Himel served as chair of the first board of directors.

Celebration of the achievements and contributions of the association is tacitly a recognition of the wisdom and foresight of the founders and of the hard work and support of the many thousands of volunteers who subsequently joined in the work of the association, whether as board members, litigation counsel representing the association, members and donors, and, of course, a succession of devoted, skillful, and drastically underpaid staff members over the ensuing decades. The financial circumstances of the association were modest in the first few years. The association was led by young lawyers providing service on a part-time basis, the first being Julian Porter, later a prominent Toronto barrister and Law Society Bencher, and the second, Sidney B. Linden, a future chief justice of the Ontario Court of Justice. It was not until the fourth year of its existence that the association was able to appoint a full-time general counsel. By the time of his appointment, A. Alan Borovoy had already distinguished himself in the field of civil liberties activism in his work at the Ontario Labour Committee for Human Rights. Borovoy brought to CCLA a strong interest in combating discrimination, in opposing religious education in the public school system, and in those particular civil liberties, such as the right of association, of particular interest to the labour movement. As the pages of this volume amply reveal, these interests and concerns, combined with other obvious objectives for civil liberties organizations, such as the protection of freedom of speech and freedom of religion, have continued to hold a place on the agenda of the association through the ensuing decades.

The growth of the association in strength and influence is, of course, the achievement of many hands, but the fact that Alan Borovoy devoted his professional life over the next four decades to building the association is a critical part of the explanation for its success. When Borovoy assumed leadership of the organization, it was a small organization, poorly funded, and with just a few hundred members struggling to get on its feet. Forty years later, the association could properly claim to be the predominant civil liberties organization in Canada, with many thousands of members and supporters and a substantial reach and influence throughout the civil liberties field.

The nature and extent of Borovoy's contribution is, of course, reflected in these pages. His personal perspective on his work is set forth in his recently published and highly entertaining memoir, *At the Barricades* (Toronto, Irwin Law, 2014). His earlier works, listed in the Endnotes, record his views on the philosophical issues underlying our civil liberties and the tactics he deployed in a career of civil liberties activism.

I first became aware of Borovoy and his prowess as a tactician when I was a teenager reading about a local incident in my hometown newspaper, the *St. Catharines Standard.* A Black family had been evicted from an Ontario Street apartment building by the landlord on the specious ground that the neighbours objected to their presence in the building. Borovoy came to the rescue and went door to door in the building, attempting to persuade the neighbours to sign a petition stating that they had no objection to a Black family living in the building. Although one neighbour maintained that he thought that renting to a Black family would "ruin the neighbourhood"—a curious claim given the neighbourhood's circumstances then and now—most signed the petition. The landlord relented and withdrew the eviction notice. I was impressed. Foolproof Borovoy stratagems for generating publicity in the anti-discrimination campaign included surveys of recruitment agencies conducted by CCLA staff posing as prospective employers. When asked if the agency was willing to discriminate against certain types of potential employees on racial grounds, invariably a majority would indicate a willingness to do so. In an all-too-recent survey, one feckless recruiter responded, "Of course, that's why people like you hire us."

Borovoy also conducted "tests" across the province, sending in two-person teams of volunteers, one Black and one white, to respond to locally advertised rental accommodations. When the Black team member first made inquiries, the accommodation was no longer available. When the white partner followed up with a subsequent inquiry, the accommodation was miraculously again on the market. It was not until I read Philip Girard's recent biography of Bora Laskin that I came to appreciate that Laskin, then a law professor and campaigning for fair accommodation legislation, had deployed the same strategy, with the co-operation of Black and white law students. The Black law student who assisted Laskin was none other than Julius Isaac, a future chief justice of the Federal Court of Canada. Such "trouble-making" by Borovoy, Laskin, and others no doubt contributed to the evolution of the multicultural and largely tolerant society of which Canadians are so proud.

Gradually, Borovoy extended the reach of the association and its advocacy beyond the borders of Ontario. Attaining some visibility for the association in Quebec posed challenges for a Toronto-based and essentially anglophone organization. Nonetheless, the association's stout (and lonely) resistance to the invocation of the *War Measures Act* in the October Crisis of 1970, chronicled within, assisted in this regard, as did the efforts of long-time board member Professor Gisèle Côté-Harper of Laval and McGill professors Patrick Healey, now a member of the Quebec Superior Court, and Frederic Bachand, a current board member. Further momentum resulted from the appointment of a bilingual daughter of Quebec as Alan Borovoy's successor as general counsel.

After Borovoy's retirement in 2009, he was succeeded by Professor and now Dean Nathalie Des Rosiers, the former president of the Law Commission of Canada and former dean of Civil Law at the University of Ottawa. Des Rosiers brought inspired leadership to the organization, building on the foundations put in place by Borovoy and strengthening the effectiveness and visibility of the organization across the country. Dean Des Rosiers recently returned to the University of Ottawa as dean of Common Law and has been succeeded by Sukanya Pillay. Pillay also has a background as a legal academic and professor at the University of Windsor Faculty of Law and a long track record of achievements in the civil liberties field. Interviews with Alan Borovoy and Nathalie Des Rosiers are contained within, and the final chapter provides Sukanya Pillay's insights into the organization's priorities and likely future developments in the area of civil liberties.

A series of distinguished Canadians have served as president of the association over the years. The first president, Keiller MacKay, was highly regarded by civil libertarians in part for his progressive decision in 1945 in *Re Drummond Wren*, a decision still read by first-year law students. The applicant owner of real property sought relief from a restrictive covenant prohibiting him from selling his property "to Jews or persons of objectionable nationality." MacKay boldly struck down the covenant on the basis that it contravened public policy. Replete with quotations from American justices Benjamin Cardozo and Oliver Wendell Holmes, Franklin Delano Roosevelt, and Winston Churchill, the decision still reads well today. Himel, together with co-counsel John Cartwright, a future chief justice of Canada, acted for the applicant. Laskin, Charles Dubin, a future chief justice of Ontario, and others provided advice behind the scenes to Himel and Cartwright.

The successor presidents to J. Keiller MacKay have included the Honourable Allan Blakeney, the former premier of Saskatchewan; Walter Pitman, the former president of Ryerson Polytechnical Institute; Harry Arthurs, mentioned above; the Honourable Walter Tarnopolsky, former law professor and justice of the

Ontario Court of Appeal; Dr. Marsha Hanen, former president of the University of Winnipeg; lawyers John Nelligan, Q.C., of Ottawa and Sidney Midanik, one of the founders of the association, and Sybil Shack, a Manitoba educator and civic leader. The Honourable Emmett Hall, former justice of the Supreme Court of Canada, served for a period of time as honourary president. In my personal experience of interacting with a series of association presidents, they have been active participants, even though often located at some distance from Toronto, in the work of the association and the deliberations of the board of directors. None has been more so than the current president, Richard Pound of Montreal, a very senior member of the Montreal Bar and, as is well-known, a former Olympian and active member of the Olympic movement.

The constituencies from which the founders of the initial board of directors were drawn—lawyers, law professors, journalists, and the clergy—continue to be well represented on the current board of directors. In the latter category, the Very Reverend Lois Wilson, the former moderator of the United Church of Canada, is a current and longstanding member of the board. Predecessors include the Roman Catholic theologian Gregory Baum. But there have been changes in board composition as well. The initial board was very Toronto-centric and male dominated. For many years now, the board membership has included substantial numbers of members from across the country, many distinguished female colleagues, and, as one would expect in contemporary Canadian society, the membership is much more ethnically diverse than the founding board. Board members have also been drawn from a broader range of constituencies having an interest in civil liberties issues.

Thus, the association's concern with freedom of expression has, of course, included an emphasis on freedom of artistic expression. An early initiative under Porter's leadership was to provide support for the Dorothy Cameron Gallery, which was, unjustly in the association's view, successfully prosecuted for a display of allegedly pornographic material. With the growth and remarkable success of the Canadian artistic community, it is gratifying that a number of Canadian artists have joined the board. The current board includes two filmmakers, David Cronenberg and Deepa Mehta, and three well-known Canadian novelists, Joseph Boyden, Katherine Govier, and Joy Kogawa.

From its early days, the association has enjoyed strong support from organized labour and continues to do so. A number of labour leaders have served on the board, including Terry Meagher of the Ontario Federation of Labour and Dennis McDermott, president of the Canadian Labour Congress, both of whom served for many years on the board. Leah Casselman, the former president of the Ontario Public Service Employees Union, currently sits on the board. The nominating committee of the board has tried to signal the bipartisan nature of its support for civil liberties by appointing politicians of all stripes, normally retired, to the board. Thus, the current board includes two former federal cabinet ministers, the Honourable Ronald Atkey, Q.C., a Conservative, and the Honourable Warren Allmand, Q.C., a Liberal, as well as the Honourable Ed Broadbent, the former leader of the federal New Democratic Party. Predecessors with strong ties to the three parties include Walter Gordon, a Liberal finance minister, Dalton Camp and Eamon Park, presidents of the Conservative and New Democratic parties respectively.

Over its five decades of existence, the association has deployed a successful litigation strategy through the efforts of volunteer counsel who have acted for the association in numerous cases at all court levels across the country. In the past year, for example, the association was actively involved in almost fifty litigation files, including cases decided, heard, decisions pending, and leave granted. Our volunteer counsel have included many of the leading lawyers of their day, such as former Supreme Court of Canada Justice Ian Binnie; the late Ian Scott, former Attorney General of Ontario; and the two John Laskins, Bora's son John I., now on the Ontario Court of Appeal, and his cousin, John B., a prominent Toronto barrister; as well as leading academics, such as Ontario Court of Appeal Justice Robert Sharpe, then dean of Law at the University of Toronto. Litigation counsel who have given of themselves so generously have also provided a strong source of board membership. Current board members who have frequently acted on behalf of the association include Frank Addario, Professor Jamie

Cameron of Osgoode Hall, Marlys Edwardh, Sydney Goldenberg, Edward L. Greenspan, Trisha Jackson, Mahmud Jamal, Andrew Lokan, Professor Kent Roach of the University of Toronto, Anil Kapoor, Jasmine Akbarali, Paul Schabas, and Kenneth Swan. Greenspan's many contributions include, remarkably, putting aside his practice for an extended period of time while campaigning across the country for the abolition of capital punishment.

Although the composition of the board has, of necessity and by design, changed greatly over time, the association, like many similar organizations, has been nourished and nurtured by stalwarts who have served as board members for many decades. Such members have provided a valuable core of stability and continuity for the general counsel of the day. Many have been mentioned above. June Callwood, a founding director, was granted an honourary life membership in recognition of her prolonged devotion to the cause. Perhaps the next longest-serving board member has been Mel Finkelstein, a Toronto accountant who supervised the association's financial matters through almost all of Borovoy's tenure and ensured needed financial stability and support for the association's activities.

Collectively, the board brings to the table an impressive range of expertise in civil liberties issues. Thus, when the federal government recently introduced contentious and highly questionable reforms to our federal electoral system, it was marvellous that both the board and the staff had access to the experience and advice of board member Jean-Pierre Kingsley, the former chief elections officer of Elections Canada. As a result of its composition, board deliberations tend to be both informed and vigorous. Elsewhere in this volume, Professor Roach provides an admirable account of the association's engagement with the Canadian Charter of Fundamental Rights and Freedoms. Borovoy remembers fondly the board debates that reflected the differences of public opinion described in Professor Roach's chapter prior to the enactment of the Charter. The leading proponents of strongly held but differing views at that time were board members Professor Donald V. Smiley, a distinguished political scientist from York University, and the Honourable Louise Arbour, then a professor of Law at Osgoode

Hall Law School and a future justice of the Supreme Court of Canada and United Nations high commissioner for human rights. It would be indiscreet to reveal the positions taken at that time by the combatants.

The contribution of hard-working staff members has been critical to the association's success, beginning with Doris Dodds, the association's first executive secretary. By way of illustration, Danielle McLaughlin has served as director of administration of the association for more than twenty-five years. Not content to simply discharge that role, Danielle also conceived and implemented the association's highly successful education program. The program is designed to assist in teaching critical thinking about civil liberties issues in the school system. It provides in-school programs for both elementary and high school students, as well as workshops for teacher-candidates in the faculties of education across Ontario, and it holds an annual conference for high school students and their teachers. A remarkable program, it annually reaches many thousands of school students, teachers, and teacher candidates, and this in the last five years has been ably expanded by the tireless efforts of our deputy director of education, April Julian. McLaughlin, having celebrated her twenty-fifth anniversary with the association, is our longest-serving staff member. Donna Gilmour, Alan's wonderful assistant for two decades, is the second. The staff complement was substantially increased under the leadership of Des Rosiers. In addition to General Counsel Pillay, the staff now includes three outstandingly dedicated lawyers: Noa Mendelsohn Aviv, Abby Deshman, and Cara Zwibel. We have recently strengthened the administrative core of the organization with the contributions of the director of administration, Rayna Zwibel, and the financial officer, Anne Lee. The contributions of these staff members and those of their colleagues and predecessors have been indispensable.

The contributions of these many individuals and the scores, indeed hundreds, of others they may be taken to represent have provided the enthusiasm, support, and energy necessary to enable the association to flourish. Giving the reader a sense of the background and identity of many, but not all, of those involved in building the association carries the risk of offence to the many others who could and, indeed, should have been mentioned. I can only ask for their understanding and forgiveness. Mentioning all of them is not feasible. Mentioning no one is a practical but unpalatable alternative.

As noted, this volume does not provide a detailed history of the association nor does it provide an extensive legal analysis of civil liberties issues. Such volumes, though worthy of course, would be principally of interest to a specialist audience. In commissioning the present work, the board of directors very much hoped that a volume could be prepared that would provide an account of the growth of Canadian civil liberties culture and of the role played by the association that would be both accessible to, and of interest to, a much broader audience. Marian Botsford Fraser has succeeded wonderfully in meeting this objective. She has masterfully portrayed, in a remarkably concise manner, the broad historical evolution of civil liberties issues in modern Canadian society and, by examining the particular preoccupations, projects, and initiatives of the association at critical moments in that history, she has provided an accurate portrayal of the association's growth from its modest beginnings to its current stature as a vigorous champion of civil liberties in contemporary Canadian society. We are all much in her debt and, as well, are indebted to the other contributors to this volume, Professor Kent Roach, Sukanya Pillay, and Joseph Boyden. On behalf of the board of directors, which I currently have the privilege of chairing, I express our appreciation for their efforts. We hope that this volume will enjoy the broad readership that it so richly deserves.

John D. McCamus
Osgoode Hall Law School, York University
Toronto, ON
July 2014

PART 1
The Foundations

INTRODUCTION
Acting for Freedom for Fifty Years

In a democracy, the majority has all the tools. It has the votes. It can do what it wants. The whole point of having legal protections for human rights and civil liberties is to use the law to constrain the abuses of the majority. So by definition you're always on the side of unpopular minorities. That's the heart of the work.

—Louise Arbour, interview, June 2013

This is the story of civil and human rights activism in Canada over the past fifty years, as seen through the prism of Canada's most prominent civil rights organization—the Canadian Civil Liberties Association, CCLA, which was founded in 1964. This book looks at the progress that we've made in Canada on some major civil and human rights concerns and at how CCLA played a seminal role in that progress. The book is not a history of the organization, but it takes as its guide CCLA's role in the narrative of our evolution as a country where fundamental rights and freedoms matter. It is addressed to curious Canadians—those who never have given a great deal of thought to statutes like the *Canadian Bill of Rights* and have forgotten or have no idea who was on whose side during the October Crisis and who only read about the workings of the Supreme Court when a big case hits the headlines. Some will read this book with a photographic memory of the events recalled here; they were members or volunteers or counsel charged with carrying CCLA's position into a Court of Appeal or the Supreme Court. Younger people might have only recently had their spirits raised, by a G20 demonstration, perhaps, or an Idle No More hashtag. The thing about civil liberties is that they are so simple and basic that we just take them for granted until they are taken away.

As with any complex endeavour, civil and human rights activism is both haunted and driven by the past. One could take as a beginning point in the larger history of Canada's engagement with fundamental freedoms the *War Measures Act*, put into place by the government of Canada in 1914. The purpose of a war measures act in any democracy is to define the extraordinary measures that a nation might take against its own citizens in the case of the most extreme peril and emergency—war. The most basic freedoms are suppressed—freedom of speech, movement, assembly, and association. (In some countries, the equivalent of a war measures act is imposed during a period of conflict and never removed. So a war measures act is a useful symbol of the battle between governments and citizens over the civil liberties prize.)

A war measures act deprives people of their fundamental freedoms as a kind of vaccine, imposing a cessation of the rules and conventions of democracy in the name of "security, defence, peace, order, and welfare," as with the Canadian *War Measures Act.* A war measures act takes away the rights enshrined in the constitutions of democracies, and the invocation of a war measures act is often the act that causes a citizenry to realize how fragile those freedoms are, and how easy it is to take them for granted. In Canada, whenever the *War Measures Act* is invoked—or its modern-day equivalent, an *Emergencies Act* enabling anti-terrorism legislation—civil liberties activism is sparked.

For the purposes of this discussion, it can be argued that civil rights activism was awakened in Canada during the First World War, and then at the end of the war during the Winnipeg General Strike, and then again in the thirties, and in 1939, when the *War Measures Act* was not only called up at the beginning of the war, but immediately after the war, to take away the rights of Japanese-Canadians. Activist groups formed and then disbanded; individuals came together and then drifted apart—because most activists are not professional activists; they are people in all walks of life who get angry or upset about something they see or read about. Activist organizations (which are very different from professional associations and unions) are a peculiar aspic made up of elected boards and prestigious honourary presidents, endlessly cheerful and devoted volunteers, and underpaid workers who are also cheerful and devoted and, it must be said, whose numbers are overwhelmingly dominated by women, at least until very recently.

Between big public campaigns that play out in rallies and vigils and the media, the fight for civil liberties becomes a chain of much smaller wars about small injustices. One pattern you see over and over again in the history of CCLA is how a small indignity against one person, in one town, becomes the spark for social change and a change in the law. Must a schoolgirl be forced to choose between learning Christian dogma or leaving the classroom? Is a Sikh boy allowed to carry his kirpan on his person during school hours? Why can't a Jamaican man find a place to stay in a city full of rooming houses? Should a man be jailed for shouting at a visiting politician? Why should a woman on welfare have to hide a male visitor in her closet?

Sometimes such indignities can be resolved by an op-ed in the newspaper, a visit by a famous writer to a politician, a speech. In many other cases, asking the simple question demands a commitment over decades to find an answer.

Occasionally achieving swift justice is the satisfying side of civil rights activism. But the flip side is not so comforting, and that is the pattern of what might be termed chronic recidivism. The history of CCLA and of fundamental freedoms in Canada is simply this: what goes around comes around. Just when you think the problem is solved, the law fixed, the story over, the same injustice rears up again in a new and unexpected form. The arbitrary powers demanded by a police commission in 1964 are alarmingly similar to the arbitrary actions taken by police in 2010. The language of a proposed bill to give police more powers in 1964 is exactly the same as the powers given to a commission in 1946. Wiretapping (meaning the bugging of rotary telephones) and the steaming open of letters stolen from mailboxes appeared to be nicely under control in 1974; yet in 2014, the government's cavalier assumption of all kinds of powers of electronic surveillance is breathtaking. And the claim is always that it's being done by police for the public good.

One century after the first *War Measures Act* in Canada, attention still must be paid to the threats to democracy. Governments are still looking for ways to take away rights and curtail liberties.

A third caveat about civil rights work is that very often, as Louise Arbour points out in the epigraph that opens this chapter, you are on the side of unpopular minorities; this means defending unpopular causes and unpleasant people. Very often what is overwhelmingly perceived as right and good is not that simple. In the rush to create a new good, a forgotten evil sometimes lurks. That is the piece to which civil rights activists must pay attention. And as Arbour has also said, the real courage is not to take on your enemies; the real courage is to take on your friends.

• • •

CCLA came into the civil liberties fray fifty years ago, in 1964, because a provincial government suddenly wanted to change the rules of arrest and imprisonment. It was actually the rebirth of an older, then-dormant, organization. What began as a question about whether or not Ontario would become a police state has grown into five decades of asking hard questions and not taking no for an answer. That first question was asked with reference to the only defence against a violation of individual freedoms that Canadians had at that time—the well-intentioned but feeble Bill of Rights, which had come into being in 1960.

Over the subsequent five decades, key moments in the timeline of civil liberties in Canada are these: the Bill of Rights (1960); October Crisis/*War Measures Act* in peacetime (1970); the birth of *The Charter of Rights and Freedoms* (1980); Supreme Court rulings on hate speech and pornography (1990); 9/11 (2000 to 2001); the G20 (2010).

Within that simple timeline, however, a complex narrative unfolds. One of the realities of being part of a small organization dedicated to a cause is that the story can change every single day, and the stories overlap and run into each other, and everything stops for a major and unexpected event that quite often then changes the game completely. Anyone with any history at all with CCLA will tell you about one favourite case or campaign or an audacious position taken by the organization. And these are rarely the same story.

Most of the signature campaigns of CCLA, and the major civil rights stories over the past fifty years, are not contained by a single decade. Many of the most important civil rights battles start small and get big: the boy with the kirpan in a Quebec schoolyard ends up in the Supreme Court of Canada; because of the complaint of a ten-year-old schoolgirl with nightmares about going to hell because she is not a Christian, religious instruction is banished from the curriculum of Ontario schools four years later. Or a complicated issue takes the form of numerous court cases emerging at different times in several provinces, and then they all end up in the Supreme Court at the same time, as in the instance of hate speech in the early 1990s.

This book does not document every single case and issue that CCLA has spoken about or been involved in. Instead, emblematic issues, cases, and stories have been chosen. Over the past fifty years, CCLA has engaged in myriad discrete battles—parade permits in the 1960s, Royal Canadian Mounted Police (RCMP) barn-burnings in the seventies, bathhouse raids and police oversight in the eighties, the public funding of religious schools and strip searches in the nineties, anti-terrorism legislation and drug dogs in schools in the 2000s, gay-straight alliances in schools, a North America security perimeter, and privacy and surveillance in this current decade. CCLA has stood on street corners, organized parades, set up tables in public squares. Far from the courtrooms, CCLA has had since the very beginning an energetic education program in schools and libraries. For the most part, this book does not tell the stories of the quiet actions of dedicated individuals, of which there have been thousands.

Instead, we have first looked at the foundations of civil liberties activism in Canada—the first *War Measures Act*, the Bill of Rights, the second *War Measures Act*, and the *Charter of Rights and Freedoms*. In the second part of the book, we have chosen to focus on five major issues that exemplify both the work of CCLA and the important civil rights issues that Canadians have tackled over the past fifty years. These issues illustrate various challenges to rights and freedoms—especially in terms of how these issues are handled in the courts, where the frame of reference is very specific and the language is very different from that used by citizens outside of the courtroom. And for several reasons, the issues illuminate and affect one another, so there is some overlap in their treatment in the chapters that follow.

Part One: The Foundations: The first chapter describes the beginnings of CCLA and the civil liberties back story, notably the creation of the Bill of Rights in 1960 and our country's record over the next twenty years in defending and supporting the freedoms it laid out. It became increasingly obvious that stronger measures were needed, a situation that dovetailed smoothly with the ambitions of Pierre Elliott Trudeau to repatriate the Constitution and create a Charter.

The fulcrum on which the evolution of civil rights rests, over the past fifty years, is the creation of the *Charter of Rights and Freedoms*, almost halfway through those five decades. The Charter was transformational. Its first two apparently simple sentences have created an endlessly rich dialogue about freedom and constraint, which has gone on for more than thirty years. In its entirety, the Charter is a theatre in which vitally important issues and extremely subtle and complex ideas affecting the daily lives of Canadians are played out. So we've asked the distinguished law professor Kent Roach, one of Canada's great experts on the Charter, and CCLA counsel in a number of important cases, to tell the story of the Charter, how and why it came into being, the controversies that it has sparked, and why it is so significant.

In its fifty-year history, CCLA has benefited from the dedication and support of hundreds of Canadians as board members and volunteers and staff. But remarkably, it has only been led by three people. A. Alan Borovoy was general counsel of CCLA for forty years and unquestionably became the voice to be reckoned with on civil liberties in Canada. He was succeeded in 2009 by Nathalie Des Rosiers; interviews with both of them appear at the end of Part One of the book.

Part Two: The Issues: There were many to choose from. These five illustrate varied aspects of CCLA's work and the range of challenges to the fundamental freedoms of the citizens living in a democracy. The abortion story unravelled in Canada over almost twenty years, between 1969 and 1988, when the book was closed, it seemed then, for good. The issue of obscenity and pornography spanned four decades and played out in cinemas and bookstores and art galleries, pitting artists against bureaucrats, and feminists against other feminists. Before and during the Second World War, Canadians became conscious of the unsavoury spectre of hate speech, and since then it has proven one of the most difficult challenges for defenders of free speech.

One of the fundamental freedoms that has informed CCLA's work almost without pause over the past fifty years is the issue of national security and police powers. Here the tension is between public security and private lives. In Chapter Six, Sukanya Pillay, CCLA's new executive director and general counsel, and an expert on national security, looks at the uncomfortable relationship between Canadians and their various police forces, security agencies, and governments.

And in the chapter entitled The Dispossessed: Rights of the Accused/Rights of the Imprisoned, we look at two of the fundamental issues of justice—capital punishment and the right to a fair trial—and profile a number of individual Canadians whose stories are forever linked to the manner in which they were shamefully treated by authorities.

Sukanya Pillay is only the third executive director and general counsel of CCLA. She ends the book by reflecting on the recent work of CCLA and identifying the most significant questions facing civil liberties activists today and in the future.

CHAPTER ONE
Building Foundations Over Twenty Years: From the Bill of Rights to the Charter

The civil liberties and fundamental freedoms bestowed by a democracy are easily taken for granted until those rights and freedoms are endangered. In democracies and repressive regimes alike, the pattern is the same: freedoms are imperilled when a government—in the name of protecting its citizens from some perceived threat by a specific group, labelled as enemy aliens or criminals or terrorists—creates a law that overrides the rights of everyone in its jurisdiction. When that happens, citizens try to address the imbalance by protesting, by challenging the law in the courts, and by looking for protective measures, such as a bill of rights.

This pattern can be traced nationally in Canada from the creation of the *War Measures Act (WMA)* in 1914, through its deployment three times between 1914 and 1970. It can be seen provincially, for example, in the attempt by the Ontario government in the mid-1960s to radically change the rules for police custody and questioning. It can be seen whenever the rights of an individual—a single mother on welfare, a student protester—or a group—such as Japanese-Canadians or Aboriginals or the patrons of a bar on a Saturday night—are violated by the actions of a government or a bureaucrat or a law enforcement agency.

In this narrative, there are recurring threads: it is always the position of governments that proposed aggressive measures would only be used against villains. It is regularly the role of civil liberties activists like CCLA to defend a marginalized (even unpalatable) group or an arcane principle in the face of formidable vested interest and/or popular sentiment. And curiously, the language of repressive measures is constant, no matter what the context—a revision of the *Criminal Code* in 1919 to deal with Communists, "minor adjustments" to a *Police Act* in the 1960s to enable better confessions from gang members, or an edict in 1970 to deal with "apprehended" insurrection.

CCLA was formed in 1964 in response to the potential abuse of police powers in Ontario. But its roots were in the uncertainty and unrest of the thirties, forties, and fifties. And everything in that period leads to the creation of the Bill of Rights in 1960, which in turn sets the stage for the repatriation of the Constitution and the creation of the *Charter of Rights and Freedoms* in 1982—after everything comes to a head during the October Crisis in 1970.

POLICE VERSUS CCLA (1964)—THE FIRST BATTLE

> "For the public good," the Ontario Government has taken an axe to the fundamental rights and liberties of this province's people. "For the public good," it proposes to trample upon Magna Carta, Habeas Corpus, the *Canadian Bill of Rights*, and the Rule of Law. The legislation...empowers the Ontario Police Commission to summon any person for questioning in secret, to deprive him of legal advice, and to keep him in prison indefinitely if he refuses to answer questions.
>
> Are we in Ontario—or are we in Ghana? In the Canada of 1964—or in the Germany of 1934?
>
> This legislation is supposed to be directed against organized crime. In fact, it is directed against every man and woman in this province. Attorney General Frederick M. Cass says of it: "The rights of a few individuals may have to be overridden for the public good." These rights, which belong to every individual, ARE the public good. Overridden for one man, they are overridden for all. Where, then, is "the public good"?

> ...This legislation could make Ontario a police state. It would give the Ontario Police Commission powers comparable with those of the OGPU [an early version of the KGB] or the Gestapo.
>
> —Editorial, *The Globe and Mail*, March 20, 1964

In March 1964, the government of Ontario threw down a gauntlet before its citizens. The Attorney General in the Progressive Conservative government of John Robarts, lawyer Frederick M. Cass, introduced Bill 99 to his caucus colleagues as a modest piece of housekeeping. In fact, Bill 99 was a piece of legislation that, in the name of addressing the burgeoning problem of organized crime (an anxiety fanned by the Liberals in the recent election) undermined the civil liberties of all citizens of Ontario.

Bill 99 was the Attorney General's response to a 220-page Ontario Police Commission (OPC) report on organized crime in Ontario, released the day before Bill 99 was introduced in the legislature. The report, written by Judge Bruce J.S. Macdonald, the recently retired first chair of the OPC, revealed that organized crime syndicates had apparently failed to take hold in Ontario to the extent predicted by politicians and law enforcement agencies. The OPC was not content with this assessment of the situation and felt it needed additional powers in order to force informers and criminals to give up more information. Judge Macdonald's report proposed that the OPC be given the authority to suspend civil liberties in the pursuit of information from informers and criminals. The OPC should have the power to investigate crime, law enforcement, and other matters, such as hate literature.

The report also recommended that all police forces in the province be regulated by the OPC, including the Ontario Provincial Police, which was not under OPC control. It contained numerous recommendations that have since become commonplace in most jurisdictions in Canada: photographs on drivers' licences, firearms registration, the use of wiretapping, and some oddities, such as the prosecution of radio and TV stations that broadcast horse-racing results.

The "necessary" new powers were spelled out in Bill 99 as

changes to section 14 of the *Police Act*, and they were radical. They included the power to apprehend individuals and keep them in custody for questioning, without legal counsel. If the person summoned refused to answer questions to the satisfaction of the commission, the OPC could "by warrant, commit the person to prison for a period not exceeding eight clear days" without any possibility of bail or appeal. If the individual still was uncooperative, a second eight-day sentence could be imposed, and further, the OPC "may commit the person to prison from time to time until the person consents to do what is required of him." And if detainees revealed any information about these proceedings, they could be ordered to pay a $2,000 fine and to spend an additional year in prison.

The draconian overhaul of the *Police Act* was justified by the OPC as necessary in order to deal with organized crime, and as such, it was insisted, would only be applicable to a small number of individuals (mostly criminals). But it was immediately clear to a wide range of interested parties that rewriting the *Police Act* to entrench these provisions would make them applicable to everyone in Ontario. The Attorney General himself was oddly ambivalent about his legislation; after tabling Bill 99 in the legislature, he immediately declared in a press conference that "it's drastic and it's dangerous and it's new and it's terrible legislation in an English common-law country." But he went on to defend the changes as a necessary means to fight the "invisible tyranny of syndicated crime."

Public outcry was instant, as was the response of MPPs of all parties; it appeared that although Bill 99 had been in draft form for a number of weeks before being tabled in the legislature, it had not actually been read by anyone on the government side, including Premier Robarts. Churches, labour groups, the Voice of Women, and eminent jurists made statements; students marched on Queen's Park.

One of those who spoke bluntly was Irving Himel, secretary of the then-dormant organization known as the Association for Civil Liberties: "The proposed amendments would introduce an alien spirit of McCarthyism into our province," Himel said, and would "literally turn Ontario into a police state."

In 1964, the Association for Civil Liberties was an organization in name only and the rights to the name were held by Himel, a Toronto lawyer who had been active on discrimination issues since the late 1940s, especially those concerning employment and real estate. (One of Himel's noted achievements was his collaboration, in 1947, with Chinese lawyer Kew Dock Yip in pushing for repeal of the *Chinese Immigration Act*, known as the Chinese Exclusion Act.)

But like many citizens of Ontario, Himel was stirred to action by Bill 99. He told *The Globe and Mail* on March 21, 1964, that the proposed legislation violated six fundamental freedoms—the right to not incriminate oneself, the right to privacy, the right to counsel, the right to public hearings when one's freedom is jeopardized, the right to freedom of expression, and the right to not make a statement to police. He added, "I think now is the right moment for Ontario to indicate its belief in the fundamental freedoms and basic human rights and introduce a bill complementing the federal Bill of Rights.... This will restore the confidence of the people in the basic rights, which they expect the legislature to uphold."

Canada's Bill of Rights had been enacted only four years previous, in 1960, by the Progressive Conservative government of John Diefenbaker, who had been pushing indefatigably for such a bill for almost thirty years. It was, in a sense, Canada's somewhat belated response to the United Nations Declaration of Human Rights (UNDHR), which had come into being in 1948, and which the Liberal Canadian government of the day had not supported wholeheartedly, to say the least.

CANADA'S BILL OF RIGHTS—GREAT CHARTER OR WEAPON OF REPRESSION?

> The Parliament of Canada, affirming that the Canadian Nation is founded upon principles that acknowledge the supremacy of God, the dignity and worth of the human person and the position of the family in a society of free men and free institutions;
>
> Affirming also that men and institutions remain free only when freedom is founded upon respect for moral and spiritual values and the rule of law;

> And being desirous of enshrining these principles and the human rights and fundamental freedoms derived from them, in a Bill of Rights which shall reflect the respect of Parliament for its constitutional authority and which shall ensure the protection of these rights and freedoms in Canada…
>
> —From the Preamble to the Bill of Rights, 1960

Many Canadians, over many years and for a variety of reasons, pushed Canada slowly and indirectly towards the imperfect, frail, and surprisingly terse statute (only five numbered points) called the Bill of Rights. Over the half-century between passing the *War Measures Act* in 1914 and passing the Bill of Rights in 1960, Canadians experienced two wars, long stretches of economic instability, and unsettling ideological clashes between employers and workers on the right to collective bargaining. These events served to create a burgeoning awareness across the country of entrenched systemic biases rooted in religious and class discrimination and racism. In his book *Canada's Rights Revolution*, historian Dominique Clément traces the myriad organizations and individuals who, from the 1930s onwards, struggled to achieve fairness and equality in Canadian laws, both federal and provincial.[1]

In the mid-twentieth century, ours was a society of deeply imbedded prejudicial ideas and practices and, at the same time, a society with unwavering respect for and trust in our own laws and institutions, all derived from English common law and the British parliamentary systems—so much so that there was great resistance in Canada to any challenges to those institutions. Progress in the realm of individual rights was incremental and erratic. The concept of individual civil and human rights was a direct challenge to the doctrine of parliamentary supremacy, which was implicit in Canada's system of parliamentary democracy until fundamentally altered in 1982 by the creation of the *Charter of Rights and Freedoms.*

Small organizations formed in opposition to the powerful status quo, in the face of unfair labour practices, an anti-immigrant bias (against anyone who was non-white, non-Christian, and "radical," a euphemism for Communist), and countless small indignities visited upon minority groups and individuals. Some organizations—the Canadian Labour Congress, the Canadian Jewish Congress, the Canadian Bar Association—formed, merged, renamed themselves, and evolved over many years into large, powerful, and sometimes contradictory voices and well-funded lobbying forces. Other small groups came together and collaborated in response to a particular situation and then disbanded or lapsed into inactivity until another insult presented itself. [2]

Fear of communism informed or was used to justify much of public policy concerning civil liberties from 1919 onwards because of the Winnipeg General Strike. On May 15, 1919, more than thirty thousand workers, including police and firefighters, went on strike for six weeks, bringing Winnipeg to a standstill and setting off labour unrest elsewhere in the country. The strike revealed for the first time the inherent power of organized labour in Canada, where the concept of collective bargaining was considered revolutionary and condemned as bolshevism of the worst kind. The government of Canada (under Prime Minister Robert Borden) responded immediately to the fear of "alien scum" by creating new provisions in the *Criminal Code*, section 98, which criminalized members and officers of any "unlawful" organization and set out severe punishments—imprisonment for up to twenty years and seizure without warrant of property.

The poet, scholar, and co-founder of the Co-operative Commonwealth Federation (CCF), Frank Scott, writing in 1932, rained contempt on the "now notorious" section 98, "which for permanent restriction of the rights of association, freedom of discussion, printing and distribution of literature, and for severity of punishment, is unequalled in the history of Canada and probably any British country for centuries past." Scott laid out the stringencies of section 98 that were directed cryptically against:

> any association whose purpose is to bring about governmental or economic change within Canada by the use of force, violence or injury to person or property...any person who prints, publishes, circulates or sells any literature which advocates the use of force...or who mails such literature

> in Canada, or who imports it by any means (whether or not he is aware of its contents) is liable to twenty years [in prison].... Finally, it is the duty of every Dominion civil servant, in any position, to seize such literature and send it to Ottawa where the Commissioner of the Royal Canadian Mounted Police will make up his mind as to whether Canadians should read it.[3]

Section 98 was used in 1931 in a trial in which the Communist Party of Canada was declared illegal, and as a result hundreds of people were deported, some to countries wherein they would face imprisonment, torture, or execution for being Communists. Scott also noted that Canada was the only country that "claims to be a democracy" to join a handful of countries—Italy, Japan, Poland, and "some of the more reactionary Balkan states"—in outlawing the Communist Party.

Mackenzie King finally revoked section 98 when the Liberal Party regained power in 1935, having failed to revoke it in earlier attempts because the move was blocked by the Senate. But immediately, Quebec's premier, Union Nationale leader Maurice Duplessis, responded with the *Padlock Act*—an *Act to Protect the Province against Communist Propaganda.* This heavy-handed statute (in effect until 1957, when it was declared unconstitutional by the Supreme Court of Canada) criminalized all forms of publications and premises supporting bolshevism and communism. It provoked the ire of civil liberties activists across the country and resulted in the creation of several new activist organizations. However, as Clément notes, possibilities for co-ordinated action in these years were frequently undermined by political divisions; fear of communism infected many groups that prohibited members of the Communist Party from joining.

And in wartime, patriotism trumped skepticism.

During both world wars, the government of Canada invoked the 1914 *War Measures Act* and instigated punitive action against entire national groups, labelling the Ukrainians in World War I and the Japanese in World War II as "enemy aliens." The government seized assets and placed thousands of people, many of them born in Canada, into what were actually called concentration camps at the time. These internments and the wholesale evacuation in 1942 of Japanese fishing communities from the West Coast of Canada appear to have been widely tolerated or ignored by Canadians at the time. (The treatment of Japanese-Canadians was enabled by a pervasive anti-Orientalism in British Columbia, where most Japanese settled initially. At the end of the war, a *Vancouver Sun* editorial declared: "What British Columbians want to know is whether the Japs can be sent out of the country and kept out.")[4]

The government's post-war proposal to "repatriate" to Japan more than ten thousand Japanese-Canadians—three-quarters of whom were Canadian citizens and half of whom were born in Canada—finally generated a widespread collaborative backlash among civil libertarians, whose critique of the earlier internment policies had been negligible. They were joined by a wide range of church groups, the CCF, and the media; a coalition was formed, which mounted a formal legal challenge. But the repatriation proposal was confirmed as perfectly legal, first by Canada's Supreme Court and second by the Judicial Committee of the Privy Council in the United Kingdom (until 1949, the Privy Council was the final arbiter on civil legal issues for Canada). The extradition plan was dropped by Mackenzie King in 1947, but not before thousands of people had been deported.

In September 1945, immediately after the end of the Second World War, the fragile equilibrium of the West was disrupted by the defection in Ottawa of Igor Gouzenko, a Soviet cipher clerk whose revelations about the extent of Soviet spying in all Western states—at first not even believed by the Royal Canadian Mounted Police (RCMP)—have come to be characterized as the beginning of the Cold War. In October, the Cabinet of the government of Canada passed a secret order-in-council (PC6444)—effectively extending the provisions of the *WMA* in peacetime—that permitted the secret incarceration and interrogation of any person suspected of being "an agent of a foreign power." This licence was further extended in February 1946 by the establishment of a Royal Commission on espionage. The sessions of this body, called the Kellock-Taschereau Commission, were held in camera, and testimony thus acquired was then used to prosecute suspects.

Clément writes that the "proceedings of the 1946 espionage commission rank alongside the October Crisis of 1970 as the most extensive abuse of individual rights in Canadian history in peacetime." Interestingly, the creation of a Royal Commission was, secretly, strongly recommended to the government by the head of the Canadian Bar Association as the only way to go in order to avoid due process. But civil liberties groups in numerous Canadian cities responded forcefully when the work of the commission became known; several new groups were formed, and according to Clément, this was one of the few occasions when Communist and non-Communist groups did work together, lobbying politicians, publishing reports, and placing advertisements in newspapers. Generally, in what was a climate of virtuous chauvinism, advocates of Communism were prevented from joining most labour associations and civil- and human-rights organizations.

These flare-ups of outrage by small citizen groups and a general sense that the recently ended war must not have been fought in vain encouraged political parties that were not in power to campaign for a Canadian bill of rights. Parties other than the Liberals were not threatened by notions that the rights of individuals would challenge the doctrine of "parliamentary supremacy." This view of democracy served the reigning Liberals well—from 1921, they formed majority governments for thirty-six years (with only one significant interruption), and under Mackenzie King consistently opposed moves to codify civil liberties in laws. Clément observes that for the CCF, first in Saskatchewan, and for Progressive Conservatives like Diefenbaker, "a bill of rights was an attractive solution to the potential abuses arising from the exercise of virtually unfettered executive power."

The Western provinces were especially interested in bills of rights. In 1946, Alberta passed a Bill of Rights that was declared invalid by the Privy Council because it concerned itself with banking, a matter under federal jurisdiction. In 1947, Manitoba failed to pass a proposed Bill of Rights, but Saskatchewan did so successfully that same year. For John Diefenbaker, a sense of injustice and the arbitrary powers of government was formulated as early as 1936, when he was a lawyer in Saskatchewan, and he started drafting a bill of rights, moved, it is said, by the evidence of systemic discrimination against non-white Canadians. On the Diefenbaker Canada Centre website, Diefenbaker, an irrepressible orator, is quoted, with implicit reference to his own ethnic origins and life in small-town Western Canada, as deploring "what it has meant in the past for some to regard those with names other than British and French origin as not being quite that kind of Canadian that those of British or French origin could claim to be."

In 1948, the Universal Declaration of Human Rights (UDHR) was adopted by the United Nations General Assembly and became the standard against which the human and civil rights values of all nations were measured. Although the UDHR was drafted largely by Canadian John Humphrey, working for the United Nations, Canada's response to the declaration as it worked its way through the UN adoption process was as convoluted and tortuous as could be imagined. Mackenzie King was prime minister; Lester Pearson the minister representing Canada at the UN. Byzantine strategizing (attempts to delay, fussing about federal/provincial jurisdictional concerns) obscured the ambivalence of the Liberal Party; acting Prime Minister Louis St. Laurent wrote in a memo that he was "particularly concerned about the uses which could be made of the text of articles 17, 18, 19 and 22 [freedom of speech, freedom of association, freedom of assembly, and the right to employment in the public service] as an undertaking not to discriminate against Communists because of their political views." Other members of Cabinet expressed concerns that the declaration "would permit the unrestricted activities of sects like Jehovah's Witnesses."[5]

Canada abstained from support of the UDHR initially, along with regimes like the USSR, Saudi Arabia, and South Africa, but supported the declaration in the final vote. This was an embarrassing moment (still referenced) in Canadian diplomacy, which set the stage for the demands from other political parties and activist groups including CCLA's predecessor, the Civil Liberties Association of Toronto, for a Canadian bill of rights. As constitutional expert, Frank R. Scott wrote in a 1949 essay, noting the Canadian government's apparent indifference to the fundamental freedoms of Canadians:

> We live under a constitution that permits the deportation of citizens born in Canada; under which persons have been denied the vote solely on grounds of race; that, in Quebec, enables an administration official to padlock a man's house for propagating Communism before he has been found guilty in a court of law and, in Prince Edward Island, has forbidden trade unions to affiliate with any bodies outside their province.... Grave doubt has been cast on the power of Parliament to legislate effectively in regards to human rights and fundamental freedoms.

Twelve years later, when Diefenbaker's Progressive Conservatives were in power, the Bill of Rights was proposed in the House of Commons, and after vigorous debate and strategic delays (twenty-four amendments were proposed by the opposition), it was passed unanimously on August 4, 1960.

John Diefenbaker spoke of the Bill of Rights as "an altar of freedom that will ensure that the minority will not be unjustly treated by the majority.... It will make individual Canadians strong in the knowledge that, under law, the State shall not interfere unjustly with the person." The Bill of Rights was invoked in courtrooms across the country within days of taking effect, and yet, simultaneously, the critique of its strength and effectiveness was articulated. It did not apply to any areas of provincial jurisdiction. As a statute, it had no more authority than any other act of Parliament and so could be repealed at any time. Diefenbaker had reluctantly acceded to the proviso insisted upon by the Liberals that the Bill of Rights did not apply to the *War Measures Act*.

A *Globe and Mail* editorial commented on August 6, 1960: "A Bill of Rights with so many loopholes, with such restricted authority, is hardly the sort of charter, of grand concept and design, for which Mr. Diefenbaker has been striving all these years. Such a charter can only take the form of an amendment to the constitution, the *British North America Act*."

Over the next two decades, the Bill of Rights indeed proved feeble as an instrument for protecting the civil liberties of individuals. But for activists in Canada in the 1960s, it provided at least a starting point and a frame of reference for the actions of governments, like that attempted by the Ontario government in 1964 with its infamous Bill 99.

THE SIXTIES—PROSPERITY, REVOLUTION, AND CIVIL LIBERTIES

The 1960s was a decade of unparalleled change in Canada, certainly by standards of preceding decades, and perhaps still a benchmark for comparison. There was, on one hand, a string of events that symbolized the beginnings of a clearly modern Canadian identity, one that shrugged off the cloak of British imperialism and deference. In 1964, we made a brand-new flag; in 1967, we mounted Expo 67, a glittering international fair; in 1968, we elected a sophisticated, charismatic prime minister. We had our own celebrated cerebral prophet, Marshall McLuhan; a hugely influential economist, John Kenneth Galbraith; and a famously eccentric and brilliant musician in Glenn Gould, who gave his last public concert in 1964. Canada was prosperous; Medicare became universal; the AutoPact was the first milestone on the long highway to free trade. We were to become, in the vision of Trudeau, the Just Society.

It was a decade during which Canada attempted to set its own course internationally, in the face of complex pressures like the Cold War, which set off deep disruptions in Asia (over the long, dark course of the Vietnam War) and in Cuba (with the Cuban Missile Crisis in 1962). There was also the Space Race and the arms race—that prolonged and terrifying chess game played with nuclear weapons mostly by the United States, Russia, and China. The dismantling of colonization in Africa and the rise of apartheid in South Africa both happened in the 1960s.

Canada was affected like a sibling by events in the United States—the assassinations of President John F. Kennedy in 1963 and Martin Luther King and Robert Kennedy in 1968; the protests against the Vietnam War, which brought draft dodgers and deserters into Canada; the civil rights uprisings against segregation, disenfranchisement, and employment inequality; and the first stirrings of the women's liberation movement towards the end of the decade. All of these movements resonated in Canada where there were parallel formations of large student groups and organized labour protest movements; there were love-ins, communes, collectives, and co-ops; a nascent Red Power movement; and mass protests, sit-ins, and parades against nuclear armament and poverty in Canada and the war in Vietnam. Politically, the ground shifted in Canada in the 1960s, the relative stasis of the two old parties jolted by the formation of the New Democratic Party (NDP) in 1961 and by the beginnings of the Quiet Revolution in Quebec in 1960, which by 1963 had its own undertow of anarchy, the Front de libération du Québec (FLQ).[6]

In 1964, the politicians of Ontario were apparently more worried about the hidden tentacles of organized crime than public expressions of social unrest. However, the government of Ontario's attempt to radically revise the province's administration of the *Criminal Code* with the blunt instrument of Bill 99 (which seemed to draw directly upon the 1945 Espionage Commission's playbook for inspiration) was a spectacular but mercifully brief fiasco for the Robarts government. Robarts's own members spoke against the legislation. Attorney General Cass fanned the controversy with remarks like the following: "The rights of a few individuals may have to be overridden for the public good.... The right of counsel is not necessarily part of the due process of law." Within four days, after various attempts by Premier Robarts to send the bill to committee, a motion from the opposition was supported by the government, the offending portions of Bill 99 that referred to section 14 of the police code were withdrawn, and Attorney General Cass had resigned.

Two months later, Robarts created a Royal Commission on Civil Rights led by Justice James Chalmers McRuer. The commission invited submissions from experts and members of the public and undertook a series of public hearings around the province at the end of 1964. In March 1968, McRuer delivered the first volumes of an almost 1500-page report and more than five hundred recommendations concerning myriad abuses of the civil liberties of citizens of Ontario.

But an immediate outcome of the Bill 99 drama was the coming together of like-minded individuals in Toronto to form a new civil liberties organization. In January 1965, the impending creation of Canadian Civil Liberties Association was announced in Toronto.

A NEW WATCHDOG

> [A civil libertarian] isn't the person who would lead a parade. He isn't even the person who would be in the parade. But he is the person who would sit at home, read about it and agree that there has to be the right to parade.
>
> —Harry Arthurs, CCLA secretary, quoted in *The Telegram*, July 18, 1966

This self-deprecating comment by Harry Arthurs, distinguished law professor, former dean of Osgoode Hall Law School, and former president of York University (so scarcely an armchair critic), speaks in an illuminating way about the modest role that CCLA intentionally carved out for itself when it was formed in the middle of an era of unprecedented volatility in the public realm. CCLA intended to be, among other things, a means "to bridge a widening gap between the policeman and the public."

The fledgling organization was also described in the media as a "watchdog" that aspired to overcome "Canadian smugness" concerning civil liberties and to pay particular attention to the needs of new Canadians. Approximately 150 people attended the first CCLA meeting on February 11, 1965, and a range of opinions was expressed, including a suggestion from law professor Dr. Edward McWhinney that there should be a new Bill of Rights to replace "the somewhat miserable apology enacted some years ago by a political leader who seems to be disappearing."[7]

The press seemed somewhat bemused by the new organization; it was described in *The Telegram* in July 1966 as both right-wing subversive and left-wing subversive: "[People] are simply mystified when they read that one day CCLA is supporting Dorothy Cameron, the following day that it is providing counsel for 40 student pickets and the day after that is supporting the rights of a self-styled Nazi to speak in Allan Gardens."

Dorothy Cameron was an artist arrested for displaying and selling paintings of nudes in her art gallery. The self-styled Nazi was John Beattie, who was beaten when five thousand protesters disrupted a Nazi rally in a Toronto park in 1965. Defending Beattie's right to speak was difficult for some CCLA members. The diverse makeup of CCLA—its founders included law professors (such as Arthurs, McWhinney, and Bora Laskin, who, in 1970, would become the first Jewish justice appointed to the Supreme Court of Canada), a rabbi and a United Church minister, journalists such as June Callwood and Pierre Berton, and young lawyers—was from the beginning a strength and a challenge. It was created as an organization in which belief in fundamental rights for the most part trumped other beliefs; over the years, this principle occasionally caused rifts and the resignations of high-profile members who found themselves at odds with positions taken by CCLA.

The first few years of CCLA's existence were somewhat inauspicious. The first order of business was the preparation of a comprehensive brief to the McRuer Commission, addressing censorship laws, the bail system, and police/public relations, and recommending a provincial ombudsman. With the exception of the Dorothy Cameron art gallery case (undertaken in 1965 by CCLA acting counsel Julian Porter, who was not representing CCLA, but CCLA supported the case, as described in Chapter Four of this book), the entity campaigned erratically and floundered financially and structurally as it struggled to somehow become a national organization even though, in fact, it had little profile or authority on matters outside Ontario. Police malfeasance, specifically the arbitrary exercise of power, was a key preoccupation, but focused primarily on such matters as parade permits and routes and whether or not the police should be able to arbitrate on signage during demonstrations. There was a protest against the transfer of elderly patients from one nursing home to another without their consent, a protest concerning the forceful removal by police of hippie demonstrators from a sit-in in Yorkville in downtown Toronto, and support for a motorcyclist member of the Black Diamond Riders denied entrance to the Canadian National Exhibition (CNE). And there was a series of small, unrelated actions such as responses to a plea from June Callwood to take up the case of a bullied schoolgirl, and to a forcefully worded request from Pierre Berton that CCLA speak out on behalf of a protestor who yelled at President Lyndon Johnson at Expo 67.

Briefs were written and presented to legislative bodies on issues that would become signature causes for the organization over time—a brief to an Ontario Committee on Religious Education and a brief to a Parliamentary committee studying hate propaganda. CCLA began very early its tradition of holding public meetings and distributing general interest pamphlets, mostly in Toronto, on subjects such as censorship in the arts, hate propaganda, expropriation, and the right to privacy. An early pamphlet on the rights of citizens under arrest was translated into a number of languages.

In the first few years, funding the work was a persistent challenge; the board of directors looked wistfully at the example of the American Civil Liberties Union (ACLU) in 1967, with more than a hundred thousand members paying ten dollars each, yielding an annual operating budget of $1 million. CCLA was adamantly opposed from the start to receiving funding from governments, and its membership numbers fluctuated wildly. There was a wish to become a national organization; the Constitution and membership strategy included the idea of open membership across the country, with local chapters as a goal, but these objectives were unevenly pursued and not consistently successful.

Between mid-1967 and the end of 1968 (declared the International Year for Human Rights by the United Nations, marking the fortieth anniversary of the UDHR), CCLA was awarded two substantial grants by foundations and received a significant anonymous legacy. A. Alan Borovoy was subsequently hired as the first full-time general counsel, and CCLA almost immediately became a force to be reckoned with. Borovoy came to CCLA after an extended period as an activist with the CCF and the Jewish Labour Committee. He brought with him to CCLA a project already underway with native groups in northwestern Ontario, an interest in the issue of religion in schools, and a longstanding relationship with organized labour. For the next forty years, Borovoy would be CCLA's general counsel and public voice.[8] A 1969 CCLA newsletter captures the excitement:

> What's got into the Canadian Civil Liberties Association?
>
> —Over 500 new members in Toronto in less than three months' time....
>
> —Four new chapters in Ottawa, London, Fredericton, and Winnipeg....
>
> —A new General Counsel, A. Alan Borovoy, whose tireless efforts on our behalf have drawn much favourable attention....
>
> —A diversified and highly committed group of men and women as officers and board members, representatives from labour, business, the professions, the arts, journalism, education, housewives, and the clergy....
>
> Civil Liberties is where the action is!

Over the years, CCLA would take on, or intervene in, major emblematic cases in Canadian courts at all levels, and very often at the Supreme Court of Canada (SCC). Often the case would be a small one, the stakes not especially high, but the principle significant. One of the issues defining civil liberties activism in Canada over fifty years is the freedom of expression of all kinds, and the first court case that Borovoy accepted on behalf of CCLA (and one of the few in which he himself acted as CCLA counsel) was a modest free speech challenge in 1969 in New Brunswick.

> The courts in New Brunswick are simply the instruments of the corporate elite. Their duty is not so much to make just decisions as to make right decisions (i.e. decisions which will further perpetuate the elite which controls and rewards them). Court appointments are political appointments. Only the naive would reject the notion that an individual becomes a justice or judge after he proves his worth to the establishment.
>
> —Tom Murphy, *Brunswickan*, December 3, 1968

The *Brunswickian* was a student paper at the University of New Brunswick in Fredericton, and Tom Murphy was a student, moved to write this piece after being called as a witness in the case of Norman Strax, a university physics teacher who was suspended from teaching after he refused to provide identification as a condition of taking books out of the library. In protest, Strax staged a forty-eight-day sit-in, which resulted in a number of students being taken briefly to jail. He was in court because he defied an injunction against entering university grounds. (Strax was an American, and he and Murphy were both members of a group called the Canadian Struggle for Democratic Society. Murphy was also the president of the Student Christian Movement, and he wrote a regular column for the newspaper.)

Murphy wrote from his experience as a witness; his column described what he observed as arbitrary and biased actions by the judge as a "mockery of justice" and concluded with the paragraph cited above. Murphy was charged with the virtually archaic crime of "scandalizing the court." The prosecution claimed that anyone who read Murphy's article would lose faith in the judicial system. The case was heard by the Appeal Division of the Supreme Court of New Brunswick, and when Murphy was unable to find counsel to represent him, Alan Borovoy was asked if he would represent Mr. Murphy on behalf of CCLA.

Borovoy attempted to enter as evidence some research done by two sociologists who had surveyed student populations (who had either read or not read the article in question) to see what their attitudes were towards the New Brunswick courts. The court refused to admit this evidence, and the justices were unmoved by the suggestion that the charge itself was arbitrary and archaic because it had not been used in New Brunswick since 1888.

The court concluded somewhat opaquely, "The question to be determined is not the effect the writer intended his article to have but the effect the article itself is calculated to have," and it found Mr. Murphy guilty of contempt and ordered him to spend ten days in jail.

The case itself is minor, but it was the first of the freedom of expression cases that CCLA would engage with directly over the next forty years. In the meantime, a nationwide threat to the civil liberties of all Canadians—one that had been simmering and stewing for almost ten years in Quebec—was about to explode.

THE OCTOBER CRISIS, 1970—RETURN OF THE *WAR MEASURES ACT*

> The revolution in Québec is not in preparation, it is in full execution. The situation is dangerous. The population has no idea of the gravity of the moment. It eerily resembles revolutions in other countries.
>
> —Montreal Mayor Jean Drapeau,
> *Le Soleil*, October 13, 1970

> I recognize, as I hope do others, that this extreme position into which the governments have been forced, is in some respects a trap. It is a well-known technique of revolutionary groups who attempt to destroy society by unjustified violence to goad the authorities into inflexible attitudes. The revolutionaries then employ this evidence of alleged authoritarianism as justification for the need to use violence in their renewed attacks on the social structure.
>
> —Pierre Elliott Trudeau, speech, October 16, 1970

> At the time of the *War Measures Act* in 1970, I had the sense that English Canada was completely tone-deaf to what was happening in Quebec...[and was] very supportive of the hard line of the federal government.... CCLA was the only organization that was very concerned about this militarization of law enforcement. [The October crisis] anchored my commitment in fundamental civil rights.
>
> —Louise Arbour, interview, June 2013

The October Crisis is an event with a timeline of hours and days. It is a Rashomon story, the telling of which depends a great deal on the perspective of the teller. At the time, it was an event that threw into sharp relief the Quebec/rest-of-Canada divide, and it happened that the Prime Minister of Canada, Pierre Elliott Trudeau, stood at the pinnacle of that divide. For an organization like CCLA, it was an unprecedented opportunity to establish leadership on a complex and divisive issue of national import. This was not a minor court case or a weekend rally. The October Crisis embraced everything from federal/provincial jurisdictional issues and personalized politics to murder; finding and holding to a clear civil liberties line[9] through a volatile drama signalled a maturation of CCLA as an organization.

For Quebeckers, the events over twenty-five days in October 1970 were the culmination of Front de libération du Québec (FLQ) actions and agitation over almost a decade, including bombs, threats, more than twenty arrests and convictions, six deaths, and the politicization of a student population ripe for incitement. Those days were an intense drama in which a generation of important provincial political leaders were implicated—Robert Bourassa (Liberal premier), René Lévesque (former member of the Liberal Party, Parti Québécois leader, and journalist), Jacques Parizeau (president of the Parti Québécois), Jean Drapeau (mayor of Montreal), and Claude Ryan (editor, *Le Devoir*). The kidnappings of the British consul, James Cross, on October 5 and deputy premier and Minister of Labour Pierre Laporte on October 10 took place in broad daylight. Concurrent with the crisis was a legislative deadlock on Medicare bills and a strike by the province's medical specialists.

The rest of Canada reacted with shock, dismay, and confusion as events unfolded and looked to Prime Minister Trudeau in Ottawa for reassurance and leadership.

Within a day of the kidnapping of James Cross and FLQ demands being made public, the governments of Bourassa and Trudeau agreed to collaborate on a strategy for dealing with the demands of the FLQ. (Cross, as a British diplomat, was under federal jurisdiction.) The key issue was whether or not to negotiate with the FLQ, whose demands included the release of prisoners, money, and flights out of Canada. On October 10, the FLQ Manifesto was read out first on a private radio station and then again on Radio-Canada (over the objections of Trudeau):

> The Front de Libération du Québec is neither the Messiah nor a modern-day Robin Hood. It is a group of Québec workers who have decided to do everything they can to assure that the people of Québec take their destiny into their own hands, once and for all. The Front de Libération du Québec wants total independence for Quebeckers, united in a free society, purged for good of its gang of rapacious sharks, the big bosses who dish out patronage and their henchmen, who have turned Québec into a private preserve of cheap labour and unscrupulous exploitation....

On October 11, the Canadian government ordered out the army as a precautionary measure in Ottawa. On October 13, Trudeau made his famous comments to a Canadian Broadcasting Corporation (CBC) reporter about "bleeding hearts who just don't like to see people with helmets and guns," and when asked how far he would go to stop the FLQ, he replied:

> Well, just watch me.... I think the society must take every means at its disposal to defend itself against the emergence of a parallel power, which defies the elected power in this country and I think that goes to any distance. So long as there is a power in here, which is challenging the elected representative of the people, then I think that power must be stopped. And I think it's only—I repeat—weak-kneed, bleeding hearts who are afraid to take these measures.

On October 14, the Bourassa government agreed to safe passage for terrorists and parole for five eligible prisoners in exchange for Cross and Laporte, but nothing else. That same evening, sixteen "eminent personalities"—including Ryan, Lévesque, Parizeau, and a number of academics—issued a petition critical of Bourassa's strategy, declaring that it "risks reducing Quebec and its government to tragic impotence." On October 15, demonstrations erupted at universities and colleges, and more than one thousand students at l'Université de Montréal signed the FLQ manifesto. That afternoon, the Quebec government called in the Canadian armed forces, and six thousand troops were on the streets of Montreal before nightfall. (At the same time, the Quebec legislature was

"Well, just watch me," was the response to reporter Tim Ralfe (right) when he asked Prime Minister Pierre Trudeau how far he was prepared to go to protect government officials against the FLQ.

debating Medicare bills and finally ordered the specialist physicians back to work. And simultaneously, some three thousand people were attending an FLQ rally in downtown Montreal.)

At 9:00 p.m., Bourassa issued a six-hour ultimatum to the FLQ. Two hours later, Bourassa signed a formal request to the government of Canada to invoke the *War Measures Act (WMA)* and sent it by car to Ottawa. (This action was used by apologists for the invocation of the *War Measures Act* as proof that the federal government was merely responding to the request of Quebec, but it is also possible that this was a step insisted upon in advance by Trudeau, who had thoroughly prepared the ground for this possibility in Ottawa, not only in his own party but also with leaders of the opposition parties.)

On October 16 at 4:00 a.m., in response to the hand-delivered written request from Bourassa (and a similar request from Mayor Drapeau and other city of Montreal officials), the federal Cabinet passed an order-in-council invoking the *War Measures Act* provisions, effective immediately, to deal with the "apprehended insurrection," making the FLQ a criminal organization. Within hours, the first arrests were made. Several hundred people were arrested within twenty-four hours.

The Cabinet's decision to act was made public early on the morning of October 16, and reaction across Canada was swift. CCLA responded immediately, instinctively, that afternoon, in advance of discussion and approval by its own board. Borovoy stated that there was no evidence that the magnitude of the intrusive response by the government of Canada had merit. Other civil liberties groups made similar statements.

In a twenty-minute speech to the nation that evening, broadcast simultaneously in French and English, Trudeau eloquently articulated his decision to invoke the *War Measures Act* to defend against what he called "a handful of self-selected dictators." "If a democratic society is to continue to exist," he said, "it must be able to root out the cancer of an armed revolutionary movement that is bent on destruction of the very basis of our freedoms."

English Canada was not fully convinced by Trudeau's rhetoric at this point. A *Globe and Mail* editorial from October 17, 1970, stated:

> Only if we can believe that the FLQ is strong enough and sufficiently armed to escalate the violence it has spawned for seven years now, only if we can believe that it is virulent enough to infect other areas of society, only then can the Government's assumption of incredible powers be tolerated. For this War Measures Act is not only drastic and dangerous, it is in itself a denial of the very rights which Mr. Trudeau once wanted to enshrine in the Constitution.

The response in Quebec was focused primarily on the actions of the government of Quebec: On Saturday, October 17, morning editorials from René Lévesque and Claude Ryan condemned Bourassa for handing power over to the government of Canada. Lévesque wrote, "Quebec no longer has a government. The pitiable excuse for a government, which we had, was blown away by the first tough blow. The Cabinet gave up its authority and now is only the puppet of the federal government."

The House of Commons sat in a rare Saturday session, and the decision to invoke the *War Measures Act* was debated for the entire day, but the vote was held over until the following Monday. Both Robert Stanfield (PC) and Tommy Douglas (NDP) voiced hesitancy and disapproval, Douglas saying that invoking the *War Measures Act* against the FLQ was like using a sledgehammer to smash a peanut. When, on the previous day, the order-in-council was first proposed, John Diefenbaker had reminded Parliament of its deeply problematic *Criminal Code* section 98, which was rashly introduced to protect Canada from Communists in 1919. Then he quoted from it, demonstrating that exactly the same offensive language was being used again. Disapproval of the decision was expressed that day in press statements and small demonstrations across the country by human rights activists, lawyers, and students.

Then, at just past six o'clock that Saturday evening, while the House was still in session, the FLQ announced through the media that Pierre Laporte had been "executed." His body was found more than six hours later, after midnight, in the trunk of a car; he had been strangled with a chain he wore around his neck.

The tenor of the debate changed instantly. When Prime Minister Trudeau arrived on Parliament Hill to speak about the

This anti-*War Measures Act* poster, issued by New Democratic Youth, was successful in calling alarmed citizens to demonstrate in Toronto's Nathan Phillips Square. While demonstrators gathered in Toronto on October 17, 1970, the Canadian armed forces patrolled the streets of a tense Montreal.

CIVIL LIBERTIES ARE NOT to be FLAUNTED

COIFFURE

death of Laporte, people greeted him by singing "O Canada." It was almost three o'clock on Sunday morning before Trudeau finally spoke. On October 19, the Parliament of Canada continued its debate and—by a vote of 190 to 16—the Cabinet's middle-of-the-night order-in-council became the *Public Order Act*, putting a state of emergency in place until the end of April 1971, to almost universal approval across the country.

But that same day, CCLA released the following statement:

> Neither when the matter was introduced in Parliament nor during statements which have followed in the media has the Government furnished the Canadian people with a statement of fact sufficient to support the conclusion that the country was on the brink of an insurrection...no reasonable person could fail to sympathize with the cruel predicament faced by the governments of Canada and Quebec...but the infringement of civil liberties is not appropriate unless it is "the only method available to prevent imminent peril to life, limb, liberty for the survival of society itself."

EXACTLY WHAT IS AN "APPREHENDED" INSURRECTION? (A. ALAN BOROVOY)

The *War Measures Act* was a weapon to be used with extreme caution. It could be invoked by Cabinet without advance approval by Parliament, and the emergency measures thus created were not governed by the Bill of Rights. Its use in peacetime had happened once before in Canadian history, immediately after the end of the Second World War, to justify the so-called repatriation of Japanese-Canadians to Japan, a country most of them had never been to.

The *War Measures Act* enabled a blanket suspension of civil liberties, giving the government broad general powers:

a) to censure, suppress, or control publications

b) to arrest, detain, exclude, or expel individuals

c) to control ports and the movement of ships

d) to control all forms of transportation

> e) to control trade, exports, imports, production, and fabrication
>
> f) to take over, control, confiscate, or dispose thereof or use any property

The *Public Order Act* of October 16, 1970, was created under the aegis of the *War Measures Act* to target one organization, in the name of an "apprehended insurrection," not an actual insurrection. This equivocation seemed implicitly to acknowledge the question of whether or not invoking the *War Measures Act* was necessary or appropriate. As Alan Borovoy asked, not just rhetorically, exactly what *is* an "apprehended" insurrection? Especially, you might ask, one that had only been in existence for a single day, according to the text of the proclamation:

> .... Whereas there is in contemporary Canadian society an element or group known as Le Front de Libération du Québec who advocate and resort to the use of force and the commission of criminal offences, including murder, threats of murder and kidnapping, as a means of or as an aid in accomplishing a governmental change within Canada and whose activities have given rise to a state of apprehended insurrection within the province of Québec.
>
> Now Know Ye that We, by and with the advice of our Privy Council for Canada, do by this Our Proclamation proclaim and declare that apprehended insurrection exists and has existed as and from the fifteenth day of October, one thousand nine hundred and seventy.

The powers to suspend civil liberties applied across the country and were spelled out in considerable detail: police forces, both provincial and municipal, the RCMP, and the army, all acting more or less independently, were given free rein to enter premises without warrant, seize materials, and arrest and hold suspect individuals without bail, and without access to counsel of their families for seven days, a time frame that could be extended by an Attorney General of a province to twenty-one days. The regulations stated:

evidence that any person

(a) attended any meeting of the unlawful association

(b) spoke publicly in advocacy for the unlawful association, or

(c) communicated statements of the unlawful association as a representative or professed representative of the unlawful association

[All of this] is, in the absence of evidence to the contrary, proof that he is a member of the unlawful association.

The possibilities for arrests on a large scale under these provisions were clear; one thinks of the rallies held in Quebec in the days immediately preceding this proclamation, at which thousands of students shouted, "FLQ! FLQ!"

After the death of Laporte, public support for Trudeau's actions was extremely high, with some polls indicating that more than 88 per cent of all Canadians approved, and in Quebec, 86 per cent. The general public accepted the statements made by the government at the time that the special measures given to the police would only be used to apprehend those suspected of membership in, or association with, the FLQ. In Toronto in late October, five thousand people came to a rally at York University in support of the government's actions.

On December 3, James Cross was found alive, and his captors were put on a plane to Cuba. By the end of December, 453 people had been arrested, and all but fifty released. Only eighteen were ever convicted. The army remained in Quebec into January.

On the day that the *Public Order Act* was approved by Parliament, and in the weeks immediately following the creation of a state of emergency, the Canadian government insisted that it would be creating legislation to permanently replace the *Public Order Act* when it expired at the end of April. Trudeau believed this was necessary because there was nothing else to choose from except either the *Criminal Code* or the *War Measures Act*. To justify his actions, the Prime Minister speculated about the need for police surveillance on university campuses. The Quebec minister of justice mused about the possibility of mandatory identity cards and intermittent press censorship. In fact, there was a great deal of press harassment, censorship, and self-censorship during and following the October Crisis, notably at CBC/Radio-Canada.

Outside of Quebec, over the next several months, the *Public Order Act* was used numerous times. It was invoked to justify the harassment of hippies in Vancouver, and the raid of a house and the confiscation of anti-war signs in Ottawa. It enabled the seizure of some printing plates from a student newspaper in Guelph, Ontario, and the confiscation of a thousand copies of a Maoist pamphlet in Toronto. The government of British Columbia declared by order-in-council on November 2, "as public policy no person teaching or instructing our youth in educational institutions receiving Government support shall continue in the employment of the educational institution if they advocate the policies of Le Front de Libération du Québec, or the overthrow of democratically elected governments by violent means." In Ontario, CCLA challenged a similarly punitive resolution concerning teachers proposed by the Toronto Board of Education, arguing that it was the role of schools to allow the free exchange of ideas, and even to play devil's advocate.

Thomas Berger, in his 1981 book *Fragile Freedoms,* comments that the casual incorporation of inflammatory language into hasty action by governments as far away as British Columbia "illustrates the way the morbid excitement of a crisis can spread and lead to the abrogation of civil liberties in places far removed from the threat.... The whole exercise reveals how unwise it is to have such extraordinary power available to any government."

But the sense of an impending national crisis did not hold. In March 1971, CCLA presented a position paper to Justice Minister John Turner, strongly urging that the government not introduce new legislation to replace the emergency powers set to expire on April 30. CCLA said the *Public Order Act* should be revoked immediately: "If the Governments of Canada and Quebec felt safe enough to withdraw the army, how can they contend that the situation is so unsafe as to warrant emergency powers?... Surely a free society in trouble would prefer to have more police with fewer powers rather than fewer police with more powers." Immediately following the meeting with Turner, Alan Borovoy told the press that the invocation of the *War Measures Act* had merely served to encourage numerous ideas for curtailing civil liberties, such as censorship of the press and police surveillance on campuses.

CCLA argued that there were sufficient powers already in the *Criminal Code* to deal with real threats to society and that, in fact, it had been regular policing that had led to the rescue of James Cross and the capture of those who had killed Laporte. It was wrong to criminalize membership in organizations like the FLQ: "We are running a grave risk of sending people to jail for five years, not for the bad conduct they have committed, but for the bad company they have kept." And the difficulty in proving non-membership in an organization, suggested the CCLA brief, was like a person being asked to find a witness to declare that one had never travelled to Europe.

The CCLA brief recommended that there should be more safeguards, not fewer, for invoking the *War Measures Act*; in addition, there should be a "recital of circumstances" justifying the declaration of a state of war or insurrection.

The consistent critical, skeptical position taken by CCLA during the October Crisis was noted in Quebec. An editorial in *Le Devoir* noted, "At the height of the crisis…one had the impression that, but for a few voices crying in the wilderness, all critical reflection had practically ceased in English-Canada." CCLA was one of those voices, and several years later, this resulted in the distinguished jurist Louise Arbour becoming a member of CCLA, "the only organization I ever joined."

Trudeau and Turner dallied publicly on the question of what they might do next, right up until the *Public Order* (Temporary Measures) *Act* expired on April 30. On April 28, *The Globe and Mail* wrote, "Never, in the six-and-a-half-month history of this sorry affair, has Mr. Trudeau established a case for invoking the *War Measures Act* and passing the *Public Order Act*. In fact, too often he has tried to cleanse himself of responsibility for both the legislation and its implementation by washing his hands in a bowl provided by Mr. Bourassa."

The *Public Order Act* was allowed to lapse at the end of April. In a statement resonating with CCLA's position, Turner announced in May that, indeed, the FLQ would undoubtedly be considered an illegal organization under the seditious conspiracy section of the *Criminal Code*. A special joint Parliamentary Committee would be established, he said, to draft new anti-terrorism legislation.

But nothing happened. It was not until 1988 that the government of Canada under Brian Mulroney replaced the *War Measures Act* with the *Emergencies Act*, a process CCLA participated in and influenced. One key difference is that, while the *War Measures Act* was specifically excluded in 1960 from the authority of the Bill of Rights, the preamble of the *Emergencies Act* incorporates references to both the *Charter of Rights and Freedoms* and the *International Covenant on Civil and Political Rights*. In addition, the *Emergencies Act* cannot be invoked without approval first by Parliament (a safeguard considered illusory by some critics).

For CCLA, the October Crisis opened up another area of concern entirely—the actions of the RCMP. Although the provisions of the *War Measures Act* were no longer in force after April 1971, the surveillance and collecting of information by police, especially the RCMP, did not come to an end. In fact, the federal government, which now feared not simply the immediate threat of terrorism but also the political danger of separatism, had almost immediately asked the RCMP to maintain a "proactive" watch on the actions of Quebec nationalist organizations, including political parties and, if necessary, to "counter" any disruptive activities. This led the RCMP on a program of infiltration, harassment, and intelligence-gathering in Quebec, and in a number of instances, independent of any instruction from government, to commit acts that were undeniably illegal. When these actions became public, two separate inquiries were undertaken almost simultaneously and even competitively—the federal government's McDonald Commission (1977–81) and the Keable Inquiry in Quebec (1978–81). The McDonald Commission presented CCLA with an opportunity to seize the initiative on a matter of national interest, as discussed at the end of this chapter.

THE 1970s—INSTABILITY, INFLATION, AND INJUSTICE

The 1970s, famously called the "me" decade by American writer Tom Wolfe, are remembered in North America as a decade of economic uncertainty, unemployment, and inflation, in contrast to the love-in vibe of the sixties.

The uncertainty in Canada in the early 1970s resonated with instability in other parts of the world—war and famine in Bangladesh from 1971, unrest in Yugoslavia over the decade, coups in Uganda (with Idi Amin taking power in 1971 and then deposed in 1979), the overthrow of Chile's left-wing government of Salvador Allende by the right-wing forces of Augusto Pinochet in 1974, and the overthrow of Haile Selassie's monarchy in Ethiopia in 1974. The balance of power in Asia rose and fell in bloodied waves. The United States abandoned its war in Vietnam, and North Vietnam gradually took over South Vietnam. In Cambodia, the Khmer Rouge under Pol Pot engineered an "agrarian socialist" revolution and the massacre of almost three million people between 1975 and 1979, when Vietnam invaded and became an occupying force for ten years.

In the Middle East, the Yom Kippur War of 1973 resulted in an oil embargo and a decade-long, worldwide energy crisis, seeding political tensions in the region. The shadow of nuclear war, so heavy in the 1960s, was gradually lightened in the 1970s, one unarmed ballistic missile at a time, by SALT, the bilateral Strategic Arms Limitation Talks, with agreements signed in 1972 and almost renewed in 1979, when the Soviet Union invaded Afghanistan.

Nixon resigned in 1974; Mao Zedong and Zhou Enlai died in 1976. In 1979, the Shah of Iran was deposed, and Margaret Thatcher was elected in Great Britain.

Canada instigated an official policy of multiculturalism in 1971 and co-hosted (in Sweden) the first international conference on the environment in 1972. We played hockey against the Russians in 1972 and hosted the Olympic Games in 1976. The spectre of the separation of Quebec became more than a chimera when René Lévesque's Parti Québécois won a majority in 1976. Canadians watched Watergate unfold in 1974 as our own government passed legislation on wiretapping. We tracked the uncertain fortunes of the Equal Rights Amendment in the United States—a constitutional amendment that would have guaranteed equal rights for women, but failed to pass the state ratification deadline of 1982. *Roe v. Wade*, the United States Supreme Court's abortion decision of 1973 (making abortion a matter of choice until the point of fetal viability outside the womb) became immediately both an activist rallying point and a judicial marker for abortion rights in Canada.

CCLA's work in the 1970s swung back and forth between big national issues and cases of individuals in Ontario who were affected by the unfair practices of the Ontario government. This pattern of engagement remains a hallmark of CCLA activism; and in many instances, what began as a plea to help a single person developed over time into a major campaign, with a range of actions. The 1970s also saw CCLA's first SCC intervention, in the Henry Morgentaler abortion clinic case of 1976 (discussed in Chapter Three); this was to become a key strategy for CCLA work for the next thirty years.

> DESERTED WIFE WHO SLEPT WITH MALE BOARDER HAS WELFARE PAYMENTS RESTORED
>
> —Headline, *The Globe and Mail*, January 1970

One longstanding source of systemic abuse of rights in Canada is welfare, where questions of entitlement and fraud have chronically undermined the support of governments for the working and unemployed poor, an injustice that historically has affected women more significantly than men. Fifty years ago, the "man in the house" standard was commonplace in welfare practices throughout Canada (until 1986 in Ontario), whereby the living arrangements of single women on welfare were probed in order to determine their eligibility, and the presence of a male boarder, friend, or lover constituted a violation of their status: "A pair of male slippers, an empty beer glass, or a stale cigar butt would inevitably provoke a sexual inquisition," a CCLA newsletter noted in reference to the case cited in the headline above, in which a woman with three children, whose husband had left her, was informed by mail (without benefit of a hearing) that her benefits would be cut off: "It appears that you are not living as a single person...."

CCLA argued this case before the Family Benefits Review Board and subsequently to the Ontario Court of Appeal, where the appeal failed. In this case, however, the woman's benefits were finally restored as a result of direct negotiations between CCLA and the minister for welfare. CCLA pursued the issue further by conducting a survey of more than a thousand welfare recipients across Canada and produced *Welfare Practices and Civil Liberties,* a report on the systemic abuse of the rights of people on welfare. Throughout the early 1970s, CCLA ran a volunteer support program at the duty desk at welfare offices in Toronto.

In 1977, the government of Ontario introduced new welfare legislation that drew a blistering response from Borovoy in the *Toronto Star*, September 9, 1977. (One of Borovoy's successful tactics over the forty years of his tenure as CCLA general counsel was his consistent rhetorical presence in newspapers, either as a columnist or in op-ed pieces.)

BILL DENIES WELFARE RECIPIENTS THE MOST FUNDAMENTAL OF RIGHTS

Poverty is not a sufficient justification to deny people their basic civil liberties. But that is exactly what the Ontario government's Bill 142 proposes to do to welfare claimants.

Until now, the welfare law has generally required advance notice when there are to be refusals, suspensions, or cancellations of assistance. The idea was to give claimants an opportunity to defend themselves before they suffered the loss of their very livelihood. But, even though such safeguards have been considered fundamental since the Magna Carta, Bill 142 has dropped this requirement altogether....

Under Bill 142, no appeals will go forward without, first, an internal review. Moreover, there is no provision for interim assistance during whatever period the government might later decide is appropriate for such reviews. Thus, it becomes possible for welfare administrators to unilaterally deprive welfare claimants of subsistence income for unacceptably long periods.... Bill 142 also proposes to explicitly deny the right of appeal where the administration decides that claimants are not fit to exercise responsibility for themselves. Thus, the administrator or a special trustee could wind up virtually controlling a claimant's whole way of life....

Moreover, in contrast with the existing law, Bill 142 would deny special disability assistance to alcoholics and drug addicts. In view of the fact that the purpose of this assistance is to address genuine need, why make such distinctions? If any persons are unable—as opposed to unwilling—to earn income, why should it matter what caused the disability? It appears that the Ontario government is reluctant to provide disability assistance to those who it believes are responsible for their disabilities. This is unwarranted sanctimony....

Bill 142 is provoking serious conflicts—political, ideological, and financial. But the minister insists nevertheless that the Bill is "fair"..."fair to [those] who pay for it" and "fair to those who need its help." Ironically, one of the Bill's most salient features is its departure from our society's accepted notions of fundamental fairness.

ABORIGINAL LIFE, RIGHTS, AND THE BILL OF RIGHTS

Between 1969 and 1974, CCLA paid particular attention to the question of Aboriginal rights. CCLA's work took two forms: first, it produced a study and report on conditions in Aboriginal communities that gave rise to small but significant improvements to problems such as access to the legal system; and second, it monitored the way that Aboriginal issues played out in the courts, especially with reference to the Bill of Rights. In both arenas, the depth of prejudice and indifference is worth taking note of, four decades later.

In 1969, a joint project with the Canadian Labour Congress (CLC) working with the Ojibwa in Kenora, Ontario, resulted directly in an increase in wage rates on the reserve and an economic development grant. In 1969, CCLA defended the rights of Mohawk demonstrators in Cornwall, Ontario, to demonstrate on disputed land. These small interventions led to a two-year CCLA study that culminated, in 1974, in "Indian Life and Canadian Law," a report based on more than two hundred affidavits that identified "a sizable gulf between our legal pretensions and the social reality" of native people.

The report described the discrimination against Aboriginal people in the assignment of public housing, which in Kenora, for example, typically benefited white families, most of which earned $10,000 or more, while impoverished native families lived in "unfit-for-human-habitation" houses: "In many of these homes, one will find rotting structures, conspicuous fire hazards, no indoor plumbing or stove, and the frequent presence of vermin." An Ontario Hydro dam constructed in 1956—on the land of the Islington Band at One Man Lake northwest of Kenora—flooded reserve land, destroying fish habitats and wiping out traplines and rice fields, resulting in the need for public welfare assistance, which had previously never been required. Ontario Hydro was granted the land in question without reference to compensation for lost livelihoods, and the band (now the Wabaseemoong Independent Nation) was never given any legal advice when agreements were signed.

One of the most basic rights denied to native people living in isolated communities was access to legal aid, and even the ability to travel to courts over great distances. Poverty and distance from courts resulted in further indignities. A resident of Grassy Narrows First Nation was picked up by police when he was with his son and told he had to report to jail immediately for non-compliance in paying a fine. He could not afford a taxi to send his son home, so he asked the police to drive his son home; two weeks later, when he was released, he learned that, instead, his son had been placed in the custody of the Children's Aid Society.

The CCLA report concluded that the problem was not merely the racist and discriminatory actions of local bureaucrats and officials but "the statutory enshrinement of empty slogans at senior levels of government. The resulting tragedy is attributable not to the isolated cruelty in the north, but to government apathy in the south."

Also in 1974, CCLA represented Joseph Fardella, a federal employee who was fired because he refused to make native children at a federally operated residential school attend mass, disobeying direct orders from school directors. CCLA counsel J. S. Midanik argued before the Federal Court of Appeal that the order was improper because it infringed on the freedom of religion rights of the native parents and their children, in conflict with the rights protected by the Bill of Rights. The Federal Court of Appeal upheld the firing of Fardella, stating that the "silence [of the parents] was held to imply their consent to the practice" of compulsory attendance at religious services. Mr. Midanik argued unsuccessfully that "the use of public resources to promote private faith in a coercive setting constitutes an infringement [and] it is not proper to infer consent from silence in a delicate matter like religious conscience."

The same month that "Indian Life and Canadian Law" was released, CCLA reported at length on *Attorney General of Canada v. Lavell*, a recent SCC case that considered the provisions of the *Indian Act* in light of the Bill of Rights.

Between 1960 and 1980, the courts seemed determined, overall, to prove that the Bill of Rights was indeed a statute of no significance or authority. The SCC found, as early as 1962, that a contentious *Lord's Day Act* was not in conflict with the Bill of Rights, thereby making it possible for Christian practices and the "sanctity of Sunday" to prevail in the province of Ontario. It was argued not only that the Bill of Rights had no authority over laws that predated it but also that it only applied to whatever laws existed at the moment of its creation, and could not be applied "forward" to new laws. In 1976, in the case of *Morgentaler v. the Queen*, the argument, put forward by Morgentaler's defence team that Canada's abortion laws constituted an infringement of the Bill of Rights, was dismissed briskly and outright by the SCC.

In one rare case, the SCC used the Bill of Rights in 1970 to defend the civil liberties of a Canadian. Joseph Drybones was an Indian who was charged with being intoxicated on the evening of April 8, 1967, in the lobby of the Old Stope Hotel in Yellowknife, Northwest Territories (NWT). Mr. Drybones, who neither spoke nor understood English, pleaded guilty to being intoxicated and to being an Indian, and therefore subject to the *Indian Act* of 1952, specifically section 94 (b), which stated that it is illegal for an Indian to be intoxicated off a reserve. Mr. Drybones was fined ten dollars, but later appealed his conviction. He appealed successfully to two higher courts—in the Northwest Territories Territorial Court and Court of Appeal—both of which dismissed the conviction. The argument accepted by the NWT higher courts was that because of this legislation, Indians in the Northwest Territories, where there are no reserves, by reason of their race, are denied "equality before the law with their fellow Canadians...," in direct defiance of the Bill of Rights. The Northwest Territories Crown appealed this decision to the SCC, which heard the case in 1969 and delivered an ambivalent 6 to 3 judgment in favour of Mr. Drybones in 1970.

The deliberations of the Supreme Court in this case demonstrate how deeply entrenched racist thinking about First Nations was at the time. The entire court considered irrelevant the fact that there were no reserves in Northwest Territories, a fact that did lead one justice to point to the absurdity that, if by law an Indian could only become intoxicated on a reserve, and there were no reserves, it would presumably also be a crime for an Indian to be intoxicated in his own house. (In the NWT at the time, it was a much lesser offence for non-natives to be intoxicated in a public place, and not a crime to be intoxicated at home.)

The majority determined that the *Indian Act* was subject to the Bill of Rights in this particular context, and so the conviction of Mr. Drybones was set aside. But three justices set out their individual reasons for determining that the *Indian Act* was not subject to the Bill of Rights, even though it resulted in discrimination because it made public intoxication a greater crime for an Indian than for any other Canadian.

The minority position was that the Bill of Rights was merely common-sense guidance, a "canon of construction" when it came to existing federal laws and did not require those laws to be altered. If that were the case, "Equality before the law...would require the Indians to be subject in every province to the same rules of law as all others in every particular, not merely in the question of drunkenness." The purpose of the Bill of Rights, they argued, was merely to declare that rights and freedoms existed, not to lead the courts to proactively create rights and freedoms.

As described ironically in the opinion of the majority, the dissenting SCC justices implicitly supported the notion that "the most glaring discriminatory legislation against a racial group would have to be construed as recognizing the right of each of its individual members 'to equality before the law,' so long as all the other members are being discriminated against in the same way."

The court ruled in a 6 to 3 decision that the Bill of Rights did apply specifically to section 94 of the *Indian Act*. Justice Emmett Hall made a point of firmly rejecting the "separate but equal" argument: "The *Canadian Bill of Rights* is not fulfilled if it merely equates Indians with Indians in terms of equality before the law, but [must affirm equality] between all Canadians whether Indian or non-Indian."

Three years later, in *Attorney General of Canada v. Lavell*, the SCC took the completely opposite position concerning the *Indian Act*. The question before the SCC, in two separate cases joined in the decision known as *Lavell*, related to the rights of Aboriginal women who married non-Aboriginal men. The first *Indian Act*, written in 1876 to expand upon the authority over Aboriginal people bestowed upon the federal government in the *British North American (BNA) Act* in 1867, unequivocally decreed that a native woman who married a non-native man had to leave the reserve and would lose her Aboriginal status. Even if a woman subsequently divorced her non-native husband, she was not permitted to return to the reserve. But the same was not true of Aboriginal men who married non-native women; men were permitted to remain on the reserve, and they continued to enjoy the benefits of status no matter whom they married.

Jeanette Lavell, a member of the Wikwemikong Band, married a non-native, and as a consequence, her name was arbitrarily struck from the Indian Register, an action that she protested unsuccessfully to the registrar. Yvonne Bédard also married a white man, and when her marriage ended in divorce, she returned with two children to the Six Nations Reserve to live in a property bequeathed to her by her mother; she was ordered by the band council to dispose of that property and leave the reserve.

More than a dozen Aboriginal organizations were present as interveners defending the *Indian Act*, and a number of women's organizations also intervened on behalf of the two women. It was a clear case of competing rights, one that CCLA, in reporting on the outcome in its newsletter, chose to present as a clash of two conflicting positions, but, interestingly, not to offer a CCLA opinion in favour of either.

In a 5 to 4 decision, the SCC determined that, in this instance, the Bill of Rights was "inoperative"; the *Indian Act* was not subject to the Bill of Rights and that "it follows that the phrase 'equality before the law' is to be construed in light of the law existing in Canada at that time."

The majority decision affirmed that an Indian woman's loss of status upon marriage to a non-native person was enshrined in the earliest versions of the statutes concerning Indians, as written here in 1869:

> Provided always that any Indian woman marrying any other than an Indian, shall cease to be an Indian within the meaning of this Act, nor shall the children issue of such marriage be considered as Indians within the meaning of this Act; Provided also, that any Indian woman marrying an Indian of another tribe, band or body shall cease to be a member of the tribe, band or body to which she formerly belonged and become a member of the tribe, band or body of which her husband is a member, and the children, issue of this marriage, shall belong to their father's tribe only.

This about-face by the SCC, concerning the respective trumping powers of the Bill of Rights and the *Indian Act*, reflected a slightly modified composition of the court; those justices who had affirmed the authority of the Bill of Rights in *Drybones* three years earlier were now in the minority. Their dissenting position was written by Justice Bora Laskin. Unless the language of the Bill of Rights was to be seen merely as "rhetorical window dressing,"

Laskin wrote, this was clearly a case of discrimination against the women on the basis of sex:

> If for the words "on account of race" there are substituted the words "on account of sex" the result must surely be the same where a federal enactment imposes disabilities or prescribes disqualifications for members of the female sex which are not imposed upon members of the male sex in the same circumstances...it is not possible to leap over the telling words of s.1 of the *Canadian Bill of Rights*, "without discrimination by reason of race, national origin, colour, religion or sex" by invoking the words "equality before the law".... Pre-existing Canadian legislation as well as subsequent Canadian legislation is expressly made subject to the commands of the *Canadian Bill of Rights*, and those commands, where they are as clear as the one which is relevant here, cannot be diluted by appeals to history....

This blatant system of discrimination against Aboriginal women was abolished in revisions to the *Indian Act* in 1985.

Also in a dissenting opinion in *Lavelle*, Justice Douglas Abbott offered the following comment as a criticism and a concern about the fate of the Bill of Rights. His conclusion is interesting because it signals precisely the course about to be undertaken by Prime Minister Trudeau in his campaign for a repatriated constitution and the creation of a charter of rights over the next eight years:

> In my view the *Canadian Bill of Rights* has substantially affected the doctrine of the supremacy of Parliament. Like any other statute it can of course be repealed or amended, or a particular law declared to be applicable notwithstanding the provisions of the Bill. In form the supremacy of Parliament is maintained but in practice I think that it has been substantially curtailed. In my opinion that result is undesirable, but that is a matter for consideration by Parliament not the courts.

POLICE VERSUS CCLA (1974)—THE BATTLE CONTINUES

A decade after CCLA was roused into existence by the excesses of police powers proposed in Ontario's Bill 99, its crusade against police abuse of power began anew and would continue for many years. From CCLA's perspective, it seemed that law enforcement agencies literally left no stone unturned in their abuse of the rights of Canadians. Rampant wiretapping, illegal raids, and dogged surveillance of a host of unsuspecting Canadians were common practices by police forces in the name of defending law and order. (The contemporary ramifications of these long-time concerns are explored in depth in Chapter Six of this book, but the following three examples illustrate how CCLA's campaigning on police-related issues took shape in the 1970s.)

In January 1974, the *Protection of Privacy Act* became law. This legislation dealt with wiretapping, which had been an issue under consideration by the government since 1969. In the months leading up to the law's enactment, wiretapping had been examined in the glare of what a CCLA newsletter referred to as the "sordid stories pouring out of Washington" about the uses and abuses of electronic bugging revealed by the Watergate scandal. CCLA appeared three times before the committee responsible for the wiretapping legislation, identifying electronic eavesdropping (here in its most primitive form, the tapping of telephone lines) as "an instrument that invades the privacy of everyone—not just the suspected." The persistent CCLA interventions were recognized as having considerable impact on the final form of the bill. CCLA's vehement criticism led Justice Minister Ron Basford to comment in the House of Commons, "The Canadian Civil Liberties Association is a responsible group that has raised questions... which it is my duty, as Minister, either to answer and convince them or consider changes in the bill."

The first draft of the bill would have permitted bugging for "all offences that may be prosecuted by indictment," which was wide open to abuse. CCLA argued that bugging should only be approved for emergencies with danger to human life; in the final version of the bill, bugging was permitted for forty-four serious offences. Police forces argued for the authority to eavesdrop for up to thirty-six hours without a judicial warrant; CCLA argued that prior warrants should be required in all circumstances. The final bill did state that judicial warrants were required for all wiretapping, including emergencies, but that in emergency situations, judges may grant a special thirty-six-hour warrant without the usual application formalities. The legislation outlawed the practice of private wiretapping.

"The *Protection of Privacy Act* is a puny response to the pervasive threats to individual privacy which are posed by modern eavesdropping devices," said CCLA when the bill was passed. "Although the outlawing of private wiretapping is a welcome step, there is still no justification for the broad bugging powers given to police in this Bill." Within two years, the government would be attempting to increase the wiretapping powers of the police. Forty years later, the threat of something as quaint as wiretapping seems as antiquated as *Dick Tracy* comic books. Surveillance has become commonplace, and the privacy implications only belatedly raised.

In May 1974, undercover police searching for drugs raided the Fort Erie Landmark Hotel near Niagara Falls, Ontario. They did not have a warrant, only a vague form of writ of assistance, acquired under the aegis of the *Narcotic Control Act*. During the raid, which took more than three hours, fifty officers (a combined force of RCMP and Niagara Regional Police) searched and detained more than a hundred people. More than thirty women were apprehended and taken into washrooms, where they were forced to strip and submit to vaginal and rectal inspections. Women who refused to comply were threatened with the presence of male police officers. The raid resulted in three charges of possession of marijuana and eight charges under the *Liquor Control Act*.

The absurdity of the raid was the subject of much mocking and incredulous coverage in the media over the next several months. A *Globe and Mail* editorial stated in July 1974 that the Niagara Regional Police had probably become "the laughingstock of its community; that is, among people who aren't afraid to go out to have a drink for fear that they'll end up stark naked and leaning spread-eagled against some washroom wall." CCLA organized a rally in Niagara Falls in June and almost 1,000 people turned up to protest and to demand action. Alan Borovoy opened the meeting by declaring, "We're here tonight to tell the police here and in every community—don't you dare ever do anything like that again." The main speaker was writer Pierre Berton, a founding member of CCLA. Berton said, "There's a basic philosophical difference between a police state and a democracy. In a police state, the police are allowed to get away with anything that means the efficient operation of the state. But in a democracy, the rights of the innocent are more important than the pursuit of the guilty."

The meeting ended with a call for an amendment to the *Narcotic Control Act* to restrict the powers of police to conduct searches and for an independent judicial investigation of the incident. CCLA also called for a new structure for citizen complaints independent of police commissions.

• • •

> What I am saying is that I am not prepared to condemn, you know, irremediably the people at the time who might have done an illegal act in order to save a city from being blown up.... Policemen break the law, sometimes, I suppose, when they drive 80 miles an hour to catch the guy who is escaping from a bank...
>
> —Pierre Elliott Trudeau, news conference, October 28, 1977

The police were indeed breaking the law in the 1970s. The RCMP, in particular, interpreted very aggressively instructions from the federal government to remain vigilant and proactive after the end of the October Crisis. The guidelines for the RCMP surveillance activities referred to "subversive, or other activities aimed at effecting secession." In 1975, the guidelines from the Cabinet authorized the RCMP security branch to "maintain internal security by discerning, monitoring, investigating, deterring, preventing and countering individuals and groups in Canada...[who] may be planning to engage in...the use of force, violence, or any criminal means, or the creation or exploitation of civil disorder...."[10]

The work was carried out by a separate security service within the RCMP, under the leadership of a civilian director-general. They burned down a barn, it was said, in order to force a meeting between a group of Quebec nationalists and visiting American activists to take place elsewhere, where eavesdropping was easier. They broke into the offices of the Parti Québécois and stole membership lists. The illegal activities were not limited to Quebec, but extended to the surveillance, including break-ins and mail tampering, of individuals and groups across Canada whom the RCMP determined were suspicious of leftish leanings. Such activities were not confined to the surveillance of Canadians in the name of national security, but were also related to espionage and counter-espionage.

In 1977, when a break-in in Montreal was investigated, both the government of Canada and the government of Quebec created commissions to examine the activities of the RCMP and its security operations. Quebec's Keable Commission (which also had a particular interest in the possible involvement of federal political parties in break-ins into Parti Québécois properties) was created first, a move that greatly unsettled both the federal government and the RCMP; the government set in motion court challenges into the rights of a province to inquire into the activities of a federal police force, a process that ended in a 1980 SCC ruling in favour of the federal government. The Trudeau government also immediately created its own royal commission, chaired by David McDonald, an Alberta Superior Court judge. That inquiry lasted for four years and cost $10 million.

CCLA engaged fully with the McDonald Commission, attempting first to persuade the commissioner that the association's lawyers be permitted to cross-examine witnesses, and subsequently engaging a team of observers across the country to attend hearings of the commission and do research for exhaustive briefs.

One of CCLA's concerns was that, in the time-honoured strategy of politicians, all of the revelations of police misconduct, including the specifics of individuals breaking the law, were merely referred to the commission, with no sense that police officers who broke the law should be charged and prosecuted. This strategy was rooted in Trudeau's unshakeable belief that politicians should not have oversight (and by implication could not be held responsible for) the actions of police forces. In language similar to his famous comment that the state had no business in the bedrooms of the nation, Trudeau laid out his position on the relationship between politicians and police to Parliament in 1977:

> [Governments]...should be kept in ignorance of the day-to-day operations of the police force and even of the security force.... It is not a matter of pleading ignorance as an excuse. It is a matter of stating as a principle that the particular minister of the day should not have a right to know what the police are doing.... That is our position. It is not one of pleading ignorance to defend the government. It is one of keeping the government's nose out of the operations of the police....

This position incensed CCLA, as did what CCLA saw as the somewhat cavalier attitude of Trudeau and other Cabinet ministers to the evidence of law-breaking and a "sizeable cover-up of illegal activity." On November 16, 1977, CCLA wrote an open letter to Prime Minister Trudeau, which was published three days later (at a cost of $8,000) as a full-page ad in *The Globe and Mail.* The letter stated that the government itself is "no longer immune from suspicion...[and is] functioning under a heavy cloud. The dissipation of that cloud cannot be postponed until the Royal Commission has concluded its lengthy deliberations."

The letter made specific demands—for example, that information on law-breaking by officers be made available to Attorneys General for investigation and prosecution and that investigations begin immediately into allegations of illegal activities in any federal agencies, including the post office and the armed forces.

Prime Minister Trudeau replied to this letter three weeks later. He criticized CCLA, dismayed that "an association with the stature of yours should have chosen to abandon thoughtfulness for polemics in its haste to enter the fray" and noting that he had also made clear in the same news conference that the police "must observe the law and if...they break the law and we discover it, they will have to pay for it." He firmly rejected the suggestion that prosecutions should begin immediately, because of the mandate of the McDonald Commission. In rhetoric that resonates uncomfortably more than thirty years later, Trudeau invoked higher considerations: "It is necessary, I suggest, for those asking these questions to bear in mind the extraordinary techniques employed by those engaged in espionage, subversion or terrorism…."

CCLA responded by suggesting that it was "improper to defend the idea of illegal break-ins," with reference to car chases and bank robberies, in the context of specific and serious revelations of a breach of the offices of a political party, notably the Parti Québécois. CCLA then turned its attention fully to the proceedings of the McDonald Commission for the next four years.

Over a period of several months, CCLA launched a public petition that laid out details of RCMP wrongdoing and demanded that normal law enforcement measures be instigated to deal with individual cases. The petition circulated through the newsletter and was sent to individual members, and it was also displayed on a table in front of the CCLA offices on Yonge Street, where prominent members of the organization solicited passersby to sign: IF YOU BELIEVE THE POLICE SHOULD OBEY THE LAW, SIGN HERE. The petition asked not only for signatures but also for a donation of one dollar, and it netted more than fifteen thousand signatures and seventeen thousand dollars.

One of CCLA's celebrity signature-collectors was Margaret Atwood, who wrote about the exercise in her 1979 novel *Life Before Man*:

> Nate sits on a folding wooden chair behind a card table, on the east side of Yonge Street a block south of Shuter Street. The afternoon sun beats down on his head. He shades his eyes with his hand; he should have worn sunglasses. He wishes he could drink beer, just one can anyway of Molson's tucked between his feet, a quick lift to the mouth. But it wouldn't look good….
>
> Nate fixes each approaching pedestrian with what he hopes is a compelling stare: *Your Country Needs You.* Most glance at the sign propped on the table and quicken their pace, trying to get past before he can rope them into anything upsetting, any commitment. RCMP WRONGDOING, the sign says, rapping the Mounties lightly across the knuckles.

CORRUPTION, or, even better, SIN, would have brought more money.

Some pause and he hands them leaflets. Occasionally he gets a nibble of interest and goes into his spiel. He's collecting signatures on a petition, he says; surely they are opposed to RCMP Wrongdoing? He mentions mail-opening but leaves out barn-burning and office-wrecking in Quebec. Most people have no barns or offices and are indifferent or hostile towards Quebec, but they do have mail.... Nate speaks quietly, without undue fervor. Anything like fanaticism must be avoided. He's supposed to represent the average decent-minded citizen. But he knows he does not. It gives him a wry satisfaction that most of those who have so far responded with any enthusiasm have come from the ranks of the black-shirted youths, obvious dope-pushers, fences and petty thieves....

"Jail the bastards," one says. "Bust into my place last weekend and went through it like a goddamn chainsaw. Didn't find nothing on me though."

LEGITIMATE DISSENT IN PERIL—THE BIRTH OF CSIS

But the report and recommendations of the McDonald Commission, finally released in 1981, failed to address satisfactorily CCLA's longstanding and steadfast objectives concerning the relationship between police, politicians, and the people. The commission refused to consider allegations against individual officers and, furthermore, recommended that there be no prosecutions of RCMP wrongdoers, a recommendation that two ministers of justice, Jean Chrétien and his successor, Mark MacGuigan, happily accepted, an acquiescence roundly condemned by Alan Borovoy: "Public respect for the rule of law cannot withstand the unwarranted immunity which the government has conferred on the RCMP."

And the proposal that a new civilian security agency be established—this would result several years later in the creation of the Canadian Security Intelligence Service (CSIS)—was, for CCLA, fundamentally the wrong approach. As Borovoy wrote in a *Globe and Mail* piece in September 1981:

> The further that security surveillance is removed from the discipline of law enforcement, the greater the risk of blurring the line between improper subversion and legitimate dissent. The virtue of the law enforcement approach...is its focus on gathering evidence of relatively definable crime.... But when security surveillance is divorced from law enforcement, investigations are more likely to involve vaguer, broader, and less definable matters. This is what imperils legitimate dissent.

In Dominique Clément's opinion, despite the organization's deep disappointment with the outcomes, CCLA's work on RCMP wrongdoing and the McDonald Commission was one of its greatest public successes, which resulted in five thousand members and "elevated CCLA to the position of one of the government's leading critics.... For the first time in its history, CCLA had justified calling itself a national organization [because] it had asserted itself aggressively on a national issue."

It is perhaps debatable that CCLA had managed, as its founders hoped in 1964, "to bridge a widening gap between the policeman and the public." But the achievement of a heightened sense of active public interest in the actions of law enforcement agencies and politicians would be re-enacted by CCLA some thirty years later when the G20 Summit landed in Toronto.

Thus by the end of the decade, CCLA had marked the territories it was most interested in defending: the rights of citizens in the face of excessive and illegal actions by police; the rights of victims of discrimination on the basis of poverty and race; the importance of due process and civilian oversight of police forces; and the rights to freedom of expression, religion, and dissent. Sometimes CCLA joined the parade, and even led a few, but the organization was increasingly dedicated to making sure that parades took place, whether agreeing with the participants or not.

• • •

> The confrontations between the institutions of the state and minorities and dissenters reveal the true face of Canadian democracy.... A strong nation will nurture diversity; a strong nation can abide dissent.
>
> —Thomas Berger, *Fragile Freedoms*

Also by the end of the 1970s, Canada was ready for a discussion about bringing control over its Constitution to Canada and primed to consider strengthening the rights and freedoms of Canadians with something more robust that the Bill of Rights. It would not be an easy discussion; in 1980, René Lévesque conducted the first referendum on sovereignty in Quebec; Quebeckers chose federalism, but there was by now a chasm between Ottawa and Quebec that would prove unbridgeable. And there was no consensus among Canadians on what the mechanisms and language of a real bill of rights should look like. The debate over several years that resulted in the final text of the *Charter of Rights and Freedoms* was complex, multi-faceted, and fiercely fought.

CHAPTER TWO
The Impact of the Charter and the Judicial Activism Debate

Kent Roach

The *Canadian Charter of Rights and Freedoms* (the Charter) was controversial from the start. It was even controversial within CCLA.

Long-time CCLA general counsel A. Alan Borovoy was a skeptic about the Charter and the increased power that it would give unelected judges.[11] Borovoy's views can usefully be contrasted with those of Thomas Berger, another prominent civil libertarian. Berger published a book in 1981 that presented the Charter as an antidote to the history of the abuse of civil liberties in Canada.[12] Berger resigned from the British Columbia Supreme Court in 1983 after being savagely criticized by Chief Justice Laskin for writing a 1981 op-ed urging that Aboriginal and treaty rights and women's rights be included in the Charter.

Borovoy did not share Berger's passion for the Charter. His views were much closer to those of Saskatchewan's NDP premier Alan Blakeney, a long-time board member of CCLA, who argued that judges were not equipped to make judgments on broad matters of social policy. Borovoy was supportive of Blakeney's arguments that legislatures should have the power to override Charter rights and judicial decisions under the Charter. The override was eventually included in section 33 (s.33) of the Charter, but only after court decisions made it necessary for Pierre Trudeau to reluctantly agree to such a change in order to obtain substantial provincial support for patriation of the Constitution from Britain with the Charter in it.

Others within CCLA were far less skeptical about the Charter. Law professor Walter Tarnopolsky was president of CCLA at the time the Charter was being drafted. Although Tarnopolsky eventually and reluctantly agreed to the override as necessary to ensure the passage of the Charter, he threatened to resign as CCLA President when Alan Borovoy proposed that CCLA come out in favour of the override during early discussions of the Charter.[13]

Despite its internal disagreements about the wisdom of enacting the Charter, CCLA greatly influenced the drafting of the Charter.[14] It was largely responsible for significantly strengthening the legal rights and remedies as well as for changes that required governments to demonstrate that the limits they placed on Charter rights were justified. CCLA has gone on to make extensive and at times successful use of the Charter. At the same time, it has never confined itself simply to the Charter or had any illusions that the mere existence of the Charter would guarantee respect for civil liberties. CCLA has been affected by the increased power of courts under the Charter and the debate about judicial activism that this power engendered, but it has always been an organization that recognized the limits of the courts and the Charter. It was always prepared to engage both courts and legislatures to improve the protection of civil liberties.

This chapter will critically address an influential critique of judicial activism and CCLA's role in it, as put forth by University of Calgary political scientists Ted Morton and Rainer Knopff. They have argued that CCLA is part of a "Court Party" of elites who are "partisans of judicial power" who have used their interventions before the courts to obtain results that could not be achieved in the legislative process.[15] Professors Morton and Knopff's critique is not simply an academic matter: it influenced the Harper government to abolish funding for interveners under the Court Challenge Program.

Part one of this chapter will suggest that Professors Morton and Knopff underestimate the sophisticated debate that

Canadians—including Canadians within CCLA—had when the Charter was drafted about the proper balance of power between courts and legislatures. The Charter that was eventually enacted in 1982 was carefully designed to avoid the extremes of either legislative or judicial supremacy and to promote balanced constitutionalism.[16] At the same time, the enactment of the Charter drew on growing concerns about police abuses of civil liberties. Many critiques of judicial activism on both the Right and the Left miss the mark by pitting the unelected judges against the elected legislators, whereas much Charter litigation and much of CCLA's advocacy is aimed at the unelected executive, most notably the police. This part of the chapter will feature case studies of CCLA's constant concern about unnecessary strip searches by the police and its advocacy, both before and after the enactment of the Charter, of a balanced approach that would give trial judges the discretion to exclude improperly obtained evidence from criminal trials.

The second part of this chapter will focus on Professors Morton and Knopff's Court Party thesis, which alleges that a number of elite groups were united in their attempt to use the Charter to impose extremist positions without regard to social interests or the need for compromise. This chapter will demonstrate that the so-called Court Party has hardly been a unified force, and that CCLA frequently found itself opposing other members of the "Court Party," including interveners representing women, religious groups, and the disabled. Moreover, interveners are a far more diverse group than the somewhat conspiratorial Court Party thesis suggests. CCLA had to compete not only with women's groups and others who opposed its positions, but also with Attorneys General from multiple provinces and groups representing the police and conservative groups. The Charter has not allowed groups such as CCLA to capture or hijack the political process; rather, it has provided another venue for people and groups to participate in a democratic process that includes both Charter litigation and the legislative process. To be sure, CCLA has used Charter interventions before the courts to good effect, but it has also always been willing to raise awareness (and funds) through the media and to participate in legislative reform. The so-called Court Party is neither. The groups identified as part of the Court Party are not a unified party. Moreover, those groups, including CCLA, do not limit their activities to litigation before the courts.

PART I:
CCLA AND THE CHARTER

> "Thanks but No Thanks"[17] to a Watered Down October 1980 Charter: "Canadians would be better off without this Charter...A document as severely flawed as this one does not deserve to be enshrined in our constitution."[18]

The fact that Canada received the Charter that it did is an interesting and largely unknown quirk of history.[19] With the exception of minority language rights, Pierre Trudeau was more committed to the idea of the Charter than its specific content.

During the summer of 1980, Trudeau allowed the Charter to be significantly watered-down in an attempt to win provincial consent to the patriation of the Constitution with the Charter. For example, the right against unreasonable search and seizure was changed to the right to searches and seizures as authorized by law. Under this standard, the open-ended search powers given to police officers under general search warrants known as writs of assistances would have been upheld under the Charter. The Charter would have been a pale imitation of the American Bill of Rights, which specifically prohibited writs of assistance as one of the grievances that led to the American Revolution. The Charter that emerged from closed-door intergovernmental bargaining during the summer of 1980 would not have served as a model for subsequent bills of rights enacted in New Zealand, South Africa, Kenya, and some Australian states.

The October 1980 draft of the Charter had a clause that preserved parliamentary supremacy and the existing law with respect to the exclusion of evidence. Under such an approach, evidence obtained unconstitutionally would still be used in criminal trials. The Charter would have effectively endorsed and continued the Supreme Court of Canada's refusal to exclude improperly obtained evidence as a remedy to enforce the 1960 *Canadian Bill of Rights*.[20] The provinces wanted legal rights and remedies watered down given their jurisdiction over policing and the administration of justice. They, not the federal government, would have to live with the consequences of the new legal rights and remedies.

The October 1980 draft also allowed reasonable limits to be placed on all Charter rights, including the watered-down rights, so long as the limits were "generally accepted in a free and democratic society with a parliamentary system of government." This was a failed attempt to win over Charter skeptics and champions of parliamentary supremacy—a large group at the time that included those on the Left, such as Saskatchewan premier Alan Blakeney, and those on the Right, such as Manitoba premier Sterling Lyon. Left- and right-wing skepticism about the Charter has been present from the start.[21]

In the end, Blakeney, Lyon, and six other provincial premiers were not assuaged by the watered down Charter. Trudeau was forced to try to persuade the United Kingdom to add the Charter and a domestic amending formula to the Canadian Constitution with only the agreement of Ontario and New Brunswick. In order to win more public support for the Charter, Trudeau allowed a special Joint Committee of the House of Commons and the Senate to hear representations from ninety-three groups during the fall of 1980 and the spring of 1981. Most of these groups, including CCLA, were extremely critical of the watered-down October 1980 Charter. The stronger Charter that was eventually enacted after the Joint Committee hearings placed a greater emphasis on the rights and remedies that individuals would have under the Charter. It was, as Trudeau had argued, more of a people's Charter, as opposed to the October 1980 draft, which was more of a government's Charter. As will be seen, the strengthened Charter that emerged from the Joint Committee responded to a growing rights consciousness in Canadian society.

CCLA was the most influential group that appeared before the Joint Committee in the fall of 1980. CCLA's sixteen-page brief, signed by Professor Walter Tarnopolsky, J.S. Midanik, Q.C., and Alan Borovoy, started boldly with a "thanks but no thanks" theme.

CANADIAN CHARTER OF RIGHTS AND FREEDOMS

Guarantee of Rights and Freedoms

Fundamental Freedoms

Democratic Rights

Mobility Rights

Legal Rights

Equality Rights

Official Languages of Canada

Minority Language Educational Rights

Enforcement

General

Application of Charter

Citation

The *Canadian Charter of Rights and Freedoms* was signed by Her Majesty Queen Elizabeth II and the Right Honourable Prime Minister Pierre E. Trudeau in Ottawa on April 17, 1982. A full text and explanation of the text can be found on the Internet by entering Your Guide to the Canadian Charter of Rights and Freedoms.

It asserted that "we believe that Canadians would be better off without this Charter. Its present defects are too serious and too numerous. A document as severely flawed as this one does not deserve to be enshrined in our constitution."[22]

STRENGTHENING SECTION ONE: "PARLIAMENT MUST FISH OR CUT BAIT. LEGISLATIVE SUPREMACY AND THE ENTRENCHMENT OF HUMAN RIGHTS CANNOT CO-EXIST"[23]

CCLA criticized the deferential version of the limitation clause, most famously denounced by women's groups as one that "a Mack Truck" could be driven through. CCLA argued that the idea of generally accepted limits in a parliamentary system of government would render the Charter toothless because "what better measure is there of what is 'generally accepted' than the decisions of Parliament and the Provincial Legislatures? Thus this Charter might well have been impotent against the internment of the Japanese-Canadians and the harassment of the Jehovah's Witnesses."[24] The brief bluntly and colourfully stated that "Parliament must either fish or cut bait. Legislative supremacy and the entrenchment of human rights cannot co-exist in this way. It is imperative that the issue of limitation be handled much differently."[25]

CCLA stressed that the government should bear the onus of demonstrating the necessity of limitations on rights, something that was later embraced in the language of s.1 of the Charter, which now provides that reasonable limits on Charter rights have to be "demonstrably justified in a free and democratic society." CCLA also suggested that s.1 should guarantee rights as well as provide for reasonable limits so as to indicate "an intention to depart from the kind of restrictive interpretations, which effectively eroded the 1960 Bill of Rights."[26] Again, this suggestion found favour, and the Charter was amended so that s.1 "guarantees the rights and freedoms" as well as provides for reasonable and demonstrably justified limits.

CCLA helped tighten s.1 of the Charter, but there was also a hint of undoubtedly Borovoy-influenced skepticism about judicial enforcement of rights in its brief. Drawing on experience under the American Bill of Rights, CCLA argued that even without a limitation clause, the courts would impose limits on even absolute rights. The Charter would never be "a recitation of absolutes" and it would not produce "extremist" or "doctrinaire" jurisprudence.[27] Implicit was the message that CCLA would also not want such jurisprudence. Indeed, CCLA did not attempt to have the limitation clause removed from the Charter. Professors Morton and Knopff have sought to portray CCLA as part of a cabal of unrepresentative extremists who were partisans of the Charter and judicial power.[28] Their approach discounts both the pragmatism and legal sophistication of CCLA, including its appreciation of the limits of any judicially enforced bill of rights.

STRENGTHENING LEGAL RIGHTS IN THE CHARTER

CCLA was concerned about the rights of the accused, and it successfully lobbied for them to be strengthened in the Charter. CCLA's approach was not based on a doctrinaire or absolutist approach, but rather on the group's considerable experience with police misconduct and the realities faced by those accused of a crime. CCLA has consistently focused on the rights of the accused under the Charter and has taken unpopular stands on issues of child pornography, unconstitutional searches that have revealed drugs and weapons, and mandatory sentences. Critics of judicial review often argue that courts have no mandate to resolve reasonable disagreements about rights. What they ignore, however, is that the truly unpopular—such as those accused of crime and prisoners—have very few who are prepared to defend their rights. In addition, political parties often have an incentive to enact populist crime control measures, and even parties that may not take the lead on such measures may be reluctant to lose votes by opposing such measures. Without some degree of judicial activism, the accused and prisoners would have few, if any, rights.

A CANADIAN *MIRANDA* RULE: "SUDDENLY DENIED THE PSYCHOLOGICAL SUPPORTS OF LIFE"[29]

CCLA argued that in the October 1980 draft of the Charter, the right to counsel should be beefed up to require that arrested or detained people—"suddenly denied the psychological supports of normal life" and "likely to be nervous, frightened and bewildered"[30]—be informed of the right to counsel. This argument responded to problems in the court's refusal to exclude improperly obtained evidence under the *Canadian Bill of Rights*. This meant assertive people who knew about their rights and refused to co-operate with the police were able to be acquitted, but not those who simply complied with police demands. A right to be informed about the right to counsel was added to the Charter, and the Canadian *Miranda* rule was created.

The Canadian *Miranda* rule is, in some respects, stronger than the American rule. It applies to those who are subject to psychological detention.[31] In most provinces, it requires that detainees be told of a toll free number that they can use to obtain free legal advice from the state.[32] The Supreme Court also adopted another suggestion from CCLA's 1980 brief inspired by *Miranda*. CCLA argued that "people should be immune from custodial interrogation" until they have reasonable opportunity to consult counsel. The Supreme Court imposed such a holding-off duty on the police in 1987.[33] CCLA was, as always, pragmatic and recognized that there could be exceptions to this right not to be interrogated in cases of "imminent peril to life or limb," a limited exception that has also found favour in the Supreme Court.[34] It also demonstrated its legal sophistication by indicating that research in the United States showed that the police were able "to sustain their conviction and crime solution rates despite Miranda."[35]

In recent years, however, the court's approach toward the Charter has been more cautious. In 2010, the court, in a 5 to 4 decision, rejected CCLA's arguments[36] that the presence of defence counsel in the interrogation room may be necessary because "during a custodial interrogation, the various factors that create the power imbalance between detainees and the state are exacerbated" because "detainees are isolated, alone, without knowledge of the law, and at the mercy of the state."[37]

STRIP SEARCHES FROM FORT ERIE TO GOLDEN

Although critics of the Charter such as Professors Morton and Knopff portray its drafting as a product of unrepresentative elites, and CCLA has never enjoyed mass membership, there was a growing rights consciousness in Canada in the 1970s.[38] The Charter, including the strengthened commitment to legal rights and remedies that CCLA promoted, did not come from nowhere. It was supported by real people who were appalled at well-publicized acts of abuse by the police.

Although supported by the vast majority at the time, Canada's invocation of martial law to respond to two terrorist kidnappings in Quebec in 1970 was soon viewed by many as an overreaction that saw almost five hundred innocent people temporarily detained without access to prompt judicial review. The overreaction of the police did not stop with the October Crisis but included illegal police behaviour such as the destruction of property and the theft of a Parti Québécois membership list.[39] In February 1981, Toronto's infamous bathhouse raids also helped convince many that constitutional restraints on the police were required. Canadians were knowledgeable about human rights abuses and this provided an environment that allowed CCLA and other groups to strengthen the Charter.

Along with the October crisis, one of the events that galvanized Canadians was a massive drug raid at the Landmark Motor Inn in Fort Erie, Ontario, in May 1974. Over 115 people were strip-searched including thirty-six women. A warrant was issued, but the RCMP officers used the powers of their general warrants or writs of assistance that did not require reasonable grounds or even suspicions in relation to particular individuals. Writs of assistance had been one of the grievances that motivated the American Revolution and had been specifically prohibited under the American Bill of Rights, a document that more Canadians were familiar with as a result of the liberal decisions of the Warren Court and popular culture.

CCLA took the lead in protesting the Fort Erie searches, which only discovered six ounces of marijuana, mostly discarded on the floor and none discovered as a result of the humiliating strip searches. The pressure was so intense that the province had to appoint a judge to conduct a public inquiry into the searches. The judge concluded that while the officers had acted in "good faith" and "lawfully," the searches were nevertheless "arbitrary," "foolish," and "unnecessary." Moreover, the police had strip-searched the patrons without "a shred of evidence" that such invasive and humiliating searches would discover evidence of a crime.[40]

CCLA used the Fort Erie searches to good effect to criticize the October 1980 draft of the Charter. It argued that the 1980 draft—which only gave people a right against *illegal*, as opposed to unreasonable, searches—would have done nothing to prevent the Fort Erie searches in which "more than thirty women were herded into washrooms, stripped, and subjected to vaginal and rectal examinations."[41] As a result of CCLA's submissions, the Charter was amended to provide a right against *unreasonable* searches and seizures.

The courts would soon strike down writs of assistances under the more substantive version of the Charter right against unreasonable searches and seizures. CCLA, however, was not a simple-minded partisan of the Charter that only focused on litigation. It asked both the Guelph and Toronto Police Services Boards to adopt policies on strip searches in recognition that police policies were often more effective in controlling police behaviour than the sporadic interventions by the courts. The policies that CCLA urged the Police Services Boards to adopt were not popular with the police, but they were also not an example of a doctrinaire or absolutist approach that would prohibit all strip searches. Instead, CCLA urged the police services boards to limit strip searches to cases where there were reasonable grounds to conclude that such invasive searches would discover weapons, evidence, or dangerous substances. CCLA also recommended that chiefs of police should prepare an annual report on strip searches and whether they were justified,[42] thereby triggering accountability, not in the courts, but in the media and civil society. CCLA was well aware that most people who were unnecessarily strip-searched by the police would not have the money or inclination to go to court to seek remedies, even under the broad remedies provision that it had successfully lobbied to be included in the Charter. Instead, CCLA consistently stressed the importance of independent civilian review of the police and urged that people who were strip-searched should be able to make complaints to independent boards who could take remedial action in a less costly fashion than the courts.[43]

Unfortunately, the Police Services Boards and the police did not take actions to prevent unnecessary and humiliating strip searches. In Ontario, gains with respect to the independent review of the police were repealed by the Mike Harris government. As is often the case, CCLA went to court when other avenues of change and reform were blocked. In 2001, the Supreme Court, in *R. v. Golden*,[44] decided, in a divided 5 to 4 judgment, that the right against unreasonable searches and seizures prohibited routine strip searches upon arrests. Consistent with CCLA's original representations to the Toronto Police Services Board, there would now have to be reasonable and probable grounds to believe that such an invasive and humiliating search would discover weapons or evidence of crime.[45] In reaching this decision, the court heard from CCLA as well as legal aid clinics representing African-Canadians and Aboriginal peoples. The court, however, was not captured by these groups. It also heard arguments about the need for strip searches from the Canadian Association of Chiefs of Police and the Attorneys General of Canada and Ontario.

CCLA, represented by criminal lawyers Frank Addario and Jonathan Dawe, did not take an absolutist position that strip searches should always be prohibited or even always require a judicial warrant. It did submit that a senior officer should approve strip searches except in exigent circumstances. It also stressed that strip searches should not be a normal part of a search following an arrest and should only be used if there were reasonable grounds to believe that they were necessary to discover weapons or evidence. CCLA cited various media reports to make its point about the need for constitutional regulation of strip searches and to indicate that "some police forces have had policies of routinely strip searching *all* arrestees."[46]

Many of CCLA's submissions are reflected in the majority judgment in *Golden*. The majority concluded that common law police powers to search arrestees should not extend so far as to include invasive and humiliating strip searches and that reasonable and probable grounds were needed to justify the searches. The majority also stressed that strip searches should generally be conducted at the police station and not, as in the Golden case, in a Subway sandwich shop, or indeed in places such as Fort Erie's Landmark Motor Hotel. Four judges, however, dissented and refused to impose new restrictions on the police and instead held that strip searches could be conducted as an incident of arrest so long as they were not performed in an unreasonable manner or for abusive reasons. The minority was influenced by the Canadian Association of Chiefs of Police's argument that police were often alone and in remote areas, and it might not be safe for them to wait to conduct strip searches.

Golden—much like CCLA's protest of the 1974 Fort Erie raids and the enactment of a right against unreasonable search and seizure—was a significant victory for CCLA. Alas, CCLA was under no illusion that either section 8 or favourable precedents from the Supreme Court were self-executing. Problems with strip searches are still frequently reported, and some police seem more inclined to follow at least the spirit of the minority judgment. The Toronto Police Service strip-searches a third of the people it arrests, amounting to over 20,000 strip searches in the last year (2013).[47] CCLA continues to advocate to the Toronto Police Service Board to change police policies on strip searches but often to no avail as that board is subject to the same malaise about municipal politics that one finds in a city that elected Rob Ford as mayor. CCLA played an important role in strengthening the Charter to better protect civil liberties, but alas, there are no guarantees, notwithstanding the language of the Charter.

REJECTING RIGHTS WITHOUT REMEDIES: "IF THE CHARTER IS TO ENJOY THE RESPECT OF THE CANADIAN PEOPLE, IT MUST BE CAPABLE OF EFFECTIVELY VINDICATING THE RIGHTS IT CREATES."[48]

CCLA argued to the Joint Committee that the October 1980 draft of the Charter was woefully deficient because it did not provide for remedies for violations of rights. CCLA embraced the common law's traditional idea that rights were in practice defined by their remedies. They argued that invalidation of laws "in the absence of compensation...may appear very hollow to the aggrieved parties and the public" and that a general remedies clause should allow the courts to award damages. They also argued that a remedy section was required to prevent the "unacceptable paradox" of citizens being capable "of challenging an act of Parliament but not an act of a police officer."[49]

CCLA was concerned, some might say obsessed, with police conduct. Most debates about judicial activism pit the unelected court against elected legislatures, whereas most Charter cases actually pit the unelected court against unelected representatives of the executive, such as the police officers. CCLA asked the Joint Committee to enact a general remedies clause that would subsequently become section 24(1) of the Charter, which allows courts and tribunals to award appropriate and just remedies. The brief argued:

> We believe an additional section should be added specifically endowing the courts with a wide range of powers to remedy violations of the Charter. Such remedies should include the power to issue corrective orders, enjoin certain acts, make declarations, exclude evidence, and award damages. The remedies section should clearly apply not only to any law which violates the Charter but also to administrative practices and common law precedents which conflict with its provisions. If the Charter is to enjoy the respect of the Canadian people, it must be capable of effectively vindicating the rights it creates.[50]

In subsequent years, the Supreme Court would stress that appropriate and just remedies under s.24(1) of the Charter would be available in response to unconstitutional acts of the executive that were often not even authorized by democratically enacted legislation. The courts would also, as CCLA suggested, apply the Charter to the common law, thereby indicating, contrary to some critics of judicial activism,[51] that not even the courts were above the restraints of the Charter.

It would take thirty years for the Supreme Court to articulate a test for awarding damages under the general remedies section that CCLA had inserted into the Charter. The court did so in a case with the assistance of a CCLA intervention that again stressed that rights would be hollow without effective remedies. The court accepted a CCLA argument that the deterrence of police misconduct was a legitimate purpose of Charter damages.[52] Both in that case and in another landmark remedies case decided in 2003,[53] the Supreme Court echoed the words of the 1980 CCLA brief, stating, "If the Charter is to enjoy the respect of the Canadian people, it must be capable of effectively vindicating the rights it creates."[54] At the same time, both decisions recognized that courts must respect the role of legislatures and the executive when devising remedies. The court's 2010 damage case even imported a "mini-section 1" into the remedies section by providing the government an opportunity to demonstrate that less drastic remedies than damages would be sufficient or that the awards of damage would harm the operation of government. In the end, the court approved the modest award of $5,000 to Vancouver lawyer Cameron Ward, who had been unconstitutionally strip-searched, while at the same time it suggested that damages would not automatically flow from all Charter violations. Unnecessary strip searches have been a long-time concern of CCLA both before and after the enactment of the Charter. Unfortunately, the passage of the Charter, and a number of successful Charter cases, has not stopped unnecessary and humiliating strip searches that occur in Canadian police stations on a daily basis.

CANADA'S COMPROMISE EXCLUSIONARY RULE: "ONE OF THE FEW PRACTICAL METHODS AVAILABLE TO A COURT FOR VINDICATING A RIGHT THAT HAS BEEN VIOLATED."[55]

One of the criticisms of the Charter and judicial activism is that they promote absolute rights claims that are hostile to compromise. Morton and Knopff have written that "the growth of courtroom rights talk undermines perhaps the fundamental perquisite of decent liberal democratic politics: the willingness to engage those with whom one disagrees in the ongoing attempt to combine diverse interests into temporarily viable governing majorities."[56] Morton and Knopff's critique of judicial activism has echoes in Prime Minister Harper's argument, made recently when introducing a Canadian Victims Bill of Rights: "The rights of criminals have received far more attention than the rights of their victims… justice is not only for the accused; it is also for the victims."[57] Such arguments trade on the idea that courts enforce the rights of the accused in an absolute manner. To be sure, CCLA has defended the rights of the accused, but it has never defended an absolutist approach to the enforcement of their rights.

In its presentation to the Joint Committee on the Constitution in late 1980, CCLA consciously sought a compromise position on the exclusion of evidence under the Charter. They argued that the watered-down October 1980 draft foreclosed judicial discretion to decide whether evidence should be excluded because it entrenched parliamentary supremacy with respect to the laws of evidence. CCLA argued for judicial discretion to decide whether exclusion was necessary on the facts of particular cases. It observed that the "sanction" of exclusion "might well represent one of the few practical methods available to a court for vindicating a right which has been violated.… While we recognize that the matter is truly controversial, we consider it again inconsistent with the notion of entrenchment to deny the judiciary the right to make the choice."[58] CCLA recognized that reasonable people could disagree about the exclusionary rule. Its argument in favour of judicial discretion foreshadowed the subsequent arguments it would make against the use of mandatory minimum sentences. CCLA may not have trusted judges in every respect, but it believed that only judges were in a position to make decisions tailored to the facts of specific cases.

In his oral presentation on behalf of CCLA, Professor Walter Tarnopolsky made it clear that CCLA was not advocating an American-style absolute exclusionary rule, but a more moderate and balanced rule that would require "exclusion in some cases but not necessarily exclusion in every case." He explained that judges would have to balance competing interests and to "weigh on the one hand the gravity of the offence, the circumstances, and on the other, the seriousness of the infringement…."[59] CCLA consciously sought to fashion a compromise between defence lawyers who may have wanted all unconstitutionally obtained evidence excluded from criminal trials and prosecutors and the police who wanted no unconstitutionally obtained evidence excluded.

"THE ADMISSION OF THIS EVIDENCE WOULD MAKE ME VOMIT, IT WAS OBTAINED IN SUCH A REPREHENSIBLE MANNER."[60]

Groups representing police and prosecutors also appeared before the Joint Committee on the Constitution. They warned of the dangers of the American approach, which required the exclusion of all unconstitutionally obtained evidence including the "fruit of the poisonous tree." These concerns were more rooted in popular culture—such as the 1983 movie *Star Chamber*, featuring Michael Douglas as a judge who would kill murderers allowed to go free because of the exclusionary rule—rather than the actual reality of the administration of the exception-laced American rule. Regardless, CCLA had no interest in defending an absolute exclusionary rule.

What is now s.24(2) of the Charter was eventually added by an amendment brought by the Progressive Conservative Party, which argued that only in cases of serious police misconduct would evidence be excluded on the basis that its "admission would bring the administration of justice into disrepute."[61] This view was echoed by Eugene Ewaschuk, then a senior Department of Justice official, who told the committee that the exclusionary remedy would, under s.24(2), only be used in response to "very blameworthy, repugnant and very reprehensive conduct"—or as he colourfully put it, when "the admission of this evidence would make me vomit, it was obtained in such a reprehensible manner."[62]

As will be seen, once CCLA succeeded in obtaining the s.24(2) compromise, it did not engage in the sort of extremist and uncompromising rights talk that critics of judicial activism on both the Left and Right criticize. It took a consistently moderate position on the exclusion of unconstitutionally obtained evidence, even when it meant arguing for a less robust exclusionary rule than the Supreme Court accepted.

THE RISE OF A MORE ABSOLUTE EXCLUSIONARY RULE

The Supreme Court, in the early years of the Charter, was not persuaded by the restrictive "vomit" test or even by warnings by CCLA and others that unconstitutionally obtained evidence should not be excluded in every case and only in response to police misconduct. The court was keen to make clear that it would interpret the Charter in a more generous manner than it had interpreted the *Canadian Bill of Rights*.[63]

The court decided its first s.24(2) case in 1985. It excluded a Breathalyzer sample that would have convicted the accused. A police officer in Moose Jaw, Saskatchewan, simply forgot to inform a drunk driving suspect of his right to counsel a week after Queen Elizabeth had proclaimed the Charter in force on April 17, 1982, in a cold and rainy ceremony in Ottawa. If the constable had informed the accused and the accused had contacted counsel, counsel would have most likely told him that he had to provide a breath sample because refusing to provide one is also a criminal offence of the same severity as providing one over the legal limit. CCLA did not intervene in the case. There were no interveners on the side of the accused. The Attorney General of Saskatchewan was well represented by James MacPherson, a future law dean and Court of Appeal judge, and Andrew Petter, a future law dean and B.C. Cabinet minister. Three other Attorneys General intervened to oppose exclusion. They all lost. The Supreme Court decided 6 to 2 that the evidence should be excluded.

Justice Estey, in a terse decision for the majority, seemed to embrace an absolute exclusionary rule by arguing that failure to exclude the evidence would "invite police officers to disregard Charter rights of the citizens and to do so with an assurance of impunity" and strip the right of right "of any meaning" so it "would have no place in the catalogue of 'legal rights' found in the Charter."[64] Justice LeDain dissented and argued that judges should balance the seriousness of the violation against the seriousness of the offence and that the violation was not that serious, especially because the police officer could have relied in good faith on *Canadian Bill of Rights* jurisprudence that would have held that the accused was not entitled to counsel before providing the Breathalyzer sample. In this and other early cases under the Charter, the Supreme Court clearly signalled that it was prepared to take a much more robust approach to interpreting the Charter than it had to interpreting the *Canadian Bill of Rights*.

In 1987, in another case that CCLA did not participate in, the Supreme Court articulated a more elaborate theory to justify the result in its 1985 Breathalyzer case. The test became known as the fair trial test. It held that courts should exclude evidence obtained through a violation of the right of counsel or other Charter violations that forced accused persons to incriminate themselves through statements or bodily substances regardless of the seriousness of the Charter violation or the offence.[65] The court's theory was that the unconstitutional compulsion of the accused would result in an unfair trial, and that an unfair trial would always bring the administration of justice into disrepute and require the exclusion of evidence. The seriousness of the violation and the offence charged would only be balanced in those cases where evidence was not conscripted from the accused. The Supreme Court's enthusiasm for the Charter and its determination to make Charter rights meaningful through robust remedies had taken it quite far from the intent of the framers of the Charter, including CCLA.

CCLA'S MODERATING INFLUENCE ON THE CANADIAN EXCLUSIONARY RULE: "NO RULES OF AUTOMATIC EXCLUSION OR INCLUSION"[66]

The Supreme Court's fair trial exclusionary rule was both controversial and complex. In 1997, the court signalled that it was prepared to reconsider its approach to s.24(2). Alan Borovoy asked me to represent CCLA in this very important Supreme Court case. I was a relatively young law professor at the time who had written on s.24(2) and had taken a position that was generally supportive of the Supreme Court's fair trial test. It is obvious from the public record of CCLA's factum in the Supreme Court that my instructions from Alan Borovoy were not to support the fair trial test that I had supported in my academic writings. Consistent with its traditional concerns, CCLA would focus on police misconduct.

The case involved a seventeen-year-old accused who had been charged with a brutal murder of a teenaged girl. Critical evidence in the case was semen obtained from the victim's vagina and a bite mark. The police arrested the accused, and the accused's lawyers gave them a letter stating that the accused did not consent to the taking of bodily samples. The police ignored this request. Under threat of force, they took pubic and other hair samples and cheek-swab samples from the accused. They also took impressions of the accused's teeth. They interrogated the accused, but did not obtain an incriminating statement. They did, however, retrieve DNA from a tissue that the sobbing accused had thrown away while he was being interrogated. The trial judge found that the accused's rights against search and seizure had been violated by the seizure of the hair, cheek swab, and teeth impressions. Nevertheless, he held that given the seriousness of the offence, the admission of the evidence would not bring the administration of justice into disrepute.

CCLA supported the accused on the appeal from his first-degree murder conviction but not on the basis eventually accepted by the court—that the hair, cheek swab and teeth impressions should be excluded as evidence that was unconstitutionally conscripted from the accused, and that their admission would affect the fairness of the trial. Rather, CCLA argued that all of the bodily samples (including the critical DNA from the discarded tissue) should be excluded because of a pattern of serious Charter violations. CCLA stressed that s.24(2) was designed to counteract double standards that would allow the police to violate the law, in this case by assaulting an accused. The state should not be allowed "to exploit its superior power over detainees without apparent sanction for such conduct."[67] As in its original brief to the Joint Committee on the Charter, CCLA stressed the "particular vulnerability of detainees who are cut off from the world."[68] It argued that violations of Charter rights that were accompanied by police threats of force were "especially serious." Moreover, the force used against the accused in obtaining the hair samples and teeth impressions was not less serious because "the accused prudently chose the path of least resistance and least indignity" and complied with the police requests.[69] Although the police were investigating a serious offence, there was no urgency. The police and the prosecutors who advised them should have paid more attention to Charter requirements in such a serious case. CCLA urged the court in reconsidering s.24(2) to pay more attention "to the need to promote compliance by public authorities with the letter and spirit of the Charter"[70] throughout the entire investigation. It stressed that there should be "no finding of good faith when police or prosecutorial conduct reveals a pattern of disregard for the Charter."[71]

The Supreme Court decided that all of the evidence except the DNA in the discarded tissue should be excluded under s.24(2), not because, as CCLA argued, the evidence came from a pattern of serious violations, but because the evidence was unconstitutionally conscripted from the accused.[72] In other words, the Supreme Court decided to retain the essence of the fair trial test that it had created in the early years of the Charter. The court's approach was generous to the accused, but at the same time, the court admitted the critical discarded tissue (containing the DNA that matched the semen found in the victim) on the basis that its seizure did not interfere with the accused's bodily integrity. CCLA's position would have required that the tissue be excluded because of the seriousness of the pattern of Charter violations.

This case and others where the Supreme Court excluded DNA seized from the accused were understandably controversial. Parliament responded quickly with new warrants that allowed the police to seize DNA samples and to take body impressions. The critical difference, however, is that the police must demonstrate to an independent judge that there are reasonable grounds to believe that a crime has been committed and that the intrusive seizures of bodily substances and impressions will provide evidence of the crime. The cases viewed in isolation may strike some as judicial activism, but the end result was not permanently to fetter the police, but to require them to get judicial warrants before they invaded a suspect's bodily integrity. What some denounced as judicial activism and a preference for the rights of criminals over those of victims can also be seen as an exercise in constitutionalism, separation of powers, and even dialogue between courts, the executive, and Parliament. The populist politics that decries the "rights of criminals" runs a real risk of undermining our commitment to the rule of law and constitutionalism.

CCLA's plea to the Supreme Court to focus on the seriousness of Charter violations and police misconduct before excluding evidence did not win the day in 1997, but it did in 2009. The case involved three police officers who arbitrarily detained and questioned a young African-Canadian man in Toronto without giving him the right to counsel before the accused handed marijuana and a loaded gun over to the police. As in the 1997 case, CCLA, this time represented by Professor Don Stuart, argued that the evidence should be excluded because the violations were serious. Consistent with its initial stance on s.24(2), CCLA maintained that there should be "no rules of automatic exclusion or inclusion." As it had unsuccessfully argued in 1997, CCLA argued that the "central consideration" under s.24(2) should be "the seriousness of the breach."[73]

CCLA did not champion an absolute exclusionary rule, but it was concerned that a failure to exclude evidence obtained by police misconduct even in serious cases would suggest that "the police ends always justify the means" and could create "public cynicism regarding the integrity of our system of law enforcement."[74] CCLA defended exclusion as the only realistic sanction for police misconduct because the "police are rarely, if ever, disciplined for Charter breaches that uncover evidence of criminality" and "civil litigation is expensive" and "highly unlikely when the plaintiff is in prison."[75] CCLA also argued that negligent breaches that ought to have been avoided were serious and "there must be a sanction for serious Charter breaches, Courts must be above law and order politics."[76]

The Supreme Court ultimately admitted the evidence of the drugs and gun in Donohue Grant's case, but it accepted CCLA's argument that the s.24(2) fair test that it had used for over twenty years to exclude conscriptive evidence, without considering the seriousness of the violation or of the offence, should be discarded. Henceforth, courts should first assess the seriousness of the Charter violation with a particular focus on the integrity of the justice system. In all cases, judges should look at the effect of the violation on Charter protected interests and the adverse effects of excluding the evidence. As CCLA suggested in its factum, appellate courts should defer to how trial judges balanced the competing factors in individual cases. This was consistent with the arguments that CCLA had made almost thirty years earlier to the Joint Committee on the Constitution, which had stressed the importance of having trial judges who were familiar with all the facts of the case decide whether exclusion of unconstitutionally obtained evidence was necessary.

The court, in *R. v. Grant*, embraced CCLA's argument that police negligence towards their obligations under the Charter or patterns of Charter violations should not be condoned.[77] It also accepted the argument that admitting evidence simply because it was reliable was inconsistent with the clear wording of s.24(2)[78] that CCLA had fought to have included in the Charter. The court admitted the drugs and the gun while noting that it might have decided differently had there been evidence of racial profiling or egregious or deliberate police misconduct. The new test articulated by the court is more in line with CCLA's consistent advocacy that trial judges should have the discretion to exclude evidence, but only when necessary to respond to police misconduct and serious Charter violations.

NOT JUST THE CHARTER: A MULTI-FACETED SEARCH FOR POLICE ACCOUNTABILITY

Much of the debate about judicial activism in Canada has focused on how the Charter has given the courts more power in relation to the legislature. To be sure, this is the case, and CCLA has successfully urged the Supreme Court to strike down a number of laws. Much Charter review, however, pits the unelected judges against the unelected executive. CCLA has always been concerned that the police, as the part of the executive authorized to carry guns and use force, should be carefully and publicly monitored. CCLA has pursued a multi-faceted quest for police accountability.

CCLA intervened successfully in two different cases in 2010 to convince the Supreme Court that judges should be able to reduce an accused's sentence as a remedy for a Charter violation or other police abuse of power,[79] and that the courts should be able to award damages under the Charter when necessary to deter Charter violations and vindicate Charter rights.[80] It was also successful in convincing the court to recognize intentional abuse of office[81] and negligence in police investigations as causes of action that would allow individuals to sue the police.[82] The Charter is important, but so too are the common law and ordinary statutes. CCLA supported attempts to have the police comply with statutory oversight systems such as Ontario's Special Investigations Unit, which investigates serious injuries caused by the police.[83] It was also active in campaigning for independent review of police complaints. CCLA was not a one trick "partisan of the Charter"[84]—it used all available means to attempt to hold the police accountable.

CCLA saw the Charter—and, in particular, the ability to exclude evidence that the police had unconstitutionally obtained—as an important means to ensure that the police would be held accountable. CCLA never favoured an absolute exclusionary rule that would exclude all evidence obtained in violation of the Charter. It consistently argued in favour of the exclusion of evidence obtained by serious and unacceptable violations of the Charter. This moderate position rejected either automatic inclusion or exclusion of improperly obtained evidence. It was not an extremist position, and it persuaded the Progressive Conservative Party to move a resolution adding s.24(2) to the Canadian Charter. The Supreme Court used a more absolute exclusionary rule than CCLA advocated until 2009 when it embraced an approach that, as CCLA had suggested, focused on whether the police had engaged in unacceptable conduct that the courts should not condone. Attempts by Prime Minister Harper to discredit the courts as automatically favouring "the rights of criminals"[85] over those of victims and society may be politically popular, but they distort the balanced nature of the Canadian exclusionary rule and CCLA's consistent defence of such an approach.

STRENGTHENED EQUALITY RIGHTS BUT NO "EXCESSIVE JUDICIAL SECOND GUESSING OF LEGISLATIVE POLICY CHOICES"[86]

The generation that was involved in the drafting of the Charter had good reasons to be skeptical about relying on Canadian judges to enforce human rights. They had witnessed the Supreme Court eviscerate the *Canadian Bill of Rights* with rulings that deferred to Parliament. Some of these rulings seem absurd today. For example, in 1978, a unanimous Court held that women—denied benefits because of pregnancy—were discriminated against on the permitted grounds of pregnancy as opposed to the prohibited grounds of gender. In making this decision, the court rejected arguments by "Miss Lynn Smith." She would later become an esteemed law dean and judge[87] and a leading advocate of a more robust and substantive vision of equality.

Although women's groups had the most influence in strengthening equality rights under the Charter, CCLA also weighed in. It argued that the grounds of discrimination should be left open-ended. The grounds specified in the October draft "hardly begin to address the spectrum of unacceptable discrimination."[88] In this way, CCLA and others left the door open to the subsequent recognition by the courts that gays and lesbians were a protected group vulnerable to discrimination. CCLA also intervened under the Charter to support a small gay and lesbian bookstore from prior censorship. Patricia Jackson of the Torys law firm argued for CCLA that customs officials were incapable of applying a community standards definition of obscenity in a manner that did not discriminate against sexual minorities.[89]

CCLA wanted strong equality rights that could grow in a living-tree manner. Nevertheless, they were also concerned that equality rights not be so broad that they would result in "excessive judicial second guessing of legislative policy choices" or "wind up dumping too many problems on the courts."[90] This part of the brief was undoubtedly written by Alan Borovoy who, in 1988, published a book that included an entire chapter about his fears that unelected and elite judges would use the Charter, as they had the American Bill of Rights, to impose "free market" policies over "social democratic" ones and subvert what Borovoy passionately believed should be a democratic choice for the people to make in elections.[91] In this way, CCLA shared the concerns of many left-wing critics of judicial activism that Canadian courts not be able to use the Charter to interfere with legitimate government regulation, as the American courts did when they attempted to constitutionalize *laissez faire* economics in the Lochner era in the early 1900s.[92]

CCLA and others were concerned that Canadian courts not follow the American example of the 1970s of restraining the "reverse discrimination" of affirmative action programs. They supported the carve-outs that were included in both equality and mobility rights in the Charter for programs designed to assist disadvantaged groups. CCLA's concern that an unrestrained approach to equality rights could lead to "excessive judicial second guessing of legislative policy choices" was reflected in the Supreme Court's first equality rights case. The court in that case stressed that only legislative distinctions that resulted in discrimination and violated the substantive equality rights of the disadvantaged would violate even an expanded section 15.[93]

CCLA'S COMPROMISE ABOUT GIVING JUDGES MORE POWER AND THE SAFETY VALVE OF THE OVERRIDE: "OUR BOARD WAS SPLIT INTO THREE"[94]

CCLA was aware of arguments stating that it was a bad idea to give judges increased power under the Charter. In its November 1980 submission to the Joint Committee, it noted that it had "avoided addressing itself to the abstract idea of whether such entrenchment is philosophically desirable" only because Parliament "has already expressed its intention to entrench our fundamental freedoms in the constitution."[95] This carefully worded sentence in the CCLA brief recognized that there were internal divisions within CCLA about the Charter project. As discussed above, CCLA's general counsel, Alan Borovoy, was concerned that the Charter would give the courts too much power over social policy and was not particularly optimistic that they would do a good job enforcing civil liberties, while its president Walter Tarnopolsky had threatened to resign if CCLA advocated the inclusion of an override clause that would allow legislatures to enact laws notwithstanding Charter rights.

When the override was eventually included in the Charter in order to win the support of all provincial governments except Quebec, CCLA board was "split into three."[96] Alan Borovoy and academics Donald Smiley and Harry Arthurs supported the override; Eddie Greenspan, Mary Eberts, and Irwin Cotler opposed it; and Tarnopolsky, Syd Midanik, and Ron Atkey pragmatically accepted that it was necessary to get the Charter passed. Surprisingly for a group that Morton and Knopff have labelled as partisans of the Charter and increased judicial power, CCLA was divided about the override.

The compromise of the section 33 override sought to avoid the extremes of either legislative or judicial supremacy. Some within CCLA saw the override as an acceptable safety valve that could be used to respond to egregious judicial decisions. They recognized that the use of the override should be subject to special democratic debate and forced reconsideration. CCLA fought in the courts, but it was no stranger to democracy: It frequently appeared before legislative committees, intervened in the media, and held rallies in support of its positions, including a rally in 1987 when Parliament voted on whether to restore the death penalty. Others in CCLA, including leading lawyers such as Eddie Greenspan and Mary Eberts, would have seen the override as a threat to the rights of the unpopular, especially the accused and women. Critics of judicial activism argue that the Canadian response to judicial activism has failed because the override has not been used. However, this is not the case.

Quebec used the override after the court struck down part of its legislation to protect the French language, but decided not to renew the override after five years and some successful appeals by anglophones to the United Nations. Alberta used the override in an attempt to prevent gay marriage, but again allowed the override to expire. The federal government probably should have used the override when it enacted in-your-face legislative replies to unpopular Supreme Court decisions recognizing a defence of extreme intoxication to sexual assault and wide-ranging access by the accused to the therapeutic records of complainants in sexual assault cases. More recently, Quebec premier Pauline Marois indicated that she was prepared to use the override to protect the proposed Quebec Charter of Values that would prohibit public employees from wearing or displaying religious symbols. Quebeckers voted her out of office shortly after, but the override remains as a potential restraint on judicial power in Canadian power.

CCLA'S PROCEDURAL AND COMPROMISE APPROACH TO ABORTION AND CAPITAL PUNISHMENT

CCLA was not only prepared to compromise on the override but also on the divisive issues of abortion and capital punishment, thus belying those such as Morton and Knopff who criticize it for engaging in rights talk that they say makes compromises between reasonable differences of opinion impossible.

In one of its first interventions in the Supreme Court, CCLA argued that Canada's abortion law was contrary to the *Canadian Bill of Rights*. It did not take a substantive due process approach, such as that taken in the American *Roe v. Wade* case that constitutionalized a substantive right to abortions in the first trimester. Rather, it stressed the procedural inequities of the Canadian law that required abortions to be approved by hospital committees and performed in hospitals, despite the fact that hospitals in some regions of Canada refused to perform abortions. This argument helped Alan Borovoy keep the support of both Emmett Hall and John Nelligan, who were members of the CCLA board who were also opposed to abortion. Again, CCLA was not immune from compromise. CCLA's procedural unfairness argument did not win the day under the *Canadian Bill of Rights*, but it eventually convinced the Supreme Court, in 1988, to strike down the abortion law under the Charter.[97]

CCLA was also well aware that it was Parliament, and not the courts, that abolished capital punishment. In 1976, parliamentarians voted 131 to 124 to repeal the death penalty in a free vote. A few months later, the Supreme Court of Canada rejected CCLA's submission that capital punishment was cruel and unusual punishment contrary to the *Canadian Bill of Rights*. The court unanimously decided that mandatory capital punishment for the murder of police officers was not arbitrary or excessive and did not violate the right against cruel and unusual punishment under the *Canadian Bill of Rights*. It rejected arguments that Edward Greenspan had made on CCLA's behalf in a thirty-nine-page factum that drew heavily on American constitutional debates about the death penalty. Chief Justice Laskin upheld the Canadian death penalty on the basis that it was available in a much narrower range of cases than in the United States. He noted, however, that Parliament was free to repeal capital punishment,[98] which of course it had just done. In 1987, another free vote on reinstating capital punishment was rejected in Parliament in a close vote. CCLA was actively engaged in opposing the political re-instatement of the death penalty. Canadian political culture—not court decisions—effectively abolished the death penalty.[99]

In 1976, the Supreme Court ignored an argument made by CCLA that would in 2001 lead it unanimously to conclude that extraditing a fugitive to face the death penalty would generally violate the Charter. The argument was simply that it was impossible to prevent all wrongful convictions. As in the abortion context, CCLA's argument deliberately avoided a "substantive due process" approach that asked the courts to embrace an absolute position on the controversial moral issues of abortion or capital punishment. Instead, CCLA argued that the death penalty was arbitrary because of the discretion that permeated criminal justice from police investigations, charging decisions, jury decisions, sentencing decisions, and decisions by the executive as to whether to extend mercy or let the prisoner hang. It added that "compounding the arbitrariness of the infliction of the death penalty is the fact that at each stage there exists the possibility of error," and it reminded the court that once a person was executed "the mistake cannot be remedied."[100] This was essentially the argument the Supreme Court would eventually accept to prohibit extradition to the death penalty almost twenty-five years later.[101] CCLA's procedural approaches to abortion and capital punishment recognized that there was a range of reasonable positions on these issues while also insisting that flaws and arbitrariness in the administration of the law should not be ignored.

Some critics of judicial activism argue that it is undemocratic for the unelected judges of the Supreme Court to prevent Parliament from bringing back the death penalty. Such arguments ignore that the judges have greater expertise about the workings and the frailties of the criminal justice system than parliamentarians. It also ignores that Parliament could still reinstate the death penalty if it was prepared to enact the legislation notwithstanding the legal rights in the Charter. Ted Morton has argued that one way to revive and legitimize the use of the override would be to tie a legislative decision to invoke it to a popular vote in a referendum.[102] The Harper government has so far avoided the divisive issues of abortion and capital punishment, but it is possible that these issues may be re-visited in the future, perhaps by relying on the populist strategy of using referendums. Although many who desire restrictions on abortion and the use of the death penalty may believe that the courts and the Charter stand in their way, it would not be impossible for them to enact their views if they had significant public support. The court has not constitutionalized pro-choice or abolitionist positions as a matter of moral fiat. Rather, following the lead of arguments that CCLA originally made in the 1970s, it has focused on procedural flaws and inequities in the administration of both restrictions on abortion and the use of capital punishment.

THE ALMOST-ABANDONED SECTION 7 OF THE CHARTER: "IT MIGHT BE POSSIBLE, WITHOUT UNDUE JEOPARDY, TO WITHDRAW THE PROPOSED SECTION 7"[103]

The Charter guarantees, in section 7, that "Everyone has the right to life, liberty and security of the person and the right not to be deprived thereof except in accordance with the principles of fundamental justice." Some have called this the section that protects legal rights, but it actually includes many more aspects of what we consider to be important to living in a democracy.

CCLA's pragmatic caution about the possibility of judicial overreaching under the Charter was reflected not only in its concerns that legitimate policy choices not be subject to "judicial second guessing" under the equality rights, but in an extraordinary concession it was prepared to make in its November 1980 brief. CCLA contemplated that if Parliament was willing to strengthen the other legal rights as it proposed (and as Parliament did), then "it may be that section 7 will no longer appear as necessary as it does now" and "it might be possible, without undue jeopardy, to withdraw s.7."[104]

Here again the negative example of the Lochner era of free market *laissez faire* constitutionalism/capitalism raised its head. CCLA was concerned that the reference to liberty in s.7 of the Charter might be interpreted to refer to "liberty of contract." To be sure, as a civil liberties organization, CCLA was concerned with liberty, but it was concerned with physical liberty of the type that was protected by the other legal rights, such as safeguards against searches, detentions, and the right to counsel. In its brief, CCLA raised concerns that s.7 of the Charter could "empower courts to strike down labour and social welfare laws on the basis of the kind of interpretation earlier American courts gave to the 14th amendment of the US constitution." CCLA did not "unreservedly predict that this would happen in Canada,"[105] but it felt compelled to point out that s.7 could be repealed to prevent even the risk that courts would move towards Lochner.

Parliament did not take up CCLA's offer to delete s.7 of the Charter. At the same time, CCLA's caution about the dangers of the section was widely shared. As detailed further in Chapter Three on abortion, the framers of the Charter believed that s.7 was neutral on questions such as substantive due process and would not lead Canadian courts to follow the path of *Roe v. Wade* in constitutionalizing a woman's right to abortion. The framers of the Charter believed that they had avoided these problems by only constitutionalizing a fair process. In its first major decision under s.7, however, the Supreme Court rejected the idea that its interpretation should be limited by the intent of the framers or the idea that the principles of fundamental justice under s.7 only guaranteed fair process as opposed to substance.[106] In 1988, the court ruled that the abortion law violated s.7, with four judges following CCLA's unsuccessful arguments in the 1970s about the procedural and geographic inequities of the law that only allowed abortions approved by hospital committees. Only one judge, Justice Bertha Wilson, following the more substantive *Roe v. Wade* approach. Justice Antonio Lamer remained sympathetic to CCLA's original position that s.7 was only a more general statement of the legal rights.

Section 7 has continued to grow and evolve, as has CCLA's approach to the section. CCLA intervened in the *Tremblay v. Daigle* decision in 1989 to stress traditional libertarian ideas that courts should not issue an injunction to prevent a woman from obtaining an abortion.[107] Two years later, CCLA argued that a law that categorically restricted the admissibility of the complainant's prior sexual conduct in a sexual assault trial violated s.7 by imposing "arbitrary" "blanket" and "unfair" restrictions on evidence that the accused could call in his defence. The court accepted CCLA's argument that the law should be struck down because it would be too uncertain and unfair to require the accused to demonstrate a violation before being exempted from the overbroad law.[108] The decision was very unpopular and Minister of Justice Kim Campbell seriously considered restoring the law with an override before deciding to re-enact a less blanket restriction accompanied with fundamental changes to sexual assault law to emphasize that "no means no."

In 2003, CCLA intervened to argue that s.7 of the Charter embraced the traditional liberal principle that the criminal law should only be used to respond to harm and that such a principle should result in the decriminalization of marijuana. It took a nuanced approach by distinguishing between harm to self and others. It argued that "where only harm to the self is in issue, it is consistent with civil liberties principles to require the state to show, at the very least, that the harm is serious, substantial or significant, before incarceration could be imposed."[109] Former CCLA vice-president and then Supreme Court Justice Louise Arbour was attracted to this harm-based approach, but the majority of the court held that there was not sufficient consensus that the harm principle was a principle of fundamental justice that should be constitutionally protected under s.7 as opposed to a philosophical precept. [110]

Although CCLA lost the marijuana case, the court in that case recognized new principles of fundamental justice that would invalidate laws that were arbitrary or grossly disproportionate. In 2005, a divided court waded into health care—the very type of social policy issue where CCLA maintained that the courts should not second-guess complex and distributive legislative choices. A narrow majority of the court held that Quebec's restrictions on the purchase of private insurance was arbitrary. Three judges in dissent echoed CCLA's fears that the court was deciding complex issues of social policy that should be left to the legislature.[111] CCLA did not intervene in the case likely because it did not think that health care was a civil liberties issue that should be resolved by courts under s.7 of the Charter.

CCLA intervened in the Insite case, which combined issues of health care and the criminal law. It argued that the application of drug offences to prevent the operation of a safe injection site on Vancouver's downtown Eastside would violate s.7 principles that prohibited arbitrary, overbroad, and grossly disproportionate laws. The Minister of Health's reluctance to approve exemptions from the criminal law would prevent access to clean needles that could stop the transmission of AIDS and other diseases. CCLA argued that while the government defined the taking of drugs as a free choice, it was really a matter of the disease of addiction. It urged the court to "consider the value that Canadians place on universal access to health care and the respect for the human dignity of all individuals, including the most marginalized in society."[112] The Supreme Court accepted the argument that the Minister's refusal to continue the exemption that allowed Insite to operate was both arbitrary and grossly disproportionate given the evidence that suggested that the safe injection site saved lives and did not increase crime. The court used its remedial powers under the Charter to order the reluctant Minister to grant the exemptions.[113] At the same time, the Minister has refused to grant new exemptions, demonstrating the continued role of executive decision and electoral powers, even in the face of an activist judicial decision in a single case.

DAY-TO-DAY DIALOGUE

In its influential November 1980 brief on the Charter, CCLA expressed concerns that too many problems might be dumped on the courts. It also recognized, in part because of the American experience of judicial review, that courts were fallible and generally not inclined to engage in "doctrinaire" or "extremist" jurisprudence. The day-to-day work of CCLA and other civil society groups demonstrates a recognition of the complex interplay or dialogue[114] that occurs between courts, society, the executive, and the legislature over the treatment of rights and freedoms in a democratic society. CCLA spends much time appearing or trying to appear before legislative committees. Sometimes, however, it is easier to get a fair hearing before the courts.

PART II:
CCLA AND THE COURT PARTY CRITIQUE OF JUDICIAL ACTIVISM

The Canadian judicial activism debate has featured accusations that the Charter has allowed a "Court Party" of "post-materialistic elites"[115] who campaigned for and are partisans of the Charter to hijack the policy-making process. Professors Morton and Knopff argued in 2000 that CCLA "is one of the key interest-group members of the Court Party"[116] through which a "new knowledge class successfully pursues its agendas through litigation and the courts."[117] In their view, this use of the courts is "deeply and fundamentally undemocratic."[118] It substitutes "coercion for government by discussion"[119] and "replaces negotiated, majoritarian compromises with the intensely held policy preferences of minorities."[120] Robert Bork similarly has railed against elites arguing "the same liberal intelligentsia dominates the jurisprudence"[121] of both the United States and Canada.

The Court Party thesis has had much influence. It inspired the Harper government's 2006 abolition of the court challenges program that funded equality and minority language litigation.[122] The abolition of the program hurt many rights-seeking groups associated with the Court Party. It did not, however, hurt CCLA, which had a long standing policy against accepting government money.[123] As Alan Borovoy summed up in his memoirs, "For $3,000 I can't be bought."[124] CCLA differed from some other interveners in its refusal to take government funds and in its skepticism about the state. The Charter presented opportunities for all, including those of the civil or economic libertarian bent, as well as other groups who sought greater protection or respect of their identities from the state.

CCLA V. OTHER MEMBERS OF THE SO-CALLED COURT PARTY

There are many problems with the Court Party thesis, but the one that deserves some attention here is how it understates the range of disagreement among interveners before the Supreme Court and even between those groups named as members of the anti-democratic Court Party. The Court Party thesis systemically ignores the fact that Attorneys General are far more frequent interveners before the court than civil society groups. It also disregards the role of interveners who represent the police, religious groups, and pro-life groups, who do not easily fall under the rubric of liberal and leftish elites.

Even within the selectively defined Court Party, there are deep divisions. Professors Morton and Knopff recognize that CCLA and women's groups disagreed over some issues, but they underestimate the extent of this disagreement. Moreover, they did not let the record influence their overall conclusions that the Court Party is an unrepresentative group of leftish elites and extremists, sheltered in the universities from majoritarian politics, that was having an unwarranted influence on the policy process.

CCLA and women's groups divided on pornography and criminal justice issues. These decisions were so profound that they inspired CCLA general counsel Alan Borovoy not "simply to disagree with your traditional allies" but to "write a whole book on the subject."[125] Borovoy's book *The New Anti-Liberals* discussed how equality claims were eclipsing traditional liberal values related to freedom of expression and fair trials. CCLA also found itself on the opposite side of the courtroom to Jewish groups on a number of cases involving anti-Semitic speech and the funding of religious schools. It also was on the opposite side of groups representing the disabled as well as pro-life groups in the Latimer case, involving the imposition of a mandatory life sentence on a man who killed his disabled daughter in the belief that it was necessary to prevent her suffering further pain. All of these divisions belie the idea that there is any unified Court Party that could capture the courts and the policy-making process. They also suggest that those within the Court Party are well aware that there is a range of reasonable views on the difficult and divisive issues raised in Charter litigation. The Court Party thesis is more an attempt by conservatives to define a common enemy than an accurate and sustained academic analysis.

CCLA V. RELIGIOUS GROUPS

CCLA's first divide from other parts of the so-called Court Party came in hate speech cases (explored in more depth in Chapter Five). In the Keegstra case, CCLA, represented by defence lawyer and future Ontario Court of Appeal judge Marc Rosenberg, was the only intervener to argue that Canada's hate propaganda law should be struck down as an unjustified violation of freedom of expression. Interveners on the other side, defending the law, included the Canadian Jewish Congress, B'Nai Brith, and the Women's Legal Education and Action Fund (LEAF). CCLA argued that the law chilled legitimate expression. It pointed to a leading case where francophone activists had been convicted at trial for circulating anti-French material in order to stimulate activism in their own community, as well as other incidents where youths were arrested for "Yankee Go Home" pamphlets. It noted that Salmon Rushdie's novel *The Satanic Verses* as well as pro-Zionist and pro-African National Congress materials had been held up in customs by claims that they constituted hate propaganda.[126] Alan Borovoy also made the historical point that the hate speech laws might have been applied to the anti-Catholic speech that earned the Jehovah's Witnesses the wrath of the Duplessis regime in 1950s Quebec.[127] CCLA also made the pragmatic argument that prosecutions of "hate-mongers" give them "a legitimacy they neither warrant nor deserve."[128]

CCLA lost in the Keegstra case, but by the narrowest of margins. Two years later, however, Marc Rosenberg made many of the same arguments when the Supreme Court struck down the false news provision on the basis that it was overbroad and chilled legitimate expression in the Ernst Zündel Holocaust denial case.[129] For his part in these cases, Alan Borovoy was unfairly accused of being a "self-hating Jew,"[130] even though his distaste for Zündel, who he believed "should have been allowed to wallow in the obscurity he so richly deserves,"[131] was obvious.

CCLA and religious groups were also on opposite sides in the Adler case in which parents who sent their children to Jewish and Christian schools argued that Ontario's funding of Catholic schools violated their equality rights and freedom of religion. CCLA intervened and argued that the funding of religious schools would harm public schools. As a result of earlier CCLA litigation, the public schools no longer attempted to indoctrinate children into the Christian faith. CCLA defended public schools as a venue where all children could "learn about other people's cultures and religions, concentrating on accepting and understanding one's differences" and thus "building a climate of tolerance, understanding and mutual respect among the children of Ontario."[132] Borovoy was aware that "if the Catholics are entitled to a certain amount of public funding for their schools, the Jews also have a persuasive claim." Nevertheless, he pragmatically, albeit reluctantly, accepted that the funding of Catholic schools was "foisted on us by history."[133]

CCLA V. WOMEN'S GROUPS

CCLA clashed with women's groups, most notably LEAF, in a number of cases in the 1990s even though the two organizations had previously worked as allies in challenging the "man in the house" restrictions on social assistance.[134]

Represented by Sheila Block, CCLA argued in the 1992 case of *R. v. Butler* that the obscenity provisions in the Criminal Code were too vague to survive Charter review (obscenity and pornography are explored further in Chapter Four). It reminded the court that the offence meant that police officers "are the effective censors" and that this could make "book selling" or "running a theatre, art gallery and library into hazardous occupations."[135] CCLA's pragmatic approach was another reminder that so-called judicial activism is not simply a matter of the unelected judges pitted against the elected legislators. It also involved unelected members of the executive who had considerable discretion in enforcing the law.

CCLA lost in its attempt to have the obscenity provisions struck down. Instead, the court was moved by arguments made by LEAF that the obscenity provisions should be refocused on violence against women and children.[136] Alan Borovoy wrote about how the court's adoption of the feminist idea that degrading material should be prohibited soon led customs officials to censor gay and lesbian pornography.[137] CCLA joined a Charter challenge to censorship in 2000 based on the *Butler* standard that degrading pornography was obscene. Block's colleague at the blue chip Torys law firm, Patricia Jackson, argued that the obscenity standard was "unintelligible," "uncertain," and failed to give "fair notice," especially when used by custom officials to justify prior restraint of the import of gay pornography.[138] The Supreme Court accepted that Little Sister's, the small gay and lesbian bookstore, had had their imports unconstitutionally profiled and seized by customs officials. The seized material included literature on HIV/AIDS prevention and novels that mainstream bookstores had no trouble importing. Nevertheless, the court refused to strike down the legislation that authorized the seizure or to reconsider the prior interpretation it gave to salvage the obscenity law.[139] The court's decision ignored that, as CCLA stressed, it was customs officials not judges who would decide in the first instance whether pornography was harmful. Predictably, Little Sister's continued to have disputes with customs officials who had trouble understanding that the pornography of sexual minorities was not obscene. These subsequent disputes were unfortunately not resolved on their merits, but by a Supreme Court decision that refused to grant the small book store advance costs to fund their continued litigation against customs censors.[140] The whole episode sadly confirmed CCLA's original prediction that successful battles against censorship could result in "emotional or financial ruin" that could "make even victory pyrrhic."[141]

In 2001, using similar arguments to those made in the 1992 obscenity case, CCLA argued that a new child pornography law was overbroad and vague. Again the Court Party of interveners was hardly a united front. CCLA joined by the Criminal Lawyers Association and the B.C. Civil Liberties Association argued that the law should be struck down. They were, however, vigorously opposed by interveners representing groups against child prostitution, the Canadian Police Association, the crime victims' group, Canadians Against Violence (CAVEAT), and the Evangelical Fellowship of Canada, not to mention intervening Attorneys General from Ontario, Quebec, Nova Scotia, New Brunswick, Manitoba, and Alberta.

CCLA quoted the testimony of Alan Borovoy in opposition to the bill in Parliament and argued that the "hasty enactment" of the law suggested that the law did not give adequate weight to "the substantial violations of thought, belief, expression and privacy" created by the offence.[142] The court refused to strike the child pornography law down, but it did read in some restrictions on it.[143] This failed to address CCLA's concern about the chilling effect of the overbroad law.

CCLA also opposed women's groups in several high profile cases involving sexual assault law. In *Seaboyer* (explored in detail in Chapter Seven), CCLA argued that restrictions on the admissibility of a complainant's prior sexual acts were too categorical and restricted the accused's ability to defend himself; LEAF, on the other hand, argued that any evidence excluded by the provision would not be relevant, or would be of limited relevance, if the equality rights of the complainant were considered.

CCLA's position was not an absolutist one that evidence of the complainant's prior sexual activity was already relevant but rather its traditional concern that legislative restrictions were overbroad, and that judges should be allowed to decide evidentiary questions on the particular facts of the case. Alan Borovoy was proud that CCLA was the only group before the court to address what should happen if the law was struck down, and that its guidelines imposed "substantial hurdles"[144] before evidence of the complainant's prior sexual acts could be admitted. The Supreme Court largely adopted CCLA's more flexible guidelines as did Parliament when it subsequently enacted a less categorical restriction on the admissibility of evidence of the complainant's prior sexual conduct, which was subsequently upheld under the Charter.

CCLA and LEAF were again on opposite sides of the courtroom in *R. v. Mills*. CCLA again argued that the restrictions on admissibility of a sexual complainant's therapeutic records was an overbroad restriction on the accused's rights; LEAF and other groups representing sexual assault centres argued that they were a necessary protection of the complainant's privacy and equality rights. CCLA, represented by Patricia Jackson, relied heavily on its prior victory in *R. v. Seaboyer*. She argued that Parliament's attempt to "pre-define issues of relevance by categorization"[145] was unconstitutional. Judges should have the discretion to balance competing concerns about the accused's rights to defend himself and the complainant's rights to privacy in the context of the particular case. The Supreme Court upheld the law from the Charter challenge, but also stressed that it left some room for the exercise of judicial discretion.[146]

As I have argued more fully elsewhere,[147] these cases were examples of a new political case where rights claims on behalf of the accused were pitted against rights claims of victims and groups disproportionately victimized by crime. The picture that emerges from these cases is far more complex and less conspiratorial than the idea that a Court Party led by CCLA and LEAF was hijacking the policy process in favour of rights and courts.

CCLA V. GROUPS REPRESENTING THE DISABLED

CCLA also intervened in the Latimer case to argue that the mandatory sentence of life imprisonment was cruel and unusual given the circumstances of the case, wherein Robert Latimer killed his disabled daughter, Tracy Latimer, because he thought that she would suffer greatly from a scheduled operation. (The Latimer case is detailed further in Chapter Seven.) CCLA based its submission on its long-standing opposition to mandatory sentences as well as the trial judge's decision to sentence Latimer to two years imprisonment instead of the mandatory life imprisonment term. It stressed that a person could be guilty of murder regardless of the motive of the killing, or even if the victim consented, and that it had "opposed other mandatory penalties on the basis that they will result in needless severity by imposing punishment on the basis of abstract formula as opposed to concrete circumstances."[148]

Groups representing the disabled saw the two-year sentence as a discriminatory double standard that reflected a view that Tracy Latimer's life was less worthy of protection because she was disabled. Borovoy took them on, arguing that the two-year sentence "hardly suggests that what [Latimer] did 'was okay'" and that it was wrong to punish Latimer "as though his deed were the outgrowth of hate rather than of love."[149] In the end, however, the Supreme Court did just that. It unanimously upheld the mandatory life imprisonment sentence. It suggested that the executive was free to grant clemency,[150] even though CCLA stressed that such discretionary relief should not save the mandatory sentence. Alan Borovoy subsequently attempted to persuade his old friend and former CCLA board member Irwin Cotler, when he was Minister of Justice, to grant clemency, but "the government apparently felt that it might be too politically costly for them to go along with us."[151] In the end, Latimer was not granted full parole until December 2010, and in 2014 he continues to fight against travel restrictions on his parole.

I represented CCLA in the Latimer case, and I recall how lonely it was on Mr. Latimer's side of the court. There was Latimer's legal team and Douglas Elliott representing the Canadian Aids Society. Sitting on the other side of the courtroom were two intervening Attorneys General, lawyers for the Council of Canadians with Disabilities, the Catholic Group for Health, Justice and Life, and the Evangelical Fellowship of Canada. My point is not that those groups should not have been represented—far from it—but only that the role of interveners, rights claims, and the political effects of the Charter are far more complex than presented by the conspiratorial Court Party thesis.

CONCLUSION

CCLA played a key role in the development of the Charter. Its "thanks but no thanks" strategy to the October 1980 draft of the Charter that had been watered down in an unsuccessful attempt to win provincial support was highly effective. CCLA can take particular credit for ensuring that the legal rights in the Charter have substantive content and that the courts can award effective remedies for their violation. One of the reasons why CCLA was so effective is that it was pragmatic, arguing for a middle-ground approach that avoided the extremes of the pre-Charter Canadian rule of automatically admitting reliable evidence even if it was improperly obtained, or the American rule of automatically excluding unconstitutionally obtained evidence. CCLA has consistently advocated this approach even when the Supreme Court was prepared to take a more absolute approach to the exclusion of evidence. To be sure, CCLA often supported the accused, but it did so more because of its concerns about police misconduct and accountability than out of any doctrinaire view that sought to maximize the accused's rights and was uncompromising of other interests.

CCLA was aware from the start that courts could make serious errors. It expressed concerns that equality rights not become so broad that it would encourage judicial second-guessing of social policy-making. Surprisingly, CCLA in November 1980 was even prepared to sacrifice s.7 of the Charter to minimize the risk of courts intruding too deeply into social policy-making. CCLA was not a monolith. Borovoy and others supported the s.33 override but others, such as Tarnopolsky and Greenspan, were opposed to it. CCLA was part of a rather sophisticated debate about whether the courts should be given more power with the Charter.

CCLA was never a simple-minded partisan of judicial power, as some critics of judicial activism and the Charter have maintained. It was well aware of the advantages and limits of both courts and legislatures. It had experienced judicial defeats on issues like capital punishment only to experience legislative victories. It knew that judicial victories such as limitations on the police powers to strip-search people were fragile and had to be supported by administrative policies, good police complaints structures, and effective remedies.

The Canadian debate about judicial activism has seen critics of the court on both the Left and the Right raise concerns that unelected judges would substitute their views for those of elected legislators. An examination of CCLA's history, however, reveals the impoverished and partial nature of this debate. The cases that CCLA was most concerned with were those that pitted police officers and other unelected members of the executive against the courts. CCLA helped ensure that under the Charter, judges would have the necessary tools to respond to police misconduct. Nevertheless, CCLA never placed all its faith in judges, and it did not ignore the need for executive power to be supervised in the legislature and discussed in the media.

CCLA was well aware that many other groups, including some that were allies in other causes, could reasonably and thoughtfully disagree with the positions that it took. It was no stranger to compromise. It fashioned a compromise procedural approach on abortion in recognition that some of its board members were opposed to abortions. It fashioned a compromise position on the exclusion of evidence that was adopted by the Progressive Conservative Party that amended the Charter to include what is now s.24(2) mandating the exclusion of unconstitutionally obtained evidence only when its admission into a criminal trial would bring the administration of justice into disrepute.

CCLA fought many battles against women's groups, religious groups, and others that are sometimes grouped together as common advocates of judicial activism. There was no united or conspiratorial Court Party that had its way with the courts. Yes, the Charter has increased judicial power in Canada, and CCLA sometimes reaped the benefits of that power. Nevertheless, CCLA was well aware of the limits of courts and the need to work not only in court but in the media and in the legislature for better protection of civil liberties.

Interviews

"OUR WHOLE MANDATE IS *TO CHANGE THE LAW.*"

A. Alan Borovoy and Marian Botsford Fraser in Conversation

A. Alan Borovoy is a lawyer, activist, and writer. In 1968, he became general counsel for CCLA, *a position he held until his retirement in July 2009. He is an Officer of the Order of Canada and has several honourary doctorates. He is the author of* The New Anti-Liberals*;* Uncivil Obedience: The Tactics and Tales of a Democratic Agitator*;* When Freedoms Collide: The Case for Our Civil Liberties*; and* Categorically Incorrect: Ethical Fallacies in Canada's War on Terror. *His memoir,* At the Barricades, *was published in March 2014.*

You joined CCLA *in 1968, when it was very much a fledgling organization, perhaps even a floundering one...so why did you join?*

I attribute it to the silver-tongued oratory of Harry Arthurs, an old friend. I was happy where I was, at the Jewish Labour Committee. In fact I was on the CCLA board at the outset, and I remember feeling they were perhaps overly conservative, over technical, lawyerly. So when they came after me, I wasn't excited; but Harry Arthurs, who was then on the board, came to see me, and he turned me around. He made it sound more challenging. Harry actually used the words "moribund organization,"...so the challenge was to do something.

CCLA had acquired an anonymous bequest at the time, and I still don't know from whom. I long suspected it was the CIA, which was giving grants to progressive organizations, which I thought was a more sophisticated development for American intelligence agencies than one would expect.

Did you have a sense of what the key issues might be, where you might go? For instance, in 1964, what got CCLA started was the question of policing powers and police oversight. Did you think that would be a key issue?

Freedom of speech always interested me, and I'd developed some ideas about that in my previous position, and I was also interested in how the welfare state could be made more responsive to civil liberties principles, those are the things that got me interested. I looked at what I thought were the fundamental freedoms of a democratic system and very early on spelled those out in the pamphlet *The fundamentals of our fundamental freedoms....*

I got involved in welfare rights almost from the beginning. I believe we were the first organization to register on that issue, which started with the one woman who was unfairly treated. Thanks to the infamous "man in the house" policy, it became a feminist issue, but that was later.

Over and over again in the history of CCLA, something begins as a small thing, an apparently isolated incident, and then becomes bigger and bigger....

For us there's no point in getting involved in a case, or an issue, unless we can produce a structural change with it. If people are just looking for a lawyer, they don't need us. There are lots of lawyers out there who will take cases. Our whole mandate is *to change the law.* So this could be with a case, or with briefs to Cabinet Ministers, and testimonies before Cabinet committees, petitions, rallies.... We even closed the Toronto libraries down at one point, in the name of free speech!

Police behaviour and oversight have always been key issues, since 1964.... Why is the relationship between police and citizens such a constant? Have things changed at all in fifty years?

I think there have been changes, and I think it behooves us to acknowledge them. It's not adequate, but the only way to measure things in history is if things have become less inadequate...so I think there are fewer problems than when I started, but there are still changes needed. For example, there's a lot more individual involvement in the handling of civilian complaints against the police now than there was. At the beginning, the cops did it all themselves. There should be more of this.

My thinking about the police underwent a lot of changes over the years, as additional issues surfaced, RCMP (Royal Canadian Mounted Police) wrongdoing for example, and ministerial responsibility. I started changing my views, or expanding them; there were things I'd never thought about earlier.

How so?

Originally, I bought the conventional wisdom that the minister in charge should not have jurisdiction over what the police do in their day-to-day activities. I thought the minister should only lay down policy guidelines, but not get involved in operational issues. But I started to ask the question: How can the minister in charge be held accountable for what police do, day to day, unless he has something to say about it, unless he knows about it?

The whole bloody thing didn't make any sense. That got played out first in 1977 with Trudeau's silly response to the concept of ministerial responsibility for the RCMP. And it got played out again in 1995, with Mike Harris at the time of the Ipperwash, when the Stoney Point Ojibway were occupying that piece of land, and the OPP (Ontario Provincial Police) went in, and Dudley George was killed.

When Mike Harris was asked about the OPP involvement there, he said it wasn't our business; we had no right to know what they were doing.

Well, I found myself saying, if he is lying, it's a very bad thing, but it's even worse if he is telling the truth. What the hell was he saying—that he's not supposed to know when the OPP was sending in all these cops against a whole community of Aboriginal people? If we decided to take on a contingent from a foreign power that was the same number of people, would anyone suggest that the politicians shouldn't have any decision-making to do, only the military?

So from such things evolved the idea of independent auditing, that a complaints system wasn't enough, that you have to have an independent agency constantly looking into what the cops are doing. Then you'll have a greater level of police accountability.

They'll still find ways to get around it of course. That's the way history goes—we come up with reforms, they figure out how to get around them.

The whole business of RCMP wrongdoing in the early 1970s led to the McDonald Commission, and eventually, in 1984, to the creation of CSIS (Canadian Security Intelligence Service). Was that a good outcome? Do you think the management of CSIS is sufficiently transparent?

Who knows? We don't know what CSIS is doing, except for SIRC (the Security Intelligence Review Committee), which has audit power. I think SIRC has started to do an interesting job by way of reporting what CSIS was doing. But the press has stopped taking an interest. One of the challenges for my successors is to find a way to make SIRC reports more newsworthy for the press.

In 1982, the Charter of Rights and Freedoms *came into being. And CCLA was very active in determining the final text. (You lost the "God" battle in the preamble, as I recall....) Initially, you were very opposed to the idea of a Charter. What were your concerns?*

Our material at the time of the Charter negotiations reflected what was the uneasy consensus in the organization. I thought the Charter was fundamentally undemocratic. Because the value judgments of appointed judges—and that's really what you have to be talking about—should not be allowed to prevail over the judgments of elected politicians. Not that quite often, of course, the judges wouldn't have better judgment, and they often have. But judges are less accountable than politicians. And I am an old-fashioned democrat.

Doesn't the way in which the Charter is constructed address that concern?

No, it can't. Well, the notwithstanding clause is an acknowledgement of that issue, or rather it's a way of building ultimate political rule into the Charter, so that addresses the problem in part. Of course that wasn't why it ended up being included. The provinces and the feds were scrapping over fundamental interests, which produced a compromise. Whenever they do the right thing, it's for the wrong reasons.

Some of our people saw the notwithstanding clause as the death knell of the Charter. I saw it as the redemption of the Charter.

How effective has the Charter been in affecting the civil liberties narrative in Canada?

To be fair, even though I never wanted it, it has definitely had an impact. But it has had less impact than some of those who dreamt about it wanted, and it's had more than others believed it would. For example, on the issue of religious instruction in the schools—that was the first big victory we had, with the Elgin County School Board case, which we took ourselves in partnership with a couple of parents. That went on for years and years, ending up in the Ontario Court of Appeal in 1988. The politicians were afraid to take it on, and the courts did, and they were very helpful.

[MBF: The school board argued it was using religious texts as a form of moral education. CCLA and the parents argued that

Christian doctrine was a form of indoctrination, and an infringement of Charter-protected freedom of religion rights, and the Court of Appeal agreed. The long-term result was that schools in Ontario, and elsewhere in the country, became secular.]

It's interesting, now, a quarter of a century later, religious instruction in schools, and the right to pray, have become issues….

It's always been a problem of how does a democracy accommodate dissent? And we had one set of interests then, and now we have a different set. It's a real challenge to figure out how to come up with a system for accommodating competing interests. Not easy.

That principle of compromise, looking for less bad things, doing less harm, balancing competing rights…that principle does seem to be a measure of how CCLA approaches cases….

That was my conscious philosophy certainly.

And quite often, historically, CCLA has gone after process issues, rather than the substantive issue in the case.

Can you give me an example?

In the Robert Latimer case, for example. CCLA did not address the question of guilt or innocence, or the merits of the act he was tried for, but focused instead on the issue of punishment….

How he was being treated by the system, yes. I just didn't want him to be jailed in that way. There's a lot of substance in that. Another example?

Well, there was the first Morgentaler case before the Supreme Court of Canada (SCC) in 1976. CCLA didn't address the issue of whether or not abortion was a good thing, but it looked at the fairness of how a woman was able to actually get an abortion across Canada.

I had a problem. My president was against abortion, our national honourary president was against abortion, and the rest of us were pro-choice. My problem was, what could we do? How could we come up with something that wasn't just milquetoast? So I came up with the idea of intervening *on process*. But that wasn't because we wished to avoid substance; it was because we couldn't get consensus any other way. A few years later our pro-choice incarnation emerged from the closet.

I believed then, and I still do, that ours was the first intervention permitted by the SCC for which there wasn't a consensus of all other parties. We came in over the objection of the Quebec prosecutor. That had never been allowed before. The precedent was set, the organization picked up on it, and the courts picked up on it.

And now sometimes at the SCC there are very large contingents of interveners on both sides; wasn't a record set recently with the number of interveners in the Whatcott case, twenty-five, including both sides?

And that's okay. You're dealing with some of the vital questions of our society. So why should the coincidence of which party litigates first determine the right to participate in those things? This is a perfectly reasonable way to handle it. We also learned that intervention can really play a vital role. If you look at the rape shield case, we made a significant contribution there.

That was the Seaboyer case, in 1991, where the existing rape shield (which limited the testimony a rape victim had to give) was struck down....

We got so much flack at the time, and yet we saved it ultimately. No one else had an unbiased interest; the prosecution and the feminist organizations just wanted to sustain the law as it was, and the accused, of course, just wanted to shoot it down and make it disappear. We were the only ones who said, shoot down the existing law, but leave something there in its place, a narrower shield.

During the past fifty years, another player has come into the civil liberties field—the human rights tribunals, and commissions, both federal and in most provinces. It seemed to me that the position of CCLA evolved on these bodies. In the beginning it seemed like a good thing, a useful relationship, and then, as they developed, CCLA's position changed.

At the beginning, specifically in Ontario, it was largely an informal co-operation between Dan Hill and me. (He was the first director of Ontario's Human Rights Commission, from 1962–72.) We would cook up these cases together. He would tell me about some problems, I would go out and find evidence and blow it up in the press, then he would come in as the great conciliator, and the matter would be resolved. If the parties couldn't agree, there would be a tribunal.

As time went on, the process took on a different form. I never quarreled with the idea of human rights tribunals. But I was opposed to having the human rights apparatus involved when it came to the freedom of expression issues. When the human rights commissions were starting to censor, I became very opposed, because that was hostile to free speech.

Giving the human rights commissions the job of dealing with hate speech...that was a decision of the politicians, bidding for support of their various constituencies. That wasn't inherent in the human rights tribunal process. I found myself in the position of vigorously opposing their hate speech measures and strongly supporting them otherwise.

In the Robert Latimer factum, there is this statement: "Canada has never embraced a simplistic and punitive notion of just deserts that ties punishment automatically to the offence committed." Do you think that statement still holds, or has the ground shifted, either in terms of public opinion or Parliament?

The current 2014 government is just awful on this score, pandering shamelessly to the lowest common denominator of their constituency. What really gets me is when they increase the mandatory minimums from four years to five years, as if that would make any difference to anyone planning to commit a crime. What conspicuous horseshit that is.

Is there a real threat to civil rights of the accused and imprisoned?

The political game constitutes a threat. The notion of a fair trial is substantially infringed upon by these mandatory minimum sentences, by making it a matter of regulation. That's hardly in keeping with any reasonable concept of a fair trial.

Did you miss a boat anywhere along the line? Were there issues CCLA should have engaged with in your time as general counsel?

I think there were...we haven't done everything. I made the decision in my career here that I wasn't going to do everything there was to do. I didn't want to be a press release mill; I wanted us to engage in newsworthy activities. I wish that we had done more Aboriginal issues, for one thing. And I wanted to get involved with more cases that dramatized the idea that pressure without reason may be irresponsible, but reason without pressure is ineffectual.

Some think that the areas that CCLA has missed are social and economic interests, that as a society, even, we've missed out on those ideas of justice.

It's an error to see an organization like this as having as its concern the whole panoply of social issues. Should we be fighting for Medicare, fair wages? I don't think so.

And I don't think we should just be in the courts. I see agitating, but for what? For more progressive legislation in the area of the fundamental freedoms, not for resolving the inequalities of income.

I've long thought that this is an organization where people who care about fundamental freedoms can form a consensus and act.

You've got to be able to raise hell—not just by saying nasty things but by *doing* something, using the tactics of lawful disruption.

"IN CIVIL LIBERTIES, AN INJUSTICE TO ONE IS AN INJUSTICE TO EVERYONE."

Nathalie Des Rosiers and Marian Botsford Fraser in Conversation

Nathalie Des Rosiers served as the general counsel for CCLA from 2009 to 2013. She is an expert in constitutional law, has taught at the University of Ottawa and Western University law schools, and has been in private practice in London, Ontario, and Montreal, Quebec. She is currently the Dean of Faculty of Law, Common Law Section, University of Ottawa. She has received the Order of Canada, the Order of Ontario, several Honourary Doctorates, and was named one of Canada's twenty-five most influential lawyers in 2011 and 2012.

What attracted you to CCLA?

I had watched Maher Arar cry on TV. I thought how awful it is that we have let this injustice happen in Canada, and I thought, if you have any talent at all, you should work to ensure that what happened to Maher Arar never happens again to anyone else.

It seemed to me there was a real necessity to reinvest in due process safeguards, and a civil liberties organization helps a democracy to do that. I've always considered CCLA to be an important organization; it has a great reputation for vigilance.

You were general counsel between 2009 and 2013. What was the most significant issue you faced while you were at CCLA?

If you are in the civil liberties business, every day is the most important! This is always difficult to answer...the fact that it would be 1,100 people arrested during the G20 is significant, but the fact that the next day you have one person who has been stopped from going to the United States because her personal mental-health information was shared by Metropolitan Toronto Police with the US border authorities also feels like a very important thing.... So it is hard to say that one thing or another is "most significant."

In civil liberties, an injustice to one is an injustice to everyone. Each injustice signifies a failure of the system. So there are many such issues: the over bureaucratization of our lives, the way that security trumps privacy, and the way that security is also deemed to trump due process and other rights; the fact that security is deemed to trump all the traditional ways in which we've been concerned about freedom of dissent.

But the G20 Summit—when 1,100 people, mostly peaceful protestors, were arrested on one weekend on the streets of downtown Toronto—that was a revelation for me. I had not expected it, and it was definitely a turning moment, in realizing that the work we were doing was important.

The G20 Summit resulted in numerous actions by CCLA: follow-up reports, participation in police and civilian inquiries, public meetings, and a class action lawsuit. So there are many strategies, many forms of activism. Is the primary objective behind all of these actions a change in legislation?

The value of CCLA is that once it has identified an issue, it works to solve it, no matter what it takes or how long it takes. So I'll give you two examples related to the G20 Summit.

That event was an example of many small things going wrong. There was bad planning. There was bad civilian oversight of policing. There was a complete lack of accountability for what was going on. There were excesses—in the bail conditions being imposed, in the power of arrest, and power being over-used. There were problems in the framework around security. There was a complete lack of transparency around regulations being passed in secret. So you look at all of this and you say, okay, let's get to work.

So first, we had success in improving the regulatory framework around the sonic cannons (long-range radar devices), which were used for crowd control during the G20 Summit. We got on commissions, made submissions, and forced a review of sonic cannons by the ministry, which concluded—surprise, surprise—that there were health issues, concerns about hearing loss related to these devices.

Then secondly, we forced the Government of Ontario to look at the *Public Works Protection Act*—a regulation which was passed secretly right before the summit, cryptically designating the G20 site as a "public works" site needing special security. Now the government is committed to repealing that Act, so we worked not only on the repeal of the Act but on the replacement legislation.

Then on all the other matters, you just write and write, and sue—if you're not listened to, you sue—it's a way of using public education, putting pressure on legislators, appearing at consultations, doing your own public consultations if you're not getting anywhere, and then eventually, if necessary, litigating.

In 1964, the issue that galvanized slumbering civil liberties activists and resulted in the creation of CCLA was a very similar problem of police action and powers, and also the oversight of police. (Who polices the police?) At that time, special measures were enacted in the name of organized crime; now these problems arise in the context of national security. Why can we not, as a society, fix that piece? Why does the relationship between citizens and police remain a constant battleground?

Every generation needs to be sensitized anew about this relationship. Police oversight gets easily shoved aside, every time there are

Masked rioters travelling north on Yonge Street smashed windows on Saturday, June 26, 2010 during Toronto's G20 Summit.

concerns about security. So 9/11 didn't change everything, but it certainly dramatically changed public perceptions around security and privacy. Decision-makers decide that security is a primary concern. That in turn empowers police and security forces to take bigger steps, to take risks, and to assert more power.

So I think it's not a surprise that it's a constant struggle. Civil liberties are the rights of minorities, people who are not popular. That's why it's essential that you stay alive as a civil liberties organization, that you are vibrant, that you're courageous and vigilant. You have to build into your organization a kind of moral fibre, so that you can be there when needed, and not be in danger of losing credibility or being co-opted. Because these are not popular causes; defending the rights of minorities, protestors, dissenters will never be popular causes.

I think the question of police oversight has had its ups and downs over time. Every generation needs a little bit of a scandal to make people realize how important it is!

In 1982, the Charter of Rights and Freedoms *was created, and elsewhere in this book we've considered how that happened, and what the impact of the Charter has been on civil liberties in this country. How would you describe the role of the Charter and its significance?*

The Charter has had three major impacts: The first, on the public education side. The Charter creates a sense, a place in which the population has embraced a rights discourse. People have come to believe they have the right to freedom of expression. That's a very good thing. As a society, we've embraced this idea, both nationally and internationally.

Secondly, the Charter has given more power to the courts to scrutinize government. Now that's just one tool among many. If the courts don't get it right, the government can always respond and try to improve legislation. So it has created an enhanced accountability framework for governments. I have no problem with that; I have no problem with governments being asked to justify their legislative choices, and choices they've made to infringe the rights of some people for the benefit of the large group. If governments can't explain well what they've done—and why—they should go back to the drawing board.

And finally, when everything fails, the Charter creates for Canadians, for CCLA, and for other groups the opportunity to build a legal challenge. You don't want legal challenges to displace political challenges and the ways you want to engage in changing minds. But at times you need—and can use—the courts to advance a cause, to ensure that there is a remedy for injustice. The Charter has made such challenges possible.

The current federal government had enacted a law-and-order agenda, and in connection with that, reservations are often expressed about the courts, the judiciary, playing a too-active role. Do you think this mindset constitutes a threat, over time, to the civil liberties of Canadians?

The real threat would be the disappearance of the democratic fibre of society. You want to have an independent court regime. And the judiciary needs to feel sufficiently secure so that, when necessary, they will challenge a government they think is not doing the right thing. This is not something new; we've had ups and downs throughout the history of Canada; we've had courts before the Charter that stood up to governments—against Duplessis, for example. It's not only a question of the Charter. It's about ensuring that you have people in the judiciary who are not afraid to call a spade a spade and are not fearful of asking tough questions and ensuring that the government is applying the law appropriately and adhering to national and international safeguards. The fact that a government wants to blame the courts has happened over history and will continue to happen. We just have to ensure that they don't go too far…so one job of a civil liberties group like CCLA is to demand compliance with the Charter. That is an important job.

In my opinion, governments will criticize the courts, but they won't defy the courts. They will not take that chance. There is still a level of respect for the Charter, because they might one day need it! The Charter, it's for everyone.

What do you think are the primary areas of concern for CCLA, and for civil rights and liberties in general in Canada, going forward from this point?

There are two big issues. First, we must realize that an immigrant country must have civil liberties for everyone and not just for Canadian citizens. So we must be really in tune with the way in which the evolving immigration regime is infringing the liberties of many, many people.

You can say that the immigration law is the new criminal law. There is a shift; in trying to pick and choose the people that we—government or society—want to stay in Canada, we are inflicting great injustices on people, through deportation, for example. In this day and age, where you live determines all of your life chances, your security, your access to jobs, to food, and to life.

The way in which immigration and the right to mobility are being framed by government in terms of security issues is a huge concern.

The second one is disparity of income and socio-economic rights. The ability to say, there is no such thing as a right to liberty if you're unable to have access to a place to sleep. The old saying by Anatole France—*The law, in its majestic equality, forbids the rich as well as the poor to sleep under bridges, to beg in the streets, and to steal bread*—still applies. The use of criminal law affects the rich and the poor very differently. When we criticize the use of criminal law, we ought not to forget that differential of impact on rich and poor.

The Charter doesn't really address those rights, does it?

The Charter is not a direct protection; it's more about civil and political rights. But under section 7—the right to life, liberty, and security of the person—and also with section 15, which deals with equality rights, more and more arguments are being made to protect derivative rights. But it is less clear, that's why we need to push there. It's not enough to only argue under the Charter, you also must make the argument for good policy.

The Charter is a floor, it is not a ceiling.

But you cannot just make these arguments at the Supreme Court, that's too late! The real strength of CCLA is the network of great lawyers, and also an incredible staff, who put out reports, create strategies, do the essential monitoring. These days, CCLA is at the Supreme Court of Canada every two weeks.

But in addition to interventions, you have to have constant engagement with people and groups with different perspectives, about how protecting freedom of dissent is important. You can't have a society that cares for civil liberties unless you have people in the society who care for it.

PART 2
The Issues

LOOR ST. W. 164
STOP
PIERRE
I LOVE YOU
DO YOU LOVE US
ENOUGH TO
LIFT
RESTRICTIONS
ON ABORTIONS
IN
TRIBUTE TO THE
YEARLY 1000 CANADIAN
WOMEN WHO DIE FROM
BACKROOM ABORTIONS

CHAPTER THREE
Life and Death Matters—Abortion

I read about a poor farmer's wife in North Carolina throwing herself under a wagon when she discovered she was going to have her ninth child, about women dying in tenements from complications of pregnancy or childbirth or terrible failed abortions which they performed with hatpins, knitting needles, bubbles of air. I read, or skipped, statistics about the increase in population, laws which had been passed in various countries for and against birth control, women who had gone to jail for advocating it.

—*Lives of Girls and Women*, Alice Munro, 182–3, 1971

Abortion is unquestionably a tragedy; it is also a tragedy to force untimely childbearing on unready women.

—June Callwood, *The Globe and Mail*, 1989

Abortion is a freighted issue in the arena of Canadian civil and human rights history. Not only is the subject itself burdened with profound emotional and moral complications for individuals, but the evolution of abortion rights in Canada happened mostly in a compressed time frame of twenty years, and ran parallel to the creation of the *Charter of Rights and Freedoms*. In 1969, access to abortion was made legal in Canada for the first time, under very specific conditions. In 1976, the Supreme Court of Canada resolutely denied that access to abortion was a fundamental human right in this country. In 1988, the Supreme Court reversed its earlier decision and struck down the *Criminal Code* provisions governing abortion in Canada.

Between 1968 and 1988 especially, a broad range of Canadians was caught up in either the abortion rights story, or the patriation of the Constitution and creation of the Charter, or both. And abortion activists were not just what are sometimes denigrated by

WE CARE! DO YOU?
ABORTION IS HARMFUL TO BABIES
THE
TORONTO
PROTECT THE

politicians as "special interest groups": Thousands of Canadians, for and against the legalization of abortion, took to the streets and signed petitions and joined hospital boards and lobbied their elected representatives. Feelings about abortion were, and are still, extremely polarized, and on occasion they have been violent. After the *Criminal Code* rules governing abortion were shot down by the Supreme Court and the government failed three times to create new legislation, abortion activism became a particularly ugly form of street theatre for a few years.

In 1975, a petition signed by more than one million Canadians was delivered to Ottawa, demanding protection of the rights of the unborn. In July 1983, an estimated 4,000 pro-choice demonstrators protested the arrest of Dr. Henry Morgentaler in Toronto for "procuring miscarriages," and exactly one month later, 1,500 anti-choice protesters demanded his clinic be shut down. In February 1985, back-to-back front page headlines in the *Toronto Star* read as follows: "3000 protesters demand abortion clinic be closed" (February 22); "5000 march in support of abortion" (February 23). During the 1990s, after abortion was removed from the *Criminal Code* by the 1988 Supreme Court decision, Morgentaler's Toronto clinic was destroyed by a bomb and three abortion providers were shot at or stabbed in Vancouver, Winnipeg, and Ancaster, Ontario. (These criminal acts mirrored similar attacks in the United States, where, since the 1990s, there have been eight murders and seventeen attempted murders of abortion providers.)

In 2013, twenty-five years after abortion regulations in the *Criminal Code* were declared unconstitutional by the 1988 *Morgentaler* decision, questions about the rights of the fetus, and the fact that abortions are legal in Canada at any time during pregnancy, surfaced in Parliament. According to January 2013 polls, public opinion on the issue of abortion remains split almost fifty-fifty, but a strong majority (59 per cent) of Canadians adamantly do not wish the issue to be reopened in the courts or in Parliament. Interestingly, it appears that neither those in favour of legalized abortion nor those opposed trust Parliament to deal with this question.

Signs of pro-life and pro-choice activists of the 1970s spell out the deep divide in public opinion on the abortion issue. The emotion-charged debate continues.

CCLA has been engaged in the abortion issue since 1976, when the organization intervened in the Supreme Court of Canada's first ruling on the abortion practice of Dr. Henry Morgentaler. But CCLA is probably the only organization in Canada that has defended *both* a woman's right to choose and the anti-abortionist's right to protest.[152]

PROCREATION, PROMISCUITY, AND THE PILL—1969

The period of time during which abortion was neither completely illegal in Canada—as it was for one hundred years prior to 1969—nor completely legal and unlegislated—as it has been since 1988—was a scant twenty years. But during those twenty years, abortion was an issue that engaged Canadians mightily, at many levels—in the courts, in the streets, during election campaigns, in the media.

The "pill" became part of the conversation about virginity, sex, and abortion around 1963, at the beginning of a profound shift in societal ideas about the role of women and their right to have premarital sex and use contraception. All forms of birth control had been labelled "obscene" in the 1892 *Criminal Code*, for "tending to corrupt morals," but from the 1920s Canadian women and medical practitioners had been quietly providing information and birth control materials. Until 1969 in Canada, chemical birth control, meaning the pill, could only be prescribed to deal with menstrual cycle irregularities, preferably those of married women. (In the 1960s it took enormous courage for a single young woman to ask for a prescription for birth control pills from a doctor, and when she did so, she rarely went to her own family doctor.) A combination of the Planned Parenthood movement, women's groups, and a coalition of churches, including Anglican, United, Presbyterian, Unitarian, and the Salvation Army methodically, systematically lobbied the government of Canada through the 1960s to remove birth control from the *Criminal Code*.

Before 1969, abortion in Canada was an offence that carried the death penalty or life imprisonment for whomever performed an abortion, be it the woman herself or a medical practitioner. However, in England in 1938, in *Rex v. Bourne*, a precedent was established for performing an abortion to protect the health of the mother, in that case a fourteen-year-old girl who was raped by five off-duty soldiers: "If the doctor is of the opinion, on reasonable grounds and with adequate knowledge, that the probable consequence of the continuance of the pregnancy will be to make the woman a physical or mental wreck, the jury are entitled to take the view that the doctor is operating for the purpose of preserving the life of the mother." The argument for abortion under such circumstances would probably also have been accepted in Canada. Between 1900 and 1972, there were just over 1,100 convictions for induced abortion in Canada; most of those convicted were laypeople, and most of them were women; physicians who conducted illegal abortions, it seems, were rarely charged, possibly because their rate of failure was lower.[153]

Socially and economically privileged women in Canada would always have been able to find a doctor willing to perform a discreet abortion, at least in urban centres. Disadvantaged women would have either attempted to perform the abortion themselves or would have gone to backstreet practitioners. Women in remote locations and without resources who were unwillingly pregnant, for whatever reason, would have had no such recourse. There are no official records documenting either the frequency of abortions or the deaths of women and infants as the result of botched abortions, unless those deaths occurred in hospitals. Until 1969, abortion was a secret; even when it was alluded to, as in Alice Munro's fiction cited above, it was distanced as a rumour, something that happened to other women in other places. The act of establishing very strict rules for obtaining a legal abortion (hospital-based, subject to approval first by a family doctor and second by a Therapeutic Abortion Committee) brought this secret into the light of day. It almost seems, in retrospect, that legalizing abortion, by bringing it into the precincts of the *Criminal Code,* was a necessary precursor to abortion becoming an unregulated medical procedure.

Several factors were pertinent to the evolution of Canada's position on the legality of abortion: The first was the technological advances from the 1960s onward, including both the introduction of birth control pills and increasingly sophisticated abortion procedures. The second was the coincidental impact of the thalidomide scandal in the early 1960s. On the market briefly between 1957 and 1962, thalidomide was a drug given to pregnant women to deal with morning sickness, which resulted in babies being born with deformed limbs, deformed hearts and eyes, blindness, and deafness. The tragedy created public sympathy for the notion of therapeutic abortions and hovered in the background of the abortion debate as legal battles on behalf of thalidomide babies ran their course over many years. The third, and most significant factor, was the direct challenge to the law by Dr. Henry Morgentaler.

The introduction into Canada's *Criminal Code* of specific clauses concerning abortion was one of several measures, including language on homosexuality and divorce, in an Omnibus Bill first proposed by Pierre Trudeau, as Justice Minister in 1967, and finally passed in May 1969 after months of difficult debate in the House of Commons and Senate.

Trudeau's intent was to modernize Canadian laws to reflect contemporary attitudes and practices. In the case of abortion, the legislation reflected the input of provincial governments and medical practitioners rather than women, and it is laden with telltale bureaucratic language and process. A physician who performs an abortion is subject to life imprisonment; a women who procures her own miscarriage is subject to two years in prison, *unless* the abortion has been performed in an accredited hospital and approved in advance by a majority of a hospital's Therapeutic Abortion Committee (TAC) finding that the continuation of pregnancy would endanger the woman's health.

It is worth noting that, in Trudeau's opinion at the time, the provisions he was proposing on abortion were appropriate and sufficient. He was not setting the stage for more flexible regulation of abortion at a later date. Indeed, when the language and provisions of the Charter were being negotiated a decade later, Trudeau firmly rejected including fetus and abortion rights in the Charter.

In section 251 of the *Criminal Code*, there was no definition or clarification of precisely what endangerment to health means, which gave considerable latitude and discretion to the therapeutic abortion committees appointed by an elected hospital board.

Hospitals were accredited and overseen by the provinces; they were not required by law to establish a TAC and/or to perform abortions. Abortions were legal, but really hard to get, a problem quickly apparent to Montreal family doctor Henry Morgentaler.

"SOCIALLY UNDESIRABLE CONDUCT SUBJECT TO PUNISHMENT": THE FIRST MORGENTALER SUPREME COURT DECISION—1974/1976[154]

Henry Morgentaler was a Montreal family physician who decided that illegal abortions were a serious problem requiring a practical, compassionate, and deliberately illegal response. He made the argument for legal abortions initially before a Parliamentary committee studying the issue in 1967. Morgentaler opened private abortion clinics first in Montreal (from 1968 onwards) and then in Ontario (from 1974) and subsequently elsewhere in the country. Morgentaler never hid his practice or his intent to perform abortions from authorities; in fact, his first clinic operated for two years in Montreal before it was raided by police. He applied for permits, which were never granted or denied. By 1973, Morgentaler was stating publicly that he had safely performed more than 5,000 abortions. Finally, in response to a tip-off from the FBI that American women were coming to Montreal for abortions, Morgentaler was arrested and charged—three times in the early 1970s in Montreal and then elsewhere in the country as he opened up clinics.

The principle charge against Morgentaler was "having procured the miscarriage of a female person by the manipulation and use of an instrument" contrary to section 251 of the *Criminal Code*, which only permitted such acts in accredited hospitals, and with the approval of a therapeutic abortion committee.

Three juries in Montreal, between 1973 and 1975, unanimously found Morgentaler "not guilty," even though he had broken the law. Defiance by a jury of existing laws is known as "jury nullification," and the fact that it was done three times clearly signalled the state of public opinion in Quebec concerning abortion at the time. (The same thing would happen a decade later in Toronto in 1984, despite instructions from the judge to the jury that a "not guilty" finding was not, technically, their job, which was to

Dr. Henry Morgentaler with supporters arrives at Montreal police station to turn himself in on March 25, 1975.

enforce the law. Defence attorney Morris Manning had audaciously suggested that the jury did have the option of using the nullification strategy.)

In 1974, Morgentaler's first acquittal by a jury was overturned by the Quebec Court of Appeal and arbitrarily replaced with a prison sentence. Morgentaler appealed this ruling to the Supreme Court of Canada (SCC), and a cohort of interveners, including CCLA, was permitted to take part.

According to Alan Borovoy, writing in *Uncivil Obedience* (1991), the granting of permission to intervene in this case was "a rather rare phenomenon," only the second time in the history of the SCC that "third-party" interveners had been allowed to participate in a criminal appeal. This was also the first time that CCLA had used the tactic of seeking intervener status, which became one of the organization's central strategies from then on.

Determining grounds for CCLA intervention, delivered by special counsel Edward Greenspan, required considerable consultation and manoeuvring by Borovoy and others. At the time there were strong, opposing positions held by members of the CCLA board concerning the right of a woman to choose to have an abortion. Consequently the CCLA intervention focused on issues of process, and specifically on the unfairness inherent in the way that the abortion laws were structured and administered across the country. In preparation for its intervention, CCLA conducted a survey of Canadian hospitals, contacting 325 hospitals, of which ninety replied, thirty-two of which indicated that they had therapeutic abortion committees (TACs).

Morgentaler's defence team and the interveners including CCLA challenged the 1969 abortion law (section 251 of the *Criminal Code*) as unconstitutional and a violation of Canada's 1960 Bill of Rights—a denial of a woman's rights to security of person, as guaranteed by the Bill of Rights, and a denial of the rights of women to a fair hearing. They also challenged the right of the Quebec Court of Appeal to overturn an acquittal by jury and impose a prison sentence.

They argued that a test of "necessity," meaning medical emergency, should determine if an abortion could be legally performed outside the framework of hospitals and TACs. They pointed out that the law on abortion was unclear regarding the meaning of "danger to health."

And finally, as part of its brief, CCLA presented extensive documentary evidence on the impact of the 1969 abortion law. The evidence showed that the possibility of getting an abortion across Canada was idiosyncratic and discriminatory, that it depended first on a pregnant woman's proximity to a hospital with a TAC and secondly on the biases and prejudices within any hospital's board-appointed TAC.

According to the data collected by CCLA, in January 1974 there were 904 hospitals in Canada. In 1973, only 261 of those hospitals had TACs; roughly half the hospitals in Ontario and British Columbia had TACs, whereas in Saskatchewan, only 10 out of 133 hospitals had TACs, and in Quebec, 24 of 133 hospitals had TACs.

The CCLA survey revealed that across the country there were widely differing interpretations of the test concerning "danger to health." One hospital required women to prove that they were suicidal, while others only asked that the wording of the applications for an abortion conform exactly to the language of the *Criminal Code*. Some hospitals required independent reports from two physicians, one of whom had to be a psychiatrist. And several TACs would only approve an abortion if the woman agreed to subsequently undergo a tubal ligation in order to ensure no further pregnancies.

There was evidence that women who had been refused an abortion by one hospital would be granted an abortion by another; in one case, a woman who had been refused an abortion while admitted to one hospital following a suicide attempt was approved for an abortion by a second hospital in a different city. The CCLA report noted that "when this committee felt justified in granting a certificate despite previous rejections...the resultant delay occasioned an increasingly hazardous operation."

The Supreme Court heard the case in late 1974, delivered its decision in early 1975, but the decision was published in 1976. It was a split decision, 6 to 3, with the majority of justices denying Morgentaler's appeal and allowing the Quebec Court of Appeal's guilty verdict and sentence to stand. Justice Brian Dickson made the following statement as a preamble to his reasons for denying the appeal:

> It seems to me to be of importance at the outset to indicate what the Court is called upon to decide in this appeal, and equally important, what it has not been called upon to decide. It has not been called upon to decide, or even to enter, the loud and continuous public debate on abortion which has been going on in this country between, at the two extremes, (i) those who would have abortion regarded in law as an act purely personal and private, of concern only to a woman and her physician, in which the state has no legitimate right to interfere, and (ii) those who speak in terms of moral absolutes and, for religious or other reasons, regard an induced abortion and destruction of a foetus, viable or not, as destruction of a human life and tantamount to murder. The values we must accept for the purposes of this appeal

> are those expressed by Parliament, which holds the view that the desire of a woman to be relieved of her pregnancy is not, of itself, justification for performing an abortion.

All the SCC justices deferred unequivocally to the authority of Parliament on the issue of abortion. Even the judgment of those justices in the minority, who would have allowed portions of Morgentaler's appeal, signalled disapproval of abortion: Chief Justice Bora Laskin wrote on behalf of the minority, "Parliament has in its judgment decreed that interference by another, or even by the pregnant woman herself, with the ordinary course of conception is *socially undesirable conduct* subject to punishment.... and the fact that there may be safe ways of terminating a pregnancy or that any woman or women claim a personal privilege to that end, becomes immaterial."

The "urgent necessity" argument was dismissed. CCLA's evidence concerning the "unevenness in the administration" of the laws governing abortions was deemed irrelevant to the case by all justices; these problems were something "for Parliament to correct and not for the courts to monitor as being a denial of equality before the law and the protection of the law." This was a matter of "administrative efficiency"; there was no reason to find section 251 unconstitutional "merely because not all persons affected by s.251 may find it feasible because of geographic or economic considerations to take shelter under its exculpating terms." The court most definitely did not think it was the job of the SCC to deal with inequalities in how the law was carried out; access to abortion was not a right.

The Quebec Court of Appeal's decision to overturn the acquittal by jury and issue a different verdict and a prison sentence was deemed legal by the majority of SCC justices, but was described as "obviously a power to be used with great circumspection." It was this aspect of the appeal that Chief Justice Laskin and two others disagreed with, finding that "the jury's verdict is not one which can be lightly interfered with, by an appellate court," and recommending that the jury's verdict of acquittal be restored.

Another point made by Chief Justice Laskin became an important marker in the evolution of abortion laws and the broader human and civil rights debate. Both Morgentaler's lawyer and CCLA had argued that the abortion legislation was unconstitutional because of the rights delineated in the Bill of Rights. But Laskin noted that the Bill of Rights is only "a statutory instrument, illustrative of Parliament's primacy within the limits of its assigned legislative authority...." In other words, the Bill of Rights was not a constitutional document, and therefore could not trump other legislation. The 1976 *Morgentaler* decision and other concurrent circumstances helped to prepare the ground for the creation of a constituted, entrenched, and binding *Canadian Charter of Rights and Freedoms*.When Morgentaler came before the Supreme Court again, in 1988, Brian Dickson was chief justice. The parameters defining "socially undesirable conduct" changed considerably over the intervening decade. The creation of the *Charter of Rights and Freedoms* irrevocably altered the terms of the debate about the rights of women. And in 1988, there was also, for the first time, a woman justice on the Supreme Court—Bertha Wilson, appointed by Prime Minister Trudeau in 1982.

"WHAT'S AT ISSUE IS NOT THE STATUTORY LAW OF ABORTIONS BUT THE COMMUNITY'S FAITH IN JURIES." (ALAN BOROVOY, CCLA LETTER TO RENÉ LEVÉSQUE, 1976)

Immediately after the SCC decision came down in 1975, Morgentaler began serving the sentence decreed by the Quebec Court of Appeal. He was in prison for ten months and was denied parole. While he was in prison, the Quebec courts instigated a second trial on different charges, at which he was again acquitted by jury.

Public and political response to the Supreme Court decision was immediate and strong, on two separate issues. First, there was the SCC decision that it was legal for a superior court to simply overturn the verdict of a jury. Politicians in Ottawa and civil liberties groups like CCLA were outraged by this ruling. The federal government consequently rushed to introduce a modification to the *Criminal Code* now known as the *Morgentaler Amendment*, which denied higher courts the right to override an acquittal (now they can only order a new trial). In a move that was clearly politically motivated, even unprecedented, Federal Minister of Justice Ron Basford applied the *Morgentaler Amendment* retroactively to Morgentaler's own case and ordered a new trial in Quebec.

Morgentaler was again acquitted quickly, in less than one hour, by a Montreal jury.

But the SCC case, despite its complete dismissal of all aspects of Morgentaler's appeal, brought the issue of abortion to a rolling boil in public discourse. On May 29, 1975, the Alliance for Life delivered to Parliament, in orange crates, the Petition of One Million, demanding protection of the rights of the unborn. In September, the government created the Badgley Commission to conduct a review of abortion practices across Canada.

Immediately prior to the elections in Quebec in 1976, CCLA wrote to René Lévesque, leader of the Parti Québécois, asking that, if he became premier, his government drop outstanding charges against Morgentaler: "What's at issue is not the statutory law of abortions but the community's faith in juries." In November 1976 the newly elected Parti Québécois announced that it would not prosecute Morgentaler further, a position that not only challenged the historic hegemony of the Catholic Church in the province but also directly resisted the authority of federal law. This was in part interpreted as Quebec flouting the authority of the federal government, but the Parti Québécois's position was also very much a response to public opinion.

The Badgley Commission reported back to Parliament in 1977. The three-person committee was only permitted to review and report on the "equitable" application of the law across Canada, not to make any recommendations concerning the underlying policy, which presumably might have undermined the *Criminal Code* provisions. The commission answered a series of specific questions about access to abortion, and did not address incendiary issues such as rights of the fetus or late-pregnancy termination.

The findings were an indictment of the abortion law and resolutely confirmed the evidence presented by CCLA to the Supreme Court in 1974. Not only were there gross variations in the application of the law from province to province but ironically, the demand for therapeutic abortions unleashed by the legalization of abortion created unmanageable pressures on hospital resources. This meant, among other things, that the time between a request for an abortion and approval could regularly be as long as eight weeks. Almost two-thirds of the hospitals surveyed by the committee introduced, with no legal justification whatsoever, the necessity of consent to an abortion by a husband, even an ex-husband. The fact that many hospitals were owned by religious denominations had an impact on the number of hospitals that would even have TACs, and the opinions of medical professionals (85 per cent of doctors surveyed were male) created additional barriers; almost half of all physicians surveyed by the committee believed that "abortion lowered the value of human life."

The conclusions of the Badgley Commission were very carefully worded: The problem, the commission said, was not the legislation itself, but incompatibility between two "equally durable" facts: "a substantial number of women seeking this operation, and a sizable proportion of the medical profession and a large number of hospital boards which on moral and professional grounds will not participate in this procedure."

This standoff was rooted, the commissioners noted obliquely, in "tolerance of widespread and entrenched social inequity for women [several hundred thousand women and their families] involved in the abortion procedure," an inequity that was eloquently articulated in substantial verbatim testimony to the committee from women who had had abortions, legal and illegal, before and after 1969. Furthermore, the committee stated its belief that the demand for abortions would increase, because of the tension in Canadian society between "two sensitive issues, abortion and family planning."

The irony was that by setting up a complicated procedure for obtaining a legal abortion, Parliament had created conditions, observed the committee, that made the likelihood of getting such an abortion "in practice illusory."

The findings of the Badgley Commission were largely under-reported and not acted upon at the time. However, the statistics found their way, in considerable detail, into the 1984 trial of

Henry Morgentaler in Ontario, and as a result into the SCC's 1988 decision.

In the interim, Canada became fiercely engaged in the patriation of the Constitution, and in the wording of the new bill of rights proposed by Prime Minister Trudeau—the Charter.

WHO IS EVERYONE?—THE *CHARTER OF RIGHTS AND FREEDOMS*

The process whereby Canada acquired the *Charter of Rights and Freedoms* was reviewed in the previous chapter of this book, with specific reference to the leadership role played by CCLA. But several aspects of that process are worth mentioning in the context of the abortion issue; these have to do with revisions to the draft Charter—presented by Trudeau in fall of 1980, and the subject of intense public attention and intervention—and with submissions from the public and organizations to the Joint Parliamentary Committee created to review the draft.

The first and most obvious change to the draft was the strengthening of the language concerning the equality of rights of women, eventually enshrined in numerous clauses throughout the Charter. Feminist groups, led by Doris Anderson (Status of Women), Mary Eberts of the Advisory Council on the Status of Women (ACSW), and others successfully lobbied to expand sections of the Charter, to rename the proposed "non-discrimination" clause as the "Equality" clause, and to specify that equality rights hold under the law and also enjoy "equal benefit of the law." The Charter's final version also included a specific guarantee of "sexual equality" notwithstanding anything else in the Charter, which was specifically designed to take precedence over the "reasonable limitations" on rights made possible in section 1.

The second issue raised during the Charter debates was whether or not abortion or fetal rights should be included. This debate circled around suggestions (both overt and covert) that a woman's right to have an abortion should actually be spelled out in the Charter, but more generally took the form of discussion about the intended meaning of the word "everyone" in the document.

There are several clauses in the Charter that assign rights and freedoms to "everyone." In some sections, the term "every citizen of Canada" or "every individual" is used, but the attention of both feminists and anti-abortion groups, in their interventions on Charter language, was on the precise meaning of the word "everyone," especially in those clauses that dealt with rights and freedoms in the largest sense. Both groups found the term "everyone" too general; feminists argued that it should be changed to "every person" in order to resonate with the definition of "person" in the 1929 Persons Case (*Edwards v. Canada [Attorney General]*), which first recognized women in Canada as "full legal persons." Anti-abortion groups argued for even more specific language: "everyone from conception until natural death…"

Archbishop MacNeil, president of the influential Canadian Conference of Catholic Bishops, sent the following statement to Trudeau in March, 1981: "Any Charter of Rights which is not founded upon respect for life from the moment of conception would be flawed by an inherent weakness.... It would be deplorable

if your Charter of Rights could, either now or in the future, be interpreted in such a way as to broaden the impact and effect of the present abortion legislation, which is already in some of its prescriptions unacceptable to us."

But Trudeau insisted unequivocally in his response to Archbishop MacNeil that the Charter would be neutral on the subject of abortion: "No provision of the Charter is reasonably capable of an interpretation that would either enshrine a right to abortion or a right to life for the unborn or deny the ability of Parliament to legislate on the matter in the context of the Criminal Code."

Anti-abortion activist Joseph Borowski, formerly a Manitoba NDP Cabinet minister, went on an eighty-day hunger strike in 1980 to protest the lack of protection for unborn children in the Charter. Between 1978 and 1989 Borowski launched a challenge, first citing the Bill of Rights and later the Charter, claiming (just like his nemesis and arch-rival Morgentaler) that the *Criminal Code* provisions for legal abortion were unconstitutional. CCLA applied to intervene in the Saskatchewan Court of the Queen's Bench in 1983, where Borowski's challenge was first heard; this location was designated for the simple and practical reason of alleviating the expenses of Borowski's lawyer, Morris Shumiatcher—himself a rather famous person, who in 1947 drafted the *Saskatchewan Bill of Rights*. CCLA was hoping to argue that, Borowski's implications to the contrary, it would be "repugnant" to interpret either the Charter or the *Bill of Rights* as intent on "barring medical treatment considered necessary for life or health."[155]

The CCLA application to intervene was denied, as was the application of the Canadian Abortion Rights Action League. CCLA declared that the absence of interveners made the Borowski case "lopsidedly uneven" and subsequently requested, without success, that federal Justice Minister Mark MacGuigan ask for a Supreme Court reference concerning the constitutionality of the abortion laws. (A Supreme Court reference can be requested by Cabinet, through the offices of the governor general, for interpretation of law or fact about the Constitution or federal or provincial legislation; recent examples are the 2004 Supreme Court reference on same-sex marriage and the 2014 references concerning abolition of the Senate, and the composition and constitutional status of the SCC itself.)

It was deeply unfair, said CCLA, that Borowski was being given his day in court on the subject of abortion, but that women cannot even intervene on an issue that affected them directly. "He, of course, is not now a fetus or the father of one. He, of course, is not now pregnant or likely to become so. Nevertheless, he enjoys special standing in this case while many women in the country do not."

Borowski's case moved very slowly through the Saskatchewan and federal courts, until it finally was rejected as moot in 1989, by the SCC, because of the 1988 *Morgentaler* decision.

In accounts of the tumultuous abortion debate in Canada over these twenty years, Morgentaler and Borowski are consistently depicted as the chief protagonists (attracting intense media attention, celebrity lawyers, and huge sums of money) in a drama about the rights of women. Even the court challenges were focused on doctors, not pregnant women.

Neither proposal to alter the meaning of "everyone" was accepted, nor was there support for any mention of abortion rights in the Charter. To date, the term "everyone" has not been interpreted by the courts to include the fetus.

"IN THIS COUNTRY, ACCESS TO AN ABORTION REQUIRES A TRAVEL AGENT—AND MONEY." (JUNE CALLWOOD, *THE GLOBE AND MAIL*, 1986)

Within weeks of the ceremonial enshrinement of the Charter in April 1982, Henry Morgentaler announced that he was opening clinics in Winnipeg and Toronto, and Borowski was defending the rights of the fetus in Regina courts. Around the country, forces for and against abortion rights mobilized; the elections of hospital boards (responsible for determining not only whether abortions would be performed, but also the very important composition of the TACs) became intensely politicized. Canadian women openly attempted to seek abortions either legally or from a private clinic. The Canadian Abortion Rights Action League not only raised funds for Morgentaler's clinics, and the expected legal costs, but also lobbied provincial governments and hospitals for improved access to abortion services.

Interpretation of the abortion law by hospitals and other institutions was alarmingly unpredictable and prejudicial. In Ontario, in 1983 for example, the Cornwall Children's Aid Society attempted to deny an abortion to a fifteen-year-old girl—one of their wards who had become pregnant as a result of rape—insisting that the Society would only permit the abortion if two doctors (in addition to a therapeutic abortion committee) declared that her life was in danger. CCLA requested that the Ontario Minister of Community and Social Services intervene, arguing that "it is a gross abuse of power for a public agency to deny a youngster medical treatment...considered necessary for her health." Before the Minister responded, the girl had travelled to Montreal to the Morgentaler Clinic.

Within a year of opening, both of the new Morgentaler clinics were raided by police, Morgentaler and others were arrested and charged, and in November 1983, the court case began in Toronto that would ultimately end up in the Supreme Court, which was always the intention of both Morgentaler and his lawyer, Morris Manning. The Toronto Morgentaler defence was a showpiece of legal gamesmanship, involving a pretrial motion to quash the indictment on constitutional grounds (which took eight months), acquittal by a jury (just like in Montreal), appeals and cross-appeals, and an order for a new trial in Ontario, before the case ascended to the Supreme Court.

"THE CONTEMPORARY VIEW [IS] THAT ABORTION IS NOT ALWAYS SOCIALLY UNDESIRABLE BEHAVIOR" (FROM THE ONTARIO COURT OF APPEAL, QUOTED IN 2ND *MORGENTALER* SCC DECISION, 1986/88)

In the pretrial phase of the Toronto court proceedings, Manning had strategically introduced all of the evidence he could muster concerning the difficulties in obtaining an abortion (as delineated in the Badgley Commission Report and elaborated upon by numerous witnesses) and the constitutional arguments, so that both issues could be incorporated as the bedrock for his case in the SCC. The grounds for this appeal were similar to the grounds of the 1976 case—necessity and equality of access—with additional arguments for right to privacy, now based on section 15 of the Charter.

There were no interveners in what was to date the most significant Charter case before the Supreme Court. Manning, it is said, preferred to go it alone and brushed aside the offers of organizations like CCLA to intervene, perhaps concerned that a cast of interveners in support of Morgentaler would attract an equally large contingent of interveners on the other side. (According to Borovoy, Manning simply did not answer his calls.) Anti-abortion activists were already focused on the Borowski case, which was expected to be considered by the SCC at almost the same time.

Manning made his arguments to the SCC over six days in November 1986. It took the court more than one year to prepare a ruling. The decision came down on January 26, 1988. It was a complex split decision from seven judges (one justice was absent because of illness and another was then removed from proceedings to prevent a tied judgment): five justices upheld Morgentaler's appeal, in three separate written rationales, and two justices would have denied the appeal.

It was an extraordinary ruling for many reasons, not least of which was that it was, on almost every point, a complete reversal of the 1976 *Morgentaler* decision. The reversal extended even to the opinions of the justices on the idea of abortion; in 1976, Justice Dickson described abortion as socially unacceptable. In 1988, he quoted the Ontario Court of Appeal in saying the exact opposite. In 1976, the formidable difficulties faced by women trying to get legal abortions, itemized by CCLA, were dismissed as mere administrative matters. In 1988, those difficulties were seen to invalidate the *Criminal Code* procedures.

The appeal was granted on very narrow grounds (the court chose not to even consider the issue of right to privacy): first, section 251 of the *Criminal Code* was deemed a denial of a woman's legal rights to "security of person" (guaranteed in section 7 of Charter) and secondly, the terms of this infringement (the means by which an abortion could be deemed legal) were found unjustifiable.

The following statement is from Chief Justice Brian Dickson's summary of the ruling by the majority:

> Section 251 clearly interferes with a woman's physical and bodily integrity. Forcing a woman, by threat of criminal sanction, to carry a foetus to term unless she meets certain criteria unrelated to her own priorities and aspirations, is a profound interference with a woman's body and thus an infringement of security of the person. A second breach of the right to security of the person occurs independently as a result of the delay in obtaining therapeutic abortions caused by the mandatory procedures of s.251, which results in a higher probability of complications and greater risk. The harm to the psychological integrity of women seeking abortions was also clearly established....
>
> One of the basic tenets of our system of criminal justice is that when Parliament creates a defence to a criminal charge, the defence should not be illusory or so difficult to attain as to be practically illusory. The procedure and restrictions stipulated in s.251 for access to therapeutic abortions make the defence illusory resulting in a failure to comply with the principles of fundamental justice.

Chief Justice Dickson enumerated at considerable length the flaws of the "unfair and arbitrary" procedure: it required the participation of at least four physicians; the term "accredited" and the need for provincial approval set up too many restrictions; "the word 'health' is vague" making it "impossible for women to know in advance what standard of health will be applied by any given committee."

In his concurring comments, Justice Jean Beetz wrote the following:

> If a rule of criminal law precludes a person from obtaining appropriate medical treatment when his or her life or health is in danger, then the state has intervened and this intervention constitutes a violation of that man's or that woman's security of the person. "Security of the person" must include a right of access to medical treatment for a

> condition representing a danger to life or health without fear of criminal sanction. If an act of Parliament forces a person whose life or health is in danger to choose between, on the one hand, the commission of a crime to obtain effective and timely medical treatment and, on the other hand, inadequate treatment or no treatment at all, the right to security of the person has been violated.

It is curious that, although the majority decisions all specifically stated that the court was not asked to rule on whether or not the word "everyone" in the Charter included the fetus (with independent rights to "life, liberty and security of person"), they all framed their decision concerning the constitutionality of section 251 of the *Criminal Code* in terms of the rights of the woman *against* the rights of the fetus, even though there was also no reference at all in section 251 to the fetus. Chief Justice Dickson wrote: "State protection of foetal interests may well be deserving of constitutional recognition under s.1." Justice Bertha Wilson declared, "The primary objective of the impugned legislation is the protection of the foetus...." Objectives like protection of the life and health of women are "ancillary."

Justice Wilson went even further and considered issues such as the viability of the fetus. She cited the principle used in the 1973 US Supreme Court decision *Roe v. Wade* to identify when, during the term of a pregnancy, the court might have an interest in the life of a fetus, what she referred to as the "developmental nature of the gestation process." Wilson declared that "the foetus should be viewed in differential and developmental terms. This view of the foetus supports a permissive approach to abortion in the early stages where the woman's autonomy would be absolute and a restrictive approach in the later stages where the states's interest in protecting the foetus would justify its prescribing conditions. The precise point in the development of the foetus at which the state's interest in its protection becomes 'compelling' should be left to the informed judgment of the legislature which is in a position to receive submissions on the subject from all the relevant disciplines."

In strong, rhetorical language, Justice Wilson also articulated what she saw as deep offence to women in section 251 of the *Criminal Code*:

> In essence, what it does is assert that the woman's capacity to reproduce is not to be subject to her own control. It is to be subject to the control of the state. She may not choose whether to exercise her existing capacity or not to exercise it.... She is truly being treated as a means—a means to an end which she does not desire but over which she has no control. She is the passive recipient of a decision made by others as to whether her body is to be used to nurture a new life. Can there be anything that comports less with human dignity and self-respect? How can a woman in this position have any sense of security with respect to her person? I believe that s.251 of the *Criminal Code* deprives the pregnant woman of her right to security of the person as well as her right to liberty.

In addition, Wilson found that section 251 failed the test of section 1 of the Charter because abortion is essentially a moral question, a question of conscience: "It is not just a medical decision; it is a profound social and ethical one as well."

Dissenting justices argued in favour of the abortion clauses of the *Criminal Code*. They noted that the "proposition that women enjoy a constitutional right to have an abortion is devoid of support in either the language, structure or history of the constitutional text, in constitutional tradition, or in the history, traditions or underlying philosophies of our society." And that the "allegation of procedural unfairness is not supported by the claim that many women wanting abortions have been unable to get them in Canada.... Any inefficiency in the administrative scheme is caused principally by forces external to the statute—the general demand for abortion irrespective of the provisions of s.251. A court cannot strike down a statutory provision on this basis."

This issue of "procedural unfairness" and "inefficiency in the administrative scheme" would surface twelve years later in a very different SCC case, that of *Little Sister's Book and Art Emporium v. Canada Customs*.

The 1988 SCC ruling in favour of Morgentaler was not an endorsement of unregulated abortion as a right of women. The ruling declared section 251 illegal, meaning it has no force and is not in effect, even though it still remains in the *Criminal Code*, as section 287.

The judgment left the door wide open for Parliament to introduce new legislation concerning abortions, and clearly the court imagined that such legislation would be proposed; the comments by Justice Wilson in particular invited Parliament to consider specifically the issue of late-term abortion in new legislation.

In October 1988, the SCC also heard the appeal of Joe Borowski, arguing for the rights of the fetus as implied in "everyone," and in February 1989 it ruled that because of the *Morgentaler* decision, and in order not to preempt the anticipated new legislation on abortion, Borowski's case was moot.

The entire country fully expected a new abortion law. Alan Borovoy wrote in 1988 about the significance of the SCC *Morgentaler* decision and what message parliamentarians should take from it:

> According to the court, the abortion law violated the procedural protections of the Charter. In some ways, however, the opinion of the judges is not nearly as significant as that of the many jurors who assessed Dr. Morgentaler's conduct in four different trials. Each time he was tried for violating Canada's abortion laws, Dr. Morgentaler was acquitted by juries of his peers.... They were, of course, unanimous.... What explains their unwillingness to convict a self-confessed abortionist? The most plausible explanation is that those jurors acted out of a visceral sense of the appropriate limits of state coercion. Even if they had been brought up to oppose abortion and respect the law, they had also been exposed to the norms of the democratic system.... The application of the law in the Morgentaler case meant intruding state power on the right of women to control their own bodies. That was something those juries were not prepared to do.
>
> No matter what kind of abortion law our parliamentarians favour, they cannot afford to ignore the remarkable

experience of the Morgentaler case. If they enact a law that juries find repugnant to enforce, our parliamentarians risk bringing the administration of justice into disrepute. This, in turn, could undermine public respect for the rule of law itself.

—*When Freedoms Collide*, 1988

STRIKING OUT ON ABORTION LAW—1988–91

The Progressive Conservative government of Brian Mulroney attempted to craft abortion laws between 1988 and 1991 and failed three times. The first bill proposed in July 1988 would have made first-term abortions legal and late-term abortions illegal. It was defeated in the House of Commons by a vote of 147 to 76, because it satisfied neither those MPs who opposed abortion outright nor those who opposed the use of the *Criminal Code*. Women MPs of all parties voted against this bill.

The second bill, Bill C-43, was not introduced in the House of Commons until November 1989. But between the two bills, public interest in abortion was galvanized (CCLA joined a coalition of twenty-five pro-choice groups), first by the still-outstanding Borowski SCC appeal and then, over four midsummer weeks, by the first SCC challenge on abortion in which a pregnant woman was the protagonist.

Chantal Daigle was a twenty-one-year-old resident of Val-d'Or, Quebec. After living for several months with Jean-Guy Tremblay, Daigle discovered that she was pregnant; but because (she averred) Tremblay had become jealous and physically abusive, Daigle decided to end both the relationship and the pregnancy and asked her doctor for an abortion. On July 7, 1989, Tremblay filed for an injunction to prevent the abortion. The injunction was granted, first by the Quebec Superior Court and second by the Quebec Court of Appeal, both of which found that the fetus had either legal rights, under the *Quebec Charter of Human Rights and Freedoms*, and/or "natural" rights, and a right determined by "custom." (Three similar injunctions were filed in 1989 by men in Alberta, Manitoba, and Ontario, but they were dismissed by lower courts.)

Daigle appealed to the Supreme Court of Canada and in her affidavit gave specific reasons for wishing to terminate the pregnancy: Tremblay "became dominant, jealous and possessive and… abused her physically." And despite knowing that she was pregnant Tremblay pushed her to the floor, threatening to "bring her into line once and for all." Daigle feared for her future "psychological and moral health" and declared, "I do not wish to have a child at the present time in light of my age, my social situation as a single person and my moral values as I want to provide for a child in a serene stable family environment in which there is no violence."

But the day before her case was to be heard by the Supreme Court—its members called back for an unprecedented emergency

sitting—Daigle went secretly to Boston to have her twenty-two-week pregnancy terminated. Despite this action (for which Daigle could have been charged with contempt of court), the SCC decided to proceed with the hearing and granted three interveners on both sides ten minutes each to state their case.

The CCLA intervention made by John B. Laskin addressed the issue of whether "coercing a woman to keep a fetus in her body against her will" was in accordance with "legal principles" and, secondly, if an injunction was appropriate—noting that dealing with these two questions did not require the court to address the issue of whether or not a fetus was a human being. CCLA argued for the principle of "individual autonomy," noting that medical procedures such as organ donation require informed consent, and expressed concern that injunctions were not appropriate in the case of abortions, because, if a precedent was created, injunctions might be used to delay and interfere with abortions at any stage in a pregnancy.

The SCC heard all arguments, retired, and very quickly returned a unanimous decision to overturn the injunction; the written decision was not issued until November 16, 1989. Daigle's appeal was upheld because the SCC found that neither the *Civil Code of Lower Canada* nor the Quebec Charter makes reference to fetal rights, nor does the Quebec Charter "include any definition of the term 'human being' or 'person'.... If the legislature had wished to accord a foetus the right to life, it is unlikely that it would have left the protection of this right in such an uncertain state. As this case demonstrates, a foetus' alleged right to life will be protected only at the discretionary request of third parties." And further that the injunction "must be set aside because the substantive rights which are alleged to support it—the rights accorded to a foetus or a potential father—do not exist."

The SCC also stated that "the Canadian Charter cannot be invoked in this case to support the injunction. This is a civil action between two private parties and there is no state action which is being impugned.... This Court should generally avoid making any unnecessary constitutional pronouncement."

In his 1992 book, *Morgentaler v. Borowski: Abortion, the*

Charter, and the Courts, F.L. Morton notes that the cases of Daigle and Borowski were "equally moot" by the time they were considered by the SCC, but they were treated very differently: "Joe Borowski had spent ten years and nearly half a million dollars to bring the issue of the rights of the unborn before the Supreme Court. He was told to try again if and when a new abortion law was enacted. Chantal Daigle had spent thirty days and had won."

Furthermore, argued Morton, the SCC had a very different mindset when it dealt with Morgentaler: "Why had the Court exercised the techniques of judicial self-restraint when ruling on the rights of the unborn, but the tools of judicial activism when dealing with the rights of the mother?"

The theme of "judicial activism" emerged persistently over the subsequent twenty-five years, with reference to the SCC's interpretation of the Charter, and was discussed in the previous chapter of this book. But both the *Morgentaler* and the *Daigle* decisions were clearly made by the SCC with the expectation that Parliament would very soon enact new legislation to deal with abortion.

Bill C-43, introduced on November 3, 1989, was considered to be a compromise bill; abortion would be dealt with in the *Criminal Code*, but it would be legal if performed by a doctor of the woman's choice; mental and psychological health were to be considered, and abortions were not restricted to accredited hospitals. But still, much of the debate over the bill was focused on the question of the rights of the fetus.

Borovoy, in a September 1989 op-ed in the *Toronto Star*, argued that "the emphasis should shift from the mysteries of embryonic life to the limits of governmental power.... The law should allow the pregnant woman herself to determine when her suffering is unbearable." He stated that "a democracy does not have to embrace the moral merits of an abortion in order to rule out state coercion as an appropriate remedy."

In classic civil libertarian style, Borovoy also defended the anti-abortionists' right to make their case: "As long as they believe what they do, they should demonstrate, remonstrate, advocate and educate. In such matters, the norms of democracy encourage persuasion but not coercion." But "despite the rights that fetuses might otherwise have, they should not be able to invoke the power of the state to keep them in the bodies of their non-consenting mothers."

Bill C-43 was passed by the House of Commons on May 22, 1990, by a vote of 140 to 131—a "free vote," except for Cabinet. But intense activism from both sides over the next seven months resulted in a tie vote (43 to 43) in January 1990 in the Senate, where a tie vote means that the legislation dies. The Progressive Conservative government announced that it would not make any further attempts to create abortion legislation, and no federal government has attempted to do so since.

Between 1988 and 1996, however, there were numerous attempts by provincial governments to limit or control abortions, either by withholding funding or by redefining medical services; in all cases—B.C., Nova Scotia, and New Brunswick—the actions taken by provincial governments were found to be unconstitutional, mostly by reason of jurisdiction.

ACRIMONIOUS AFTERMATH—RIGHTS OF THE FETUS, RIGHTS OF PICKETERS

In 1997, the issue of fetal rights surfaced in another guise—that of the right to protect a fetus from the addictions of the woman bearing the fetus, addictions that had caused two previous children to be born permanently disabled and to become wards of the state. In the case of *Winnipeg Child and Family Services (Northwest Area) v. D.F.G*, CCLA was one of sixteen interveners, and it argued that to restrain the rights of a pregnant woman would represent a "dramatic rewriting of the law, a rewriting with vast ramifications for the civil liberties of pregnant women." The argument acknowledged the difficulty of the situation but stated: "On balance…it is less undesirable that the law and Canadian society accept the consequences for the foetus of non-interference with the woman's freedom of choice and liberty than that it expose others in less severe circumstances to unwarranted encroachments."

The SCC ruled that the court did not have the right to assume parental responsibility, and that:

> A pregnant woman and her unborn child are one and to make orders protecting fetuses would radically impinge on the fundamental liberties of the mother, both as to lifestyle choices and how and as to where she chooses to live and be. The invasion of liberty involved in making court orders affecting the unborn child is far greater than the invasion of liberty involved in court orders relating to born children.

The woman did, in fact, receive some treatment for her addictions during the course of the pregnancy and delivered a healthy child.

The CCLA argument also anticipated a later case, that of *Dobson v. Dobson*, 1999, in observing that extending the court's duty of care to a fetus could "expose the woman to an action by her child after its birth for damage suffered *in utero.*" In *Dobson v. Dobson,* a woman in the twenty-seventh week of pregnancy was involved in a motor vehicle accident that resulted in an immediate Caesarean delivery of the fetus, which suffered permanent mental and physical impairment as a result of the collision. The argument in favour of allowing liability was inspired by practical insurance-claim considerations (although interpreted as a fetal rights issue by two religious groups intervening), but was denied by the SCC. The two women justices, McLachlin and L'Heureux-Dubé, chose to make the following additional comments in agreeing with the majority:

> The intrusion upon the pregnant woman's autonomy worked by the proposed common law rule would also violate her right to equal treatment. Canadians generally enjoy the full right to decide what they will eat or drink, where they will work and other personal matters. Pregnant women, however, would not enjoy that right. In addition to the usual duties of prudent conduct imposed on all who engage in life's various activities, pregnant women would be subject to a host of additional restrictions.... To say women choose pregnancy is no answer. Pregnancy is essentially related to womanhood. It is an inexorable and essential fact of human history that women and only women become pregnant.

> Women should not be penalized because it is their sex that bears children....

• • •

Over time, the CCLA board came to support the principle of a woman's right to choose, and thus to proceed with ease in the pro-choice movement. But there was one issue related to the abortion debate on which CCLA found itself greatly at odds with other activists and with some of its own members. This had to do with the right to protest against both abortion clinics and abortion practitioners. In April 1993, the government of Ontario ordered a complete ban on all abortion protests—outside abortion clinics, hospitals, and in proximity to the homes of doctors who performed abortions. Ontario Attorney General Marion Boyd applied for a court order permanently barring such protests "within 500 feet" in specific cities—Toronto, London, Brantford, Kingston, and North Bay. The injunction detailed actions such as "assaulting, harassing... intimidating" and "using insulting abusive or defamatory language or gestures." The government sought damages of $500,000 against members of the anti-abortion movement.

In a letter to Marion Boyd in June 1993, CCLA protested the injunction, despite expressing sympathy with much of what the government was attempting to achieve, and noting that, indeed, many of the pickets had been unacceptable and their actions should be curbed. But CCLA questioned "whether the government should be taking the unusual step of applying for civil remedies in a dispute among citizens...." Actual offences, acts of mischief, intimidation, or vandalism should simply be prosecuted. But injunctions are "particularly contentious instruments" and cast too wide a net; this was often the case with labour injunctions: "the terms of the proposed injunction in this case are so broad that they could arguably prohibit even silent, peaceful, informational picketing...." And "at what point do unkind words become 'insulting' or 'abusive'? Imagine the impact of such a precedent on the picket lines of environmentalists, consumer boycotters, and Aboriginal activists."

CCLA recommended the use of criminal prosecutions instead of injunctions and suggested that "peaceful, non-obstructive picketing" be permitted within 500 feet of premises and that there should be no injunctions against picketing the homes of abortion practitioners.

The draft of the CCLA letter to Boyd was circulated to board members before it was sent, and it was the subject of a special board meeting. The position received strong and contradictory responses from CCLA Board members:

> —What if a particular group were suddenly to object to doctors who treat AIDS patients, or Black patients, or native peoples, or Jewish patients. Should a civilized and civil libertarian government allow doctors to be intimidated...that smacks too much of Nazi Germany.
>
> —Is the picketing to communicate or is the picketing to harass?...A one person picket is communicating information. Six, seven, eight or more pickets can be intimidation and harassment. It is not the message, but rather the method.

Michele Landsberg, columnist for the *Toronto Star*, was outraged. In her April 27, 1993, column she wrote: "Maybe these free-speech advocates, who are so worried about the rights of the anti-choice militants, suffer from a reality deficit. Maybe they've never been "free-speeched" by a praying, shrieking, fetus-wielding crowd of vigilantes...." CCLA stuck to the high road: "...it is worth re-stating our commitment to ensuring that clinic staff and patients are fully protected in the exercise of their lawful rights. But those rights were won, in the very recent past, largely because the "pro-choice" movement was able to exercise a vigorous right of free speech and assembly. These freedoms remain the best hope there is that fairness will prevail."

In September 1994, Boyd was granted the right to impose temporary injunctions limiting protesters to 150 metres from the homes of nine abortion providers in Ontario, and limiting pickets to a distance of between 9 and 18 metres from some clinics (the Morgentaler clinic already had a 150-metre distance guaranteed). In 2014, in downtown Toronto, there are still small huddles of protesters holding placards across the street from one modest "women's clinic" at the corner of Parliament and Gerrard streets, and on May 9, 2014, the annual March for Life drew approximately 7,000 people to Parliament Hill in Ottawa.

"LET SLEEPING DOGS LIE"—THE ABORTION ISSUE IN 2014

> The decision [to have an abortion] is one that will have profound psychological, economic and social consequences for the pregnant woman. The circumstances giving rise to it can be complex and varied and there may be, and usually are, powerful considerations militating in opposite directions. It is a decision that deeply reflects the way the woman thinks about herself and her relationship to others and to society at large. It is not just a medical decision; it is a profound social and ethical one as well. Her response to it will be the response of the whole person.
>
> It is probably impossible for a man to respond, even imaginatively, to such a dilemma not just because it is outside the realm of his personal experience (although this is, of course, the case) but because he can relate to it only by objectifying it, thereby eliminating the subjective elements of the female psyche which are at the heart of the dilemma.
>
> —Justice Bertha Wilson, 1988 *Morgentaler* SCC Decision

Canada is currently the only country in the world in which abortion is simply a legal medical procedure, no more and no less. There remains access to abortion issues, notably in Prince Edward Island, where no hospitals perform abortions and there are no abortion clinics. New Brunswick, in defiance of federal law, does not pay for abortions performed in private clinics. The statistics concerning abortion indicate that the number of abortions performed has consistently declined since 1997, with approximately 70,000 abortions performed annually, approximately fourteen abortions per 1,000 women of childbearing age, and that 90 per cent of abortions are performed within the first twelve weeks of pregnancy. According to the Abortion Rights Coalition of Canada (ARCC) there are virtually no maternal deaths during legal abortions.

As Justice Wilson's comments above suggest, no one wants to have to undergo an abortion. But there remains consistently strong support in Canada for abortion rights, and a firm resistance to the idea of introducing legislation to control abortion. "Canadians have mixed feelings about abortion but the attitude is: 'Let sleeping dogs lie,'" said Mario Canseco, vice-president of Angus Reid Public Opinion, in January 2013, twenty-five years after the *Morgentaler* decision. The Angus Reid poll showed that many Canadians, 45 per cent of those surveyed, erroneously believe that (as is the case in the United States), a woman can have an abortion in Canada only during the first twelve weeks of pregnancy. A very small number (5 per cent) of Canadians think abortion should be illegal; 35 per cent said there should be no restrictions on a woman's access to abortion. Roughly 50 per cent of the individuals polled indicated that they thought there should be some restrictions on abortions (related either to fetal defects, cause of pregnancy, such as rape, or viability of the fetus).

And yet, since 1989, there have been forty-five attempts to introduce legislation via private member's bills into the House of Commons on the subject of abortion or fetal rights. For example, in 2010, a private member's bill (called Roxanne's Law, in reference to a young woman who was murdered) tried to make it unlawful to "coerce" or attempt to "coerce" a female into getting an abortion. "Coercion" was defined to include "conduct that is intentionally and purposely aimed at directing the female person who has not chosen to have an abortion to have an abortion." CCLA expressed opposition to this bill, as "not helpful in addressing the question of violence against women." It described the proposed legislation as redundant: "A young pregnant woman has the right to choose whether to carry a pregnancy to term *or* to terminate it. Whichever option she chooses, she should not be subjected to harassment, intimidation, threats or the removal of financial support. The *Criminal Code* already prohibits all of these activities."

As recently as November 2012, a motion was introduced putatively to deal with the "problem" of sex-selective abortions in Canada. In the spring of 2013, pressure from Conservative Party MPs to be able to address the issue of abortion in the House of

Commons resulted in a rift in the ranks of the party. In spring 2014, Liberal leader Justin Trudeau declared that all Liberal candidates would be required, if elected, to support a woman's right to choose; historically, abortion votes in Parliament have been free votes.

The current debate in Canada is coloured by events south of the border. In March 2013, the Arkansas House of Representatives passed the *Human Heartbeat Protection Act*, which bans abortions after twelve weeks (which is when a fetal heartbeat is detectable), except to save the mother's life, or in pregnancies resulting from rape or incest. This act, and similar "personhood" bills in other states—which would protect the rights of the zygote (the first four days after sperm and ovum have united)—directly contravene *Roe v. Wade*, which sets the date at which a fetus can survive outside its mother (between twenty-three and twenty-four weeks) as the point at which states have the power to ban abortions outright. The rapidly evolving sophistication of reproductive and fetal technologies will undoubtedly create increased pressures on the definition of fetal viability. Anti-abortion activism in Canada follows closely such trends in the United States and has become extremely sophisticated, imbedding its message in websites with anodyne names such as Abortion in Canada and The Interim.

Henry Morgentaler (who had controversially been awarded the Order of Canada in 2008) died in May 2013, and his final SCC appeal, concerning the funding of abortions in New Brunswick, died with him. Even at the moment of death, Morgentaler was a polarizing figure. One straightforward tribute to Morgentaler came from long-retired Conservative Cabinet Minister Barbara McDougall, who took the issue right back to where it started, in the lives of girls and women:

> Henry Morgentaler changed things. Not many mortal men (or women) can make that claim, but the changes he set in motion in Canada have had a profound effect on virtually the whole of Canadian society, no more so than on women in their child-bearing years.
>
> I remember back when dark whispers of back alley and coat hanger abortions haunted the dreams of teenagers who

> were, or wanted to be, sexually active—promiscuous, our parents would have called it; daring, the rest of us would have claimed.... It is not "society" or the church and almost never the father who will see the fetus through babyhood and childhood to adulthood—it is the mother, the woman who bears the child, sometimes with help, sometimes not.
>
> Without question there is a profoundly moral decision to be made on whether or not to end a pregnancy. The only issue is who makes it. The State, that bears no responsibility? The father, who may or may not involve himself in the consequences? I fervently believe it is the Mother's decision alone, after discussing it (or not) with people she respects. Do we honestly think so little of a woman's ability to judge for herself that we would remove from her control over the most important moral choice she will make in her lifetime?
>
> —*The Globe and Mail*, May 30, 2013

Abortion for half the population is not a theoretical issue, but a life and death matter. Like other life and death matters—capital punishment and euthanasia—abortion has implications that run far deeper than civil liberties and freedoms that might seem more theoretical, or matters of principle in democratic societies where, when there is clash of values (on issues such as freedom of speech for example, or police malfeasance) resolution does not involve body and soul.

But at the same time, abortion as an issue is a virtual template for the evolution of civil rights in Canada over the last fifty years. It is emblematic of the nexus of personal and political values, a war of competing rights, when a deeply felt, most intimate moment in someone's life is laid bare in courtrooms and in placards on street corners. With the two Morgentaler SCC cases bookending the creation of the Charter, abortion, as much as any single issue, illustrates how profoundly our society and the tenor of public debate and the playbook for legal and political engagements changed over two decades, and yet, at the same time, how the values we hold as Canadians, which find their most extreme opposition on the matter of abortion, are curiously immutable.

For CCLA abortion was a test of the organization's maturity, its capacity for embracing competing views, its ingenuity at finding the best path through a forest of possibilities. It was a test of convictions, personal and legal. It pitted individual activists and like-minded organizations against one another; for women who were both feminists and defenders of civil liberties, for example, defending the rights of anti-choice protestors was a crucible on which ideologies and loyalties and deep friendships faltered. This would not be the last time that CCLA would find itself championing a difficult and unpopular cause, and making enemies of friends—the defence of obscenity and pornography was also a battlefield imbedded with landmines.

CHAPTER FOUR

Lady Chatterley's Lover, Macho Sluts, One Dad, Two Dads—Defining Obscenity, Defending Pornography

I really think that we are much better qualified to deal with increasing the seasonal tariff on cabbages and cucumbers than to pass moral judgment on literature coming into the country.

—George Nowlan, Minister of National Revenue,
Canadian House of Commons, 1958

Bear, take me to the bottom of the ocean with you, bear, swim with me, bear, put your arms around me, enclose me, swim, down, down, down with me.

—Marian Engel, *Bear*,
1976 Governor General's Award Winner

A person who picks up a gun to rob a bank knows beforehand that such conduct will run afoul of the criminal law. But a person who writes, publishes or distributes a particular book may not know that the book in question will ultimately be considered an "undue exploitation of sex."

—A. Alan Borovoy, *When Freedoms Collide,* 1988

Is a novel about sex with a bear pornography or literature? Are paintings of naked old men with very young girls obscene or just disturbing? Does it matter to Canadians in general if forty copies of a lesbian S&M magazine are available in a bookstore? These are some of the questions that Canadians have asked over the past fifty years, either in the privacy of their own homes or, frequently, in the courts. As a society, we're not at ease with images and ideas that challenge taboos. We are also blessed with the instinct to protect the vulnerable. We struggle to maintain balance between being punitive or permissive, and as individual citizens, parliamentarians, police, and the judiciary in a multicultural society, we are guided whether we know it or not by arcane codes derived from religions and diverse cultures, by our understanding of fundamental rights and freedoms in a democracy. All this grappling with virtue and vice happens in an increasingly affluent economy driven by capitalism and technological change, floodlit by game-changing movements, such as feminism and gender-identity rights, pushing up hard against inherently conservative institutions such as the courts and the police.

Cultural shifts in Canadian society have been unprecedented over the past fifty years; police officers who once tracked down unexpurgated editions of *Lady Chatterley's Lover* and scooped up nudes from the art galleries of Toronto now assume aliases in child exploitation chat rooms on the Internet. For people neither implicated in criminal acts nor even particularly interested in the materials themselves, the shift in the terms of discourse may come as a shock: In 1962, *Lady Chatterley's Lover* was a prohibited book and *Playboy* (neither *Penthouse* nor *Hustler* existed) was a relatively straightforward, even cheerful compendium of mainstream male erotic fantasies; in 2014, the most horrific, exploitative, unimaginable images and videos are available for viewing and downloading merely by typing one or two sexually charged words into any search engine on an iPad. These materials escape even old-fashioned classification; the Ontario Film Review Board reviewed 3,000 adult sex DVDs between January 2012 and 2013, for distribution to cable networks and retail outlets only. But this form of licensing has no impact whatsoever on digital sharing and downloading, the two most pervasive means of distributing pornography. Current concerns about obscenity/pornography are mostly with the digital transmission of materials portraying and derived from criminal acts with children.

The context for what might be deemed pornographic or obscene also evolved immeasurably between the mid-sixties and mid-eighties, a period to a large degree informed by the emergence of feminism and by burgeoning public awareness of what was labelled the "new pornography"—explicit materials depicting violence and sexual abuse of women and children. This issue came to a boil in the courts in the early 1990s, at exactly the same time that the issue of hate speech was before the courts. What began in the early sixties as a relatively simple conversation on a definition of obscenity is now split into several strands: adult pornography/erotica, child pornography, and the rapidly changing forms of distribution of both. In today's *Criminal Code*, the term pornography is only used with reference to the exploitation of children; the term obscenity is used to cover adult materials.[156]

Arrests and seizures through the 1980s and early 1990s were about objects—such as works of art, books and magazines, and videotapes—both in terms of their content and their availability; there were regular Canada Customs interventions in materials, especially non-heterosexual materials, that were being mailed to bookstores. But even though there are still occasional Customs seizures and attempts to ban books, the marketplace for obscene and pornographic materials and their production and distribution is now overwhelmingly virtual. And while laws are constantly being fiddled with to catch up to technology, and governments worldwide conduct merciless surveillance on Internet users, controls on content in most democracies are virtually non-existent, except as undertaken by providers such as Google, iTunes, and Amazon, which find themselves called out by consumers both for exercising censorship (prohibiting gay-positive materials) and supporting hate speech (allowing anti-gay apps).

The position of CCLA on what is obscene or pornographic has not shifted over fifty years: the law should be used to punish people who commit crimes, not to make artifacts and ideas illegal. Limiting freedom of expression will not stop pornographers. CCLA has made the argument for freedom of expression in a multitude of court cases. It is not difficult to defend a novel or a painting; the artistic community is generally very open-minded, the argument for artistic merit not hard to create, although a rigorous anti-censorship position finds even the defence of artistic merit superfluous.

But a defence of violent, exploitative pornography is difficult. In the 1990s, in two major Supreme Court of Canada (SCC) court cases in particular, CCLA stood against the emerging and very powerful lobby focused on violence against women. Feminists who opposed censorship found themselves at war with feminists who supported censorship as a means to deal with violence against women; long-time allies and friends stood on opposite sides of a deep chasm. The argument about obscenity was no longer just about morality, it was about equality. The issue was no longer about corrupting innocent minds, it was about causing harm to women and children. And in the courts, this was no longer a simple matter of defining something as obscene, yes or no; as with all civil- and human-rights issues in Canada, the legal challenges were fundamentally altered by the appearance of the Charter in 1982, which introduced a two-step review of all legislation that dealt in any way with freedom of expression: Does the law inhibit freedom? If so, can the limitation be justified?

The court cases dealing with obscene and pornographic materials make interesting close reading, because they demonstrate, first, how the judiciary interpreted its role in society before and after the Charter; second, how the definition evolved as the debate shifted to deal with different forms of material; and finally, how the courts were pushed and pulled in their decisions by social movements. The sometimes arcane language of the courtroom unwittingly reveals what is at the heart of this debate about sex and vulnerable people.

Until the end of the twentieth century, Canada's battle with obscenity was a story of artists, bookstores, and street-level porn merchants pitted against morality squads and the courts in cases concerned with specific books, films, or videos. With the advent of that emporium without borders called the Internet, and a major shift in the means of production and distribution of pornography, including child pornography, the public debate became more complex, more heated. But regardless of the material or the individuals being charged, the fundamental issue is always the definition of obscenity, a definition that changed dramatically in this country between the early 1960s and the present day.

"BUT I KNOW IT WHEN I SEE IT." (US SUPREME COURT JUSTICE POTTER STEWART, 1964)

For CCLA and other civil libertarians, the problem with defining obscenity is precisely that: What is it and who determines that? And who is "guilty" of obscenity? An obscenity court case, prior to the invention of the Internet, took the following form: A citizen would complain about something that to his or her mind seemed obscene, most typically a book, a film, or a magazine. A member of a police force would respond to the complaint and seize the offending materials, perhaps shut down a bookstore, and often charges would be laid.

This pattern is identical to the process whereby obscenity was first defined in English courts in Victorian England.

For almost a century, the court-honoured definition of obscenity in Canadian law was drawn from a case referenced always as the Hicklin Test. In *Regina v. Hicklin* (1868), the document that offended two justices (one named Benjamin Hicklin) of the borough of Wolverhampton, was an anti-Catholic pamphlet entitled "The Confessional Unmasked; Shewing the depravity of the Romish priesthood, the iniquity of the Confessional, and the questions put to females in confession." Between 2,000 and 3,000 copies of this pamphlet (in Latin, with "free" English translation) were both bought and sold, for the price of one shilling, by a Protestant metal broker named Henry Scott, whose motives for doing so are embedded in the pamphlet's title.

The pamphlet was deemed "obscene in fact as relating to impure and filthy acts, words, and ideas." It is an odd document; with Latin and English texts side by side, in the name of a high-minded exposé of priests, described as "prurient inquisitors" and compared to anacondas, the compiler of the material pulls what are described as excerpts from commentaries by Roman Catholic authorities on the kinds of questions that might arise during confession—Is it a mortal sin to have sex with the woman on top? Is it a mortal sin "for a man to rub his ____ against the hinder vessel of his wife"? Is oral sex a "new species of luxury"? And is it actually sodomy if the man doesn't "spend" when "the connection takes place in the hinder vessel"? (Probably not, appears to be the conclusion.)

The two magistrates ordered that the pamphlets be burned; Scott appealed their ruling, which was overturned by the borough Recorder, subject to a review by the Court of the Queen's Bench.

The judges of the Court of the Queen's Bench, with due and learned reference to the very rich tradition of the bawdy in English literature "from Chaucer to Byron—Dryden's translation, for instance, of the sixth satire of Juvenal," ruled that:

> the test of obscenity is this, *whether the tendency of the matter charged as obscenity is to deprave and corrupt those whose minds are open to such immoral influences, and into whose hands a publication of this sort may fall.* Now, with regard to this work, it is quite certain that it would suggest to the minds of the young of either sex, or even to persons of more advanced years, thoughts of a most impure and libidinous character.

If the author of the pamphlet is trying to expose the hypocrisy of the confessional, where such thoughts are likely "to do mischief" to the minds and imaginations of the innocent, it surely follows, said the judges, that mischief will also be done by the pamphlet itself, with its paragraphs "one following upon another, each involving some impure practices, some of them of the most filthy and disgusting and unnatural description it is possible to imagine."

Furthermore, the justices found Mr. Scott's motive (to prevent people from becoming Roman Catholics) irrelevant and indeed questionable: "The probability is, that nine hundred and ninety-nine out of every thousand into whose hands this work would fall would never be exposed to the chance of being converted to the Roman Catholic religion."

The pamphlet was deemed obscene: "Here we have a certain and positive evil produced for the purpose of effecting an uncertain, remote, and very doubtful good." The ruling of Mr. Hicklin and his fellow magistrate that the pamphlets be burned was obviously not fulfilled, because "The Confessional Unmasked" has recently been uploaded to the Internet by the University of Michigan.

The note of elitist, almost biblical paternalism—*You shall not do evil that good may come*—underlying the Hicklin Test informed all subsequent rulings on obscenity in Great Britain, the United States, and Canada (where there were few) for almost one hundred years. The definition of obscenity has always bedevilled lawmakers and judges, and, as Justice Stewart's comment above reveals, their attempts to do so, despite reference to grand notions of good and evil and "community standards," spring from their own instincts and beliefs.

In 1959, a new definition of obscenity was inserted into Canada's *Criminal Code*: "any publication a dominant characteristic of which is the undue exploitation of sex, or of sex and any one or more of the following subjects, namely, crime, horror, cruelty and violence, shall be deemed to be obscene." Obscene materials of all kinds, even crime comics (depicting real or fictitious events), were the targets of this section of the *Criminal Code*. Over the next fifty years, parliamentarians, the courts, civil libertarians, and citizens would attempt to interpret and apply, first, this amorphous test for obscenity, and second, a much later definition of child pornography.

THE 1960s—DIRT FOR DIRT'S SAKE

> The author then minutely describes with unholy satisfaction more than fifteen adulterous scenes in the henhouse, the brushwood of the nearby fields, or the living quarters of the game keeper. Nothing is left even to the most vivid imagination. All the episodes are brutally described, and the conversation between the two lovers is of a low and vulgar character. Words are used that no decent person would dare speak without, in my view, offending the moral sense of anyone who believes in the ordinary standards of decency, self-respect and dignity.... I must say that I believe that this book has been over-glorified.
>
> —Justice Taschereau, about
> *Lady Chatterley's Lover,* SCC, Larry Brodie, 1962

> You'll have to kill me first before you take my pictures.
>
> —Toronto gallery owner Dorothy Cameron, 1966

D.H. Lawrence's *Lady Chatterley's Lover* was first published privately in Italy in 1928, and only became available in 1960 as an unexpurgated edition, which was found to be not obscene in the United Kingdom and in Australia before it made its way to Canada, where several copies were seized in Montreal. Two lower courts found the book obscene and the issue was the subject of Supreme Court case *Brody, Dansky, Rubin v. The Queen [1962]*. The court ruled in a close 5 to 4 decision, first that the Hicklin Test was now to be considered obsolete, because of the 1959 amendments to the *Criminal Code*, and second that *Lady Chatterley's Lover* did not rely overwhelmingly on obscene material, and therefore the book as a whole was not obscene, even though "there are isolated passages which, when read alone, do unduly exploit sex."

The terms of the obscenity debate for the next forty years were set in this courtroom. The social-improvement intent of the 1959 legislation was noted with approval by the court: the new test "manifests the well-publicized and commonly known intention of Parliament to strike more effectively at the corruption of public morals by obscene publications." Justices who found the book not to be obscene were receptive to the defence of literary and artistic merit, presented by writers Hugh MacLennan and Morley Callaghan. Those who dissented pointed to the "allure" of the word "unexpurgated" on the cover, and appear to have quantified the evidence of obscenity, finding it on 250 pages of the book, one dissenting justice decrying Lawrence's "unholy satisfaction" in depicting "more than fifteen adulterous scenes." And the elusive, richly ambiguous notion of "community standards" was introduced into the debate: "obscenity is not to be determined by the fact that a publication may offend the prude or excite the frustrated; it must be offensive to community standards or be likely to deprave or corrupt a recognizable segment of the public."

EROS 65—THE DOROTHY CAMERON GALLERY

In Toronto, in 1965, within months of its establishment, CCLA found its first freedom of expression case to support. Dorothy Cameron Gallery mounted an exhibition called Eros 65. It was a collection of sculptures, paintings, and drawings by twenty-one artists (Harold Towne, Joyce Wieland, Greg Curnoe, among others) on the subject of sexual love. On May 21, 1965, and again on May 26, members of the Morality Bureau of the Metropolitan Toronto Police came to the gallery, the second time with a search warrant, when they confiscated seven works of art by three artists (five by Robert Markle and one each by Lawrence Chaplin and Fred Ross). The Ontario Court of Appeal outline of the facts of the case states that the police described gallery owner and artist Dorothy Cameron as "dramatic...a demonstrative person...emotional," who, when told that the pictures would be seized and that she would be charged with " knowingly, without lawful justification or excuse, exposing obscene pictures to public view'...threw herself against the wall with her arms out and exclaimed, 'You'll have to kill me first before you take my pictures.'" The pictures, described by a police witness as "variously depicting nude figures in attitudes of sexual invitation or in positions or acts of sexual intercourse or in acts of lesbianism, [and] of base purpose and their obscenity was flagrant."

A magistrate's court found the images obscene and fined Cameron fifty dollars for each image. Cameron, with her lawyer Julian Porter, who was at the time also CCLA's part-time counsel, appealed to the Ontario Court of Appeal, where four of five judges ruled to dismiss Cameron's appeal. The works are described in great detail by the justices as having "a strong sexual connotation"—"Three...portray acts of lesbianism; [one] purports to show a male nude figure and a female nude figure with the female figure grasping the nude male's genitalia with her right hand." The works were for sale, at prices that now seem modest indeed—$100, $140, $160.

Porter's argument relied, in part, on a collection of catalogues of works of art and on expert witnesses such as artist Doris McCarthy and art historian Mary Bagnani. Cameron herself never testified. Porter also argued that the public good would be served by the exhibition, because of the impact on artists: "The repercussions which would result from proscribing or inhibiting the creative instincts of artists, by curtailing the freedom of artists to disseminate the concepts of their imaginations, are without measure."

The majority of the Court of Appeal justices, in a decision written by Justice Aylesworth, unequivocally supported the ruling of the magistrate and declared the works obscene:

> Some sense of morality is essential to the well-being of a country and to its healthy life as a community; anything that tends to offend that sense of morality by the exploitation of sex as a dominant characteristic of the work constitutes an undue exploitation of the subject. The magistrate had ample evidence by proper inference or otherwise including, of course, the drawings themselves, to reach the conclusion that these drawings were obscene. I, too, am left in no doubt as to their being obscene. They lie not in any gray area of doubt; they are of base purpose and their obscenity is flagrant.

In addition, the majority did not believe that the public good was served in any way by the exhibition, mocking the idea:

> I take it to mean that so long as there is artistic merit in a drawing, the public good is served no matter how much or to what degree sex is exploited, no matter how filthy, prurient or degrading the treatment of sex is portrayed as emanating from the instincts and imagination of the artist.... This is carrying the concept of "civil liberties" much too far.... The nature and extent of the obscenity indulged in is relevant to a decision as to whether or not the defence has been established.

The judgment acknowledged the 1962 *Brodie* decision, in which the Hicklin Test was declared "obsolete" and *Lady Chatterley's Lover* found not to be obscene; it also acknowledged the 1964 case against Coles bookstore, in which John Cleland's

Fanny Hill—Memoirs of a Woman of Pleasure was also found not to be obscene, despite the opinion of two of five judges that the book was "nothing but a chronological succession of venereal adventures, wallowing in sex and dripping with sensuality and lewdness. It was plain unvarnished dirt for dirt's sake...."

But the seven works of art from Cameron's gallery were deemed obscene and no defence of their quality as works of art could save them:

> Artistic merit, however, does not excuse obscenity...where there is a clear and unequivocal offence against community standards obscenity is established and artistic merit will not obliterate it. To hold [otherwise] would be to substitute complete licence for accepted community standards of decency and morality.

As is often the case with higher court decisions, the minority opinion is what resonates years later. Justice Bora Laskin argued strongly that evidence and the opinion of experts are essential: "Especially in non-jury trials, the Court should be exposed to the persuasion of evidence and extrinsic materials to counterbalance the ineradicable subjective factor residing in the application of any legal standard of obscenity, however objective the standard purports to be...."

This conundrum—How reliable is the "I know it when I see it" judgment?—will define almost every freedom of expression case to come before Canadian courts over the next fifty years, whether the subject is obscenity or hate literature. The corollary issue—When does ordinary or simple become excessive?—was also articulated by Justice Laskin:

> Since obscenity itself requires proof of undue exploitation of sex, to which artistic or literary merit and purpose are relevant, I think there is a hopeless entanglement created by the superimposition of the pre-existing defence of public good upon a new definition of obscenity. No doubt, it is possible to distinguish simple obscenity and excessive obscenity for the purposes of the defence of public good, if only because Parliament has so ordained. Nonetheless, it strikes me as

> somewhat arch, in the circumstances of the definition of obscenity with which we now have to deal, to be called on to assess the obscene character of a publication or drawing at two levels; one marked simple or ordinary, and the second marked excessive or undue.

The judgment is silent on whether or not the images were to be destroyed or returned to Cameron, who subsequently closed her gallery and returned to the business of being an artist full-time. (An attempt by Cameron's legal team to appeal the case to the Supreme Court of Canada was unsuccessful.)

The 1960s marked the beginning of great changes in Canadian attitudes to and laws governing intimate aspects of our lives—contraception, divorce, homosexuality, abortion. Our culture exploded with books, films, music, and changes in how we dressed and walked down the street; it was as if our white-gloved, buttoned-down post-war identity had been let off its leash. But that sense of freedom came with new challenges and fears. It seemed that while we were ready to explore the idea that "the state has no business in the bedrooms of the nation," as Trudeau declared in 1967, there was less certainty about the role of the state in our movie theatres, bathhouses, bookshelves, and libraries.

1970s AND 1980s—SEX + DEGRADATION = OBSCENITY

> [Pornography is material that] reinforces some unhealthy tendencies in Canadian society...[reinforces] male-female stereotypes to the detriment of both sexes...and attempts to make degradation, humiliation, victimization, and violence in human relationships appear normal and acceptable.
>
> —Standing Committee on Justice and Legal Affairs, *Report on Pornography*, 1978 (MacGuigan Report)

> [There] are magazines, films and videos produced solely for the purpose of entertainment whose depiction of women in particular, but also, in some cases, men and young people,

demeans them, perpetuates lies about aspects of their humanity and denies the validity of their aspirations to be treated as full and equal citizens within the community.

—*Pornography and Prostitution in Canada*, 1985 (Fraser Report)

Over the next twenty years, the issue of obscenity, in the courts, took the form of skirmishes with provincial film censorship boards and endless cases, it seems, involving small bookstores, alternative publications, cinemas, and grubby video outlets. There was nothing coherent or logical about the erratic swooping down on individual artists and small businesses. In CCLA newsletters, a

pattern of such ambushes can be traced. In 1970–71 in Toronto, about fifteen bookstore clerks were arrested by the Metro Toronto Police Morality Squad on charges of possession and distribution of obscene materials, despite the fact that they were mere employees, with no financial interest in the stores and no control over what the bookstores sold. Over that one year, bookstore clerks spent a total of seventy-seven hours in jail and paid out more than $2,000 in bail deposits. (The names of the bookstores and the nature of the so-called obscene material are not identified in the newsletter.)

CCLA sent a delegation to the Metro Toronto Police Commission in November 1970, suggesting that, rather than arresting "powerless employees," the police had the option provided by the *Criminal Code* to prosecute a book, instead of prosecuting a person. "To whatever extent the Police Commission feels obliged to enforce these questionable laws, it ought to do so in a manner which minimizes the impositions upon the freedoms of those concerned," said CCLA. The delegation also questioned the practice of pretrial arrests and incarcerations: "None of these people has yet been found guilty of a criminal offence. Thus, in the eyes of the law, they are still innocent.... It is cruel social policy, indeed, that would launch criminal prosecutions against hapless sales clerks who are making no profits and exercising no discretion."

TANGLING OVER TANGOS

Film censorship has been exercised by provinces in Canada since 1911, when Ontario enacted regulation. Historically in Canada, as elsewhere in the world, it has been linked to moral standards informed by religious constituencies and has been criticized, not only for prudishness and a dearth of artistic sophistication, but also because censorship has been seen as an unjustified infringement of individual rights. Film censorship has been a tool that could be wielded for political and social control; in times of war, censorship of film and other media is regularly expanded to include "propaganda."

The SCC 1978 decision in *Nova Scotia Board of Censors v. McNeil* is considered a landmark pre-Charter case. The Nova

Scotia Board of Censors barred the sensational film *Last Tango in Paris* by director Bernardo Bertolucci from exhibition in the province, refused to give any reasons for this decision, and was taken to court by Gerard McNeil, a journalist. CCLA intervened in this case on the grounds that the Nova Scotia Board of Censors' action was an infringement of freedom of expression rights, but the CCLA intervention did not inform either the majority or minority position, both of which considered only whether or not the provincial board of censors was stepping into federal *Criminal Code* territory.

The SCC majority determined that the Nova Scotia Board of Censors was merely regulating trade, not making a decision on moral grounds (which it clearly was). The ruling stated that Nova Scotia's *Theatres and Amusements Act* was did not contravene federal jurisdiction because:

> [It is] not concerned with creating a criminal offence or providing for its punishment, but rather...regulating a business within the Province as to prevent the exhibition in its theatres of performances which do not comply with the standards of propriety established by the Board.... Legislation which authorizes the establishment and enforcement of a local standard of morality in the exhibition of films is not necessarily "an invasion of the federal criminal field...."

This judgment (which, like most obscenity decisions, was close, at 5 to 4) seems to go to considerable lengths to deny what was actually going on. But on behalf of four dissenting justices, Bora Laskin, who was by then chief justice of the SCC, demurred:

> What is involved...is an unqualified power in the Nova Scotia Board to determine the fitness of films for public viewing on considerations that may extend beyond the moral and may include the political, the social and the religious.... The Board is asserting authority to protect public morals, to safeguard the public from exposure to films, to ideas and images in films, that it regards as morally offensive, as indecent, probably as obscene. The determination

> of what is decent or indecent or obscene in conduct or in a publication, what is morally fit for public viewing, whether in films, in art or in a live performance, is, as such, within the exclusive power of the Parliament of Canada under its enumerated authority to legislate in relation to the criminal law.

Justice Laskin pointed to the vast possibilities for abuse in the role of provincial film censorship bodies, an issue that would continue to engage CCLA over the next three decades; as recently as 2004, CCLA intervened in a provincial film board case, discussed later in this chapter. Film censorship in Canada now takes the form of classification by provincial bodies, according to community standards, but as already noted, the influence of such boards is greatly diminished by the availability of unclassified materials online.

Curiously, *Last Tango in Paris* had already been declared *not* obscene in 1974, by the Manitoba Court of Appeal, in the Odeon Morton case. The metaphor offered by the court in that case, concerning obscenity, is salutary:

> In that connection I find assistance in a homely image presented by John Hirsch during the course of his testimony. It consisted of the relationship between a coat and its buttons. *Last Tango in Paris*—the film in its entirety—may be regarded as the coat. The sexual scenes are the buttons. Now buttons have an essential role to play in a coat. But they are not the coat, and it would be a transparent error to treat them as if they were. The viewer who condemns *Last Tango* merely on the basis of its sexual episodes has judged the buttons and not the coat.

Towards the end of the 1970s, parliamentarians began to wrestle with defining and punishing obscene materials. In 1978, a Justice Committee Report chaired by Mark MacGuigan, who chaired the House of Commons Justice and Legal Affairs Committee, recommended the introduction of the idea of "degradation" into the definition of obscenity:

> [Obscene material] reinforces some unhealthy tendencies in Canadian society...[reinforces] male-female stereotypes to the detriment of both sexes...and attempts to make degradation, humiliation, victimization, and violence in human relationships appear normal and acceptable. A society which holds that egalitarianism, non-violence, consensualism, and mutuality are basic to any human interaction, whether sexual or other, is clearly justified in controlling and prohibiting any medium of depiction, description or advocacy which violates these principles.

In response to this report and the bill devised incorporating it, CCLA held one of its periodic meetings on the issue. This one was called "The Federal Bill on Obscenity: Welcome protection or needless repression?" and it featured Mark MacGuigan debating Louise Arbour, then a professor of law at Osgoode Hall Law School and a member of the CCLA board. The proposed Bill C-51 died on the order paper, twice. The government (both Liberal and Progressive Conservative parties) tried seven times between 1978 and 1988 to create legislation dealing with obscenity and pornography. The last attempt was the very controversial Bill C-54 in 1988, which proposed changes to the *Criminal Code* derived from the recommendations of the Fraser Committee, discussed later in the chapter.

In the turn from the 1970s into the 1980s, Canada's gay and lesbian community found itself in the spotlight and consequently in the courts. Two almost simultaneous events embody the hostility between law enforcement bodies and the community.* [157]

Between 1977 and 1983, the radical gay magazine *The Body Politic* was a reluctant partner in a legal dance, as the result of two articles on the subject of sex between adult men and boys. CCLA intervened in the first appeal to the Ontario Superior Court. As *The Body Politic* reported in November 1983: "After almost six years,

* The issue of terminology is important; what historically were "gay and lesbian" issues have become LGBTQ issues. As Brenda Cossman wrote in a 2013 article: "...I use the term 'gay and lesbian,' not LGBT. This is intentional for a number of reasons. First, the early censorship struggles were really about gay and lesbian—not bisexual or transgender representations. Second, and more importantly, the legitimacy that has been acquired for gay and lesbian sexual representations does not equate with legitimacy for transgender representations." I have followed suit in this book.

ENOUGH IS ENOUGH

Last night, about 200 cops raided every major Toronto gay bath: The Roman, The Club, the Richmond Street Health Emporium, and the Barracks.

273 men were arrested on bawdy house charges.

Doors were needlessly smashed in, mirrors and glass broken, and lockers torn open with crowbars.

Men were pushed around, insulted, made fun of. One cop raiding the Barracks said: "Too bad these showers weren't hooked up to gas."

If you've ever gone to the baths or know someone who has,

PROTEST!

YONGE AND WELLESLEY MIDNIGHT RALLY TONIGHT!

Angry protesters turned out on February 15, 1981 to boo Police Chief Jack Ackroyd after police raided four downtown Toronto bathhouses and arrested more than 250 people.

two provincial court trials, three other separate court actions, six appeals, two trips to the Supreme Court of Canada, and more than $100,000 in legal bills, it was finally over. What had begun on December 30, 1977, with a bang…ended with a whimper…. The 'Men Loving Boys Loving Men' case had come to an end at last. And *The Body Politic* had won. For good."

Operation Soap: In February 1981, more than one hundred and fifty police officers, some alleged to be armed with crowbars, simultaneously descended upon four gay bathhouses in downtown Toronto. More than two hundred and fifty men were arrested and charged on "common bawdy-house" charges. CCLA demanded a public inquiry, noting that most of those arrested were mere "found-ins" participating voluntarily in sexual activity. None of Toronto's police leadership thought an inquiry was necessary; Ontario's solicitor general also refused to call an inquiry; finally, after thousands of people joined two demonstrations and a protracted media campaign, Toronto's City Council commissioned a study into the relationship between the police and the gay community.

The battle between gay and lesbian bookstores across the country and Canada Customs also began at this time.

BAD ATTITUDES AND STRANGE BEDFELLOWS—WOMEN FOR AND AGAINST CENSORSHIP AND ONE ANOTHER

> [Women] are exploited, portrayed as desiring pleasure from pain, by being humiliated and treated only as an object of male domination sexually, or in cruel or violent bondage. Women are portrayed in these films as pining away their lives waiting for a huge male penis to come along, on the person of a so-called sex therapist, or window washer, supposedly to transport them into complete sexual ecstasy. Or even more false and degrading one is led to believe their raison d'être is to savour semen as a life elixir, or that they secretly desire to be forcefully taken by a male.
>
> —SCC case, *R. v. Ramsingh*, 1984

> Feminism and civil liberties are inextricable. The goal of both is a society in which individuals are treated justly. Civil libertarians who oppose censorship are fighting on behalf of feminists, not against them.
>
> —June Callwood, 1985

In addition to court cases, efforts to both define and manage obscene and/or pornographic materials (in the current *Criminal Code*, the word "pornography" is used only in reference to child pornography; otherwise, the issue is obscenity) have been made repeatedly by Parliament. Between 1981 and 1985, two major commissions ran almost simultaneously in Canada; their concerns overlapped, and they issued very large reports within eight months of one another: the Badgley Committee on Sexual Offences against Children and Youth, and the Fraser Committee on Pornography and Prostitution.

The groundswell of what is known as "second-wave feminism"—the first-wave being in the early twentieth century—began in the mid-1960s in Canada and elsewhere, and by the mid-1980s was a dominant voice in rights and freedoms debates. Through two organizations in particular—the National Action Committee on the Status of Women (NAC, formed in 1971 as a response to government inertia on the Royal Commission on the Status of Women in Canada's 167 recommendations) and LEAF (the Legal Education and Action Fund, formed in 1985 as a response to Charter language on equality for women under the law)—feminists in Canada articulated and lobbied for the rights of women on such issues as abortion, pornography, violence against women, family law, and lesbian rights.

The issue of obscenity/pornography was an especially divisive, complex issue for Canadian feminists in the 1980s. Consider this description of one year, by writer Varda Burstyn:

> 1984...was marked by the cross-country travels of the Special Committee on Pornography and Prostitution (the Fraser committee) and the hundreds of briefs presented to it by all kinds of interest groups; by the trial of those accused of bombing Red Hot Video, a Vancouver porn outlet; by the passing of municipal bylaws restricting a display of pornography and, in one case, their overturning by a provincial appeal court; by the declaration of the Ontario Board of Censors as unconstitutional by the provincial appeal court; by the new expansion of the board's powers, notwithstanding the legal opinion, by the Ontario government; by the censoring of progressive artists' work in Toronto and Vancouver; by the trial of Doctors Henry Morgentaler, Leslie Smoling and Robert Scott, physicians at a Toronto abortion clinic, for conspiring to procure an abortion, their sensational acquittal by a jury and the decision to appeal that acquittal; by an injunction against Vancouver prostitutes, forbidding them to work in the west end of Vancouver, forcing them into the gritty skid row districts of that city; by a similar injunction at this writing being considered in Halifax; by the mass arrests of gay men in Montreal bars and baths; by the extraordinary entrapment of gay men in Orillia, Ontario; by the Alberta government's attempts to eliminate

> sex education; by the report of the Badgley Commission on Sexual Offences against Children and Youth; by trials of sexually explicit material—both commercial and artistic—in a series of courts; and, as the year drew to a close, by the country-wide banning of the December issue of *Penthouse* magazine—containing bondage photos of women—by the Canadian government and the charging of several of its distributors by the Ontario Attorney General.[158]

In this period, two factions formed: feminists who favoured legislation censoring pornography and punishing obscenity (because both were seen as degrading and likely to incite violence against women) and feminists who were opposed to censorship (because they did not believe that attempts to control obscenity would have any impact on violence against women). During the same time frame, these two factions also faced off as interveners in SCC cases dealing with hate literature and the testimony of rape victims, subjects dealt with later in this book.

Feelings ran deep. Two of Canada's great feminist activists, June Callwood and Doris Anderson, disagreed so profoundly that they had to agree not to discuss pornography at all. Women who worked side by side raising money for the defence of Henry Morgentaler spoke bitterly about one another's views on pornography. As Callwood, a founding member of CCLA, wrote in 1985 about this schism:

> Those who oppose censorship sometimes imagine their opponents are simpletons who believe the porn industry will collapse under the impact of new, tougher laws and that men, once the influence of pornography is removed, will immediately stop hurting women. [Feminists in the pro-censorship camp] see stiffened censorship laws as symbolic of society's determination to end the abuse and humiliation of women, a legal torpedo across the bows.... Most wounding is the accusation...that civil libertarians don't know, or don't care, that women are beaten and raped.

Callwood also pointed out that the language used to define obscenity ("community standards," "undue exploitation") does not result in consensus: "In the more than 30 years since obscenity was defined in the *Criminal Code*, there has never been a unanimous decision of the court on an obscenity case."

The federal government's Fraser Committee on Pornography and Prostitution, created in 1983 and reporting in 1985, was a battleground for this clash. The committee undertook extensive legal research on subjects such as prostitution, sexually transmitted disease, and pornography and prostitution laws in other jurisdictions; it did a content analysis of sexually explicit videos; and it held consultations with Canadians across the country. The result was a 753-page report, with 105 recommendations.[159] The CCLA brief to the committee (presented by Louise Arbour and Alan Borovoy) began thus: "The CCLA has no hesitation in joining with NAC in an unequivocal denunciation of the 'new pornography'.... It is necessary to distinguish, however, between moral condemnation and legal prohibition. The former is easy; the latter is fraught with difficulty." The brief asks a question that is never answered: If "undue" exploitation of sex is illegal, what would be a "due" exploitation of sex?

And where do learned justices stand on "community standards"? CCLA argued that this much-used concept was more fallacy than fact. In the voyage of *Lady Chatterley's Lover* through three levels of the Canadian courts in the early sixties, for example, thirteen justices considered whether or not the novel was obscene. Eight of those justices declared that it was; it happened that the five who said it was not obscene formed the majority in the final decision by the SCC in 1962. As CCLA argued, "If the most eminent legal experts in the community disagree so sharply about what constitutes an 'undue exploitation of sex,' how is the lay citizen supposed to make such judgments?"

In fact, it is most often the police (and Customs officials) who declare a book or a film "obscene" and put citizens in the position of choosing between not writing a book or creating a painting, or not showing a film or selling a video or magazine, and lengthy, expensive, emotionally draining court proceedings. The combination of two traditionally conservative agencies—police and the courts—defines and enforces community standards.

The other foundation argument in obscenity/pornography law that formed in the seventies and eighties concerned the question of harm—the role that access to pornography might play in causing people to become aggressive and commit illegal acts. The anti-censorship position is that no academic, statistical, or experimental study can be definitive concerning transgressive actions that take place far removed from the study or the laboratory, despite the existence of many studies and reports attempting to prove so. The Fraser Report also concluded that it is not possible to prove direct harm from pornography; the committee stated that it was "not prepared to state, solely on the basis of the evidence and research it has seen, that pornography is a significant causal factor in the commission of some forms of violent crime, in the sexual abuse of children, or the disintegration of communities and society."

And yet this notion persisted, in the numerous attempts to create legislation after the Fraser Report was delivered, and in court cases and public discourse. The argument that violent and otherwise degrading materials could result in harm to women and children, thereby offending the gender equality premises in the new Charter, was the position taken by LEAF in the pornography debate; pornography is "a systemic practice of exploitation and subordination based on sex that differentially harms women."[160]

An op-ed by Alan Borovoy in *The Toronto Star* in May 1985 acknowledged that some legal restrictions made sense—concerning materials depicting actual crimes; the "very existence of a legal market could act as an incentive" for committing such crimes. And an argument can be made for restrictions on public displays, and what is accessible to children. But, wrote Borovoy, "The answer to bad material is not suppression but good material," and the role of the law in the realm of pornography should be reduced, given the "definitional quagmire that has bedeviled these laws since their very inception."

With Bill C-54, the Mulroney government made its final attempt to deal with pornography in legislation. The bill, based in part on the recommendations of the Fraser Commission, proposed different punishments for different kinds of offences, determined by different kinds of pornography—child pornography, sexually

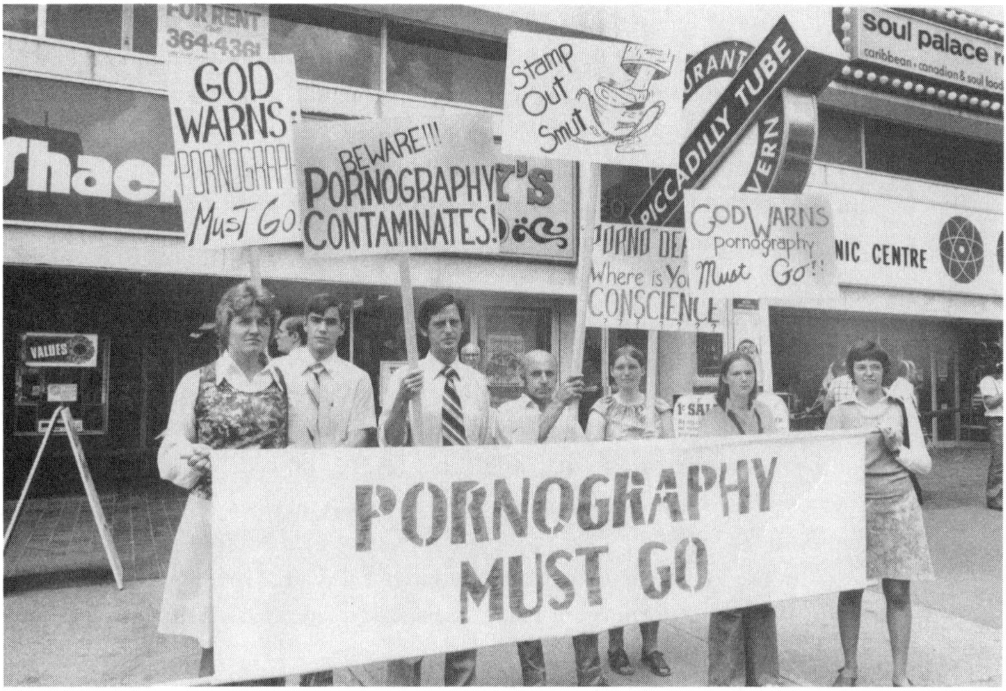

violent or degrading material. Some offences (excluding child pornography and pornography depicting physical harm) would have been eligible for the defence of artistic merit, or scientific or educational purposes. But Bill C-54 would have also punished non-violent, non-degrading sexual acts between consenting people, and was seen by CCLA and others to be a serious challenge to civil liberties.

Against pornography, protesters from the newly formed Toronto Chapter of the International Family Association march on the Yonge Street strip in Toronto, July 4, 1975. Their claim was that pornography "is harmful to children and the future of the family, and one ought to be able to walk on Yonge Street without shame."

In response to Bill C-54, CCLA initiated a campaign that engaged librarians, as the proposed legislation might have resulted in sentences of up to ten years for those having on their bookshelves such books as Vladimir Nabokov's *Lolita,* the ancient classics *Satyricon* (reputed to be by Gaius Petronius) and *The Decameron* (Giovanni Boccaccio), and Plato's *Symposium*, not to mention texts like Marian Engel's novel *Bear* or even Ayn Rand's *The Fountainhead.*

Concerned librarians wrote to federal Justice Minister Ray Hnatyshyn and were not mollified by assurances that it was unlikely that librarians would be charged. The chair and chief executive officer of the Toronto Public Library Board asked the advice of CCLA; Alan Borovoy suggested: "They should reply with action. I proposed that they close down the Toronto Public Library system." As a result, on International Human Rights Day, December 10, 1987, twenty-eight of the thirty-two public libraries in Toronto were closed—one left open in each of four districts—and librarians joined writers and artists such as Margaret Atwood and David Cronenberg in a symposium on the pornography legislation. The Art Gallery of Ontario also joined the protest and planned to label and drape works of art that might be deemed obscene under the new legislation. Bill C-54 languished and died on the order paper in October 1988.

In 1993, the hastily cobbled together Bill C-128, which dealt only with child pornography and is discussed later, passed quickly.

THE 1990s—THERE MUST BE A RIGHT TO DEPICT THE DARK SIDE OF LIFE

> The problem is that we know so little of the consequences we are seeking to avoid. Do obscene movies spawn immoral conduct? Do they degrade women? Do they promote violence? The most that can be said, I think, is that the public has concluded that exposure to material which degrades the human dimensions of life to a subhuman or merely physical dimension and thereby contributes to a process of moral desensitization must be harmful in some way. It must therefore be controlled when it gets out of hand, when it becomes "undue."
>
> —Justice Bertha Wilson, SCC Decision, *Towne Cinema* case concerning the movie *Dracula Sucks*, 1985

During the 1980s, feminist groups for and against censorship rallied their forces; there were demonstrations, positions declared, books and articles and op-eds and counter op-eds produced. A number of cases were in play, in the lower courts, some involving pornographic videos and seedy storefronts, others aspiring to somewhat higher literary and artistic definition. The battle lines were confusing: when anti-censorship feminists firebombed the Red Hot Video stores, the radical gay magazine *The Body Politic* defended the stores and was denounced by its readership. The question percolating below the surface: Which freedom of expression case would become the first test of the 1982 *Charter of Rights and Freedoms*?

During 1991–92, the Supreme Court considered the case of Donald Victor Butler, who opened a Winnipeg store dealing in hardcore video sales and rentals in August 1987 and was immediately charged with between 250 and 350 counts of possessing obscene materials for purpose of sale. The trial judge ruled that only eight counts of obscenity should stand, determining that the remaining material was not obscene and deserved the protection of the Charter because it:

> reflects consensual activity by adult individuals not involving force, duress or cruelty.... I am unable to conclude that the depiction of the human body or any of its parts, no matter how explicitly presented, or the visual presentation of masturbation, group sex or other heterosexual or homosexual activity, including incestuous relations, *prima facie* relate to sufficiently specific concerns which are pressing and substantial in a free and democratic society to justify restricting or limiting the basic freedom permitting them to be expressed.

The Crown appealed this decision to the Manitoba Court of Appeal, where the majority of justices disagreed with the trial judge and determined all of the material was obscene and did not deserve the protection of the Charter because it was despicable: "It consists in the undue exploitation of sex and the degradation of human sexuality.... The form of the activity is not one which the Charter was designed or intended to protect."

The subsequent appeal to the Supreme Court by Butler was the first test of the *Criminal Code* obscenity provisions against the *Charter of Rights and Freedoms*. The *Criminal Code* (still the 1959 version) defined as obscene all materials "a dominant characteristic of which is the undue exploitation of sex, or of sex and any one or more of the following subjects, namely, crime, horror, cruelty and violence." The only possible defence was serving "the public good."

The *Butler* decision was the first unanimous decision on obscenity by the SCC. It is a complicated decision imbued with a sense of its own historical importance. (During the same time frame, the SCC had also been considering the Keegstra case, the first major post-Charter decision about hate speech, discussed in Chapter Five of this book; *Keegstra* is quoted in the *Butler* decision.)

The most important aspect of the decision was the testing of the obscenity sections of the *Criminal Code* against the Charter. The court determined that the obscenity provisions of the code did pass the tests set by the Charter. But the judgment is confusing concerning the actual charges against Butler; the SCC disagreed with the Manitoba Court of Appeal's reasons for convicting Butler and permitted Butler's appeal, ordering a new trial. Butler was convicted at retrial in 1993.

The SCC considered only the constitutional issues, not the individual charges. With reference to a raft of earlier decisions, the decision defined community standards more specifically: not "what Canadians would not tolerate being exposed to *themselves* [my italics], but what they would not tolerate *other* Canadians being exposed to."

The SCC then determined that "degrading or dehumanizing sex" would fail the community standards test, but not because it was morally offensive, but because "it is perceived by public opinion to be harmful to society, particularly to women. While the accuracy of this perception is not susceptible of exact proof, there is a substantial body of opinion that holds that the portrayal of persons being subjected to degrading or dehumanizing sexual treatment results in harm, particularly to women and therefore to society as a whole."

These two sentences are why the *Butler* decision was perceived as a victory for feminists; the principles of harm to women, and equality (society as a whole), had entered the discourse on obscenity.

Justice John Sopinka, in writing the decision, considered what is called the "internal necessities" test—the defence on artistic grounds. The 1959 *Criminal Code* makes no mention of an artistic defence, referring only to a consideration of "public good," but judges in obscenity cases since *Lady Chatterley's Lover* in 1962 routinely had determined that, since materials must be examined in their entirety to determine if their obscenity is disproportionate (undue), this amounts to an artistic defence: Does the exploitation of sex advance plot or theme, or is it merely "dirt for dirt's sake"? Consider not only the buttons, but the whole coat.

Sopinka (no doubt aware that this would become the landmark decision on pornography) suggested that pornography be divided into three categories—explicit sex with violence, explicit sex without violence but which subjects people to degrading or dehumanizing treatment, and explicit sex without violence that is neither degrading nor dehumanizing. He found that s.163(8) of the *Criminal Code* covered the first two categories, but not the third. This tripartite categorization now also became part of the pornography discourse, to be used in subsequent SCC considerations of obscene materials.

Sopinka noted that it is difficult to prove the risk of harm and stated that this should not be a matter for the "individual tastes" of judges; the norm, or arbiter, is the community as a whole. And yet, it is still the courts:

> that must determine as best they can what the community would tolerate others being exposed to on the basis of the degree of harm that may flow from such exposure. Harm in this context means that it predisposes persons to act in an anti-social manner as, for example, the physical or mental mistreatment of women by men, or, what is perhaps debatable, the reverse. Anti-social conduct for this purpose is conduct which society formally recognizes as incompatible with its proper functioning. The stronger the inference of a risk of harm the lesser the likelihood of tolerance. The inference may be drawn from the material itself or from the material and other evidence. Similarly evidence as to the community standards is desirable but not essential.

The Fraser Committee had objected to the well-established tendency of the courts to determine criminal charges on the basis of community standards or "majoritarian impulses." CCLA and Manitoba Association for Rights and Liberties, in their joint *Butler* submission presented by Sheila Block, argued that vagueness in the definition of obscenity, coupled with tasking judges and juries with the responsibility of articulating "contemporary Canadian standards" of tolerance resulted in an unreliable "I know it when I see it" form of justice. CCLA pointed out that a review of obscenity cases since 1959 revealed a mixed record of convictions overturned and successful prosecutions based on these two elusive factors.

Sopinka argued that s.163(8) of the *Criminal Code* was acceptable as a standard, even though neither obscenity nor indecency is actually defined. But because of the Charter, it was no longer appropriate for Parliament to impose moral standards: "The prevention of 'dirt for dirt's sake' is not a legitimate objective which would justify the violation of one of the most fundamental freedoms enshrined in the Charter." Nonetheless, Parliament does have "the right to legislate on the basis of some fundamental conception of morality for the purposes of safeguarding the values which are integral to a free and democratic society." And the avoidance of harm to society is the overriding objective of s.163 of the *Criminal Code.*

Sopinka went back to the 1978 report on pornography by the Standing Committee on Justice and Legal Affairs (MacGuigan Report) for his definition of harmful material as "attempts to make degradation, humiliation, victimization, and violence in human relationships appear normal and acceptable." Yet the Fraser Committee, seven years later, had concluded that research on harm to both individuals and society was of "very limited use" because it is "so inadequate and chaotic."

Sopinka did not agree with the Fraser Committee conclusions. He argued that even though community standards had changed since 1959, the purpose of the legislation was still "the protection of society from harms caused by the exposure to obscene materials." He stated that pornography is a threat to "true equality" between the sexes and that the "message of obscenity which degrades and dehumanizes is analogous to that of hate propaganda." However, while criminal proceedings against purveyors of hate literature sometimes generate a combination of publicity and sympathy for the accused, the same is not true for those accused in obscenity cases; in the words of Chief Justice Brian Dickson in the 1990 *Keegstra* hate literature ruling, "Pornography is not dignified by its suppression."

Justice Sopinka responded at length to the brief by CCLA and the Manitoba Association for Rights and Liberties. He rejected their argument that it was possible to fulfill the objectives of obscenity legislation in ways other than "outright prohibition," such as restricting access, if, as the court determined, the objective is avoidance of harm "caused by the degradation which many women feel as 'victims' of the message of obscenity, and of the negative impact exposure to such material has on perceptions and attitudes towards women.... Once Parliament has reasonably concluded that certain acts are harmful to certain groups in society and to society in general, it would be inconsistent, if not hypocritical, to argue that such acts could be committed in more restrictive conditions."

He also rejected CCLA's suggestions for approaches such as counselling, shelters, campaigns, education.... "It is noteworthy that many of the above suggested alternatives are in the form of *responses* to the harm engendered by negative attitudes against women. The role of the impugned provision is to control the dissemination of the very images that contribute to such attitudes.... Given the gravity of the harm, and the threat to the values at stake, I do not believe that the measure chosen by Parliament is equalled by the alternatives which have been suggested," useful though they might be.

The *Butler* decision made no specific mention of the LEAF intervention, but the language of the decision resonated strongly with arguments that LEAF made to the court. Although the decision never referred to one of LEAF's key points, arguing the relevance of the sections in the Charter referring to equality of rights, the judgment itself considered the issue of harm from the perspective of those who might be victimized in the making of pornography, not those who might see it, and referred specifically to "egalitarianism" and "true equality."

The *Butler* decision did not recognize pornography as a deeply engrained feature of Canadian society, only as something that makes men do bad things to women. Furthermore, admittedly because of the material subject to review, the *Butler* decision considered only mainstream, heterosexual pornography, the product of the "burgeoning pornographic industry." It used the example of pornography from an earlier Manitoba case (*R. v. Ramsingh*, 1984) quoted above: "Women…pining away their lives waiting for a huge male penis to come along…."

Justice Sopinka declared that "the values which underlie the protection of freedom of expression relate to the search for truth, participation in the political process, and individual self-fulfilment," which "only in its most base aspect, that of physical arousal, is engaged by pornography." He stated unequivocally: "In my view, the kind of expression which is sought to be advanced does not stand on an equal footing with other kinds of expression which directly engage the 'core' of the freedom of expression values."

For different reasons, in fact, both pro- and anti-censorship interveners would have preferred that pornography/obscenity not be regulated by legislation at all, and both groups made the argument for systemic changes, not criminalization. However, the *Butler* decision changed the rules for dealing with pornography and was at the time seen as a triumph for pro-censorship forces, feminist and conservative.

But while the feminist pro-censorship position was being woven into the pornography discourse in the name of equality, a pattern of discrimination and inequality was building for lesbians, gay men, and their bookstores. The seizure by Customs officials of books and magazines ordered by Glad Day Bookshop in Toronto and Little Sister's Book and Art Emporium in Vancouver "for undue exploitation of sex" began in the mid-1980s. A 1987 challenge by Little Sister's of a seizure ended with a surprise admission of error by Canada Customs, but only after the entire shipment had been incinerated, apparently a common practice. Between

1987–88, Little Sister's was bombed, twice. Between 1992–93, Glad Day Bookshop faced two separate criminal trials; in the first (*Hayes*), the store was found guilty of selling materials depicting "sub-human" sex; in the second (*Scythe*), it was found guilty in an Ontario court of possession and sale of one low-gloss American quarterly, *Bad Attitudes,* which Justice Paris determined "flashes every light and blows every whistle of obscenity."

Little Sister's first statement of claim, in the Supreme Court of British Columbia, was filed jointly with the BCCLA (British Columbia Civil Liberties Association) in 1990, but delays and postponements by the Crown pushed the first trial date back to October 1994, a hiatus that straddled the SCC *Butler* considerations, and required a revision of strategy by counsel Joseph Arvay, who had expected that Little Sister's would mount the first Charter challenge of the *Criminal Code*'s obscenity provisions. Little Sister's engagement with the courts (described later) would take place over the next ten years.

"BETTER LATE THAN NEVER"—THE CHILD PORNOGRAPHY LEGISLATION

> When people hear the words "child pornography," they invariably conjure images of real children being unlawfully abused. If the child porn law had been confined to materials involving such abuse of real children, there would be no controversy regarding this subject. Such a law would enjoy universal support. It would directly address the legitimate goal of the exercise: the protection of children.
>
> —CCLA Submission to Parliamentary Committee
> Reviewing Bill C-2, 2005

It took Parliament fifteen years, between 1978 and 1993, to get legislation dealing with the issues of obscenity and child pornography through the House (in response to the several commissions and committee reports). Numerous bills were proposed, and were either highly controversial or died on the order paper. Finally, in 1993, Bill C-128 resulted in child pornography and obscenity being split into two distinct parts of s.163 of the *Criminal Code*, and subsequent prosecutions and legislation deal with the two issues separately. (Henceforth, the term "pornography" is only used in the phrase "child pornography.")

Legislators decried Bill C-128 even as they voted for it; it was a "better late than never" bill, they said, passed despite expert witnesses that said it was "extremely offensive to the Charter." The new section of the *Criminal Code* defining child pornography received royal assent in June 1993, and before the end of that year was used to seize a collection of paintings and drawings in Toronto.

AFTER "AFTER THE BATH"—THE ELI LANGER CASE

In fact, it was Eli Langer's paintings and drawings that were on trial, not Mr. Langer himself. During the court proceedings, a small courtroom in Toronto was invaded by a group of very large, brilliantly red and black paintings, which stood along the walls of the courtroom as evidence and silent witnesses.

Mr. Langer's works had been on display at Mercer Union, a small artist-run gallery in Toronto in December 1993. A review in *The Globe and Mail* on December 14, 1993, apparently drew the ire of readers who contacted police, who then went to Mercer Union, located at the time on the fifth floor of an Adelaide West building, and confiscated thirty-five drawings and five paintings. The paintings and drawings by young artist Eli Langer (twenty-six years old) were indeed shocking—the drawings for the explicitness of their depiction of children involved in sexual acts, including sodomy and fellatio, the paintings less for their detail, and more for the kinetic interaction of images on a very large scale. The theme of invasion was also depicted in what seemed to be domestic break-ins; troubling aspects of the images were the depiction of very old naked men with very young naked children, and the uncertainty of the emotional states of the children depicted. (These were entirely works of the imagination; Langer used no models in the creation of the works.)

The gallery acknowledged, somewhat obscurely, the transgressive nature of the works in its news release, referring to "sexual ambiguity" in images "largely informed by intuitive personal and social drives, exploring the phenomenon of intimacy where it exists without the compensation of social or cultural consent." In other words, Langer was consciously defying widely held taboos.

The Globe and Mail reviewer, Kate Taylor, was dismissive of the exhibition as a "self-conscious, juvenile prodding of its own excrement," although she did say that Langer paints "marvelously well."

The brand-new legislation was directed specifically at visual depictions of child pornography, defined as the representation of someone under the age of eighteen, or appearing to be under the age of eighteen, engaged in explicit sexual activity. The only grounds for dismissal were "if the representation that is alleged to constitute child pornography has artistic merit or an educational, scientific or medical purpose."

At first, Langer and the gallery director were charged under the new child pornography provisions of the *Criminal Code*, which had only been passed as Bill C-128 the previous summer. But, declaring this a test case of the new legislation, the Crown withdrew charges against Langer and the gallery director and instead invoked the forfeiture provision to charge the works themselves, seeking "judicial interpretation of the new child pornography legislation without placing any individual in jeopardy of a criminal conviction."

The Langer case was heard in the Ontario Superior Court by Justice David McCombs. There were expert witnesses (concerning pedophilia and art) and four interveners—CCLA, PEN Canada, and the Canadian Conference of the Arts (CCA)—for the defence, and Canadians for Decency for the prosecution. (One of the witnesses for the Crown was artist Ronald Bloore, the husband of artist and former gallery owner Anne Cameron; Bloore turned out to be somewhat of a Trojan horse, seeking revenge for the treatment of Cameron by the court in 1965.)

Justice McCombs undertook the task of a challenge to the child pornography definition with relish, and his decision is a fancy piece of footwork that makes the defence of artistic intent work both for and against Mr. Langer.

Justice McCombs acknowledged that the new definition of child pornography "reaches well beyond the proscription of depictions of actual child sexual abuse (a violent act)," and also criminalizes depictions of children engaging in explicit sexual activity (which in itself would not be a crime), images of adults depicted as children engaging in explicit sexual activity, and works of the imagination in which neither children nor adults are used to create the images.

The combination of vagueness and breadth of the definition concerned CCLA, which intervened on the constitutional questions, arguing that there was no justification for permitting the new section of the *Criminal Code*. Special counsels Sheila Block and Mark Gannage for CCLA noted first the haste with which the legislation had been enacted, with little consultation, criticizing both the absence of specific definitions and the breadth of the acts to be defined as child pornography, including private depictions of legal sex between seventeen-year-olds. The CCLA factum listed well-known works of art that could become illegal as a result—the important Canadian Broadcasting Corporation (CBC) drama about sexual abuse of orphans, *The Boys of St. Vincent*; Nabokov's *Lolita*; the painting "After the Bath" by Victorian artist Paul Peel on display at the Art Gallery of Ontario; a film like Zeffirelli's *Romeo and Juliet*; even Plato's *The Symposium*.

McCombs accepted that Langer's work had artistic merit—that "the purpose of the work is not to condone child sexual abuse, but to lament the reality of it"—but was not convinced that the artistic community's definition of artistic merit would necessarily coincide with "community standards of tolerance." And that "where the safety of children is concerned, community standards of tolerance based on the risk of harm are more important than freedom of expression, no matter how 'fundamental' that freedom may be to a free and democratic society." He reasserted the *Butler* decision, finding that the new definition of child pornography infringed on freedom of expression, but was a reasonable limit on it: the purpose of section 163.1 was "pressing and substantial and the legislation satisfies all elements of the proportionality test...." And because its objective is protecting children from harm, it should be upheld.

However, McCombs determined that Mr. Langer, as "statutory

party to these proceedings," was entitled to have the seizure of his work subjected to constitutional scrutiny, under s.8 of the Charter: everyone has the right to be secure against unreasonable search or seizure. He concluded that the defence of artistic merit could be applied to forfeiture and that Langer's work had artistic merit (in the unanimous opinion of the art experts of both the Crown and defence), and that, in part because the drawings and paintings had a "frightening quality," they would not be used by pedophiles, and therefore, the Langer works did not "pose a realistic risk of harm to children."

Langer's works were returned to him, and the SCC refused to consider a request to appeal made by the Ontario Attorney General. The decision is odd, because it sets up a contradiction between community standards and artistic merit, first, and then determines that community standards and the need to protect children are most important, and are what confirms the justifiable infringement on freedom of expression. But when McCombs transferred the argument to the forfeiture, he found that the artistic merit of the work was undeniable, and further stated that Langer's paintings and drawings would do no harm.

FLOGGING, FUN, AND FORTITUDE—THE CASE OF JOHN ROBIN SHARPE

In 1995, photographs and materials on disc brought from Amsterdam by John Robin Sharpe of Vancouver (including Mr. Sharpe's own work, "Sam Paloc's Boyabuse—Flogging, Fun and Fortitude: A Collection of Kiddiekink Classics") were seized at the border. Mr. Sharpe was charged with illegal possession and with possession of child pornography for purposes of distribution and sale. The issue before the SCC was only whether or not possession of child pornography was illegal. Both the trial judge and the majority of the British Columbia Court of Appeal had ruled that prohibiting the "simple" possession of child pornography as defined in the *Criminal Code* was "not justifiable in a free and democratic society" because it failed the Charter tests. There was considerable interest in the case, because the two B.C. courts had literally overturned the very recently written child pornography sections of the *Criminal Code*; the nineteen interveners included Attorneys General of six provinces and a dozen organizations, including CCLA.

The SCC decision came in 2001; the law was upheld, with a couple of minor exceptions read into it, and Sharpe was sent back to the Supreme Court of B.C. for trial on all of the charges. In its decision, the SCC reviewed the overall constitutional issues, and also explored and redefined the opposing tensions inherent in the consideration of such material—causing harm and the artistic merit defence. It also acknowledged that the original trial judge had "courageously" addressed some of the implications of the SCC's recent *Butler* decision; the *Butler* decision ruled that no proof of harm was necessary; the trial judge thought otherwise. The B.C. Court of Appeal's concern about the "hallmark of tyranny" was also referred to more than once.

The six justices in the majority in the *Sharpe* decision (who included Louise Arbour) went some distance to consider the freedom of expression issues caused by the child pornography legislation. The decision written by Chief Justice Beverley McLachlin argued both for a narrower definition of materials (excluding "deeply personal" work and materials created by teenagers) and for a generous interpretation of the possible defences, including artistic merit and public good. The three dissenting judges found the law constitutional as it was and did not accept the majority's arguments for "reading in" exceptions. By spelling out (known as "reading in") in the decision exactly what the exceptions to the law should be and how they should be interpreted, the majority of justices were acknowledging the law's weaknesses, but preferring to suggest minor changes in interpretation to throwing the law out altogether.

The court was not moved by CCLA's Special Counsel Sheila Block's position (referring to the Fraser Committee Report) that there is not conclusive scientific evidence concerning the harm that child pornography might cause beyond the harm clearly caused if children were used in the production of such material. In the decision, Justice Beverley McLachlin noted, "Complex human behaviour may not lend itself to precise scientific demonstration," and the judgment further stated that there is "clear and uncontradicted evidence" that pedophiles use child pornography to "groom" children for sexual activity, thus obviously causing harm.

However, the court also chose to use the test of artistic merit against the principle of causing harm, because if the idea of causing harm were to be interpreted broadly, it could also be used to censor political ideas and opinions that were "unpopular, distasteful or contrary to the mainstream" that might also change attitudes. Harm had also now become something quite different from the erosion of moral standards—"causing depravity" in a presumably uneducated population—which was the measure of the old Hicklin Test.

Artistic merit should not be determined, McLachlin wrote, as it was in the *Langer* decision by Justice McCombs, simply with reference to community standards, but should include such factors as the opinion of experts and the intention of the creator, means of production, display and distribution, and the form and content of the work, its "connections with artistic conventions, traditions or styles." Even bad art has artistic merit.

But once artistic merit had been "objectively established," the bar was suddenly very low: "I conclude that 'artistic merit' should be interpreted as including any expression that may reasonably be viewed as art. Any objectively established artistic value, however small, suffices to support the defence. Simply put, artists, so long as they are producing art, should not fear prosecution…."

Simply put, indeed. Apart from an apparently flawed understanding of how artists work—Are they sometimes "producing art," but not always?—this simplification glossed over the fact that it is not only artists who are prosecuted, but booksellers and shopkeepers who have no way of determining whether or not material that comes into their possession might, after the fact, by anyone from a disapproving customer to a SCC judge, be defined as obscene.

In upholding the law, while insisting on a liberal interpretation of the possible defences, and setting out the two exceptions, McLachlin made the following assurances:

> Families need not fear prosecution for taking pictures of bare-bottomed toddlers at the beach or children playing in the backyard, given the requirement that the dominant purpose be sexual. As case law develops, greater certainty may be expected, further reducing the law's chilling effect. On the record before us, the chilling effect, while not insignificant, does not appear to represent a major cost as it relates to the vast majority of material captured under s.163.1(4).

The SCC decision set the stage for the retrial of Sharpe in B.C. He was found guilty of possessing pornographic photos of children and was sentenced to four months of house arrest, but his personally written materials were deemed not to be advocating sexual crimes and, indeed, to have artistic merit, "irrespective of whether the work is considered pornographic."

This conclusion outraged critics of the decision, who could not countenance the possibility that the content of Sharpe's creepy and apparently endless musings on the subject of sex with children could be thus excused from prosecution. Several years later, in 2004, Sharpe was found guilty of indecent assault, because of an incident twenty years earlier with a fourteen-year-old hitchhiker.

Sharpe became a lightning rod for the free speech conflict, a position he seemed to revel in and exploit. It cannot be denied, from a perusal of the interminable (and disturbing) materials on his website, that Sharpe writes coherently and persuasively. He describes himself as "the nation's most notorious child pornographer" and his profile is featured on Evil Unveiled, a website dedicated to pedophile activism.

It seemed in the *Sharpe* decision that the SCC was moving towards a position more liberal than conservative on the *Criminal Code* definitions of obscenity and pornography, accepting that the code should not criminalize such things as materials produced by teenagers engaged in lawful sexual acts, for their own purposes, and accepting a very broad notion of "artistic merit" as a defence in child pornography cases.

But between 2003 and 2007, Parliament became increasingly concerned with the proliferation of child pornography on the Internet, and the related issue of Internet "luring," and it attempted over several years to draft legislation to address this. In 2005, Parliament also passed legislation removing the words "artistic merit" from the child pornography section of the *Criminal Code*, and substituting the following language:

> 163.1 (6) No person shall be convicted of an offence under this section if the act that is alleged to constitute the offence
>
> (*a*) has a legitimate purpose related to the administration of justice or to science, medicine, education or art; and
>
> (*b*) does not pose an undue risk of harm to persons under the age of eighteen years.

But Bill C-2 made another significant change to the existing legislation, in criminalizing "*any* written material whose dominant characteristic is the description, for a sexual purpose, of sexual activity with a person under the age of 18 years"—*not only* those materials advocating or counselling the commission of a criminal offence.

CCLA's position on this revision to the legislation was presented in a brief to the Parliamentary Committee and disregarded:

> The history of the law of pornography and obscenity overflows with situations in which legitimate and even important forms of expression have been casualties of the campaigns to stamp out "smut." It is essential, therefore, that we be especially careful, every time we attempt to draw that critical line, to ensure that there is adequate protection for freedom of expression. There should be no consideration of suppressing expression, unless there is demonstrable harm to an overriding interest.... The law against child pornography should be narrowed so that it applies only to material, the creation of which involved—or is held out to have involved—the unlawful abuse, for such purposes, of a real child.

OF CABBAGES AND CUCUMBERS—LITTLE SISTER'S AND BIG CUSTOMS

> I bitterly resent the attempt to marginalize, trivialize and even criminalize what I have to say because I happen to be a lesbian. I happen to be a novelist. I happen to have bookstores and publishers who are dedicated to producing my work. The assumption is, therefore, that there must be something pornographic because of my sexual orientation, and I think that is a shocking way to deal with my community.
>
> —Jane Rule, *Little Sister's* trial, 1994

> Because [*Macho Sluts*] is sexually explicit, it would be ridiculous for me to claim that arousal is not one of the effects that I intended to have upon some readers.... I use sexuality in the fiction partly as a way to intrigue the reader and engage their attention. I also attempt, as a writer, to disturb....
>
> —Pat Califia, author,
> *Macho Sluts, Little Sister's* trial, 1994

Between 1994 and 2005, Little Sister's Book and Art Emporium, the long-established storefront on Davie Street in downtown Vancouver, fought a battle with Canada Customs in the courts of British Columbia and at the SCC. Little Sister's opened in 1983 and specializes in books, magazines, and videos for a gay and lesbian clientele, including fiction and erotica, academic publications dealing with homosexuality, and HIV/AIDS safe-sex instructional materials. Most of this material is imported from the United States and is subject to perusal by Canada Customs officials, who, according to tariff code 9956 and an illustrated guide (Memorandum D9-1-1), can seize and examine any shipment of goods coming into Canada, looking for anything that is obscene according to s.163(8) of the *Criminal Code*. In their case, Little Sister's identified 271 items that had been seized by Customs between 1984 and 1994, seventy-seven of those more than once.[161]

Like provincial film classification boards, Canada Customs is a form of "prior restraint" censorship, in which, prior to the *Little Sister's* decision, once materials had been seized by Customs and declared obscene, the onus was on the owner or distributor of the materials to prove that they are not obscene, a process made almost impossible by the lengthy and obscure internal process of review used by Canada Customs, and also by their practice of often unceremoniously simply destroying shipments of which they have taken possession.

Shipments destined for Little Sister's bookstore were not merely seized. They were delayed and confiscated. They were subsequently often misclassified, and even classified as both obscene and not obscene. They were frequently damaged or destroyed. Shipments destined to other bookstores, often containing some of the same titles, were not targeted. And mainstream literature—such as books by well-known authors like Salman Rushdie, Bret Easton Ellis (his violently misogynistic *American Psycho)*, and Madonna (*Sex)*—was given the equivalent of a VIP pass and admitted to Canada.

The Little Sister's case targeted both the Minister of Justice and the Attorney General of Canada, and also what was, at the time, the Minister of National Revenue, responsible for Canada Customs. The proceedings in Vancouver took almost two years to get underway, because of delaying tactics by the Crown; the trial itself took two months. The case was led by Joseph Arvay, with the British Columbia Civil Liberties Association (BCCLA), who made two fundamental arguments: first, that Canada Customs was unfairly discriminating against Little Sister's, by systematically targeting their shipments (materials intended for Little Sister's that were held by Customs could often be found in the Vancouver Public Library). Second, Arvay made the argument that the SCC *Butler* decision established an obscenity standard that was prejudicial of gay and lesbian materials which, he argued, were intrinsically different from heterosexual materials in portrayals of certain practices, including sado-masochism, and that the equality rights of gays and lesbians as defined in the *Charter of Rights and Freedoms* were being denied.

The Vancouver trial reads like an astute exercise in the education of a judge and the general public in the practices, grievances, and celebrities of the Canadian gay and lesbian community. Witnesses included the American lesbian writer and S&M activist Pat Califia; the Vancouver artist Persimmon Blackbridge; Robin Hand, publisher of *Lezzie Smut,* a Vancouver-based "sex zine;" and academics specializing in gay and lesbian studies. Customs officials were asked to read aloud from books like *American Psycho* by Bret Easton Ellis and Kathy Acker's *Empire of the Senseless.* There were discussions about anal penetration and leather sexuality.

Arvay also called as witnesses to the artistic merit defence writers like Jane Rule, Nino Ricci, and Pierre Berton, the latter a founding member of CCLA, who stated that anything that was written should be considered literature, and that all books should be judged only by a panel of peers. Berton's opinion that Customs officials were ill-prepared to determine the merits of books was echoed in a quote in the later SCC decision, in which Justice Ian Binnie referred to a statement made almost fifty years earlier; in 1958, in the House of Commons, the Minister of National Revenue, Mr. George Nowlan, stated, concerning the difficulties that Customs officials had in determining whether or not goods were obscene:

> Last year I had submitted to me six lithographs for inclusion in this year's calendars. They were six nudes. They had been passed on by all these officers. Three of the nudes were absolutely nude and three had some sort of diaphanous wrapping around their bodies. One of the senior officers said the three which had the diaphanous clothing could be admitted because they were semi-clothed. Another officer said their posture was indecent and they should not be admitted, but the nudes could be admitted because their posture was not indecent.
>
> That is an example of the judgment that has to be exercised and the kind of artistic skill that has to be passed upon by customs officers. *I really think that we are much better qualified to deal with increasing the seasonal tariff on cabbages and cucumbers than to pass moral judgment*

on literature coming into the country [emphasis added by Justice Binnie].

The decision by B.C. Supreme Court Justice Smith was issued in January 1996. He did not find that the rules governing the role of Canada Customs were unconstitutional. Nor did he accept that there was discrimination against gay and lesbian materials on the basis of sexuality: "The point is that homosexual obscenity is proscribed because it is obscene, not because it is homosexual." He did condemn the practices of Canada Customs as clear and systemic violation of both the freedom of expression rights and the equality rights of gays and lesbians. Not only was there targeting of Little Sister's by Customs officials but there were bureaucratic delays and errors, and "the classifying officers are neither adequately trained to make decisions on obscenity nor are they routinely provided with the time and evidences necessary to make such decisions." But the impact on gays and lesbians, while disproportionate, was not the fault of the legislation itself, but rather the implementation of the legislation, a judgment that echoed the 1976 *Morgentaler* decision.

The B.C. Court of Appeal agreed with the findings of the trial judge; Little Sister's was permitted to take an appeal to the Supreme Court of Canada. The ritual of a post-Charter freedom of expression case was by now well established. The first question is always: Are the defendants' freedom of expression rights, as set out in section 2(b) of the Charter, infringed upon by the relevant section of the *Criminal Code* or other Act (in this case, the Customs Code)? If the answer is yes, the second question is: Is this limitation of freedom of expression reasonable, under the terms of section 1 of the Charter?

One of eight interveners, CCLA's Special Counsel Patricia Jackson, took on the obscenity definitions laid out in the Butler case and the legal issues related to the Charter. Questions raised by CCLA included the following: Can a line be drawn between "acceptable and unacceptable discourse about sex"? If "community standards" are invoked to determine whether or not something is obscene, such standards, as interpreted by a judge or jury, rest upon "moral assumptions" and favour the opinions of the majority over minority viewpoints. The fact that it is Customs officials and police who administer *Criminal Code* definitions is problematic, because officials "take an over-inclusive view of obscenity."

CCLA intervention also took issue with the question of a causal relationship between obscene material and harm to society. "As a society, we do not in other circumstances assume that simple exposure to the depiction of an act encourages its replication. The implications of so doing for freedom of expression would be frightening, given the long-time fascination of our society with expressive material (both with and without artistic merit) that depicts acts of violence, often in brutal and casual forms that would, if they took place in actuality, attract the most severe criminal penalties...."

Two feminist organizations also intervened in the Little Sister's case before the Supreme Court. In stark contrast to their position in the Butler case (when they argued that all violent pornography was harmful to women), LEAF argued here that sado-masochistic materials in same-sex erotica might have an emancipating effect. But Equality Now argued for the protection of gays and lesbians from the harmful effects of sado-masochistic pornography.

The Supreme Court decision on Little Sister's appeal was released in December 2000. The court was clearly sympathetic to the long battle between Little Sister's and Customs, and the charge of prejudicial treatment:

> The appellants were put in the position of supplicants to the government in a 15-year crusade to obtain the entry into Canada of expressive material. Whereas Customs aims to examine approximately eight per cent of goods coming across the border, the trial judge found that "virtually all imported mail addressed to Little Sister's is examined...." His conclusion, supported by numerous examples, was that untrained Customs officials were too quick to equate homosexuality with obscenity.

That sympathy resulted in sharp criticisms of the practices of Customs, and the "reverse onus" implications of the *Criminal Code*, meaning that the accused is required to prove that the material is not obscene, an expensive and time-consuming exercise.

But the SCC upheld in no uncertain terms the *Butler* definitions of obscenity, and stated that there was no discrimination against gays and lesbians inherent in either the *Butler* decision or the *Criminal Code* obscenity definitions. And the SCC also stated that even though freedom of expression rights under the Charter were contravened by the relevant sections of the *Customs Tariff*, this denial of rights was justifiable. It was the job of Parliament to protect the public from the harmful impact of violent pornography, and that obligation to protect did not stop at the border.

In its decision, the SCC took exception to the argument that the idea of community standard was a form of majority opinion ganging up on minorities. Justice Binnie wrote:

> [A] person's constitutionally protected space does not shrink by virtue of his or her geographical location or participation in a certain context or community, or indeed by the taste of a particular judge or jury. It is not necessarily in the interest of the minority to disaggregate community standards. The appellants have in mind a special standard related to their lesbian and gay target audience. The fact is, however, that they operate a bookstore in a very public place open to anyone who happens by, including potentially outraged individuals of the local community who might wish to have the bookstore closed down altogether. If "special standards" are to apply, whose "special standard" is it to be? *There is some safety in numbers, and a national constituency that is made up of many different minorities is a guarantee of tolerance for minority expression.*

Binnie also dismissed the arguments made by LEAF, which, he said, made the assumption that the *Butler* test is "gender-based" when in fact the harm test in *Butler* is "gender-neutral" and that, therefore, gay and lesbian culture as such does not constitute a general exemption from the *Butler* test. Many commentators on the *Butler* decision argued that in fact the arguments in *Butler* were entirely focused on the possibility of harm to women and children and ignored gay and lesbian issues.

But there was clearly discrimination on the basis of sexual

orientation by Customs: “The administration of the Act, however, was characterized by conduct of Customs officials that was oppressive and dismissive of the appellants’ freedom of expression. Its effect—whether intended or not—was to isolate and disparage the appellants on the basis of their sexual orientation.” Binnie itemized the many ways in which Customs officials were guilty of prejudicial and discriminatory behaviour, and concluded, simply: “The burden of proving obscenity rests on the Crown or other person who alleges it.”

That is where sympathy ended. The decision noted (somewhat feebly) that Canada Customs had apparently made improvements to its administration of the rules in the six years since the case had begun, hoped that these improvements addressed the problems, and, in effect, invited Little Sister’s to launch another case, if not.

In his dissenting opinion, Justice Frank Iacobucci wrote, “The need for structural reform is reinforced by Customs’ long history of excessive, inappropriate censorship. Before the appellants launched this case, Customs illegally prohibited depictions of anal penetration; it systematically targeted Little Sister’s and other alternative bookstores; it favoured books by mainstream authors like Bret Easton Ellis and Madonna, in comparison to gay and lesbian authors; and it failed to consider artistic merit in spite of *Butler*’s clear instruction to always err on the side of protecting expressive freedom….”

What was the impact of the Supreme Court’s *Little Sister’s* decision? According to the bookstore itself, the revision of Canada Customs guidelines on obscene materials led almost immediately to even more discriminatory treatment. Little Sister’s co-owner Jim Deva wrote in 2006:

> Within two months of the ruling, Customs came out with a new set of guidelines to help its agents identify pornography…not only had Customs not made the necessary changes, but its new guidelines would lead to more, not fewer, seizures…. Within three months of the Supreme Court’s decision, Customs attacked us with renewed vigour. Our shipments were delayed, our imports seized—it was business as usual at Canada Customs…. It seemed that

> Customs had learned enough about our sexual practices during our previous court case to use the information against us in the new guidelines.

In 2006, Little Sister's decided that another legal challenge was merited, but first, it would apply to the Supreme Court to be granted costs in advance of bringing a case of discrimination by Canada Customs for seizure of four books. Their request was swiftly dismissed, and the bookstore did not pursue the case. Like Glad Day Bookshop, Little Sister's found the costs to a small business of years and years of litigation were ultimately overly punitive and could not be sustained—winning battles, but never quite winning the war.

Glad Day Bookshop was at the SCC in 2004, with CCLA as an intervener, on a case that centred on the obligation of a bookstore to submit a video to the Ontario Film Review Board. In 2000, an undercover provincial inspector had purchased from the bookstore a copy of the video *Descent*, which had not been approved by the film board. The SCC made short shrift of the provincial regulations and determined that while classification of films is useful, censorship is not, pointing out, "Other expressive media in Ontario do not have to be approved by a government authority before they are circulated to the public. The Ontario government has not created boards that must approve books, plays, art exhibitions, concerts or other forms of performance, before the public may have access to them." Nor did the Ontario government submit any evidence that moving picture images are more powerful or disturbing than other media. The film board's role as censor was found unconstitutional under the Charter. The system of "prior restraint" in this case was not justifiable, and the decision noted the reality that the Ontario Film Review Board had no authority over material received by mail or downloaded from the Internet.

COMMUNITY STANDARDS IN 2014—PRIDE AND PREJUDICE

In 2013, Little Sister's celebrated thirty years in business with a comment on their website: "Today you can find those same magazines and books we got into so much trouble for in just about any major bookstore chain, easily found online and in libraries in every city large and small. It's simply a different world today—at least socially in Canada."

Another comment from the *Little Sister's* decision in 2000 is worth noting: "[With] the exponential growth of pornographic sites on the Internet, the barrier to the passage across the border of hard copy material may someday be seen as of marginal importance to the enforcement of anti-obscenity laws."

The border has indeed become irrelevant. In the past decade or so, there has been remarkably little discussion of obscenity; the emphasis is almost entirely on child pornography distributed on the Internet. And while the Little Sister's case was not, overtly, about gender equality, the case and its considerable public profile—especially in cities like Vancouver and Toronto at the time, when there was media coverage and fundraising campaigns in the gay community and also in the arts community at large—undoubtedly contributed to a shift in Canadian "community standards" concerning the gay and lesbian community. This would take shape in the years immediately after the *Little Sister's* decision, in the arena of same-sex marriage. It has evolved more recently into a recognition of a more complex form of gender equality: the current acronym LGBTQ embraces lesbian, gay, transgender, transsexual, two-spirited, queer, questioning, intersex, and asexual. As Brenda Cossman noted in a recent article:

> The ways in which gay and lesbian sexual representation had been successfully redefined and legitimized meant that it was becoming more difficult to argue that such representations in and of themselves were degrading or dehumanizing. After two decades of contestations, 'community standards' had indeed changed.

Discrimination lingers in school boards. In 2002, CCLA intervened in the SCC case determining if the curriculum of a B.C. school should include books written for elementary school-aged children on the subject of same-sex parents. The books were *Asha's Mums, Belinda's Bouquet*, and *One Dad, Two Dads, Brown Dads, Blue Dads,* proposed to the Surrey District School Board by a teacher of kindergarten and grade one in 1997, and turned down by the board on the following grounds—the books didn't help to achieve the board's mandated learning outcomes; they were controversial, and the opinions of objecting parents had to be respected; and K-1 children were too young to deal with the ideas and scenarios in the books. As the SCC judgment observed: "Behind all these considerations hovered the moral and religious concerns of some parents and the Board with the morality of homosexual relationships."

Chief Justice McLachlin wrote the majority position, which found the actions of the school board to be functioning beyond its purview in disallowing this material from the classroom; in it, she said simply, "A secular school system cannot exclude certain lawful family models simply on the ground that one group of parents finds them morally questionable."

The two dissenting justices noted, "The moral status of same-sex relationships is controversial...." Nevertheless, within three years, thanks to the SCC same-sex marriage reference in 2004, Canada was the fourth country in the world to make same-sex marriages legal, and it was the first outside Europe to do so.

• • •

In November 1965, when the verdict was about to be pronounced on whether or not the pictures displayed by artist Dorothy Cameron in her Toronto gallery were obscene, the magistrate, Mr. Hayes, asked Ms. Cameron's counsel if he had anything to say in her defence. Mr. Fleming made the following remarks:

> .... The accused lady has never been convicted of this offence or, I'm sure, of any offence.... The police offered...a day or two before this trial took place to drop all the charges if this lady would undertake not to show the pictures again. Now, of course, Your Worship, the gallery is not continuing.... It's been closed on account of financial trouble and that was known at the time. So that, the accused lady had absolutely nothing to gain but the principles in this matter by saying no. She couldn't give that indication because, though she

> had no gallery to show the pictures in, it would be tantamount to admitting that there was something wrong with the pictures.... She felt there was a principle for which she should stand up and fight and stand up and fight she did.

In obscenity and pornography cases that involve individual artists, works of art, booksellers, and publications, the reason for defying and testing the law is frequently such a matter of principle. (Admittedly, commercial interests often are also at stake.) But the unifying thread in this activist narrative is the belief that even, or especially, images and ideas that are marginal or transgressive or dangerous deserve protection. When they are examined under that strange microscope labelled "the public good" or "community standards," they face the countervailing principle that certain members of society must be protected. In the 1960s, books and images and movies had to be found excessive or acceptable on an invisible scale between "undue" and "not undue" exploitation. Fifty years later, the test is somewhat more rigorous, thanks to a half-century of jurisprudence enhanced by the introduction into the debate of the Charter. But in every case, sooner or later, a bastion of justices must pronounce their definition of community standards. The debate has broadened since 1982 to embrace the language of equal rights and the notion of competing rights, but it is surely impossible to codify something as nebulous and chameleon-like as community standards. The images in Dorothy Cameron's art gallery were small, abstract black-and-white depictions of nude adult bodies in tender embraces; some of the material in Little Sister's banned shipments unrepentantly challenged conventional ideas about sexuality and sexual practices; the exhibits in recent Internet child-pornography cases defy description.

The role of CCLA over fifty years of defending work labelled obscene or pornographic, and the individuals who either create them or make them available to the public, is that of interlocutor, or in courtrooms, intervener. It is to persist with questions about the implications of changes to the law. The public at large, that embodiment of community standards, is not drawn to activism on a grand scale in defence of this challenge to freedom of expression. The public marches and gathers *en masse* to defend broader rights issues; the annual Pride celebration in Toronto, for example, which attracts millions of visitors and is a joyous celebration, playfully transgressive, began as a protest in response to the Operation Soap bathhouse raids of 1981.

Not surprisingly, the issues of obscenity and pornography are not inseparable from the subject of hate speech, another realm where there often appear to be competing rights: Does the right to freedom of expression trump the right not to be discriminated against? These two issues were in the Supreme Court of Canada during the same time frame, in the late eighties and early nineties. Once again, CCLA and LEAF found themselves in opposition as interveners. With hate speech, however, the public perception of good and evil, to be simplistic, is somewhat different. Unlike purveyors of hate speech, pornographers, by and large, do not look to the general public for support; as Chief Justice Brian Dickson remarked in the *Keegstra* decision in 1991: "Pornography is not dignified by its suppression."

Artists and writers, however, like Jane Rule and Marian Engel and D.H. Lawrence, push the boundaries of taste, take artistic risks, and emerge as heroes; purveyors of hate speech like Ernst Zündel and James Keegstra thrive on the attention they get from being taken though the courts and seek recognition as martyrs.

CHAPTER FIVE
Spreading False News, Hatred, or Contempt—Freedom of Speech or Freedom to Hate?

[Every] society from time to time draws lines at the point where the intolerable and the impermissible coincide. In a free society such as our own, where the privilege of speech can induce ideas that may change the very order itself, there is a bias weighted heavily in favour of the maximum of rhetoric whatever the cost and consequences. But that bias stops this side of injury to the community itself and to individual members or identifiable groups innocently caught in verbal cross-fire that goes beyond legitimate debate.

—Report of the Special Committee
on Hate Propaganda in Canada, 1966

Remarkably, pre-Hitler Germany had laws very much like the Canadian anti-hate law. Moreover, those laws were enforced with some vigour. During the fifteen years before Hitler came to power, there were more than two hundred prosecutions based on anti-Semitic speech.... As subsequent history so painfully testifies, this type of legislation proved ineffectual on the one occasion when there was a real argument for it.

—A. Alan Borovoy, *When Freedoms Collide*, 1988

It is not about freedom of expression. It's about freedom to hate, in my opinion.

—Senator Nancy Ruth, June 2013

[The] remedy to be applied is more speech, not enforced silence.

—US Supreme Court Decision, 1927

Hate speech disturbs, but should it be suppressed? As a society and as individuals we are offended and alarmed by the ugliness and viciousness of hate speech. And so the impetus to prosecute or punish such speech in some way has remained constant in Canada, despite the surprisingly small number of actual criminal cases.

Activities labelled as hate speech—in the *Criminal Code*, the crimes of publishing false news, advocating genocide, and promoting hate—are distinctive in the annals of crime and punishment because they concern imputed crimes against groups, not crimes against individuals. The libel or defamation of an individual, a hate crime (like torching a synagogue or mosque), and even the discrimination against individuals in employment and housing (because of perceived minority status) deal with actual harm done to one person or more than one person. But publishing false news, and related charges concerning writings or speech or materials communicated electronically that might harm or that intend to harm a group, have been difficult to prove and to prosecute, and over the period of fifty years, the means for both claiming and punishing them in Canada have changed. But punish we do.

It's a small, notorious group of men who carry the hate-speech banner in Canada: You know the names—Keegstra, Ross, Taylor, Whatcott, Zündel—only because, having first attracted the attention of local courts around the country by their actions, they have successfully, and noisily, pursued appeals to the Supreme Court. There is a section of the *Criminal Code* that specifically makes *advocating* genocide a crime, but denial of genocide is not a crime in Canada (which it is in Germany, for example). However, denial of the Holocaust has been the most frequent issue in hate propaganda cases.

In the defence of hate speech—the defence of the indefensible—liberals and conservatives come together or at least have some common ground. The libertarian tradition is historically associated with conservative ideologies. Liberals support freedom of expression, but hate speech is a difficult right for liberals to uphold, because its defence often contradicts directly the rights of minorities. Unquestionably this discomfort is exploited by individuals who defy hate speech restrictions. Purveyors of hate speech demand the protection of organizations like CCLA and PEN Canada, and portray themselves as martyrs to the cause of freedom of speech. Douglas Christie, a B.C. lawyer who represented many hate-speech defendants, described Canada in 1985 as "one great big internment camp."

The other interesting characteristic of hate propaganda in Canada is that it springs almost exclusively from white supremacist, neo-Nazi organizations. The spray of rhetorical bullets is directed from that one source at a range of targets—non-white immigrants; Jewish and Muslim communities; the lesbian, gay, bisexual, and transgender (LGBT) community; and abortion—the same individuals are active on many fronts.

The fundamental position of CCLA on hate speech has always been the same: fight hate speech with more words, not more censorship. In court cases, CCLA is often the only intervener arguing for the principle of more freedom of expression. In the landmark Supreme Court of Canada (SCC) hate-speech cases in the early 1990s, CCLA faced off against the Canadian Jewish Congress, B'Nai Brith, and the Women's Legal Education and Action Fund (LEAF).

Because of CCLA's preference on such issues for remedies outside the courts, the organization was an enthusiastic supporter of the creation of the human rights codes and commissions in Canada in the 1970s; as the role and use of these statutes evolved over the years to include hate speech, CCLA found itself in opposition to the human rights tribunals, at least on the specific issue of hate speech.

NEVER AGAIN—THE BURDEN OF HISTORY AND HATE SPEECH IN CANADA

> For embattled minorities freedom of expression may be one of the only instruments available to impress their interests on an otherwise apathetic society.
>
> —CCLA *Keegstra* brief to SCC, 1990

Prohibitions on spreading false news are stitched into many cultures, tightly entwined with notions of religious and social order.

The phrase itself has a Chaucerian ring and indeed is taken from an English law enacted in 1275 known as *De Scandalis Magnatum,* which prohibited "any false News or Tales, whereby discord, or occasion of discord or slander may grow between the King and his People, or the Great Men of the Realm." Although the crime of spreading false news was dropped from English law in 1887, it was embedded in the earliest version of Canada's *Criminal Code* in 1892 as section 181.

In its original setting, those worthy of protection are only royalty and "great men"—the landed gentry. But in Canada, Everyman was worthy of protection: "Everyone who wilfully publishes a statement, tale or news that he knows is false and that causes or is likely to cause injury or mischief *to a public interest* is guilty of an indictable offence and liable to imprisonment for a term not exceeding two years." As early as the 1930s, a Manitoba statute prohibited the dissemination of Nazi literature. In 1948, because "disregard and contempt for human rights have resulted in barbarous acts which have outraged the conscience of mankind," the Universal Declaration of Human Rights (drafted by Canadian John Humphrey, and initially opposed by Canada at the United Nations) was adopted by most nations. In the period during which Canada's human rights consciousness seems to have been awakened, just prior to, during, and after the Second World War, concerns about the impact of "false news" first settled on religious groups.

In 1951, a member of the Jehovah's Witnesses in Quebec was charged *(Boucher v. the King)* with "seditious libel" for a pamphlet he distributed that accused Quebeckers and Catholics of attacking Jehovah's Witnesses. *The Watchtower* pamphlet was entitled "Quebec's Burning Hate for God and Christ and Freedom Is the Shame of all Canada," and it was written as a commentary on the perceived "vindictive persecution" of Jehovah's Witnesses, who distributed religious materials and bibles and held private services and public meetings without permits, and who "for this exercise of what has been taken for granted to be the unchallengeable rights of Canadians, have been assaulted and beaten and their bibles and publications torn up and destroyed, by individuals and by mobs...

and in hundreds have been charged with public offences and held to exorbitant bail."

The pamphlet claimed that the actions of police and the courts were not impartial, but were carried out "under priestly influence." The case was dismissed because there was deemed to be no proof that Boucher was intending to incite disorder or acts of violence. Again in 1951, the same pamphlet was the subject of a prosecution (under section 181 of the *Criminal Code*) for spreading false news, in *R. v. Carrier,* and again the Supreme Court acquitted, holding that s.181 was also "circumscribed," and could not be applied to a pamphlet that was not specifically intended to "arouse disorder." In 1953, the *Criminal Code* was revised to include anti-hate propaganda specifically, in addition to seditious libel and false news.

But the most significant changes to the *Criminal Code* on the subject of hate crimes were proposed by a Special Committee on Hate Propaganda in Canada, known as the Cohen Committee, because it was chaired by Dean Maxwell Cohen, Q.C., dean of the Faculty of Law, McGill University. Pierre Trudeau was also on the committee assembled by Liberal Justice Minister Guy Favreau, which in 1966 published a unanimous report, recommending that hate crimes be dealt with in specific terms in the *Criminal Code*. The Cohen Committee noted that while it appeared that only "a small number of persons and a somewhat larger number of organizations, extremist in outlook and dedicated to the preaching and spreading of hatred and contempt against certain identifiable minority groups in Canada" existed, it would be a mistake not to take such groups seriously. With reference to "what is known to have been the result of hate propaganda in other countries, particularly in the 1930s when such material and ideas played a significant role in the creation of a climate of malice, destructive to the central values of Judaic-Christian society," and the fact that "minority groups in at least eight Provinces have been subjected to these vicious attacks," the committee recommended action.[162]

However, the Cohen Committee readily acknowledged that creating a new "criminal remedy for group defamation" was a radical choice: "we realize it goes beyond what has hitherto been thought by many to be the *proper sphere for criminal law,* for such group defamation requires no breach of the peace, and no showing of likely injury to the reputation of any person."

Despite this carefully expressed reservation, in the 1970 revision of the *Criminal Code* (Trudeau was now prime minister) these recommendations became what are now sections 318–20 of the *Criminal Code*, dealing with the crimes of advocating genocide and inciting violence with hate propaganda.

From the mid-1970s, a rash of white-supremacist sentiment spread, erratically, across Canada, through the dogged efforts of a small number of individuals who knew one another. Groups such as the Western Guard Party, the Nationalist Party of Canada, and even the Ku Klux Klan became active in Canada, and transmission of propaganda by telephone, videocassette, and later the Internet became problematic. In 1984, a House of Commons Special Committee on Participation of Visible Minorities in Canadian Society produced a report entitled *Equality Now!*, which suggested that a combination of factors such as economic stress and recently increased immigration "have produced an atmosphere that may be ripe for racially motivated incidents" and identified "a recent upsurge in hate propaganda.... Not only is it anti-Semitic and anti-Black, as in the 1960s, but it is also now anti-Roman Catholic, anti-East Indian, anti-Aboriginal people and anti-French." The report stated that "Canada has become a major source of supply of hate propaganda that finds its way to Europe, and especially to West Germany...."[163]

In 1977, the *Canadian Human Rights Act (CHRA)* was created. The Act is the mechanism whereby individual Canadians can make a complaint against individuals or institutions and corporations about "discriminatory practices" based on race, gender, religion, and so forth. Most of the provisions of the *Human Rights Act* concern conditions of employment and the right to belong to an organization such as a union, for example. The anomaly in the *Human Rights Act* has been section 13, concerning use of the telephone (and later the Internet) to communicate messages of hate. The human rights codes of Alberta, British Columbia, Saskatchewan, and the Northwest Territories also have provisions similar to section 13 of the *CHRA*. The federal act only deals with

Le raciste, c'est l'autre!
BADO

federal areas of responsibility; most provinces, with the exception of British Columbia, also have their own human rights commissions. In 2013, as discussed later, section 13 was almost simultaneously declared constitutional by the SCC and removed from the *CHRA* as the result of a private member's bill in Parliament.

But the emphasis of all non-criminal human rights mechanisms in Canada—through a somewhat laborious and lengthy process of filing a complaint that is heard first by a commission and then, after a process of mediation and adjudication, by members of a non-judicial tribunal—is preventative rather than punitive; there are no criminal charges, the courts are not engaged, and the punishment is in the form of fines and awards. If an order of the human rights tribunal is defied, an appeals process does engage first the Federal Court, and finally the SCC.

In the early years of the human rights codes and tribunals, Alan Borovoy and CCLA applauded the tribunals as a non-criminalizing approach to hate speech. In the CCLA *Keegstra* brief, for example, it was noted that CCLA "has frequently made submissions to government recommending more vigourous and imaginative programmes for administering our various human rights statues. Canadian experience demonstrates that the fall-out from stronger programmes against racist *deeds* is often to weaken further the impact of racist *words.*" In his book *When Freedoms Collide,* Alan Borovoy is unequivocal in his enthusiasm for conciliation instead of confrontation: "Human rights commissions are more likely than the courts to develop the flexibility and imagination to advance the cause. This is not to say that the commissions *will* perform in an acceptable manner; it is to say that the courts are *less* likely to do so."

But over the next twenty years, as the human rights commissions became increasingly activist on issues like hate crimes, CCLA took a critical stance against the inclusion of hate crimes in the purview of human rights commissions.

Before the *Charter of Rights and Freedoms* took effect in 1982, free expression jurisprudence mostly was concerned, as in the cases noted above, with the expression of views that might be deemed dangerously "political." But in 1982, the Charter was signed into law, entrenching a range of potentially conflicting rights and freedoms, as discussed in the second chapter of this book. The Charter enshrined a much broader notion of freedom of expression that the courts have had to come to terms with. Section 2 is as follows:

> Everyone has the following fundamental freedoms:
>
> a) freedom of conscience and religion;
>
> b) freedom of thought, belief, opinion and expression, including freedom of the press and other media of communication;
>
> c) freedom of peaceful assembly; and
>
> d) freedom of association.

In dealing with challenges to section 2 of the Charter, in cases concerned not only with hate speech, but also those dealing with obscenity and child pornography, the courts have struggled with terms like "core values" and "community standards," and argued whether or not words such as *obscenity* and *hate* are clearly defined in legislation. A reading of these cases catches the judiciary in the act, not merely of parsing the *Criminal Code*, but also of revealing their own instincts, biases, and feelings about issues. The result is that the public good is often defined by private predilections, in rhetoric tinged at times with something approaching religious fervour.

Overall, the impulse of the courts has been to support the premise that hate speech is not defensible in the name of freedom of expression, and that those accused of disseminating it should be punished. The court of public opinion is divided, and in recent years, the Internet has thrown up a whole new set of challenges.

In the 1980s and early 1990s a hornet's nest of hate-speech cases hit the courts, along with equally incendiary cases on abortion, pornography, and the controversial "rape-shield" legislation discussed in other chapters of this book. In his book, *When Freedoms Collide* Alan Borovoy describes one six-month period in the mid-1980s:

> During the first six months of 1985, the Canadian public endured a grotesque spectacle—the back-to-back trials of pamphleteer Ernst Zündel in Toronto, Ontario and of high school teacher James Keegstra in Red Deer, Alberta.... Day after day, these trials were major news events in the Canadian media. We were subjected to detailed cross-examinations of concentration camp survivors. They were asked how they knew that their fellow prisoners were gassed and even how they knew that those prisoners were dead.... It would be hard to imagine an obscenity that could parallel the deliberate denial of the genocide suffered by the Jews of Europe.

When these cases arrived at the Supreme Court, CCLA was there to defend the right to espouse such propaganda in Canada. Borovoy argued that "freedom of speech is often most necessary when it creates some level of tension or unrest." He recalled Martin Luther King's description of his tactics as an exercise in "constructive tensions" and asked the question: "how does a blunt instrument like the criminal law distinguish between destructive hatred and constructive tension?"

THE EMBLEMATIC HATE-SPEECH CASES—"DEEP-FELT EMOTIONS OF DETESTATION, CALUMNY AND VILIFICATION" (CHIEF JUSTICE DICKSON, CANADA (HUMAN RIGHTS COMMISSION) V. TAYLOR, [1990])

In the early 1990s, the SCC considered three important hate speech cases almost simultaneously; the decisions refer to them as companion cases, and there are cross-citations. It seems likely that some form of horse-trading took place during deliberations, and interestingly, all cases were split decisions, 4 to 3 each time. The cases were those of James Keegstra, an Alberta schoolteacher; John Ross Taylor and the Western Guard Party; and in 1992, Ernst Zündel—the first of two times Zündel managed to attract the attention of the SCC. (The lesser-known case of Donald Andrews of the Nationalist Party of Canada was also considered in 1990.)

All three cases concerned either denial of the Holocaust or related neo-Nazi ideas, but each case was heard under different auspices of either the *Criminal Code* or the federal *Human Rights Act*. A *Criminal Code* violation is more serious, requires the consent of provincial Attorneys General for prosecution, and also requires proof not only of the expression of hatred, but also the intent to *cause* hatred. A *Human Rights Act* violation only becomes a criminal case if orders for penalties issued by a human rights tribunal are defied. CCLA was one of several interveners in each case, and in each case, the sole intervener arguing for striking down the relevant legislation.

TEACHING HATRED: JAMES KEEGSTRA

> Jews always deceive Christians.... Jews may lie and perjure to condemn a Christian.... Jews must divide what they overcharge Christians.... [A Jew] who kills a Christian pleases God the same as one who offers incense to him.
>
> —From "Facts are Facts,"
> a Booklet Given to Students by James Keegstra

James Keegstra was charged under section 319 of the *Criminal Code*. Keegstra taught high school in Eckville, Alberta, from the early 1970s until he was dismissed in 1982 and charged in 1984 with "unlawfully promoting hatred against an identifiable group by communicating anti-Semitic statements to his students." Keegstra described Jews to his students as "treacherous," "subversive," "sadistic," "money-loving," "power hungry," and "child killers." According to the SCC majority position written by then Chief Justice Brian Dickson, Keegstra taught that "Jewish people seek to destroy Christianity and are responsible for depressions, anarchy, chaos, wars and revolution..." and that Jews "created the Holocaust to gain sympathy and, in contrast to the open and honest Christians, were said to be deceptive, secretive and inherently evil."

Keegstra punished his students by lowering their grades if they did not accept his theories in class and feed them back to him in exams. He was found guilty by a jury, and he appealed his conviction successfully to the Alberta Court of Appeal on the grounds that section 319 of the *Criminal Code* violated his Charter rights. The Alberta Court of the Queen's Bench then appealed this decision to the SCC.

In its brief to the SCC, CCLA argued that "hatred" is a very broad term—everything from "mere dislike to acrimony, antagonism, aversion, bitterness, enmity, hostility, ill-will, malice, rancour, spite and vindictiveness." Legitimate grievance might well be defined as hate speech: if, because of the government's position on land claims, "a native leader expressed with bitter invective, indiscriminate animosity towards white people...[d]espite the arguable impropriety of the native leader's comments, a democratic society would have no business punishing such expression. Yet that is precisely the risk created by this section."

The CCLA brief looked again at the Cohen Committee Report from 1965, which, while recognizing that the actual number of hate groups was small at the time, was laced with anxiety about what might happen in the future: "given a certain set of socio-economic circumstances, such as a deepening of emotional tensions or the setting in of a severe business recession...such 'hate' could mushroom into a real and monstrous threat to our way of life."

This "what if..." mindset has informed the courts' consideration of the threat of harm from hate propaganda for almost fifty years. It is rooted in a deep-seated lack of confidence in the capacity of society for discriminating thought and judgment. Again from the influential Cohen Committee Report, a bleak and incriminating comment on the "critical faculties of individuals":

> While holding that over the long run, the human mind is repelled by blatant falsehood and seeks the good, it is too often true, in the short run, that emotion displaces reason and individuals perversely reject the demonstrations of truth put before them and forsake the good they know. The successes of modern advertising, the triumph of impudent propaganda such as Hitler's, have qualified sharply our belief in the rationality of man. We know that under strain and pressure in times of irritation and frustration, the individual is swayed and even swept away by hysterical, emotional appeals. We act irresponsibly if we ignore the way in which

> emotion can drive reason from the field.... Those who urged a century ago that men should be allowed to express themselves with utter freedom even though the heavens fall did so with great confidence that they would not fall. That degree of confidence is not open to us today.

Such deep pessimism about human nature was firmly countered by the views expressed in 1965 by Daniel Hill, first director of the Ontario Human Rights Commission. His laid-back statement resonated with statistics about actual crime rates in the face of recurring hysteria about crime and was noted by CCLA: "The Canadian public is relatively immune to extremist, anti-Semitic, and other 'hate' materials."

But on the issue of hate speech, the courts err on the side of suspicion rather than finding faith in human nature.

As with the pornography cases discussed previously, the protection of groups from hate propaganda became, in 1990, an equality issue, thanks to the interventions of LEAF.[164] The Charter is rich with equality provisions, notably section 15. The position taken by LEAF in its Keegstra intervention was based on section 15:

> LEAF submits that for the purpose of constitutional analysis, the willful public promotion of group hatred is properly understood as a practice of inequality. For example, anti-Semitism promotes the inequality of Jews on the basis of religion and ethnicity. White supremacy promotes inequality on the basis of race, colour and sometimes ethnic origin.... Hate propaganda...is a practice of discrimination similar to sexual harassment and other discriminatory acts that take a verbal form, such as signs reading "Whites Only" or advertisements stating that a position is open only to men.

LEAF argued that hate speech is a violent form of expression that is not protected by the Charter and that in what was clearly a collision of competing values, and in the context of Canada's multicultural heritage (protected in section 27 of the Charter), "freedom of expression ought to accommodate the guarantee of equality."

In language that contradicts directly the position of CCLA, LEAF argued, "Protection from hate propaganda is necessary to protect the freedom of expression and the inherent dignity and worth of all human beings in society." LEAF dismissed the "marketplace of ideas" argument, because, they said, there is no equality between teachers and their students: "The power imbalance, with its opportunity for abuse, renders the concept inappropriate."

In a 4 to 3 ruling, the SCC ruled that section 319 was a "justifiable" infringement of freedom of expression rights and that Keegstra was therefore guilty of promoting hatred.

In Keegstra's case, and other hate-speech cases, the SCC undertook a two-step review: first to determine if the section of the *Criminal Code* is in fact an infringement of freedom of expression rights (as spelled out in section 2 of the Charter), and if it is, to determine whether that infringement is justified, according to the terms of section 1 of the Charter. The preference of the SCC in these cases appeared to be not to spend a great deal of time arguing (except over issues related to the definition of words like hate and obscenity) whether or not there is an infringement of rights, but to declare that yes, clearly, there is, and then to spend the greater part of their deliberation on whether or not the infringement (meaning a specific section of the *Criminal Code*) is justified. In almost all such cases, SCC justices have examined the *Criminal Code* provisions under the *Oakes* test; *Oakes* was a 1986 case in which Chief Justice Dickson first set out a three-part test of the reasonableness (or in fact, the legality) of any infringement of rights. If the section of the *Criminal Code* does not pass this three-step test, it is tossed out of the Code and the case dismissed. If, however, the section of the *Criminal Code* is found to be reasonable and justifiable by the court, either the conviction stands, or the case is referred back to the provincial courts for retrial.

The court, as revealed in Dickson's decision, took considerable care to explore the qualitative aspects of speech deserving protection, moving away from the pre-Charter focus on political expression, which was seen to have an impact on "the maintenance and operations of the institutions of democratic government," and considering instead broader "individual and societal values...." So the danger was now not to governments but to people. The justices reviewed the "convictions fueling freedom of expression" that were identified in an earlier case, *Irwin Toy* (1989): seeking and attaining truth; participating in social and political decision-making; and "diversity in forms of individual self-fulfillment and human flourishing [which] ought to be cultivated in a tolerant and welcoming environment for the sake of both those who convey a meaning and those to whom meaning is conveyed."

Chief Justice Dickson also considered section 27 of the Charter, which affirms Canada's multicultural vision as relevant to the goal of "eradicating hate propaganda from society." He stated his personal opinion that "expression intended to promote the hatred of identifiable groups is of limited importance when measured against free expression values." He resisted the idea that "rationality" will ultimately expose falsehood in the "unregulated marketplace of ideas," and concluded that it was very unlikely that "statements intended to promote hatred against an identifiable group are true, or that their vision of society will lead to a better world. To portray such statements as crucial to truth and the betterment of the political and social milieu is therefore misguided."

Furthermore, hate speech is "wholly inimical" to the "democratic aspirations" of the Charter's guarantee of free expression. And Dickson concluded that in rejecting hate propaganda, the courts and Parliament would be applauded for "a meaningful expression on behalf of the vast majority of citizens."

In her dissenting opinion on behalf of three justices, Justice Beverly McLachlin took as a mantra a position articulated in a 1927 US Supreme Court (SCOTUS) case: "If there be time to expose through discussion the falsehood and fallacies, to avert the evil by the processes of education, *the remedy to be applied is more speech, not enforced silence*." McLachlin favoured the "rationale of self-actualization," in a generous interpretation of the kinds of speech worthy of protection, and stated that the Charter embraces the American test of clear and present danger.

In her argument for breadth, McLachlin insisted that there could be speech expressing hatred that actually has value to democracy. She referred to the hypothetical example in the CCLA argument, of a native leader angry about the actions of white Europeans on land claims issues. Or *Buzzanga* (1979), another case cited by CCLA, in which two residents of Essex County, Ontario, were hoping to get fellow francophones engaged on the subject of French schools. They wrote and distributed a satirical pamphlet, purportedly from an anti-francophone bigot, with the intent of showing what attitudes might exist in the anglophone community:

> WAKE UP CANADIANS YOUR FUTURE IS AT STAKE! IT IS YOUR TAX DOLLARS THAT SUBSIDIZE THE ACTIVITIES OF THE FRENCH MINORITY OF ESSEX COUNTY.... IF WE GIVE THEM A SCHOOL, WHAT WILL THEY DEMAND NEXT...INDEPENDENT CITY STATES? CONSIDER THE ETHNIC PROBLEM OF THE UNITED STATES AND TAKE HEED

The satiric intent of the two francophone men, Buzzanga and Durocher, was not apparent to readers, and they were charged (bizarrely) with incitement to hatred of francophones. The three justices of the Ontario Court of Appeal ruled that they were not "wilfully" inciting hatred, upheld their appeal, and ordered a new trial. "Is it unimaginable that questions of public policy should involve speech of this kind?" asked McLachlin. "Experience shows that in actual cases it may be difficult to draw the line between speech which has value to democracy or social issues and speech which does not."

McLachlin doubted that suppressing hate speech would encourage multiculturalism and discourage racism. She quoted Alan Borovoy's comments about anti-hate laws in pre-Nazi Germany that open this chapter.

The CCLA brief provided McLachlin with examples of legitimate speech that had already been unjustly caught in the net of section 319: Leon Uris's pro-Zionist novel *The Haj* (should be banned); Salman Rushdie's *Satanic Verses* was stopped at the border, as was a film entitled *Nelson Mandela.* Students were arrested in 1986 for distributing pamphlets containing the words "Yankee Go Home." McLachlin argued that fear of prosecution would most certainly lead to self-censorship:

> Novelists may steer clear of controversial characterizations of ethnic characteristics, such as Shakespeare's portrayal of Shylock in *The Merchant of Venice*. Scientists may well think twice before researching and publishing results of research suggesting difference between ethnic or racial groups.... Political debate on crucial issues such as immigration, educational language rights, foreign ownership and trade may be tempered. These matters go to the heart of the traditional justifications for protecting freedom of expression.

She also approvingly quoted Alan Borovoy on the efficacy of the human rights codes: "[a]part from collateral matters such as obstructing complaint investigations, the criminal process can safely be eliminated from human rights matters."

The fundamental points of disagreement between Justices Dickson and McLachlin were, first, the value of protecting opinions, ideas, and falsehood that in themselves clearly have no value; second, the impact of such opinions on targeted groups; and third, the collateral impact of such cases. McLachlin was prepared to go to great lengths to defend indefensible speech. Dickson was not; he also thought that the "disapproval" of the SCC and appropriate legislation were useful to society: "hate propaganda legislation and trials are a means by which the values beneficial to a free and democratic society can be publicized."

McLachlin despaired of unwarranted publicity given by court proceedings to the likes of Keegstra and Zündel, and indeed newspaper reports at the time stated that Zündel claimed he'd gotten "a million dollars' worth of publicity" from his trials. She noted an "unmistakable hint of the joy of martyrdom" in the white supremacist literature of Donald Andrews: "The Holocaust Hoax has been so ingrained in the minds of the hated 'goyim' by now that in some countries...challenging its validity can land you in jail." (Andrews also lost an appeal to the SCC in 1990 after his conviction for distributing the *Nationalist Reporter* and letters and stickers with messages such as "Nigger go home," "Hoax on the Holocaust," "Israel stinks," and "Hitler was right. Communism is Jewish.")

As noted in the CCLA brief, when the courts take the "rantings of hatemongers" seriously, absurdities result. During Ernst

Zündel's false news prosecution discussed later, his claim that Auschwitz was a Jewish country club was solemnly debated. The vice-president of the Royal Bank of Canada was required to testify that no, he was not in fact part of a Jewish conspiracy engineering international Communism.

The SCC upheld section 319 of the *Criminal Code* as a justifiable infringement on Keegstra's freedom of expression rights. Keegstra's actual sentence, a $5,000 fine, was not addressed in the SCC decision, and was subsequently overturned by the Alberta Court of Appeal and replaced with a suspended sentence of one year and two hundred hours of community service.

According to research reported by writer Richard Moon, surprisingly few prosecutions have been brought under section 319, with even fewer convictions: between 1994 and 2004, there were ninety-three prosecutions, thirty-two convictions, twenty-seven resulting in prison sentences and five in conditional sentences. Speculation varies on the reasons for this small number; one reason may be that getting the consent of an Attorney General to prosecute is a barrier, which in turn discourages persistent police investigations.[165]

WHITE POWER MESSAGES—JOHN ROSS TAYLOR AND THE WESTERN GUARD

> There is a conspiracy which controls and programmes Canadian society.... The conspirators are Jews.
>
> —Summary of Western Guard Party's Recorded Messages

For thirteen years beginning in 1977, John Ross Taylor and the Western Guard Party dallied with the Canadian Human Rights Commission (CHRC) and the courts in a persistent use of recorded telephone messages that purported to reveal the existence of a Jewish Communist conspiracy in Canada. Through a series of complaints, cease and desist orders—under section 13(1) of the *Canadian Human Rights Act*—issued and then defied, subsequent fines, suspended sentences, prison time served, more recorded messages, appeals and counter-appeals, the case finally made its way via the Federal Court to the Supreme Court, and a judgment in 1990. (The creation of the Charter in 1982 provided a brand-new route of appeal for Taylor and his associates.)

The recorded messages could be heard by calling a telephone number printed on a white card (with a maple leaf), distributed to individuals in crowds and placed under doorways. The number also appeared in telephone books beside the words "White Power Message."

Section 13(1) of the *Canadian Human Rights Act (CHRA)*, at this time, dealt only with messages "communicated telephonically." According to some commentators, the hate speech messages recorded by Taylor in the early seventies were actually instrumental in the inclusion of a hate-speech provision in the *CHRA* when it was created in 1977. Section 13(1) was amended in 2001 to apply also to matters "communicated by means of a computer or a group of interconnected or related computers, including the Internet, or any similar means of communication," but not to "matters communicated in whole or in part by means of the facilities of a broadcasting undertaking."

The human rights tribunal identified and summarized as follows a "recurring theme" in telephone messages written and recorded by Taylor:

> There is a conspiracy which controls and programmes Canadian society...our books, our schools and our media are controlled by the conspirators. The conspirators cause unemployment and inflation; they weaken us by encouraging perversion, laziness, drug use and race mixing. They become enriched by stealing our property. They have founded communism which is responsible for many of our economic problems such as the postal strike.... The conspirators are Jews.

The Supreme Court justices in 1990, and subsequently, have found favour with section 13(1) of the *CHRA*, and approved the practice of using such legislation instead of the courts for dealing with hate speech. One of the main arguments repeatedly made in favour of legislation like section 13 is that its purpose is the protection and compensation of victims, not the punishment of perpetrators. As Justice Dickson wrote in the *Taylor* decision, "the aim of human rights legislation, and of s.13(1), is not to bring the full force of the state's power against a blameworthy individual for the purpose of imposing punishment. Instead, provisions found in human rights statutes generally operate in a less confrontational manner, allowing for a conciliatory settlement if possible and, where discrimination exists, gearing remedial responses more towards compensating the victim." Because this approach lacks the "fatally broad scope" of prosecutions under the *Criminal Code* it is less likely to capture anything other than actual hate speech delivered in a very specific way.

Given the tendency towards repeat offences, and a deliberative use of both the commission and the courts by individuals like Taylor and Ernst Zündel, one might question this faith in the conciliatory effectiveness of human rights statutes.

CCLA's brief argued that the meaning of hatred was "inherently vague," and that section 13 should only be used if the telephone was used to "harass" people. It argued also that telephonic messages created in order to reduce discrimination might be captured because "intent" was not specified. Since the 1970s, for example, CCLA, in an effort to expose discriminatory business practices in Ontario, regularly conducted telephone surveys of employment and real estate agencies, posing as employers wanting to advertise for "whites only" or as potential renters.

Chief Justice Dickson, again writing the majority position in a 4 to 3 decision, disagreed that the language was vague: "The phrase 'hatred or contempt'...refers only to unusually strong and deep-felt emotions of detestation, calumny and vilification and, as long as human rights tribunals continue to be well aware of the purpose of s.13(1) and pay heed to the ardent and extreme nature of feeling described in that phrase, there is little danger that subjective opinion as to offensiveness will supplant the proper meaning of the section."

Justice McLachlin, again dissenting (in part), argued that section 13(1) overreaches because it:

> catches speech which is neither intended nor calculated to foster discrimination. It catches speech which may be

> entirely accurate and truthful; speech which merely seeks to air legitimate group grievances; speech which merely exposes to ridicule; speech which merely communicates the information by telephone to a single person who has the power to hang up the phone if he or she does not like the message; private speech between consenting participants. In short, s.13(1) *seriously overshoots the mark, going beyond what can be defended as a reasonable limit on free speech justified by the need to combat discrimination against members of particular groups.* [italics mine]

The SCC majority ruled that section 13(1) was a reasonable infringement of Taylor's freedom of expression rights. The decision, and the tests that it proposed for determining both the nature of hate and the effect of hate speech on intended targets, became the touchstone for analysis of hate propaganda cases in the courts, and in human rights tribunal considerations up to and including the *Whatcott* decision in 2013, which was about a section in the *Saskatchewan Human Rights Code*.

"A CREEP LIKE ZÜNDEL..." (ALAN BOROVOY, CCLA NEWSLETTER, 1992)

> Many countries of the Anglo-Saxon world...are today facing the gravest danger in their history, the danger posed by the alien races in their midst. Unless something is done in Britain to halt the immigration and assimilation of Africans and Asians into our country, we are faced in the near future, quite apart from the bloodshed of racial conflict, with the biological alteration and destruction of the British people as they have existed here since the coming of the Saxons. In short, we are threatened with the irrecoverable loss of our European culture and racial heritage. But what happens if a man dares to speak of the race problem, of its biological and political implications? He is branded as that most heinous of creatures, a "racialist." And what is racialism, of course, but the very hallmark of the Nazi! They (so everyone is told,

> anyway) murdered Six Million Jews because of racialism, so it must be a very evil thing indeed.
>
> —From *Did Six Million Really Die?*

The pamphlet that sent Ernst Zündel to prison for 15 months in 1988—*Did Six Million Really Die?*—can still be purchased on Amazon.ca, in a version updated in 2011. Zündel published the pamphlet, which was written by a British man called Richard Harwood (a pseudonym), and added a preface and postscript. Among other things, the pamphlet argued that "extermination" of Jews in fact referred to a "straightforward emigration" policy, that *The Diary of Anne Frank* was a "hoax among many hoaxes,"

that those who died in "work camps" such as Auschwitz died of starvation or diseases like typhus, and that "an avalanche of fabricated extermination literature" was produced to prove the "brazen fantasy of the six million" in order to procure war reparation payments from Germany.

Zündel was convicted by a jury twice for publishing this pamphlet, and his appeal claiming that section 181 of the *Criminal Code* was unconstitutional was rejected twice by the Ontario Court of Appeal. In the course of the second trial, the claims in the pamphlet were enumerated as eighty-five separate statements, and were refuted through the presentation of evidence and testimony, one by one. (Zündel admitted during his second trial that he had been writing "those things" for twenty-five years. He was acquitted of publishing a second pamphlet—*The West, War, and Islam!*).

Having recently declared in the Keegstra case that section 319 of the *Criminal Code* was a reasonable infringement of freedom of expression, the SCC, again in a 4 to 3 decision, determined in the case of Ernst Zündel that section 181 of the *Criminal Code* was not, thus overturning Zündel's conviction.

The incongruities of the hate-speech laws were thrown into relief by the Keegstra and Zündel cases. The two men drew on each other's material. Keegstra appeared as a character witness in Zündel's 1985 trial. The same lawyer represented them. Yet one was found guilty, the other not guilty, because they were charged under different sections of the Code. (The close votes by the SCC are also worth noting; although the arguments were not identical, the majority/minority flip happened because Justice L'Heureux-Dubé changed her position.)

Justice McLachlin wrote the majority opinion. (Both the majority and dissenting opinions displayed plenty of rhetorical flourish; hate speech is a ready-made target for editorializing.) McLachlin observed that this clause of the *Criminal Code* can hardly be deemed essential; it had only been invoked three times since 1892. Even George Burbidge, the Canadian jurist who drafted the 1892 *Criminal Code*, was critical of the offence, according to Canadian legal scholar and poet F.R. Scott; in a 1952 article on False News he noted that Burbidge admitted that its

James Keegstra, former Eckville, Alberta teacher, leaves the Red Deer, Alberta courthouse with his lawyer, Doug Christie (right) in 1985.

"definition is very vague and the doctrine exceedingly doubtful." Section 181 was declared anachronistic by the Law Reform Commission of Canada in 1986, and indeed no other country in the world at the time had a similar law. McLachlin argued that examples of such laws, in Denmark, Italy, and Germany, cited in the dissenting opinion, had "minimal relevance" to this appeal.

So, McLachlin wrote:

> While s.181 may be capable of serving legitimate purposes, Parliament has identified no social problem, much less one of pressing concern, justifying it. The provision originally focused on the prevention of deliberate slanderous statements against the nobles of the realm to preserve political harmony in the state. To suggest now that its objective is to combat hate propaganda or racism is to go beyond its

Ernst Zündel (right) was also represented by Doug Christie. The pair were met by a group of sign-carrying supporters as they left a Toronto courthouse in 1987. Doug Christie, sometimes called Counsel for the Damned, was a controversial figure himself. Some believe—because he represented neo-Nazis and white supremists such as Wolfgang Droege, Paul Fromm, and John Ross Taylor—he shared his clients' views. Others claim he was a courageous defender of free speech; that was his battle.

history and its wording and to adopt the "shifting purpose" analysis this Court has rejected. Such an objective, moreover, hardly seems capable of being described as a "nuisance," the rubric under which Parliament has placed s.181, nor as the offence's target of mere "mischief" to a public interest.

McLachlin found no evidence that Parliament ever intended section 181 to be used to protect the freedom of speech of minority or disadvantaged groups, which is one of the purposes of section 2(b) of the Charter. The "proscription of false news was originally intended to protect the mighty and the powerful from discord or slander; there is nothing to suggest any legislative intention to transform s.181

from a mechanism for the maintenance of the status quo into a device for the protection of 'vulnerable social groups.'" She compared the language of s.319(2), "hatred against any identifiable group," to the much vaguer, weaker language of s.181, "mischief to a public interest."

Justices Cory and Iacobucci wrote the dissenting opinion in the 4 to 3 decision, arguing for section 181's precision. "The citizen knows that to be at risk under this section, he must wilfully publish a false statement knowing it to be false. Further, the publication of those statements must injure or be likely to injure the public interest...." They defined "public interest" as those rights that are protected by the Charter. They argued that the precedent of "shifting purpose," which McLachlin said had been resisted by the SCC, in fact was adopted by the SCC in its decisions on obscenity and pornography, like *Butler*. "Just as the community standards test as applied to the obscenity law 'must necessarily respond to changing mores,' so too should the test to define 'injury to a public interest' take into account the changing values of Canadian society. Those values encompass multiculturalism and equality, precepts specifically included in the provisions of the Charter."

They argued that "it would be impossible to deny the harm caused by the wilful publication of deliberate lies which are likely to injure the public interest.... To deliberately lie about the indescribable suffering and death inflicted upon the Jews by Hitler is the foulest of falsehoods and the essence of cruelty."

Section 181 was removed from the *Criminal Code*. It is interesting to speculate what would have happened to Zündel's convictions if he had been charged instead under section 319.

The overturning of the convictions of Zündel was seen as a distinctly mixed blessing by CCLA. As Alan Borovoy noted in a 1992 CCLA newsletter, "If the section had been upheld, it could have threatened free speech; since it was struck down, a creep like Zündel will try to portray the result as a vindication of his malevolent obscenities." Zündel was indeed emboldened by his victory and created mischief in Canada for another fifteen years. He applied for Canadian citizenship and was rejected, and his appeal to the SCC on that issue was refused a hearing in 2000. In

1995, his fortified house in Toronto was fire-bombed; no charges were ever laid. In 1997, he was accused by the Canadian Human Rights Commission under section 13(1) of the *Human Rights Act* of distributing hate literature on his website. CCLA spoke against section 13 at this point, because of its vagueness and possible misapplication: "truthful internet discussions of racial, religious, or ethnic warfare in Bosnia, Rwanda, or Northern Ireland could very well run afoul of the federal *Human Rights Act*. Couldn't such discussions be seen as 'likely to expose' Serbs, Croats, Muslims, Hutus, Tutsis, Catholics or Protestants to hatred or contempt?"

The CHRC argued that because the Internet used telephone technology, section 13 should apply to websites. In 2001, the language of section 13 was expanded to include reference to the Internet, just before the CHRC made its decision on Zündel. He was ordered to "cease and desist" from publishing this material.

Zündel moved to the United States in 2000, but in 2003, US immigration officials sent him back to Canada, where Citizenship and Immigration officials filed a national security certificate stating that Zündel was a threat to national security and requesting that he be deported back to Germany, where he was wanted on hate crime charges. In 2004, the SCC refused to hear Zündel's appeal on this, and in 2005, a federal court justice deemed that Zündel was indeed a threat to national security because of his connections with neo-Nazi and white supremacist groups. He was deported, taken into custody immediately upon arrival in Frankfurt, and charged with nineteen counts of inciting racial hatred, including denial of the Holocaust, which is a crime in Germany (unlike in Canada). Zündel was convicted and sentenced to serve five years in prison; he was released in 2010 and is still barred from returning to Canada.

As Borovoy concluded, Zündel became no more than a "trivial irritation" but one who consistently exploited the judicial system to claim rights of freedom of speech and citizenship.

MORE TEACHING HATRED—MALCOLM ROSS AND DR. HEROD'S ABORTION CLINIC

The cover of *The Real Holocaust: The Attack on Unborn Children and Life Itself*, by Malcolm Ross (1983), is a drawing of a man throwing tiny coffins into a grave in front of "Dr. Herod's Abortion Clinic." In the background, three men ride camels beneath a cross-shaped star; the caption reads: "Fewer and fewer will escape if we can keep Christians from listening to the Wise Men!" Thus denial of the Holocaust itself is conflated with anti-abortion rhetoric.

Malcolm Ross was a teacher with the New Brunswick School Board District 5, in Moncton. He published four anti-Semitic pamphlets between 1978 and 1989, and concerns about his activities outside school hours were expressed as early as 1976. A Moncton resident, David Attis, filed a complaint with the New Brunswick Human Rights Commission, saying that he and his children were discriminated against for more than ten years, under section 5 of the New Brunswick *Human Rights Act.* Mr. Ross did not have a homeroom at the time the complaint was filed; he was a "modified resource teacher." The New Brunswick Human Rights Board of Inquiry found that Ross spoke of Jews as "the synagogue of Satan" and that he accused Judaism of teaching that "Jesus Christ is a bastard, a lewd deceiver, a false prophet who is burning in Hell" and that "the Virgin Mary is a whore." The board characterized Ross's primary purpose as being "to attack the truthfulness, integrity, dignity and motives of Jewish persons." It also noted Ross's notoriety in Moncton and beyond, given media coverage of his views.

The "almost indifferent response" of the local school board to the complaints about Mr. Ross had become a public issue; the Human Rights Board of Inquiry found "an atmosphere where anti-Jewish sentiments flourished and where Jewish students were subject to a 'poisoned environment...which has greatly interfered with the educational services provided.'" Students testified to the derision of Jewish students, the carving of swastikas into the desks of Jewish students, being mocked with the Heil Hitler salute. The school board took the position that a teacher is entitled to do what he likes in his spare time, and only reluctantly monitored

Mr. Ross when he was in a classroom. A "gag order" was imposed temporarily on Ross; immediately after it was lifted, he appeared on television discussing his views.

The New Brunswick Human Rights Board of Inquiry made an order with a series of recommendations, which were appealed through the New Brunswick courts and finally to the SCC by Ross and his attorney, Douglas Christie, who had also appeared on behalf of Keegstra and Zündel. CCLA intervened; Special Counsel Edward Greenspan argued that Ross should not be prosecuted for his publications and opinions, but that it was appropriate that he be removed from the classroom because of his behaviour. The unanimous decision of the SCC, written by Justice LaForest, was that the Human Rights Board of Inquiry overstepped its jurisdiction on one issue, but otherwise was entitled to make the orders it did.

The Ross case demonstrates provincial human rights tribunals taking action on a hate-propaganda issue by dealing with the issue on its own terms, within the community. Even the consideration of the case by the courts, despite Ross's efforts to invoke Charter protection, resolved the case on those terms.

In the post 9/11 decade, the focus of both hate propaganda and complaints broadened to include Islamic targets and complainants. Controversies—such as the publication, by Ezra Levant in 2005, of the *Jyllands-Posten* Muhammad cartoons; and publication, by *MacLean's* magazine in 2006, of an excerpt from a book by Mark Steyn that was critical of Islam—ran their course through the courts of public and media opinion, and were resolved through mediation or dismissed by provincial human rights commissions.

However, the so-called Danish cartoons furor became emblematic, for CCLA, of a very serious problem with the human rights codes and commissions. Alan Borovoy's op-ed in the *Calgary Herald*, March 2006, called for a radical rethinking of the mandates of human rights commissions.

HEARING COMPLAINT ALTERS RIGHTS BODY'S MANDATE
A. Alan Borovoy, March 16, 2006

The furor over those Danish cartoons simply refuses to die. It has even migrated to Canada.

In Alberta, both the Western Standard and The Jewish Free Press have republished the cartoons. This provoked a response from the Canadian Muslim community that could develop into a legal quagmire.

The Islamic Supreme Council of Canada has filed complaints under Alberta's Human Rights Act. Presumably, the group is hoping the Alberta Human Rights Commission will take action under the section of the act that targets material "likely to expose" any person to "hatred or contempt" on the basis of religion and certain other grounds.

Despite my considerable involvement in pressuring the Ontario government, many years ago, to create Canada's first human rights commission, I regret this use of the law. It's one thing to invoke the law against discriminatory deeds; it's another thing entirely to employ it against discriminatory words.

During the years when my colleagues and I were labouring to create such commissions, we never imagined that they might ultimately be used against freedom of speech.

Admittedly, we always supported narrow restrictions against speech that advertises or facilitates prohibited discrimination in areas such as jobs or housing. Thus, for example, we had no objection to stopping business operations from effectively advertising "no Blacks, Aboriginals, or Muslims need apply."

Indeed, we have long believed such enactments should be read in this narrow way.

In recent years, however, there has been a growing movement in favour of a broader interpretation. Many now see such provisions as a more general restriction against the transmission of certain news and opinion.

Consider, therefore, the sheer magnitude of what could be triggered by upholding the current complaint. This provision of the Human Rights Act contains no defence for truth or reasonable belief in the truth; nor does it require an intent to foment hatred or contempt.

What, then, would be the fate of newspaper and magazine articles that truthfully describe the conflicts in Rwanda, Bosnia, Northern Ireland, and Israel? Some such articles would be "likely to expose" at least one of the contesting parties to hatred or contempt on the basis of "religious beliefs," "ancestry" or "place of origin." Thus, this provision has the capacity to authorize pervasive censorship.

Hardly the role we had envisioned for human rights commissions. There should be no question of the right to publish the impugned cartoons.

Religious prophets no less than political leaders or even deities must be legally permissible targets of satire or even scorn. This is the essence of free speech in a democracy.

No ideology—political, religious or philosophical—can be immune. It would be best, therefore, to change the provisions of the Human Rights Act to remove any such ambiguities of interpretation.

But questions of legality cannot adequately resolve the response to these cartoons. Just because such cartoons must be legally permissible does not make them morally acceptable. There is no contradiction between legally defending and morally denouncing any particular material.

For moral purposes, the issue is whether the material gratuitously offends. Civilized people should not look kindly upon those who inflict hurt when there is no legitimate reason to do so.

Even at that, great care must be taken. Legitimate purposes must not be confined to those which we may like or admire. Democrats must acknowledge and defend the moral propriety of expressing satire and criticism even when they personally don't like it.

Thus, our civilization has acknowledged the moral acceptability—and sometimes, even the greatness—of literature bitterly critical of various religious and political beliefs.

A free culture cannot protect people against material that hurts. It can't even morally condemn the material simply because it hurts. But, if it gratuitously hurts, such condemnation becomes appropriate.

In attempting to spell out the applicable criteria, I leave to others the formidable task of passing moral judgment on these particular publications. For me, the overriding issue is the distinction between legally censoring and morally censuring.

THE "HALLMARKS OF HATE" AND THE FATE OF SECTION 13 OF THE CANADIAN HUMAN RIGHTS CODE

Excerpt from the Canadian Immigrant's Poem

Canadian crazy!
He pay all year,
To keep welfare
running here.

We think Canada
damn good place!
Too damn good for
the white man race.

—Posted on Marc Lemire's website, Stormfront.org, 2004

Between the *Taylor* decision affirming the constitutionality of section 13 of the *Canadian Human Rights Act (CHRA)* in 1991 and the removal of section 13 from the *CHRA* in 2013, the freedom of speech/hate propaganda debate for the most part circled around section 13 and similar provincial statutes. Two significant amendments were made to the section over this period; the first was the introduction of a monetary penalty (not to exceed $10,000) in 1998, and the second in 2001, referenced earlier, was altering the language of the statute to cover communications via the Internet.

The section 13 hate-speech complaints have historically been a very small percentage of the CHRC work, approximately 2 per cent of the commission's complaints and convictions, according to

Richard Moon, in his 2008 *Report to the Canadian Human Rights Commission Concerning section 13 of the Canadian Human Rights Act and the Regulation of Hate Speech on the Internet.* In that report, Moon recommended that section 13 be abolished, and that the focus on hate-speech propaganda be limited to virulent speech actually intended to incite acts of violence, and dealt with only by the *Criminal Code*. He made reference to the commission's "hallmarks of hate" identified by CHRC tribunals after the *Taylor* decision by the SCC. The list—described by the tribunal as "by no means exhaustive"—was composed of the following attributes:

> (a) The targeted group is portrayed as a powerful menace that is taking control of the major institutions in society and depriving others of their livelihoods, safety, freedom of speech and general well-being; (b) The messages use 'true stories,' news reports, pictures and references from purportedly reputable sources to make negative generalization about the targeted group; (c) The targeted group is portrayed as preying upon children, the aged, the vulnerable, etc.; (d) The targeted group is blamed for the current problems in society and the world; (e) The targeted group is portrayed as dangerous or violent by nature; (f) The messages convey the idea that members of the targeted group are devoid of any redeeming qualities and are innately evil; (g) The messages communicate the idea that nothing but the banishment, segregation or eradication of this group of people will save others from the harm being done by this group; (h) The targeted group is de-humanized through comparisons to and associations with animals, vermin, excrement, and other noxious substances; (i) Highly inflammatory and derogatory language is used in the messages to create a tone of extreme hatred and contempt; (j) The messages trivialize or celebrate past persecution or tragedy involving members of the targeted group; and (k) The messages contain "Calls to take violent action against the targeted group."

While Moon was researching and writing his report, the CHRC was deliberating the case of *Warman v. Lemire*.

Between 2002 and 2010, one man, Richard Warman, an Ottawa-based lawyer who had once been an employee of the Canadian Human Rights Commission, personally brought more than a dozen complaints under section 13 to the Human Rights Commission. At least ten of his complaints were successful, resulting in monetary penalties and cease-and-desist orders from the tribunal. But the case of *Warman v. Lemire* brought the crusade of Mr. Warman and the power of section 13 to a halt.

Marc Lemire is still in his thirties. He was briefly a reservist in the Canadian military; he ran once for the position of school trustee in Toronto; he has had a long association with the now-defunct Heritage Front, and with a number of websites on which neo-Nazi and white supremacist material is posted. His Freedom-site website proudly declares that it has been online "constantly" since 1996, and currently hosts memorial material in honour of Doug Christie, who died in 2013, the ubiquitous lawyer for white supremacists ("Doug Christie's first meeting with Ernst Zündel—1984" is one video featured). The site for the most part celebrates Lemire's section 13 triumphs.

In 2004, Richard Warman filed a number of complaints against Marc Lemire; most of them were for web-based pieces of writing (including the "Canadian Immigrant's Poem" excerpt above). The complaints were eventually bundled into one case heard by Canadian human rights tribunal member Athanasios D. Hadjis, whose ruling came down in 2009. Mr. Hadjis dealt separately with every single one of Warman's examples of hate literature and propaganda, including articles and columns by figures such as Doug Christie, press releases from the Heritage Front, an op-ed entitled "Ottawa is Dangerous," and he systematically found that none of this material could be defined as hate literature. Here is Mr. Hadjis on the Ottawa op-ed, which was basically a lament that the Liberals had won the most recent federal election:

> While I agree that the terms used with respect to these MPs are unkind and mean-spirited...[the writer's] remarks do not express the unusually strong and deep-felt emotions of detestation, calumny, and vilification contemplated by s.13, as interpreted by the Supreme Court in *Taylor*.... There is

> no call to action, and the few epithets used (e.g. "jack-asses" or "cheese sniffers") do not target specific groups or invoke historical injury. I find therefore that the complaint with respect to the *Vox Populi* article has not been substantiated.

The article "AIDS Secrets: What the Government and the Media Don't Want You to Know," however, was deemed by Mr. Hadjis to be both deeply offensive and inflammatory. HIV/AIDS is described by Lemire as a "killer loose in the land," which "emerged into our world over a decade ago, rising like an angel of death out of the oozing rivers of body fluids that spilled like fetid waterfalls into the streets of America from the sick and sleazy pleasure houses of the 'liberated' homosexuals." If the truth about AIDS were revealed by the government and medical establishment, it would "have the potential of waking up the sleeping American people—and our masters in Washington, New York and Tel Aviv cannot allow that to happen."

Furthermore, Blacks are "between 14 and 20 times more likely to be infected than are Whites…." Readers are advised to "Avoid all contact with known homosexuals…. Even if you must sacrifice status or money to do it, it is wise to avoid repeated close contact with those in high-risk groups, including Blacks, Third World immigrants, homosexuals, and drug users."

Lemire argued that the article was based on "true facts" and was merely intended to "generate discussion." Mr. Hadjis demurred, and found this article was likely to expose Blacks and homosexuals to hatred or contempt. In preparation for this hearing, Lemire filed a challenge with every single Attorney General in Canada, claiming that section 13 was a violation of his Charter rights, and this became the issue that Mr. Hadjis was required to decide.

Hadjis noted at length the changes that had been made to section 13 since it was declared constitutional in 1990 by the SCC. On the specific issue of the financial penalty, Hadjis agreed with Lemire that the confidence expressed by the *Taylor* decision in the conciliatory impact of the Human Rights Act process was misplaced: "The evidence before me demonstrates that the situation is not as the Court contemplated…."

Section 13(1) now played a significant and more than "minimal" role by imposing both financial and moral sanctions.

The Canadian Human Rights Commission subsequently appealed the decision of its own tribunal at the Federal Court of Canada, where CCLA appeared as an intervener, arguing for the removal of section 13 from the Act. The problem, said CCLA, is one of overkill: section 13 and its provincial counterparts "reach deeply into morality, politics, history and current affairs, in a manner that courts and tribunals have found notoriously difficult to balance against freedom of expression concerns." The amendment to the *CHRA* allowing a penalty to be imposed has resulted in the imposition of penalties in every single section 13 complaint brought before the tribunal. Furthermore, CCLA noted, complainants are not given the opportunity, for the most part, to take part in a conciliatory, preventative, and remedial process. (Lemire testified that he had sought both mediation and settlement, but Warman and the commission refused both options.) And the extension of the authority of section 13 to include the Internet made its possible application unreasonably broad.

In October 2012, the Federal Court upheld the constitutionality of section 13, but declared that the penalty amendment was unconstitutional. By then, the repeal of section 13 from the *CHRA* was already the subject of a private member's bill, which had been passed by the House of Commons. And the case of Saskatchewan anti-homosexuality (and anti-abortion) activist William Whatcott was being appealed to the SCC.

SODOMY IN SASKATCHEWAN—WILLIAM WHATCOTT

> If Saskatchewan's sodomites have their way, your school board will be celebrating buggery too!
>
> —William Whatcott

> In a robust democracy, polemical expression such as Whatcott's flyers may be denounced and countered, but should not be banned.
>
> —CCLA factum, Whatcott

William Whatcott is a Licensed Practical Nurse (once suspended and fined $17,000 for abortion clinic harassment); he is a member of the Christian Truth Activists. Prior to this case, he was arrested twenty times and served one six-month jail sentence, in Ontario, for violating the "bubble" outside abortion clinics (a praying-and-protesting proximity restriction that CCLA had opposed in the past); in 2001, he organized a heterosexual pride parade in Regina that captured the attention of Jon Stewart and *The Daily Show*. Whatcott has run several times for public office, including for mayorships of both Edmonton and Regina. His protests mostly concern abortion and homosexuality, although he also has denounced Mohammed as a violent man, distributing pamphlets illustrated with an image of a beheaded young woman.

In 2005, Whatcott's pamphlets on the subject of "Sodomy in our Public Schools" and others, distributed in Regina and Saskatoon in 2001 and 2002, attracted complaints to the Saskatchewan Human Rights Commission. Whatcott was charged under section 14 of the *Saskatchewan Human Rights Code*; the tribunal found that the pamphlets "exposed persons to hatred and ridicule on the basis of their sexual orientation." The ruling of the tribunal was upheld by the Queen's Court Bench, but overturned by the Saskatchewan Court of Appeal, which found that section 14 was constitutional, but the flyers did not meet the test for hatred. And so, Whatcott made his way to the SCC in 2011.

Whatcott had two kinds of flyers: the first was a written text, and the second was a note scribbled on the classified section of *Perceptions,* a Saskatchewan gay magazine. The pamphlets warned that "if Saskatchewan's sodomites have their way, your school board will be celebrating buggery too!... Break the silence! Sodomites are 430 times more likely to acquire AIDS and 3 times more likely to sexually abuse children!" But "Sodomites and lesbians can be saved.... The Church of Jesus Christ is blessed with many ex-Sodomites and other types of sex addicts...."

The notes scribbled on the pages of the gay magazine pointed out that "the ads with men advertising as bottoms are men who want to get sodomized...." Whatcott's name and phone number were on the pamphlets.

The SCC judgment on *Whatcott* was written by Justice Rothstein. Like Mr. Hadjis in the Lemire/CHRC section 13 case being determined concurrently, Justice Rothstein returned to the *Taylor* decision (which had declared section 13 constitutional) for guidance on how to define or interpret hate, and what the purpose of the materials might be, and what their effect might be. He proposed three principles:

First, courts are directed to apply the hate speech prohibitions objectively…the reference in *Taylor* to "unusually strong and deep-felt emotions" should not be interpreted as imposing a subjective test…courts must ask whether a reasonable person, aware of the context and circumstances surrounding the expression, would view it as exposing the protected group to hatred.

Second, the term "hatred" or "hatred and contempt" is to be interpreted as being restricted to extreme manifestations of the emotion as described by the words *detestation* and *vilification*. This filters out expression, which, while repugnant and offensive, does not incite the level of abhorrence that risks causing discrimination or other harmful effects.

Third, tribunals must focus their analysis on the possible effect of the expression at issue. Is the expression likely to expose the targeted person or group to hatred by others? Repugnancy alone is not, in itself, serious enough to justify restricting the expression…. It is irrelevant whether the author of the expression intended to incite hatred or discriminatory treatment or other harmful conduct towards the protected group. The key is to determine the *likely* effect of the expression on its audience, keeping in mind the legislative objectives to reduce or eliminate discrimination.

Rothstein also returned, as his predecessors did in 1990, to the 1966 Cohen Report and noted with sadness:

> The Cohen Committee wrote at a time when the experiences of fascism in Italy and National Socialism in Germany were in recent memory. Almost fifty years later, I cannot say that those examples have proven to be isolated and unrepeated at our current point in history. One need only look to the former Yugoslavia, Cambodia, Rwanda, Darfur, or Uganda to see more recent examples of attempted cleansing

> or genocide on the basis of religion, ethnicity or sexual orientation. In terms of the effects of disseminating hateful messages, there is today the added impact of the Internet.

He declared that hate speech not only had the power to marginalize a group, but forced its members "to argue for their basic humanity or social standing, as a precondition to participating in the deliberative aspects of our democracy." He gave this example:

> The suggestion that homosexual conduct should not be discussed in schools because homosexuals are pedophiles requires the protected group to first defeat the absolutist position that all homosexuals are pedophiles in order to justify a level of societal standing that would then permit participation in the larger debate of whether homosexual conduct should be discussed in schools. In this way, the expression inhibits the protected group from interacting and participating in free expression and public debate.

And so the purpose of hate speech legislation is "pressing and substantial." But he declared that hate speech must be directed at a group, not just one person: "protecting the emotions of an individual group member is not rationally connected to the overall purpose of reducing discrimination."

Justice Rothstein found that Saskatchewan's section 14 met all of these criteria, but he turned next to the question of the language of the statute. He noted that critics (like CCLA) had found that "the words *ridicules, belittles* or *affronts the dignity of*...lower the threshold of the test to capture 'hurt feelings' and 'affronts to dignity' that are not tied to the objective of eliminating discrimination." He agreed that such expression did not "rise to the level of ardent and extreme feelings that were found essential to the constitutionality of s.13(1) of the *CHRA* in *Taylor.*" Rothstein ruled that those words should be removed from section 14 of the Saskatchewan *Human Rights Act*.

Rothstein was not moved by Whatcott's defences that his material is critical of the "sin, not the sinner" and that the opinion in his flyers "relates to the discovery of truth and sexual politics... [and] are his commentary on a social policy debate...." Whatcott had argued that freedom of expression "does not restrict public debate to articulate elites"; Rothstein countered, "With respect, the definition does not require that the expression be scholarly, rational, objective or inoffensive. The definition of 'hatred' does not differentiate between the literate and illiterate, eloquent or inarticulate. Whether or not a publisher of hateful expression is sincere in his or her beliefs, or lacks the sophistication to realize that prohibitions such as s.14(1)(b) of the Code exist, the aim of the prohibition remains the protection of vulnerable groups."

Furthermore, the impact of section 14 is minimal; there are no fines or penalties such as imprisonment. Indeed, section 14(1)(b) of the Saskatchewan Code "is conciliatory and remedial. In cases such as the present, the process under the legislation can provide guidance to individuals like Mr. Whatcott, so that they can continue expressing their views in a way that avoids falling within the narrow scope of expression captured by the statutory prohibition."

Justice Rothstein did find that section 14 imposed a restriction on Mr. Whatcott's freedom to express his religious beliefs:

> It was not in dispute that Mr. Whatcott sincerely believes that his religion requires him to proselytize homosexuals. To this end, he appears to employ expression of an extreme and graphic nature to make his point more compelling. [Thus the hatred definition] will substantially interfere with Mr. Whatcott's ability to disseminate his belief by display or publication of those representations.

But this infringement is justified. "Mr. Whatcott and others are free to preach against same-sex activities, to urge its censorship from the public school curriculum and to seek to convert others to their point of view. Their freedom to express those views is unlimited, except by the narrow requirement that they not be conveyed through hate speech."

The SCC upheld section 14 of the Saskatchewan *Human Rights Act* as constitutional, once certain phrases were removed, and found that two of the four pamphlets did not constitute hate speech. The two written flyers qualified as hate speech because they contained the "hallmarks" of hatred...expression that "delegitimizes homosexuals by referring to them as filthy or dirty sex addicts and by comparing them to pedophiles, a traditionally reviled group in society." However the scribbled commentary on the classified ad reprints was ruled "potentially offensive but lawful." The court also adjusted the compensation awarded to the complainants; only those who received the two written pamphlets were awarded compensation (of either $2,500 or $5,000 depending on when the complaints were received).

The *Whatcott* decision came down on February 27, 2013, six months after the Federal Court found section 13 of the *CHRA* constitutional.

In the meantime, Bill C-304, the private member's bill that would remove section 13 from the *CHRA*, made its way through Parliament between passage by the House of Commons in the summer of 2012 to passage by the Senate in June 2013.

CCLA testified before a Senate committee on Bill C-304, stating that section 13 had proved ineffective in dealing with discrimination and that "it shouldn't be on the books anymore.... We really encourage countering hateful speech, rather than trying to censor it.... Section 13 is not something that minority groups were already embracing and making use of."

Liberal Senator Nancy Ruth told reporters that she left the Senate "heartbroken" after Bill C-304 passed, because it leaves wide open many possibilities for discrimination based on sex, disability, and age. "This is a victory for hate speech.... It is not about freedom of expression. It's about freedom to hate, in my opinion."

• • •

There is no question that the purveyors of hate speech continue to pluck away at the fabric of our society; as the Cohen Report noted in 1966, "Hate is as old as man and doubtless as durable." When the Cohen Report recommendations were being transformed into legislation on hate speech, in 1969, Eamon Park, Dr. Wilson Head, and Professor Graham Parker spoke on behalf of CCLA to the Senate standing committee on legal and constitutional affairs:

> This issue sets two of the most cherished values of a democratic society in conflict with each other. The right of free speech runs into conflict with the right to live in dignity. Civil libertarians, of necessity are committed to both....
>
> By its very nature, freedom of speech implies certain risks. To generate support for our grievances, we might ignite passions and tempers. In fact our most vital social reforms have often been accompanied by bitter social tension...too much tension can spawn violence: too little tension can prolong injustice....
>
> The welfare of our target groups and ultimate social peace of this country are far more threatened by conditions of inequality than by hate literature....

That final comment rings true almost fifty years later.

In the summer of 1965, messages of hate fluttered down like confetti on crowds of teenagers waiting to get into a Beatles concert in Maple Leaf Gardens; during the World Cup in the summer of 2014, social media messages were infected with words such as "Nazi" and "puto." The methodology has changed; the message has not.

It is important to recognize that hate crimes in the *Criminal Code* include damage to property, mischief, such as graffiti, and that if any criminal offence is deemed to have been committed as an act of hate, the sentence is heavier.

According to recent Statscan reports, 19 per cent of Canadians in 2011 identified as members of a visible minority and 38 per cent of the population of Toronto, Montreal and Vancouver were visible minorities. In 2012, there were 1,414 police-reported criminal incidents motivated by hate in Canada (up slightly from 2011, as a result of improved reporting and public awareness campaigns). Such crimes represent considerably less than one per cent of all reported crimes in Canada. Most were committed by young men against young men, most taking the form of "mischief"; half of the incidents were motivated by race and/or ethnicity (mostly Black), 30 per cent by religion (mostly Jewish), and 13 per cent by hatred of sexual orientation.

Actual hate-speech crimes are mercifully rare. This is

encouraging and perhaps surprising given the attention in media to issues of race and ethnicity, especially in the reporting of international political stories, the reporting of crime, and the attention invariably given to individuals espousing hate propaganda.

As with the issue of pornography, there is immeasurably greater value in revealing and knowing than in suppressing. As former CCLA general counsel Nathalie Des Rosiers wrote in 2010:

> Being pro-free speech does not mean being pro-hate, it means being an active anti-racism advocate. One can refuse to ban speech but must then decide to challenge it and to undermine it. The best way to firmly protect a society against discrimination and anti-Semitism is to invest firmly in its democratic and human rights reflexes. It could very well be that the responsibility for freedom exacts a more active anti-discrimination commitment. There are added responsibilities that come with wishing to live in a free society: one must work for both equality and liberty.

Freedom of speech is a "canary in the coalmine" issue for any government, be it a regime or a democracy. When the right to speak freely is arbitrarily removed, it signals deeper problems; the government that fears its power is being challenged suspends the rights of a free press or suddenly blocks access to the Internet. Such strategies have been the hallmark of authoritarian regimes for centuries. But since September 2001, the so-called "war against terror" has dramatically and dangerously changed the rules for democratic nations, including Canada.

CHAPTER SIX
9/11, National Security, Counter-Terrorism, and CCLA

Sukanya Pillay

> *On the one hand stands the manifest evil of terrorism and the random and arbitrary taking of innocent lives, rippling out in an ever-widening spiral of loss and fear. Governments, expressing the will of the governed, need the legal tools to effectively meet this challenge.*
>
> *On the other hand stands the need to ensure that those legal tools do not undermine values that are fundamental to our democratic society—liberty, the rule of law, and the principles of fundamental justice—values that lie at the heart of the Canadian constitutional order and the international instruments that Canada has signed. In the end, it would be a pyrrhic victory if terrorism were defeated at the cost of sacrificing our commitment to those values. Parliament's challenge is to draft laws that effectively combat terrorism and conform to the requirements of our Constitution and our international commitments.*
>
> —Suresh v. Canada (Minister of Citizenship and Immigration) 1 S.C.R. 3, 2002 SCC 1

In the years following the 9/11 terrorist attacks in the United States, much of the national security discussion worldwide has been framed in terms of striking a balance between security and human rights. Abrogations of civil liberties have been presented as necessary trade-offs in the fight against terrorism, even though such abrogations may not provide any meaningful gains for national security.

Canada is not immune from this polemic. Since 9/11, Canada has been implicated in crises that raise serious questions about the state of some of our core democratic values: *habeas corpus**; due process; presumption of innocence; freedom from torture; accountability and redress; the right of the accused to know and challenge the case against him or her; natural justice and fairness; and equality and non-discrimination. These values lie at the heart of Canada's constitutional order and our international legal commitments and were presumed to inform Canada's actions. Indeed, since its inception CCLA has worked to protect these very values and to demand compliance with legal rights throughout the various national security crises in Canada.

While many Canadians may recall the FLQ Crisis in 1970, it has too often been overlooked that Canada also suffered a terrorist attack in 1985, when 329 people were killed in the bombing of Air India Flight 182. The Federal Commission of Inquiry looking into the Air India tragedy released its report in 2010, with findings on the serious failures of Canada's intelligence agencies—including the RCMP, Canadian Security Intelligence Service (CSIS), and the Communications Security Establishment Canada (CSEC)—to share information in a manner that could have thwarted the attack and the resulting deaths. The lessons of the Air India tragedy and the recommendations of the Inquiry are extremely important in 2014, as we argue for efficiency and propriety in our calls for accountability of national security agencies.

The ongoing Edward Snowden revelations about the widespread surveillance of citizens by all nations have urgently reinforced the need for agency accountability. Mass collection of personal information in the United States, the United Kingdom and Canada, constituting the digital existences of entire populations—and with no accounting of how or why or to what uses such information was gathered—is indicative of just how powerful intelligence agencies have become post 9/11. And although the agencies have increased in powers, there has been no commensurate increase in any oversight, review, or accountability mechanism of these agencies.

In Canada, the fight against terror has also taken a toll on other

* The right of a detained person to be brought before a judge so that the legality of the detention and deprivation of liberty can be determined.

rights. For example, our treatment of refugees, asylum seekers, and permanent residents has changed. Applicants have too often been viewed as potential security threats rather than as vulnerable individuals fleeing persecution or valuable and contributing members to society. Similarly, many Muslims, Sikhs, Arab Canadians, and South Asian Canadians have experienced discrimination and targeting, as they have been unfairly conflated with al-Qaeda and terrorists, which has reinforced unwanted confusion among the general public. Warrantless surveillance and the listing of people on No Fly lists, Asset Freeze lists, and United Nations Terrorist lists have been devastating to individuals and their families and are inconsistent with principles of transparency and accountability, let alone due process and fairness.

Throughout the past thirteen years, CCLA has consistently and categorically condemned terrorists and terrorist acts and insisted that the State has a legal duty to protect its citizens and lands from the threat of terrorism. To do so, the State must have the proper legal tools available. But CCLA has also pointed out that the legitimate ends of counter-terrorism do not necessarily justify *any* means, particularly when it comes to abrogations of civil liberties. In our view, civil liberties and human rights can be instrumental in effectively fighting, preventing, prosecuting, and punishing terrorist acts. But not everyone has agreed with us.

There are many stories to be told of how CCLA has worked to uphold and protect civil liberties in the aftermath of 9/11. This chapter will focus only on a few of the key crises that have transpired in Canada and the role CCLA has played. Indeed, some of the key cases such as the Omar Khadr case are discussed elsewhere in this book. Our view has been that civil liberties and human rights are not antithetical to national security, but rather are "part of the same seamless web of protection," in the words of the *Berlin Declaration on Upholding Human Rights While Combatting Terrorism.*

The first part of this chapter will consider the initial response of Canada to 9/11, with the speedy passing of the *Anti-Terrorism Act, 2001*, which amended many statutes and created new powers and new crimes. A particular focus will be on the exceptional powers of Investigative Hearings, Preventive Detention, Recognizance with Conditions, and Secret Evidence, which after expiring, were recently reintroduced.

The second part of this chapter will examine the emergence of immigration detention in counter-terrorism efforts, including: the use of Security Certificates; the information used to issue these Certificates; the lack of due process and other procedural safeguards guaranteed in the *Charter of Rights and Freedoms*.

The third part of this chapter will deal with the use of torture in global counter terror efforts, how this has affected Canada, and Canada's apparent turnaround of its commitment to the absolute prohibition against torture. The absolute prohibition against torture is a peremptory norm of international law. The findings of the Commissions of Inquiry into the cases of Maher Arar, Abdullah Almalki, Ahmad Abou-Elmaati, and Muayyed Nureddin; the case of the alleged transfer by Canada of Afghan detainees to the risk of torture, CCLA's fights against *non-refoulement**, and the emergence of Ministerial Directives on the use of torture-procured information together suggest a concerning dilution of the commitment to the absolute prohibition against torture.

And finally discussed, is the rise of listing practices and the effects of mistakes on individual lives illustrated by the case of Abousfian Abdelrazik, who—to paraphrase Federal Court Justice Zinn who heard his case—woke up and found himself in the "Kafkaesque nightmare" of being on an international list of terrorists pursuant to the United Nations (UN) 1267 Sanctions Regime.

NATIONAL SECURITY, COUNTER-TERRORISM, AND CIVIL LIBERTIES PROTECTIONS

As the FLQ Crisis in Quebec demonstrated, national security threats often provoke extreme reactions in governments. During the FLQ Crisis, when the Trudeau government applied the *War Measures Act*, CCLA, while unequivocally condemning the heinous kidnappings and murder by the FLQ, was a rare voice among civil society organizations when it questioned the introduction of laws and powers that disproportionately restrained

* The principle means that no individuals can be expelled or returned (*refouler*) to a place or territory where they might be threatened or tortured.

civil liberties. CCLA argued that existing powers of criminal law were sufficient to deal with the deplorable threats, and that introducing exceptional State powers would pose a new threat to democracy. Once introduced, exceptional powers are very difficult to repeal, and the damage done to democracy can be very difficult to repair. CCLA's position would prove prescient regarding the terror attacks that would shake the world in 2001.

PASSING THE *ANTI-TERRORISM ACT, 2001*

Following the devastating September 11, 2001 terrorist attacks in the United States, countries around the world committed to international co-operation to fight, thwart, and punish terrorists. A UN Security Council Resolution (1373), supported by Canada, called upon all States to co-operate in international policing, information sharing, restricting of financing, and clamping down on any abuses of the asylum process. This was done as a means of ensuring that any networks enabling transnational terrorist activities would be disabled. Countries that had previously violated human rights and civil liberties began to claim that any dissent was "terrorism." By doing so, they sought to ideologically transform oppressive and illegal acts into some sort of justifiable "counter-terrorism." On the other hand, Western democracies that had traditionally championed fundamental democratic rights, began to depart from their tradition of rights protection, which had been carefully developed over the past five decades. Phrases such as "extraordinary rendition" and "waterboarding" entered the common parlance, indicating wholesale failure of the absolute prohibition against torture, as well as of due process and fair trial rights. Suddenly, the very framework that had been crafted precisely in response to the barbarous and horrific acts that had threatened international peace and security was seen as being insufficient to deal with the new threats posed by al-Qaeda. The lessons of terrorist attacks in other parts of the world, as well as the effective strategies that respected rights, were ignored.

Canada too, was taking steps that veered away from these lessons and legal commitments. By October 2001, Parliament had introduced an omnibus bill, the *Anti-Terrorism Act (ATA)*,

2001, which was passed with breakneck speed that December. CCLA questioned the many new powers and crimes created by the legislation, as well as the absolute lack of opportunity to properly assess and debate the bill, as would behoove a mature democracy. In hindsight, it is arguable that the *ATA*, through its extensive amendments to the *Criminal Code* and other legislation,[166] contributed to a climate in which the fabric of civil liberties in Canada is somewhat frayed.[167]

The *ATA* created provisions allowing for investigative hearings, preventive detentions, listing, and reporting. It embraced a definition of terrorism that included a motive and ideology clause that we felt was so overbroad and vague it could endanger legitimate political expression and free speech.[168]

In addition to the effect on the rights of due process, CCLA was seriously concerned about the impact of the new anti-terrorism law upon the right to equality and the right to be free from discrimination based on the grounds of ethnic or national origin. The impact of the post 9/11 climate upon Arabs, South Asians, and Muslims living in Canada who were unfairly tainted after the al-Qaeda attacks, is of serious concern. Individuals who appeared to be of these ethnicities were viewed with suspicion, not only by the State but also by civilians and neighbours.[169] In the years following the 9/11 attacks, CCLA continued to champion the need for civil liberties protections as a prerequisite for national security and effective counter-terrorism.

CCLA appeared before Parliamentary Committees regarding various pieces of counter-terror legislation, made submissions to two Federal Commissions of Inquiry, and intervened in important national security cases, such as those of Omar Khadr and the Named Individuals held under Security Certificates. CCLA also held conferences designed to engage and educate the public on topics such as national security; the reliance upon secret evidence and placing of individuals on exclusionary lists, including the No Fly list; and a panel discussion assessing 9/11 on its tenth anniversary.

In 2012, CCLA co-hosted a conference entitled "The Social Cost of National Security," where discussions were centred around the impact of counter-terrorism legislation upon immigration, security, privacy, employment; the dangers of Islamaphobia; government complicity in torture and secret evidence; and the need for oversight, review, and accountability of intelligence agencies. Ben Emmerson, the UN Special Rapporteur on counter-terrorism, delivered the keynote speech in which he reviewed the dilutions and threats to civil liberties in the post 9/11 era. He affirmed the importance of observing international human rights standards in the implementation of counter-terrorism measures. He stressed that the protection of both the rule of law and human rights is crucial to challenging the spread of terrorism.

INVESTIGATIVE HEARINGS AND PREVENTIVE DETENTION

> *The danger in the "war on terrorism" lies not only in the actual damage the terrorists can do to us but what we can do to our own legal and political institutions by way of shock, anger, anticipation, opportunism or overreaction.*
>
> —*Application* under Section 83.28 of the *Criminal Code*

The most controversial provisions introduced by the *ATA* were: investigative powers; preventive detention; and release on an undertaking to re-appear (i.e. recognizance) subject to strict conditions. These provisions were considered so extreme that they were subject to sunset clauses, with an expiry date set for 2007. But against the protests of CCLA and other Canadian civil liberties organizations, the provisions were reintroduced into law in 2013 and are again subject to sunset clauses. As far as CCLA is concerned, the sunset clauses are no comfort. Nor do we find persuasive the arguments that no preventive detention and only one investigative hearing was used. The renewal of these powers, even with an expiry date, threatens to normalize exceptional powers that run contrary to democratic principles.

In April 2011, when the renewal of the provisions was being proposed by the government, I wrote an op-ed outlining CCLA's major arguments against the renewal of the provisions. We were seriously concerned that individuals had no right to know or challenge the evidence against them—which meant these people could not challenge the basis upon which they had been brought to an investigative hearing. Further, the inability to challenge evidence rendered the person helpless to challenge the veracity of that evidence, and also whether the evidence had been obtained from a third State known to use or condone torture.

The fact that an individual's testimony could not be used against the individual in Canada in future proceedings (except as evidence of perjury) did nothing to prevent a foreign State from doing so. Also, the stigma could negatively affect these people and their families both in Canada and abroad. From a pragmatic perspective, CCLA was also concerned that if an individual later turned out to be a suspect in Canada, the State may have disqualified potentially relevant evidence.

Finally, as the op-ed pointed out, "forcing testimony is not a guarantee that you will get the truth." We went on to note that lawyers in other jurisdictions such as the United Kingdom had argued that similar measures were not only undemocratic, but could impede effective counter-terror efforts.

We argued that the powers of investigative hearings, preventive detention, and recognizance with conditions were not only contrary to democratic principles and legal safeguards, they also seemed counter-productive to effective surveillance of crime. If an individual was indeed suspected of knowing about terrorist activities and brought in for an investigative hearing, would that not tip off his co-terrorists? If the individual were indeed a suspect, would it not be better to lawfully gather evidence, criminally charge and prosecute in order to seek conviction and punishment? The whole process seemed full of holes that gave extra powers at the high cost of legal safeguards and democratic principles, with no discernable gain in security.

The detection, arrest, and ultimate convictions in 2006 of the "home-grown" Toronto 18, young men who were accused of a bombing plot, were an example of effective policing that did not need either the controversial tools of investigative hearings or preventive detention. Had an investigative hearing been used, one can wonder whether the members of the Toronto 18 would have evaded justice and remained free to carry out heinous plots elsewhere.

CCLA objected to the use of preventive detention on the grounds that the *Criminal Code* already contained provisions that would enable police to detain individuals suspected of being involved in or conspiring to carry out imminent threats to public safety. Further, preventive detention and even bail-like conditions that could result in house arrest without access to the Internet, would all impede surveillance. CCLA argued that if an individual was suspected of being involved in terrorist actions, it would be far more prudent to conduct surveillance pursuant to a warrant, to collect lawful evidence that could be used to prosecute, convict, and punish anyone actually guilty of terrorist crimes, including conspiracy.

In 2011 and 2013, when the renewal of these provisions was again on the table, CCLA availed itself of the recently released findings of the Major Commission Report, which examined the Air India bombing of flight 182. Retired Justice John Major underscored the benefits of electronic surveillance in countering terrorism. However, the renewal of the provisions—that had expired under the sunset clause—seemed to obstruct this very important tool—as lawful surveillance would be impeded.

The Supreme Court of Canada (SCC)* in 2004 ruled that the provisions in the sunset clause were not unconstitutional, but also that such evidence could not be used for deportation purposes. The renewed provisions in 2013 did not include that caveat. It is also worth noting that the dissent in this case found that the Attorney General had done exactly what was feared such excess powers would allow: namely, that during a criminal trial the Crown had tried, in secret, to use the investigative hearing provision to compel a witness to testify outside of the criminal trial process.

SECRET EVIDENCE

The 2001 *ATA* also amended the *Canada Evidence Act* to permit non-disclosure of "harmful" information, which essentially resulted in secret evidence and even secret trials about whether evidence would be disclosed to the accused. In a terrorism trial, it became impermissible for a trial judge to view any evidence that

* In the case, *Application under s.83.28 of the Criminal Code (Re)*, [2004] 2 S.C.R. 248, 2004 SCC 42

was marked as protected by the "national security privilege." Only a federal court judge could review the evidence in bifurcation (i.e. split) of the trial process, to determine whether or not there was anything in the secret evidence that could or should be shared with the trial judge.

CCLA intervened in the case of *R. v. Ahmad* to argue that bifurcating the trial and preventing the trial judge from accessing the secret evidence was a denial of fundamental justice. The SCC held that it would not strike down the bifurcation process, but if the trial judge in a specific case felt that the accused was being denied the right to a fair trial, the trial could be stayed. It is arguable that the court, while recognizing the importance of national security, was loath to curtail due process and fair trial rights.

SECURITY CERTIFICATES

Security Certificates had been used since 1978 to prevent people suspected of illegal or terrorist activities from entering Canada, pursuant to the relevant immigration laws in effect during each time period. After 9/11, Security Certificates were administered under the *Immigration and Refugee Protection Act, 2001* (*IRPA*). From the outset they were controversial.[170]

Under the *IRPA*, the Minister of Public Safety and the Minister of Citizenship receive information from CSIS regarding the inadmissibility of an individual. Neither minister independently assesses the information, but relies upon CSIS for its accuracy. If the ministers agree that the individual is inadmissible, they jointly sign a Security Certificate. Then the individual is arrested, and the ministers refer the certificate to the Federal Court, where a judge reviews the evidence and determines the reasonableness (i.e., whether to uphold or to vacate the certificate) of the Security Certificate. If upheld, deportation proceedings begin.

Security Certificates were used against non-Canadians, including permanent residents who were suspected of posing a threat to Canadian national security. These people were considered "inadmissible" and subject to deportation orders. If the individual had refugee status, then the courts would intervene to determine whether deportations would result in a violation of the principle of *non-refoulement* (not to "remove" a refugee to the risk of torture, a fundamental principle of international refugee law).

Pending their deportations, five Arab-Canadian men against whom the Security Certificates were initially used, were subject to ongoing detention and in some cases to house arrest that included strict conditions such as electronic ankle bracelets.

All five men claimed innocence. They further claimed that if they were deported to their countries of origin, they would be tortured. The information that had formed the basis of the case against each of them was withheld from them on the grounds of national security. To challenge the case and to prove innocence in such circumstances was akin to trying to play tennis with your hands tied behind your back. Security Certificate hearings were held "*ex parte*" (without the presence of the person subject to the allegations) and "*in camera*" (in private and not accessible to the public or media). These secret hearings were criticized for depriving an individual of fundamental justice and due process.

Furthermore, individuals who were detained could not seek a review of their detention until the reasonableness of the Security Certificate had been determined. This resulted in individuals being detained indefinitely, again violating standard due process rights as well as, arguably, the Charter right to be free from cruel and unusual punishment.

The individual had to rely completely on the Federal Court judge presiding over the hearing of the Security Certificate to represent his or her interest. The judge, in turn, relied upon the minister to provide the evidence, with no guarantee that all the evidence was actually being provided, or that it was accurate. Moreover, the judge was also ruling on whether to disclose evidence in light of national security concerns.

In 2007, the Supreme Court of Canada heard the merged claims of Hassan Almrei, Mohamed Harkat, and Adil Charkaoui in the case that would come to be known as Charkaoui 1 *(Charkaoui v. Minister of Citizenship and Immigration*), 2007. At issue was the constitutionality of the hearing process given that the individual was not permitted to attend the *ex parte, in camera* hearings, and was therefore deprived of knowing the full case against him and the opportunity to give a full response and defence. The fact that the individual was provided with a brief summary of the case, the appellants argued, was unsatisfactory. The information was scant, usually whatever was already in the public domain, and the ministers' evidence was not provided and remained secret, due to national security concerns.

The court found that individuals had the right to the protections of section 7 of the Charter (to life, liberty, and security of the person and not to be deprived thereof, except in accordance with principles of fundamental justice), that this section must provide "meaningful protection," and that national security could not "erode the essence of the section 7 protection."

CCLA intervened in *Charkaoui* to argue the need to comply with section 7 in the Security Certificate proceedings. Standing relatively alone among the other interveners, CCLA argued in favour of the court using a mechanism that had enjoyed success in the United Kingdom; the creation of Special Advocates—security-cleared top lawyers who could have access to the national security evidence and argue the interests of the individual. The Supreme Court also noted that the use of special advocates had been considered with favour by Canadian academics, citing in particular Professor Kent Roach's comment that "special advocates constitute one example of an approach that is a more proportionate response to reconciling the need to keep some information secret and the need to ensure as much fairness and adversarial challenge as possible."

While the court held that the Security Certificate scheme was unconstitutional, it suspended its declaration for one year to provide Parliament with opportunity to legislate a new process.

Following Charkaoui 1, the *IRPA* was amended to provide for the use of Special Advocates, assigning them to each individual's case. Accordingly, the national security information at issue was provided to the Special Advocates. The Special Advocates would be allowed to attend the ex parte hearings, have access to the national security information or evidence, and be expected to represent the interest of the individual at the hearings by accessing and testing the information and evidence.

Because of national security considerations, this evidence was provided to the Special Advocates who would be allowed to attend the *ex parte* hearings, have access to the national security information or evidence, and be expected to represent the interest of the individual at the hearings by accessing and testing the information and evidence. Special Advocates could cross examine witnesses, and they were also permitted to challenge the ministers' claims that evidence could not be disclosed for fear of harming national security.

CCLA continued to be concerned that the introduction of the Special Advocates did not cure all the problems. We recognized the vital importance of keeping national security information secret. However, because Special Advocates were not permitted to consult with the Named Individual or his or her counsel, we remained concerned that the individual's defence was bifurcated in this way between the counsel and the Special Advocate—with each one having access to different portions of case, and with communications between them being constrained and restricted.

In 2013, CCLA intervened in the case of Harkat (an Algerian refugee claimant issued a Security Certificate in 2002), arguing again that the due process and fair trial rights of the Named Individual were unjustifiably restrained—namely the right to know the case against him, and the right to answer that case—and that communications structures should be opened to allow close co-operation between the Special Advocates and counsel. In CCLA's view, because of the top-level security clearance of the Special Advocates, national security would still be protected. The Special Advocate already represents the Named Individual's interests in an adversarial process with government, and being able to communicate with Counsel would ensure fairer defence for the Named Individual. A further guarantee is that Special Advocates and government counsel are bound by their ethical duties not to disclose classified information. The provisions restricting communication, therefore, are an unjustifiable constraint upon the Named Individual's right to answer and defence.

In 2012, CCLA drafted its statement on Security Certificates, later included in our report to the UN Committee Against Torture, on the occasion of its consideration of Canada's State Report on its implementation of the *UN Convention Against Torture*:

> The CCLA continues to be concerned that Canada's Security Certificate process unjustifiably impairs key constitutional rights, including due process and compliance with the principles of fundamental justice.
>
> We are concerned that Named Individuals continue to be unaware of the full details of the case against them, and continue to be impaired in making a full defence. We argue that the introduction of Special Advocates does not cure these concerns, because the Special Advocate is also constrained in communications with the Named Individual.
>
> We are concerned that evidence obtained from torture has been found by Canadian courts to have formed the bases of some Certificates.
>
> We are concerned that Named Individuals face possible deportation to countries, where these individuals fear they risk being tortured.
>
> Finally we are concerned that by using Certificates against non-Canadians, we are creating a second tier of justice for non-Canadians or permanent residents.

THE CASE OF HASSAN ALMREI

The case of Hassan Almrei illustrates our concerns. Mr. Almrei was subject to a Security Certificate for eight years before a Federal Court judge threw out the Certificate in 2009.

The Special Advocates' work on behalf of Mr. Almrei demonstrated the unreliability of certain secret sources and resulted in the Federal Court rejecting the "secret evidence" used against him. The Special Advocates also presented information to the court that had not been previously introduced, and which was relevant to the allegations made against Mr. Almrei.

On December 14, 2009, the Federal Court held that the Security Certificate used against Mr. Almrei was "unreasonable." The court vacated the certificate that had kept Hassan Almrei in detention for eight years (including incarceration for over seven years and strict house arrest for almost one year) and ordered his release.

Justice Mosley's eighty-nine page decision was critical of the information used to renew the Security Certificate against Mr. Almrei over the years and of the information advanced by the minister and by CSIS. He found that there was no evidence linking Mr. Almrei to al-Qaeda; that the minister and CSIS may have relied upon information obtained by torture; and that the minister had tried to link Mr. Almrei to information that could justify a certificate in 2001, but that was no longer satisfactory in 2008 (the year the Security Certificate was last renewed).

Justice Mosley also found that the information provided by the minister and CSIS relied upon non-credible human sources, was incomplete, speculative, outdated, misleading in important areas, reliant upon unverified sources such as Wikipedia, improperly researched, lacking in primary sources, and reliant upon reports containing erroneous information and serious contradictions. Further, Justice Mosley found that CSIS and the ministers had breached their duty of candour to the court because they failed to properly assess all the evidence and information before them, and failed to forward to the court exculpatory evidence or evidence unfavourable to the government's case.

In the case of Adil Charkaoui, the Supreme Court of Canada found that part of the underlying basis of the Security Certificate against him included information from interrogations of Abu Zubayda, who had been tortured—with the result that the Canadian government undertook to disregard the Abu Zubayda "torture" information. In 2014, Mr. Jaballah, Mr. Mahjoub, and Mr. Harkat had cases before the courts challenging the constitutionality of their certificates.

CCLA spoke out in Canada and during the UNCAT review of Canada's State reports about our concerns that CSIS has reportedly provided the ministers with information procured from torture. Justice Blanchard, in another Security Certificate case, wrote that in his view, CSIS policies and practices "do not provide for an effective mechanism to ensure that such information is actually excluded from the evidence relied on by the ministers" in their decision to issue a Security Certificate.[171]

TORTURE

Canada's position on torture changed after 9/11, from a commitment to the absolute prohibition against torture to a seeming willingness to consider (if not use) the fruits of torture in acquiring intelligence information, as well as a willingness to consider possibilities of deportation to the risk of torture.

A FIRST WAVERING ON THE PROHIBITION AGAINST TORTURE

In one of the first cases following 9/11, the Supreme Court of Canada recognized the absolute prohibition against torture, which is a peremptory norm of international law and applies in Canada. In *Suresh v. Canada (Minister of Citizenship and Immigration)*, a unanimous decision of the court ordered a new deportation hearing for Manickavagasam Suresh, a Sri Lankan refugee. The reasoning of the court takes a dangerous turn. It starts by recognizing the abhorrent reaction Canadians would have to torture,[172] takes note of the post 9/11 context and the fact that Canadians are no longer isolated from events in the rest of world, and goes on to recognize that to lose our values while fighting terrorism would render any victory pyrrhic.

The court went on to state, "Torture has as its end the denial of a person's humanity, this end is outside the domain of a legitimate criminal justice system. Torture is an instrument of terror and not of justice." CCLA's position by 2010 when Nathalie Des Rosiers was General Counsel and I was National Security Director, was that torture dehumanizes the victim, dehumanizes the torturer, and dehumanizes the society that accepts it.

The court also recognized that the Charter guarantee of fundamental justice applies even to "deprivations of the right to life, liberty, and security of person" where these violations were committed by another State, provided there is a causal connection to Canada—that is, "where the deprivation is an entirely foreseeable consequence" of Canada's direct actions. The court went on to say that extraditing or deporting a person to torture would be inconsistent with fundamental justice.

However, later in the decision, the Supreme Court opened

a window to the possibility that in "exceptional circumstances" deportation to torture might be justified. The court went on to frame this potential within the construct of a balancing test that would be applied on a case-by-case basis. In our view, this contravenes both Canada's legal commitments under the Charter and under international law. In subsequent years, decisions by the European Court of Human Rights rejected the Canadian "balancing test" of Suresh.

A Canadian judicial inquiry concluded that Maher Arar was not a terrorist.

DID CANADA CONTRIBUTE TO TORTURE?

Maher Arar

Maher Arar is a Syrian-Canadian who, when returning from a vacation in Tunisia via the United States, was arrested by US officials at JFK airport, held for approximately ten days, and then "extraordinarily rendered" to Syria. There he was imprisoned in a tiny cell, and tortured for close to a year. Throughout Mr. Arar's ordeal, his wife, Dr. Monia Mazigh, along with many supporters, continued a highly public campaign proclaiming his innocence and calling upon Canada to bring him home. (The case of Maher Arar is discussed at length in Chapter Seven.)

After his return to Canada, a Federal Commission of Inquiry into the Actions of Canadian Officials in Relation to Maher Arar was constituted and presided over by Justice Dennis O'Connor. After painstaking review, testimony, evidence, and submissions, the Commission exonerated Mr. Arar of any wrongdoing. This case is discussed at length in the next chapter.

The Commission, however, found fault with the actions of

both CSIS and the RCMP, which had wrongly labelled Mr. Arar a suspect in terrorism, and then passed on this information to US and Syrian officials. Justice O'Connor was very clear in his recommendations about the need for Canadian agencies *not* to find individuals guilty by association and to be careful when passing on information domestically and internationally. He affirmed the importance of using caveats, and the need to ensure that agreements of information exchanged with domestic and foreign agencies be reduced to the writing of Memoranda of Understanding (MOUs), which have clear parameters regarding purpose, use, dissemination, and destruction. Justice O'Connor issued a series of recommendations relating to Mr. Arar's specific case, and in a separate report, under the terms of the Commission of Inquiry, made recommendations for a new review mechanism for the RCMP's National Security Activities. This second report contained extremely useful recommendations to fill existing accountability gaps. The report recognizes that post 9/11, because many agencies work together in an integrated fashion, while not all of them have either effective oversight or review, there should be an integrated review mechanism of their activities.

Abdullah Almalki, Ahmad Abou-Elmaati, and Muayyed Nureddin

Justice O'Connor also recommended that a separate inquiry be held to probe allegations that three other Canadian-Arab men—Abdullah Almalki, Ahmad Abou-Elmaati, and Muayyed Nureddin—had also been tortured during their separate detentions in Syria. This inquiry was presided over by retired Supreme Court Justice Frank Iacobucci.

Justice Iacobucci defined his mandate as an inquiry to conclude whether or not these men had been tortured in Syria, and in the case of one of them, also in Egypt, where he had been transferred; and whether or not Canadian officials had directly or indirectly contributed to their torture. The Iacobucci Inquiry was conducted very differently from the O'Connor Inquiry, with less transparency. Justice Iacobucci restricted the access of the three men and their counsel to the proceedings. Further, the Iacobucci

Inquiry, unlike the O'Connor Inquiry, was not mandated to make recommendations.

Nevertheless, the Iacobucci Inquiry made very helpful findings, directed to Canadian agencies, regarding the collection and sharing of information with foreign agencies. CCLA agreed with these findings, contained in thirteen chapters of the Inquiry's report. In the years since the O'Connor recommendations and the Iacobucci findings were made, CCLA has consistently argued that the Canadian public deserves to know the status of implementation regarding both.

Regarding the Iacobucci Inquiry, Justice Iacobucci found that each of the men had been tortured in Syria during their travels in the region, and that Mr. Abou-Elmaati had also been tortured in Egypt.

In each case, Justice Iacobucci found that CSIS, the RCMP, and the Department of Foreign Affairs and International Trade Canada (DFAIT) had indirectly contributed to the conditions experienced by each of the men. The information these agencies had passed on was "inflammatory, unqualified, and potentially inaccurate," given that they knew, or ought to have known, that these men were being detained and interrogated in countries known to use torture during interrogation.

Subsequently CCLA has adopted a number of the Iacobucci Commission's findings and submitted them to both the UN Committee against Torture and the Office of the Privacy Commissioner of Canada. We argued that Canadian agencies cannot pass on information that is not qualified, to foreign agencies; that agencies must be very careful in labelling individuals given the deleterious consequences (the labelling of Mr. Abou-Elmaati and Mr. Almalki as "imminent threats" was found to have contributed to their mistreatment and torture by Syrian officials); and that Canadians agencies cannot recycle imported intelligence without assessing its accuracy. Further, we submitted that DFAIT officials visiting Canadians held abroad must be trained to identify signs of torture and serious human rights abuses. Detainees held in countries known to torture are extremely vulnerable and often their fear of reprisal against themselves or their families can prevent them from alerting DFAIT to torture. Finally, Justice Iacobucci found that DFAIT should persist in gaining access to dual-citizenship Canadians detained abroad, even when the detaining country denies them access.

CCLA also agreed with the findings that information should not be exchanged or solicited from a foreign government known to engage in torture or other serious human rights abuses.

Afghan Detainees

In 2008, a storm broke out concerning the allegation that Canada, during its participation in the International Security Assistance Force (ISAF) in Afghanistan, had transferred Afghans who had been detained by Canadians to the Afghan National Directorate of Security (NDS) and to the Afghan Police, who had then allegedly tortured these detainees.

CCLA intervened in 2008 in the Federal Court of Appeal to

argue that the *Canadian Charter of Rights and Freedoms* should apply to the actions of Canadians abroad. The Federal Court of Appeal disagreed and said the Charter did not apply, but that the rules of international law did. The Supreme Court of Canada refused to hear an appeal.

Alongside the ruling of the Federal Court of Appeal, international humanitarian law (IHL) applied to this case because the countries constituting the ISAF were governed by a Memorandum of Understanding that stated that the detainees were to be treated as prisoners of war. Under IHL, prisoners of war are not to be tortured, nor are they to be transferred to another detaining power that may torture them. The transferring nation (in this case, Canada) has a duty to carry out inspections to ensure that torture is not taking place. If there is a suspicion of torture, then the transferring State must take measures to ensure that the receiving state corrects the situation, or returns the transferees. Further, as CCLA pointed out in its submissions to the UN Committee against Torture in 2012, the principle of *non-refoulement* would prevent transfer to torture.

In October 2011, the UN Assistance Mission in Afghanistan released a report documenting serious evidence of the torture of detainees in Afghanistan. In interviewing 379 detainees, between 2010 and 2011, the UN Mission received first-hand accounts of torture at the hands of the NDS and Afghan police. CCLA again called for the prompt investigation of new allegations of torture, a prompt identification of systemic causes and remedies provided to victims, and for a public inquiry. As of September 2014, no public inquiry had yet been held.

Are We Eroding the Principle of *Non-refoulement*?

Part of the absolute prohibition against torture includes the principle of *non-refoulement*, which declares that no individual will be expelled or returned ("refouler") to a place or territory where they might be threatened or tortured. The principle is entrenched in international refugee law, in the 1951 Convention on the Status Relating to Refugees, but it has also come to be recognized as a principle of international human rights law and the laws of war. As such, any removal of an individual to the risk of torture—whether the individual is a refugee, a prisoner of war, or even a wanted suspect—would violate *non-refoulement.*

In 2010, CCLA intervened in the Supreme Court of Canada to argue against the *refoulement* of a refugee to Romania, his country of origin, where he feared persecution, including torture, on the basis that he was Roma. The case was remitted to the Minister to reconsider, but did not squarely address the non-refoulement issue. CCLA had also argued that the principle of non-refoulement, which had in contemporary law been associated with the 1951 Refugee Convention, had evolved and was also firmly a principle of international human rights law and of international humanitarian law (ie the laws of war), with the net effect that any return of any individual to torture would be proscribed. From 2009 to 2012, CCLA argued that the transfer of Afghan detainees to places where there was a risk they would be tortured, violated Canadian obligations pursuant to the United Nations Committee Against Torture (UNCAT), to which Canada is a party.

In the national security context, we continued to be concerned about the deportation of individuals to the risk of torture. In our 2012 submissions, CCLA argued that diplomatic assurances are flawed for a number of reasons. The assurances suggest a recognition that the receiving country does engage in torture and will create an exception for the deportee—which is tantamount to implicitly condoning the torture or illegal treatment of other detainees in the receiving country. We also pointed out that diplomatic assurances are not legally binding, and that their very use suggests an undermining of international legal protections against the removal to torture and risk of torture. We even quoted with favour the Canadian Supreme Court in *Suresh,* stating that while diplomatic assurances may be used against the death penalty, which might be legal in other jurisdictions, "We would signal the difficulty in relying too heavily on assurances by a State that it will refrain from torture in the future, when it has engaged in illegal torture or allowed others to do so on its territory in the past."[173]

We have also argued against extradition where there is a risk of torture, unfair trial, or a trial that will rely on evidence obtained from torture. This does not mean impunity for the requested individual. Rather, it is part of international law that States have a duty to prosecute an international war criminal and where there is a risk of torture upon extradition, the State's duty to prosecute is engaged. Deportation or extradition in the face of a risk of torture, in our view, violates the principle of *non-refoulement* and undermines the absolute prohibition against torture.

CCLA also intervened in another extradition case—the Hassan Diab case—in which evidence allegedly linking a 1981 bombing of a Paris synagogue to Ottawa professor, Hassan Diab, resulted in France's request for Mr. Diab's extradition. There were also concerns that evidence procured from torture had factored into the request for Mr. Diab's extradition. Mr. Diab has always professed his innocence, yet the extradition judge, while finding the evidence before him "manifestly unreliable," committed Mr. Diab to extradition. CCLA intervened in 2013 in the Ontario Court of Appeal to argue that given the severe consequences of extradition and the threats to liberty and security of the person, an extradition judge must engage in a limited, qualitative assessment of the evidence. Further, we argued that Canada should not extradite if there was concern that the receiving state may rely on torture. As is our usual practice, CCLA did not take a position on the specific facts, but we led on the principle and the correct application of the law, which in this case concerned both non-refoulement and proper test for extradition. Citing the Supreme Court of Canada in previous iterations of the extradition test, CCLA argued that if the evidence "is so unreliable that the judge would conclude that it would be dangerous or unsafe to convict, then the case should not go to a jury and is therefore not sufficient to meet the test for committal." Anil Kapoor, an expert criminal and national security lawyer (and now Board member) who had acted for CCLA several times before, again superbly argued the Diab case for us in 2013. Unfortunately, the Ontario Court of Appeal decided in favour of extradition in deference to the decision-making power of the minister and appears to rely upon the Suresh exception to torture. The case is likely to be appealed to the Supreme Court of Canada, and if so, CCLA will also seek leave to intervene.

INFORMATION TAINTED BY TORTURE

In December 2011, the *Montreal Gazette* unearthed a memo written in 2008 by former CSIS director, Jim Judd, arguing in favour of using information procured through torture, or "torture leads" that are subsequently corroborated in the Security Certificate process. CCLA was very concerned about this memo. We spoke out against it with the media, wrote op-eds, and then reaffirmed our position in no uncertain terms with this statement:

> There have been recent media stories about CSIS considering use of information either procured from torture, or transferring information to a country where it could be used to torture a detainee.
>
> CCLA's position is clear: Canada cannot be complicit in torture. Torture is illegal in Canadian law and in international law:
>
> 1) This means that no evidence procured through torture can ever be used as evidence in a Canadian courtroom, or to deprive a person of his or her liberty.
>
> 2) Canada cannot pass on information to a foreign country, knowing that it may result in the torture of a detainee. Four Canadian-Arab men—Maher Arar, Abdullah Almalki, Ahmad Abou-Elmaati, and Muayyed Nurredin—were detained and tortured abroad due to direct or indirect faulty sharing of information by Canadian officials with foreign agencies. Two Federal Commissions of Inquiry have made detailed and specific recommendations (O'Connor Commission) and specific comments (Iacobucci Commission): CCLA believes the information-sharing recommendations and comments of the O'Connor and Iacobucci Commissions must be followed to ensure that Canada is not complicit in the torture of detainees held abroad.
>
> 3) Finally, the Minister of Public Safety has repeated that Canada will not "dither," and that information procured from torture may be relied upon to "prevent a mass terror

> event." CCLA believes that Canada must not encourage foreign countries to torture. Canadian police always act upon tips of mass threat—for example an anonymous phone call of a bomb threat will result in police first evacuating the public space, searching for a bomb, and—if a bomb exists—deactivating and disposing of the bomb in a safe manner. CCLA believes that the comments of the Minister of Public Safety—which conflate the need to act to prevent a mass terror attack, with a supposed need for torture information—is a harmful syllogism that undermines respect for the law and undermines respect for human life and human dignity—which respect is at the heart of the absolute legal prohibition against torture.

I wrote an op-ed in which we argued against torture and sought to debunk the so-called "ticking-bomb" theory:

> Nor does torture occur in a vacuum. Invariably it is accompanied by a host of serious human rights violations including the encouragement of security and law enforcement officials to engage in brutal, vicious behaviour.
>
> In addition to being immoral and illegal, information procured from torture can also be unreliable.
>
> The US army manual (2006) states that "torture is a poor technique that yields unreliable results, may damage subsequent collection efforts, and can induce the source to say what he thinks the collector wants to hear."
>
> The debate on torture has amplified in the United States amid allegations of "coercive techniques" at Abu Ghraib and Guantanamo Bay. Although many have championed "coercive interrogation," prominent Americans such as Col. Dwight Sullivan, US military commissions head defence lawyer, and Senator John McCain say "waterboarding" Khalid Shaikh Mohammed provided "false and misleading information," and only the lawful interrogation of other detainees provided useful information.
>
> Indeed, history teaches that lawful interrogation is more successful than unlawful methods.

Human rights lawyers have long argued that torture is unreliable. Individuals being tortured are prone to say whatever they believe torturers want to hear, in order to stop their suffering.

In other cases, individuals are trained to provide false information to intentionally mislead their torturers. And in yet other cases, an individual wholly innocent of the suspicions against him or her, may mistakenly be tortured.

Proponents of torture argue that torture may sometimes be the only way to get life-saving information. We disagree.

The so-called "ticking bomb" theory is predicated upon layers of speculation that the individual is not innocent but actually has salient information about a threat, that torture will get the individual to talk and tell the truth.

Experienced interrogators, including retired US army and FBI officials, have dismissed the ticking bomb scenario as rife with flawed premises.

At the CCLA, we believe that our Canadian Constitution, our Criminal Code and our commitment to the international legal prohibition against torture is what will ultimately protect Canadian life and security, and what will always set us apart from terrorists.

ACCOUNTABILITY, SIGNALS INTELLIGENCE, EDWARD SNOWDEN REVELATIONS

Edward Snowden's 2013 revelations exposed the massive surveillance capabilities available through new technologies to intelligence agencies, in particular the US National Security Agency (NSA), and the massive scale on which surveillance and collection of personal information was being conducted. The dragnet use of new technologies allegedly enabled the NSA to collect metadata of mass populations. Arguably, the entire digital existences of individuals are in the possession of the NSA and the United Kingdom's Government Communications Headquarters (GCHQ). Canada was also implicated through its membership in the Five Eyes—a signals intelligence "partnership" of Canada, the United States, United Kingdom, Australia, and New Zealand.

CCLA had long been concerned about accountability failures regarding intelligence agencies. While we recognized the crucial role and need for intelligence, particularly as a means of counter-terror and international co-operation, this does not mean that States, including Canada, should have *carte blanche* regarding surveillance. Surveillance activities must be conducted pursuant to legitimate aims, checks, and balances. Legal accountability serves as a check on this vast power, and is an important component in maintaining public confidence in the use of such powers by the State.

Following 9/11, the importance of intelligence agencies in counter-terror had accelerated, but the increased powers had not been accompanied by commensurate accountability mechanisms. The grave mistakes of CSIS and the RCMP in the case of Maher Arar and in failing to avert the Air India bombing were revealed by federal commissions of review, examining the role of Canadian officials and agencies. In his Arar Commission Reports, Justice

O'Connor had recommended an "integrated review mechanism" that would be able to review the integrated activities of the agencies. Between 2009 and 2014, CCLA repeatedly, in its legal submissions and advocacy, called for the implementation of the recommendations of all three federal commissions of inquiry, as well as a review of which provisions had and had not been implemented.[174]

In our view, intelligence agencies must operate within a democratic construct. The right to privacy is situated in the *Canadian Charter of Rights and Freedoms*, section 8, which states that "everyone has the right to be free of unreasonable search and seizure." In 1988, the SCC recognized in *R. v. Dyment* that the right to privacy lies at the heart of a modern democratic State. Privacy is one of those rights that is essential for other rights such as freedom of expression, opinion, and association to be enjoyed. It is also a prerequisite for true moral autonomy, as opposed to coerced behaviour in order to avoid being targeted. In 2010, when CCLA appeared before the Parliamentary Committee on Bill C42 (re: amendments to the *Aeronautics Act*), we argued that the right to privacy included the right to be free from unlawful intrusion by the State, and that all individuals were entitled to a sphere of privacy around them in which they would be free to pursue lawful endeavours and in which the State could not unlawfully intrude.

CCLA's position was that any intrusion into privacy must be absolutely necessary for a lawful purpose, be proportional and of minimal impairment, be collected only for the purpose prescribed and not used for secondary purposes. Moreover, the information must be subject to strict controls regarding storage, access, dissemination, and destruction, and that these controls would apply to all such uses by and between domestic agencies and with foreign agencies. Further, individuals need to be properly informed that personal information is being collected.

The Snowden revelations regarding the activities of Communications Security Establishment Canada (CSEC) highlighted accountability gaps in its governing legislation, as well as serious accountability limitations regarding the oversight and review provided by the commissioner.

From CCLA's perspective, accountability provides two essential functions. First, accountability is used to determine the propriety of an intelligence agency's functions. Is the agency operating within democratic ideals? The post World War II and Cold War histories demonstrated how excessive surveillance undermines democracy and fundamental rights and freedoms. A police State is one that believes it must know everything about everybody all the time—essentially everybody is a suspect. This is a radical departure from a democratic State, which seeks to conduct lawful surveillance on particular targets suspected of criminal activity. Mass surveillance is difficult to reconcile with civil liberties and, in turn, with a free and democratic society. Further, as demonstrated by the Snowden revelations regarding the NSA spying on German officials and CSEC spying on Brazil, once the spy genie is out of the bottle, all hell can break loose. Not only can the public lose confidence in the State, but international partners can also lose confidence in one another. This is at odds with the co-operation needed to effectively counter terror and to ensure international peace and security.

The second and related function of accountability is to determine the efficiency of intelligence agencies. For example, the failures of the RCMP and CSIS to properly share information and intelligence resulted in a failure to thwart the bombing of Air India Flight 182. The failures of CSIS and the RCMP to properly provide caveats in information they shared with the United States, along with their errors in sharing information with States known to torture, resulted in the rendition and torture of Maher Arar. Mass collection and storage of information on individuals may not actually have any real gains in terms of identifying, thwarting, prosecuting, and punishing real terrorists. William Binney (a former highly ranked NSA intelligence officer turned whistleblower, who resigned after thirty years of service with NSA) has stated that mass surveillance is like looking for a needle in a haystack, all the while creating more hay.

Propriety and efficiency are also important considerations in the context of the transnational operations of Canadian and foreign agencies. In November 2013, the Federal Court released an astounding decision, revealing that, over the years, CSIS had intentionally withheld information from the court when it received warrants to spy on Canadians abroad, and that it would be tasking its Five Eyes partners to spy for them. Justice Mosley's decision was scathing of this practice, and it reinforced for many Canadians the utter necessity of ensuring accountability and protecting the rights of Canadians.

Before the Edward Snowden revelations, plans for a Canada/US Security Perimeter were announced, with goals of "increased information sharing and pooling" and "integrated policing," among others. CCLA was seriously concerned that this arrangement, without review or oversight and with no parliamentary debate, could result in serious violations of privacy and a potential dilution of Canadian standards to match lower US standards. We joined with our colleagues, the ACLU (US) and Privacy International (UK), to draft twelve core legal principles that should apply, the twelfth of which stated:

> Foreign Information Sharing and Mutual Assistance: Steps must be taken to ensure that domestic law enforcement can never use foreign law enforcement to circumvent legal safeguards that apply to the domestic agency. A law enforcement agency must not carry out surveillance on one country's citizens on behalf of another country's law enforcement agencies in circumstances where those agencies are prohibited from carrying out such surveillance on their own.

We also supported and signed on to a set of principles drafted by Canadian advocates and NGOs regarding privacy in this context.

In 2013, CCLA joined its partners in the International Network of Civil Liberties Organizations—Liberty (UK), ACLU (US), HCLU (Hungary), EIRP (Egypt), ICCL (Ireland), SALRC (South Africa), CELS (Argentina)—to bring an action before the Investigatory Powers Tribunal against the GCHQ Tempora program in the United Kingdom. The central claim was that as foreign human rights organizations, we had reason to believe that contrary to relevant provisions in the *European Convention on Human Rights,* British Intelligence Services used Tempora to monitor our private communications that were sent to, received from, transferred via, or processed in the United Kingdom. In 2014, this case was ongoing in the United Kingdom.

In 2013, CCLA also joined with our INCLO partners to support the ACLU regarding the thematic hearing it requested before the Inter-American Commission on Human Rights, challenging the legality of the NSA's Prism program. The hearing took place in fall 2013, and we are awaiting the decision.

CCLA was also extremely concerned by claims emanating from Edward Snowden's revelations that during the G20/G8 meetings in Toronto, CSEC had permitted the NSA to carry out activities in Canada. CCLA has not rushed to claim that CSEC acted illegally, as we do not yet have the full set of facts. Even if the actions were not technically afoul of the legislation, this begs the question of whether the legislation is potent enough to protect the rights of Canadians vis-à-vis the technological advancements and transnational partnerships of Canadians, particularly given that most of these actions take place behind a cloak of secrecy. We have filed an access to information request to obtain any MOUs regarding CSEC and the NSA.

In April 2014, CCLA appeared before the Senate Committee on National Security to argue that the sweeping powers of the Canada Border Services Agency (CBSA), including law enforcement and detention, and the ability to initiate inadmissibility hearings by referral, required heightened and commensurate review mechanisms that could be both self-initiated and complaints driven. We based our submissions on the accountability recommendations made by Justice O'Connor in his second report of the Arar Inquiry.

LISTING

Listing is the process by which governments place individuals on lists that can result in the individual being labelled as highly suspicious (e.g., Maher Arar was on such a "watch list"); these lists include no-fly lists, and even lists that can result in the freezing of assets, and that can make the contribution of any funds to a listed individual a crime.

Early on, after these provisions were introduced in the *ATA*, Canadian Liban Hussein was listed and had his assets frozen and his business shut down. Just as suddenly, almost three months later and with no explanation, he was informed that he was no longer considered suspicious by Canada, and he was removed from these lists. However, his lawyer at the time indicated that his business was bankrupt, he had been stigmatized, and his life had been seriously affected.

In 2010, CCLA studied the Canadian No Fly List—the Passenger Protect Program—and an internal audit revealing that the process for adding an individual's name to the list was prone to serious errors, reaffirmed the concerns we had over listing, recourse, and redress.

An internationally known Canadian case that indicated the devastation caused by listing is that of Abousfian Abdelrazik. Abdelrazik was a refugee and a Canadian citizen who returned to Sudan in 2001 to see his dying mother. While there, the Sudanese government told him he couldn't leave. Over the course of the next six years, he was detained off and on, and allegedly tortured. He spent the end of his time in Sudan in the Canadian Embassy, afraid to leave for fear of continued detention and torture.

His lawyers in Canada had been trying to get him home, and apparently the Sudanese government had agreed to release him, but Canada refused to accept him because he was on the UN 1267 list (also known as the No Fly List). The list predated 9/11 but operated with renewed vigour and secrecy after the 9/11 attacks. Many people were unaware they were listed until they were suddenly prevented from flying or their assets were frozen.

Mr. Abdelrazik's lawyers, including Paul Champ and Yaver Hameed, argued that pursuant to Article 6 of the *Canadian Charter of Rights and Freedoms* (regarding mobility rights), every citizen has the right to remain in or to re-enter Canada.

Justice Zinn, in his Federal Court decision on the case, ordered that Mr. Abdelrazik be brought home, and that Canada should charter a plane if necessary to do so. In rendering his decision, Justice Zinn found that CSIS had "directly or indirectly" requested the detention of Mr. Abdelrazik in Sudan, and condemned Canada's role in the detention:

> An allegation that Canada was complicit in a foreign nation detaining a Canadian citizen is very serious, particularly when no charges are pending against him and in circumstances where he had previously fled that country as a Convention refugee. However, in my view, the evidence before the Court establishes, on the balance of probabilities, that the recommendation for the detention of Mr. Abdelrazik by Sudan came either directly or indirectly from CSIS.

Back in Canada, unable to earn money and grounded, Mr. Abdelrazik still dealt with the ramifications of being on the list. The problem with UN 1267—similar to any listing process—was that there was no right to know which State had forwarded names to be listed, or what evidence had been submitted. There was no real opportunity to challenge the listing, and yet clearly many rights of an individual were affected. Justice Zinn equated learning that one is on UN 1267 to a "Kafkaesque nightmare."

At CCLA we saw an opportunity. We held a conference on UN 1267 and invited Mr. Abdelrazik's lawyers and other members of Canadian and US civil society who had been working on listing, and particularly on UN 1267. In the fall of 2011, Canadian judge, Kimberly Probst, had just been appointed as the UN 1267 ombudsperson. Although she had no real power to affect change herself, she had the ability to review evidence and information pertaining to the case, to hear from individuals, and to make recommendations to the States. We emailed Ms. Probst an invitation, and she accepted.

The Conference provided an opportunity for Ms. Probst to speak directly with Paul Champ who was representing Mr. Abdelrazik in his long ordeal to have his name removed from the list and to hear the concerns of CCLA and other Canadian and US civil society organizations, which had been working and writing on these issues. Carmen Cheung had written an excellent report on UN 1267, and she also participated in the conference. In December 2011, Mr. Abdelrazik was finally de-listed from the UN 1267 regime. (He has sued the Federal government for their contribution to his detention and torture in Sudan.)

Protesters gather outside the passport office on Victoria Street in Toronto in 2009 to demand Ottawa's help in bringing Abousfian Abdelrazik home to Canada.

CONCLUDING REMARKS

In the years since 9/11, there has arguably been a dilution of Canada's commitment to civil liberties. Legal guarantees have been viewed as dispensable luxuries in the fight against terrorism. However, CCLA has taken the view that civil liberties and human rights are prerequisites for effective counter-terrorism.

What has been the impact upon Canada? Outside the parameters of counter-terrorism, if such parameters can be drawn, is there a negative impact resulting from an erosion of civil liberties? We argue that the climate created by the erosion of civil liberties has negative repercussions throughout various spheres of State action.

It is arguable that the G20 police abuses and arrests might never have happened if it had not been for the prior nine years of counter-terrorism efforts eroding civil liberties commitments. Indeed, CCLA board member and scholar Professor Kent Roach has written elsewhere on this point. (Kent Roach, Chapter 3, page 49 *Putting the State on Trial: The Policing of Protest during the G20 Summit,* Edited by Margaret E. Beare, Nathalie Des Rosiers, and Abigail C. Deshman, UBC Press, Forthcoming.)

The G20 protests marked the greatest number of mass arrests in Canadian history. This begs the question of whether, prior to 9/11, law enforcement would have been so emboldened as to arrest and detain ordinary Canadians, the majority of whom were either engaged in their lawful right to peacefully protest, or just happened to be in the vicinity when they were taken to holding cells.

CCLA and its team of volunteers monitored the protests during that week in June 2010. Some of our monitors were arrested and detained in cells. In the days that followed, we helped draft complaints to the Office of the Independent Police Review Director, we wrote reports, we participated in hearings on the G20 in Toronto and in Montreal, and we continued to intervene in cases emanating from the G20 proceedings in Toronto.

Civil liberties violations in Northern Ireland during the Troubles, which included (but were not limited to) arrests and detentions on a massive scale, were shown to contribute to greater sympathy and even recruitment for the IRA. It is important for democratic societies to heed the lessons of the past in which terrorist threats were most successfully quelled by strategies that upheld human rights and civil liberties standards. Otherwise the dilution or erosion of our legal protections—the use of contaminated information, the tactics of a surveillance State, and the massive and unjustifiable intrusions of privacy, failures of due process, fair trial, and the principles of fundamental justice—will creep into other spheres of State action. This can undermine public confidence and trust in the State and threaten to alter our free and democratic society. We can only maintain our freedom if we vigilantly protect it.

CHAPTER SEVEN
The Dispossessed: Rights of the Accused/ Rights of the Imprisoned

As a civil liberties organization, you have to be very concerned about the danger of convicting an innocent person. Wrongful convictions are the biggest stain on a criminal justice system....
—Louise Arbour, interview, June 2013

...Say goodbye to Ashley
Miss me but don't be sad
I'm not sad I'm happy and glad
I'm free, where I want to be
No more caged up Ashley...
—Ashley Smith, from her poem
"My Life," October 1, 2006
(New Brunswick Youth Centre)

In the last weeks of 2013, the five-person jury of an Ontario coroner's inquest delivered its verdict and 104 recommendations concerning the death of Ashley Smith, who died in solitary confinement in a cell at the Grand Valley Institution for Women in October 2007. Three front-line corrections officers and one supervisor were initially charged with criminal negligence in the death of Ashley Smith. Those charges never made it past a preliminary hearing in November 2008, when, following the submission of new medical evidence, they were abruptly stayed. But not before those in the courtroom saw a fourteen-minute fragment of a video presented by the prosecution on computer screens.[175]

A handheld video camera is turned on and a male voice establishes the day, time, location. In the courtroom, we see what he sees, and he sees what three or four other correctional officers huddled around and behind him see, a scene framed by the window in the door of D150, cell #1, in "seg" at Grand Valley Institution for Women.

It is 6:48 a.m. on Friday, October 19, 2007. All four seg cells are occupied: Ashley Smith in #1. There are fifteen other prisoners in "max" at GVI and 102 in "gen pop." There are three "cx 2s" on duty in seg; this is a world of acronyms, euphemisms, truncated words, and severed feelings.

What we see:

In the corner of the cell farthest from the door, a young woman is wedged between a bed frame (no bedding or mattress) and the concrete wall. She is face-down, on her knees; we see only her rounded back—she's wearing a short, colourless "suicide gown," which looks like the smock you wear at the hairdresser's except that theoretically it cannot be torn or shredded to make a ligature. We see the young woman's bowed head of thick, dark hair, and when she twists her head, we see the side of her face, her right cheek, which is undeniably purple.

The only sound from inside the cell is a ragged gasping of breath. Long intake. Silence. Long intake. Silence. Silence. Intake. Silence.

The only sound, at first, outside the cell is an occasional comment or aside from a guard. In the twelve minutes that follow, there will be two radio requests and one phone call to people at some remove from seg on the other side of many locked doors, in or through the sally port, in or through the bubble....

The only sound in the courtroom is silence. The judge and the mother are both wiping away tears. A special constable slides a Kleenex box over to the mother. Minutes pass.

At 6:51, there is a loud knock on the cell door.

"Ashley."

"Ashley."

"Ashley!"

"Ashley/Ashley!" [overlapping] Ashley!"

"Get up!"

"Hey! You said you were only going to leave that on for a little bit...."

"Ashley!"

"Sit up and come over here so I can take it off."

"Can you get it off yourself?"

At 6:52, maybe we hear a single intake of breath, then silence.

Four more minutes pass. We gaze at Ashley's curved spine, her hair, her dark purple cheek; she does not move; maybe there is the end of a piece of cloth visible beside her cheek; we cannot see her hands. The guards murmur among themselves as they watch intently.

At 6:56:50, one guard asks by radio that the cell door be opened. Someone in the sally port touches a computer screen and the door opens.

The camera follows three or four people into the cell. The view is obscured by bodies; there are shouts to Ashley, and chat; it is possible that one of the guards removes a "ligature," then they all retreat and we hear the cell door slam shut.

Again we watch, with the guards.

At 6:58, a guard calls by telephone for a nurse to be sent down immediately (there is no overnight medical staff; they only come on duty at seven in the morning).

At 7:00, someone radios for the cell door to be opened, again, and three or four guards enter the cell; there is a lot of noise—how do we know if she isn't breathing; does anyone have a CPR mask? We hear screaming from the inmate in the cell next door; a guard yells, "Shut up!"; a toilet flushes. We see Ashley pulled out from beside the bed, we see the bodies and uniforms of the guards, and the tape (which actually runs on through turning Ashley over, trying to administer CPR, the arrival of a nurse, and removal of Ashley from the cell) is stopped.

But Ashley Smith has died before our eyes.

She was nineteen. She had been in prison since she was fifteen, when she was first sent to a juvenile facility in New Brunswick for throwing apples at a postal worker. Between 2003 and 2006, mostly in segregation, she was the subject of close to 800 incident reports, more than 500 institutional charges, and 168 self-harm incidents. She was moved to a federal penitentiary at age eighteen, and in one year moved seventeen times, including nine transfers between federal correctional institutions, and she was in segregation the entire time. At Grand Valley, she was on a suicide watch, under Direct Observation (DO), meaning that a guard was posted outside her door 24/7, and guards were instructed never to take their eyes off her. Her death might simply have been buried as a statistic, labelled as a suicide.

It took fierce determination of the Smith family and their lawyers, and pressure from organizations like the Elizabeth Fry Society, the John Howard Society, and CCLA to force a coroner's inquest with a broad scope for inquiry, an objective almost crippled by the intransigence of Correctional Services Canada (which resisted submitting evidence of all kinds), but the outcome was a thorough one-year inquest and a verdict—from a jury of five young women—of homicide, in a document poignantly entitled "Touching the Death of Ashley Smith."

The case of Ashley Smith laid bare profound systemic issues concerning the rights of the imprisoned in Canada, a subject that, like the rights of the accused, rarely attracts the attention and concern of the public at large. Public sympathy is for the most part directed towards victims, not those labelled as criminals. The principles of fair trial, fair sentencing, and humane incarceration have to be fought for and protected; these principles are one of the cornerstones of the work of CCLA.

And while the battleground for this campaign is very often the courtroom, and the weapons are the words of the *Criminal Code*, the Charter, legal precedents and legislation, and the testimony of witnesses and experts, these are not abstract matters of theory and principle. These are the complex stories of individuals—things they have done, things done to them—that challenge our assumptions about what kind of society we have created. The stories are seldom straightforward, and they are often disturbing in some way; the action that begins everything either very small or cataclysmic.

Thousands of these individuals pass through police custody and courtrooms and prisons every month, and we neither know of them nor care about them. But some cases pull the general public into their wake because of the enormity of the instigating incident or the extenuating circumstances of the narrative, and these cases become emblematic. There are other cases, in which the main character is virtually anonymous and quickly forgotten, but the particulars of the case become woven into the texture of jurisprudence and legislation because they change how matters are perceived and outcomes are determined.

In Canadian jurisprudence, there are both extremes. Most Canadians have never heard of the names Drybones or Golden or Seaboyer, and yet their cases matter for some reason. Others, like Robert Latimer, Maher Arar, Omar Khadr, and Ashley Smith, have become talismanic.

These stories cover violations of the bodies and minds of Canadians, everything from strip searches to torture. They are about the loss of dignity and the loss of rights enshrined in the Charter. For CCLA, they raise questions about the responsibilities of institutions like Correctional Services Canada (CSC), the Royal Canadian Mounted Police (RCMP), Canadian Security Intelligence Service (CSIS), and the Canadian government, both in Canada and internationally.

Ashley Smith is buried in Moncton, New Brunswick.

DEMOCRACY AND THE "ROYAL PREROGATIVE OF MERCY"—THE DEATH PENALTY

> It is respectfully submitted that the reluctant, unpredictable and spotty application of the death penalty deprives it of the least capacity to serve its supposed penal functions. As a deterrent, it is wholly incredible; as an instrument of retribution, it is inadequate, haphazard and unjust. The few men whom it kills die for no reason. Capital punishment is inanely sentimental and anti-rational. There exist no coherent or non-invidious reasons for choosing anyone to hang by the neck until he is dead.
>
> —CCLA Factum, Supreme Court of Canada, *Miller et al. v. The Queen*, 1976

> Dear Sirs:
>
> You should change the name of your outfit to "Civil Liberties for Murderers and Rapists."
>
> According to reports in the American and Canadian Papers, 80% of the Public favor Capital Punishment.... We sing about our Democratic Gov't—The will of the majority—Of the People—For the people—By the People. There is no such thing—All that counts is the Private Opinion of our so-called leaders.... Only the murderers and rapists have civil rights. Their victims have none—They are dead....
>
> Yours in disgust, Herbert P. Brightmore
>
> —From Letter to CCLA, April 13, 1976

In the spring of 1975, a man named René Vaillancourt was scheduled to be "hanged from the neck until he is dead" (in the words of the *Criminal Code* at the time) for the murder of a policeman in Toronto, during his getaway from a bank robbery. The accused had come from Montreal, stolen a car, and had this to say: "I drive around the city and look for a bank to rob." He robbed a bank, left in his stolen car, which he subsequently abandoned, and when confronted on foot by Officer Leslie Maitland, he threatened to shoot him and did so, two bullets to the chest. When he heard that the officer had died, Vaillancourt said, "I want to plead guilty now and get my sentence; I wish I were dead."

The defence entered a plea of insanity, and Vaillancourt was subsequently examined by three psychiatrists for the prosecution, without his permission or a court order (for which no legal provision existed), while awaiting trial in the Don Jail in Toronto. He was thrice condemned to hang—by the trial judge, by the Ontario Court of Appeal, and finally by the Supreme Court of Canada on February 13, 1975, which allowed the evidence of Vaillancourt's soundness of mind while admitting it was illegally obtained, noting that "all a court can do is to express regret that no such provision exists and that therefore no Court order had been obtained."

Vaillancourt was not alone in waiting to hang in the spring of 1975. Seven other men were also condemned to death, and by mid-1976, the number stood at eleven. All were convicted for the murder of an on-duty police officer or a prison employee; they awaited execution in Ontario, Quebec, Manitoba, New Brunswick, and B.C. Winding its way through the courts in B.C. at that moment was the case of John Henry Miller and Vincent John Roger Cockrell, who in March 1974 in Cloverdale, B.C., had lured an RCMP officer named Roger Pierlet into pulling them over (by throwing a beer bottle through a window of the courthouse), and when he came to the window of their car, shot him with a .22 rifle. (Miller held the gun; Cockrell pulled the trigger.)

No one had been executed in Canada since 1962, when Ronald Turpin and Arthur Lucas were hanged side by side in Toronto's Don Jail (all civilian executions in Canada were hangings, within the precincts of prisons). From 1963 onwards, the government of Canada, through the Cabinets of Diefenbaker, Pearson, and Trudeau, had consistently exercised the royal prerogative of mercy, and commuted all death sentences into sentences of life imprisonment. In 1967, Parliament enacted legislation that created a five-year moratorium on the death penalty as a sentence, except in the case of the murders of police and prison employees.

Protestors against the capital punishment of Ronald Turpin and Arthur Lucas dispersed in tears moments after notices of their hangings were posted on the door of Toronto's Don Jail. They had picketed for four hours in the bitter cold.

HANGING IS ALSO MURDER
TWO WRON
DO NOT MAK
A RIGHT

That moratorium was extended for an additional five years and was due to expire in 1978. Since 1968, nine murderers had been first sentenced to death and then granted mercy by Cabinet.

But in spring 1975, the case of René Vaillancourt galvanized public attention and the attention of politicians. Support for the death penalty in Canada has always been strong; polls conducted during 1975–76, when the subject was being debated in Parliament, indicated that support was as high as 80 per cent. A majority of Canadians, it seems, have always supported the death penalty, and the levels of support are very similar to those in Great Britain, which abolished the death penalty for murder in 1965, and to those in the United States, where 32 states currently perform executions by lethal injection.

Matters of life and death were on the minds of Canadians in 1975. A month after supporting the death sentence of René Vaillancourt, in March, the Supreme Court of Canada (SCC) denied the appeal of Henry Morgentaler, who was subsequently sent to prison for performing abortions. In mid-March, a petition with 100,000 signatures of people who supported capital punishment was sent to Conservative MP John Reynolds, who presented it to Parliament, where he became a vociferous leader of the pro-death-penalty position. By the time the petition reached Parliament, it contained 200,000 signatures. In May 1975, the anti-abortion "Petition of One Million" was presented in Parliament.

CCLA seized the moment. On April 15, 1975, CCLA organized an "ad-hoc delegation of concerned citizens"—thirty Canadians, led by former Supreme Court Justice (and then president of CCLA) Emmett Hall, to go to Ottawa and meet with Solicitor General Warren Allmand and other members of Cabinet. The delegation brief described the case of Vaillancourt as a catalyst, but made it clear that "our interest in the issue transcends the fate of one man. While we support the commutation of his death sentence, we are seeking the abolition of all death sentences." CCLA quoted international statistics supporting their position that the death penalty had no effect as a deterrent. It was a short statement that made little comment on the case itself.

The delegation—composed of leaders from numerous

religions, politicians, lawyers, union leaders, and writers—was CCLA's first strike at the death penalty. It was a timely intervention; within days, the original date of Vaillancourt's execution was postponed, in order that his case could be considered by Cabinet—this while Solicitor General Warren Allmand frankly declared that if Cabinet did not commute the sentence, he would resign. Over this period, the Cabinet, most members of which were declared abolitionists, took care not to merely rubber-stamp a plea to commute a sentence; each case was considered on merits. Factors such as the (non-binding) sentencing recommendations of jury members were reviewed. In the case of Vaillancourt, two members of the jury recommended clemency; the remainder refused to make any recommendation either for or against clemency.

On May 23, Prime Minister Trudeau signalled that he would be bringing forward legislation to have the death penalty removed from the *Criminal Code*. "On the one hand, we think that laws relating to the protection of the citizen must be strengthened—gun laws, laws relating to parole or conditional absences and that type of thing—but on the other hand, I suppose there is a reluctance on the part of the Government to face the necessity of hanging somebody." When challenged by a student (at a Lindsay, Ontario, high school event) that almost 80 per cent of Canadians favoured the death penalty for murderers and so Parliament should act accordingly, Trudeau replied that a responsible government "doesn't work by public opinion polls or referendums."

In October 1975, three scheduled executions, including that of Vaillancourt, were again postponed. Public sentiment was coalescing in favour of the death penalty. Several police forces spoke in favour of it, and when Solicitor General Warren Allmand announced to a delegation of Ontario police officers that an abolition bill would be presented in Parliament, members of the delegation walked out of the room.

In April 1976, as Parliament awaited the death penalty legislation, CCLA placed an advertisement in *The Globe and Mail*, which consisted of a strong "statement of conscience" opposing capital punishment and the names of 140 prominent Canadians who supported the statement:

> Capital punishment is an exercise in senseless violence. The killing of even the worst killers will gain nothing for society that could not be gained by less violent means, for example, by imprisonment.... We share the grief of those whose dear ones have been murdered. We share the anxiety about the innocent victims of brutal crimes. But understandable distress must not divert us from facing facts.

The advertisement (which also asked for donations to CCLA) generated a vitriolic response from readers, many of whom chose to cut out and mail the advertisement to CCLA with their comments scrawled across it—"Bullfeathers; I am not a sadist. I know the horror to look at the barrel! Do you? An eye for an eye, and we hope it may be yours. Naïve garbage!"—and handwritten and typed letters, some with religious pamphlets enclosed:

> Dear Sirs:
>
> The drivel that continuously spouts from you "liberals" is truly laughable. Like true masochists, you stick up for degenerate criminals by deploring capital punishment. Why should taxpayers have to support crazies like Lucas and Bruce for 50 years? The deterrence issue is a red-herring; the crux of the capital punishment issue revolves around permanently removing from society all dangerous types. Instead of crusading for murderers, rapists and mental cases, stick up for courageous policemen who risk their life trying to protect us from your heroes. Face it, your kind of liberalism is the reason that Canada is in so much trouble.... In response to your advertizement in the Globe and Mail, April 6 issue, I've sent a letter to my M.P. asking for retention of the death penalty and removal of the gun control legislation from the House.
>
> Yours truly, Brian Haeberle, April 6, 1976

While Parliament was preparing to debate the death penalty legislation, the case of Miller and Cockreill was before the SCC with CCLA as an intervener. Bizarrely, even as the vote was taking place in Parliament to abolish the death penalty, the SCC was considering the merits of hanging as a sentence for capital murder with reference to the 1960 Bill of Rights and deliberating on whether or not execution was "cruel and unusual punishment."

The CCLA factum was a lengthy document that reviewed thoroughly both the legal points concerning the definitions of "cruel" and "unusual" and the effectiveness of the death penalty as a deterrent, compared to life imprisonment, concluding that "the punishment of death is not a fit sentence and is excessive in the light of commonly accepted penal purposes."

Further, "Death is an absolute denial of the accused person's humanity…." The CCLA argument relied to a considerable degree on a recent decision in the Supreme Court of the United States, *Furman v. State of Georgia*, a decision that found so many problems with the application of the death penalty that the death penalty was completely suspended in the United States between 1972 and 1976—a decision that, while it did not sway the SCC in this case, undoubtedly had some impact on the debate of Canada's politicians.

On July 14, 1976, in a free vote, the Parliament of Canada passed Bill C-84, which removed the death penalty from Canada's *Criminal Code*. It was an exceptionally close vote—130 to 124. As a result, the sentences of eleven men on death row were immediately commuted; three of them, including René Vaillancourt, had been scheduled to hang on the day that the House voted. The death penalty was replaced with a twenty-five-year sentence for first-degree murder, with eligibility for parole, on recommendation of a panel of three judges, after ten years, and a mandatory ten-year sentence for second-degree murder, the difference being premeditation. (Certain military crimes were still eligible for a death sentence in 1976, but those were removed in 1988.)

But the SCC deliberations concerning Miller and Cockreill continued. The court noted that it was not merely a matter of academic concern, because the decision affected the parole rights of the appellants. The court summarily rejected all grounds of the appeal (articulated by the defence and CCLA) and refused to consider the words "cruel" and "unusual" separately; these words should be treated as "interacting expressions colouring each other, so to speak, and hence to be considered together as a compendious expression of a norm."

The merits of the death penalty were found "not offensive" to the relevant sections of the Bill of Rights, and the appeals of Miller and Cockreill were dismissed. But Miller and Cockreill had been saved by the will of Parliament. The effect of the simultaneous actions of Parliament and the SCC was "a sentence of imprisonment for life for first-degree murder without eligibility for parole until he has served twenty-five years of his sentence." The Act came into force on July 26, 1976.

When Parliament voted to abolish the death penalty, between 75 and 80 per cent of Canadians favoured its retention.

It was also noted in newspaper reports at the time that members of Parliament left the next day for the opening of the Olympic Games in Montreal. And that John Diefenbaker, a long-time, fervent abolitionist, had voted against the bill, because he believed that the death penalty should remain in place in the instance of the murdering of the monarch, and sedition and treason. "I only hope the result will not encourage those who wish to assassinate themselves into history," Diefenbaker was quoted as saying in *The Globe and Mail*.

In 1987, when the Progressive Conservatives led by Brian Mulroney were in power, a bill to reinstate the death penalty was introduced by Deputy Prime Minister Don Mazankowski, over the objections of both Mulroney and Joe Clark. The bill was defeated in June 1987 by a vote of 148 to 127.

An Angus Reid survey conducted in 2012 indicated that 63 per cent of Canadians were in favour of the death penalty in some circumstances. That poll was conducted shortly after a Conservative senator, Pierre Hugues Boisvenu, whose daughter had been raped and murdered in 2002, stated that all imprisoned serial killers should be given a rope with which to hang themselves. Support for the death penalty was tempered, when the option of life imprisonment was added, and support varied considerably across the political and geographic spectrum.

Civil libertarians and human rights activists also have concerns about Canada's shifting position concerning the rights of

Canadians sentenced to death in other jurisdictions. In 2010, CCLA supported the appeal of Ronald Allen Smith, a Canadian who was on death row in the state of Montana, under extreme conditions of solitary confinement and denial of due process, for more than twenty-seven years. Smith is the only Canadian sentenced to death in the United States. He has been scheduled for execution five times, and each time, a stay of execution has been ordered.

Until 2007, the government of Canada had communicated regularly with Smith; from 1997 onwards, consular officials repeatedly requested clemency, on humanitarian grounds, for Smith. But in 2007, the Conservative government of Stephen Harper introduced a new policy for dealing with Canadians abroad: "[That] multiple murderers and mass murderers who are convicted in a democracy that adheres to the rule of law cannot necessarily count on a plea for clemency from the Canadian government and patriation back to this country." Lawyers for Smith appealed this position in the Federal Court of Canada, where the government's position concerning clemency was deemed incoherent, and the government was ordered to revert to its previous policy, a decision the government did not appeal.

Smith's petition in 2010 to the Ninth Circuit United States Court of Appeal for the commutation of his death sentence was rejected, in a split decision. CCLA, as a "friend of the court," invoked international legal standards and argued that "unduly protracted death row incarceration can amount to cruel and unusual punishment contrary to the Eighth Amendment, particularly where the state bears some responsibility for the inordinate length of the confinement."

As recently as March 2013, a bid to terminate the use of the death penalty in Montana failed. The government of Canada no longer automatically makes an appeal for clemency for Canadian citizens but, in the name of "respect" for other jurisdictions, merely reviews matters on a case-by-case basis.

The "law-and-order agenda" of the current government raises red flags for CCLA. Recent changes to Canada's *Citizenship Act*, giving the government the power to revoke the Canadian citizenship of people with dual citizenship if they fight against Canadian armed forces or are convicted overseas of terrorism-related charges, are a concern for the rights of Canadians abroad. However, thus far a review of the death penalty has not been instigated.

RIGHT TO A FAIR TRIAL—SEABOYER AND THE CASE OF THE DISAPPEARING RAPE SHIELD

> There was no question that a rape shield law was required to protect victims of rape from a long history in common law, of unconscionable abuse in cross-examination, the sole purpose of which was to humiliate and attack the credibility of women, building on stereotypes about their past sexual history. But that piece of legislation went too far.... [CCLA] endorses the general approach, the sentiment, the necessity, but as with everything, it's not an act of faith. This bill did not draw the line appropriately.
>
> It was the first time I understood that the real courage is not to take on your enemies but to take on your friends.
>
> —Louise Arbour, interview, June 2013

The common law approach to the admissibility of evidence of a complainant's past history of sexual conduct was based upon two propositions:

> (a) An "unchaste" woman was more likely to consent to an act of intercourse.
>
> (b) An "unchaste" woman was less likely to speak the truth under oath.
>
> —Ontario Court of Appeal, *Seaboyer* decision (quoted in CCLA SCC brief), 1987

The SCC *R. v. Seaboyer* decision was a pivotal and precarious moment in the treatment of rape in Canadian courts. Again CCLA and Women's Legal Education and Action Fund (LEAF) faced one another as interveners on opposing sides. Again the battle was one of competing rights—the right of a woman accusing a man of rape not to be victimized by the trial itself versus the right of a man accused of rape to a fair trial. At issue were two brief clauses in the *Criminal Code* that had only been introduced very recently, and which were the crux of what is known as the "rape-shield" law. In fact, "rape-shield" as such does not exist, and always appears in quotation marks in Supreme Court decisions. Rape *as such* is no longer named as a crime in Canada's *Criminal Code*.

In the 1970s and 1980s, Canadians struggled to bring Canada's laws governing the act of rape into line with emerging ideas of equality for women. As we became more sophisticated as a society in general, as the feminist movement matured, the *Criminal Code* attracted scrutiny and incredulity. Here is what the law was in the early 1970s:

> A male person commits rape when he has sexual intercourse with a female person who is not his wife,
>
> (a) without her consent, or
>
> (b) with her consent if the consent
>
> > (i) is extorted by threats or fear of bodily harm,
> >
> > (ii) is obtained by impersonating her husband, or
> >
> > (iii) is obtained by false or fraudulent representations as to the nature and quality of the act.

This definition of rape conjures up images of Elizabethan disguise dramas in which women are easily fooled by impersonation and tricked into having sex. It also makes rape within marriage legal, and commentators at the time noted that the jurisprudence on rape cases historically mostly dealt with the "problem" of unchaste, morally suspect women falsely accusing men of rape.

Improvements to the *Criminal Code* were first made in 1976, but still a 1982 *Report of the Federal/Provincial Task Force on Uniform Rules of Evidence* laid out the evidence considered relevant to the question of whether or not a woman (as the assumption was at the time) had consented to sex:

> Other acts of sexual intercourse with the accused,
>
> The opinion of a witness that the complainant is a prostitute, and specific incidents of the complainant's prostitution,
>
> The complainant's general reputation as a common prostitute,
>
> The complainant's general reputation for unchastity or "notoriously bad character for chastity," and
>
> Evidence that the complainant "is in the habit of submitting her body to different men, without discrimination, whether for pay or not."

As recently as 1983, before the Charter took effect, in *R. v. Konkin,* the SCC ordered a new trial of a man convicted of rape in Alberta, because in the opinion of the majority of SCC justices, the trial judge "erred" in not allowing evidence of *post-offence* sexual activity by the woman. Justice Bertha Wilson, in dissenting from that decision, referred to Canadian court cases from 1877 and 1896, which had set the tone for the next century for how "unchaste" women might be treated by the Canadian justice system—with references to admissibility of "evidence of specific acts of lewdness and unchastity with men other than the prisoner."

The majority of justices in *Konkin* ruled that the trial judge had suppressed the post-offence evidence of sexual activity on principle, which they considered an error in reading the law at the time. But Justice Wilson interpreted the trial judge's ruling as a demonstration of his compassion—he believed that the sexual activity of the woman after being raped was a result of the trauma of being raped.

Also in 1983, further changes were made to Canada's *Criminal Code* in response to public consultation. The word *rape*, as a crime, was removed and replaced with the gender-neutral terms "sexual assault" and "aggravated sexual assault" in order to acknowledge the larger fact that rape is a violent crime and deserved stronger penalties. Sexual assault within marriage was no longer protected. New language was also introduced to cover the circumstances in which the previous sexual activity of a complainant was relevant. Section 277 firmly addressed the issue of a complainant's credibility, and declared that no evidence of "sexual reputation general or specific" could be introduced to discredit a complainant.

But section 276 was less straightforward. It excluded all evidence of previous sexual activity, except for three reasons: rebuttal of other evidence presented by the prosecution; evidence concerning the identity of the person charged; and, most controversially, "evidence of sexual activity that took place on the same occasion as the sexual activity that forms the subject-matter of the charge, where that evidence relates to the consent that the accused alleges he believed was given by the complainant."

These changes to the *Criminal Code* were welcomed by feminists and human rights activists in 1983. With sections 276 and 277, it appeared that the privacy and reputation of a woman accusing a man of sexual assault were at last protected, and that, perhaps, it was recognized that "No" really did mean "No."

But in 1984, a young man named Steven Seaboyer was found guilty of the sexual assault of a woman he met in a bar, and his case wound its way up to the SCC by the winter of 1991. (The SCC was also ruling simultaneously on *R. v. Gayme*, in which an 18-year-old man was found guilty of the sexual assault of a 15-year-old girl.) Because, in both cases, a judge presiding over a preliminary hearing (not the actual trial) ruled that the previous sexual activity of the complainant could not be introduced as evidence, the SCC was asked to consider if the laws preventing the introduction of such evidence (sections 276 and 277) were constitutional. By now, the Charter was the lens through which the *Criminal Code* was inspected.

The CCLA position (presented to the SCC by lawyer Daniel V. MacDonald, but written largely by Louise Arbour, then on the board of CCLA) was that section 277 was constitutional, but that section 276 was unconstitutional and could not be "saved" as justifiable; that it should be struck down, but that the court should offer guidance on what might replace it. The position taken by CCLA was very unpopular with feminists, and indeed, the CCLA brief made reference to fears (deemed erroneous by CCLA) that striking down the clause would invoke exactly those historical attitudes concerning the fallibility of "unchaste" women. But CCLA explicitly argued in its presentation, and stated publicly, that it would behoove the SCC, in its decision, to set out the principles that might guide revised laws.

LEAF argued to preserve the existing laws, fearing that to overturn them would once again subject women to "demeaning and dehumanizing experiences" in the trial process, that the trial would "trivialize her violation" and deter women from reporting sexual assault. "Evidence of past sexual history transforms the courtroom into a sexual spectacle."

LEAF asserted that the existing laws were "more than fair" in balancing the rights of the accused against the "equality rights of women and children."

The majority (7 to 2) position of the SCC, written by Justice Beverley McLachlin, closely followed the arguments, conclusions, and remedy proposed by CCLA. The fundamental position of the court was simply that "the rules of evidence should permit the judge and jury to get at the truth and properly determine the issues." Only relevant evidence should be permitted, but it is the trial judge who "must balance the value of the evidence against its potential prejudice.... The prejudice must substantially outweigh the value of the evidence before a judge can exclude evidence relevant to a defence allowed by law."

Section 277 was deemed constitutional and was not touched. But the court determined that section 276 "misdefines the evil to be addressed as evidence of sexual activity, when in fact the evil to be addressed is the narrower evil of the *misuse* of evidence of sexual activity for irrelevant and misleading purposes—the inference that the complainant consented to the act or that she is an unreliable witness," resulting in "a blanket prohibition of evidence of sexual activity, regardless of whether the evidence is tendered for an illegitimate purpose or for a valid one."

Section 276, wrote McLachlin, did not ensure a fair trial because the important principle that an innocent person should not be convicted was undermined by a failure to look at the limits on evidence from that perspective; "the right to present one's case should not be curtailed absent an assurance that the curtailment is clearly justified by even stronger contrary considerations."

Like CCLA, the court addressed the fears that older rules of evidence would be reintroduced if section 276 was struck down. "Evidence of sexual conduct and reputation in itself cannot be regarded as logically probative of either the complainant's credibility or consent. The twin myths which section 276 sought to eradicate have no place in a rational and just system of law."

However, it seemed the court was not going to leave this possibility to chance. Unlike other SCC decisions (notably *Morgentaler*, 1988), the *Seaboyer* ruling did not just strike down the law and leave it to Parliament to deal with the lack of a law. Instead, the SCC went directly to articulating very specific principles for new legislation to replace section 276. Evidence that a complainant had had consensual sex in the past could not be used merely to find that she was either more likely to have had sex with the defendant, or that she was an unreliable witness. Such evidence had to apply explicitly to an issue in the trial, and its relevance had to be established before it could be admitted. Juries had to be warned against concluding "either that the complainant might have consented to the act alleged, or that the complainant is less worthy of credit."

The *Seaboyer* judgment is also remembered for the lengthy and fierce dissenting position written by Justice L'Heureux-Dubé and supported by Justice Gonthier. A litany of the history of sexual assault crimes, the low number of such crimes reported, and the significance of ten stereotypes informing such cases led Justice L'Heureux-Dubé to the following conclusion: "Sexual history evidence excluded by s.276 of the *Criminal Code* is mostly irrelevant and, moreover, so prejudicial that its exclusion both at common law and under the *Canadian Charter of Rights and Freedoms* is mandated." The guidelines for new legislation proposed in the majority position were dismissed by L'Heureux-Dubé: "Any optimism that the guidelines will be effectively and consistently applied in a manner that is cognizant of both the objectives of Parliament and the infirmities of the common law is badly misplaced.... They are entirely too broad and support the very stereotype and myth that they are meant to eradicate."

Response to the *Seaboyer* decision was instant. "Court ruling 'chilling' outraged feminists say" was the headline in the *Toronto Star* on August 24, 1991. Doris Anderson wrote in a *Star* column on August 26: "The Supreme Court decreed that our society is now sophisticated, and people are no longer prejudiced in sexual assault cases.... How out of touch can they be?... In our society the idea prevails that rape doesn't happen to nice women."

There were demonstrations in Toronto and Ottawa; protesters reportedly threw blood at the Supreme Court building in Ottawa.

Almost immediately, new legislation was proposed that incorporated the principles laid out by the SCC. There were broad consultations on the drafting of Bill C-49, which was unusual in that it contained a preamble, in which Parliament recognized "the unique character of the offence of sexual assault and how sexual assault and, more particularly, the fear of sexual assault affect the lives of the people of Canada," and stated that Parliament wishes to "encourage the reporting of incidents of sexual violence or abuse, and to provide for the prosecution of offenders within a framework of laws that are consistent with the principles of fundamental justice and that are fair to complainants as well as to accused persons...."

Bill C-49 became law in less than a year. The revised section 276 of the *Criminal Code* specifies eight conditions that must be taken into account before a judge, *in camera*, allows any evidence of sexual activity to be considered, including not only the rights of the accused but "society's interest in encouraging the reporting of sexual assault offences" and "the risk that the evidence may unduly arouse sentiments of prejudice, sympathy or hostility in the jury," and any threat to the privacy and the dignity of the complainant.

The constitutionality of the revisions of the *Criminal Code* was affirmed unanimously by the SCC in 2000 in *R. v. Darrach*, a decision written by Justice Gonthier. (Louise Arbour was by this time on the SCC.)

There is recognition by both feminists and civil libertarians that the revised law is far stronger than the earlier law. But recently, first in 2010 and again in January 2014, there have been murmurings in the Conservative caucus in Parliament about whether or not the word "rape" should be reintroduced into the *Criminal Code*, along with very heavy mandatory minimum sentences.

RIGHT TO A FAIR SENTENCE—ROBERT LATIMER, "SALT OF THE EARTH"—"I STILL FEEL THAT WHAT I DID WAS RIGHT"

> [Our] community must be sufficiently humane to recognize extenuating circumstances when they arise. *This is not to treat disabled people as other than human; it is to treat Robert Latimer as other than criminal.*
>
> —CCLA Letter to Alan Rock, November 1994

"This was on 24th October, right?"

"Uh-huh."

"Did you give her any pills or medication?"

"No."

"You mentioned earlier, you put a hose in the truck."

"Uh-huh."

"Tell me again which window you put it through."

"The rear sliding window."

"Where was the end of the hose?"

"Sticking a foot or two inside. Towards the driver's side, up to the roof."

"Bob, could you see any fumes or gases coming out of the end of the hose?"

"It fogged up the windows."

"Bob, did she vomit or salivate, anything like that?"

"No." [Shakes head]

"She just went to sleep?"

"She jerked three or four times. She's had worse seizures. I thought, if she cried, I'd pull her out. She didn't."

"You didn't want to see her suffer?"

[Shakes head]

"And what happened was exactly as you hoped it would."

"Uh-huh."

"Can you tell us how you feel now that Tracy is dead?"

"It's better. Soon as Laura saw her she was happy for her. She was loose. She was always stiff and in pain. She was always awake and in pain."

—From Statement of Robert William Latimer
Taken November 4,1993 09:35 hrs.
North Battleford, Saskatchewan Sub/Div.

Robert Latimer is described as a "salt of the earth" kind of guy. He and his wife, Laura, have a canola and wheat farm west of Saskatoon. Between 1980 and 1993, they had four children. The first child was Tracy, born in 1980; as a result of oxygen deprivation during delivery, she was born clinically dead and suffered from brain damage and cerebral palsy. Tracy's cerebral palsy was rare in that it involved her full body. She had seizures every day, had the mental capacity of a three-month-old baby, could laugh and cry but understood no words. She recognized family members but not her own name. She had no control over her body or bodily functions and was in constant pain. Her spine eventually curved more than 73 degrees. As described by Chief Justice Edward Bayda, who dissented in the first Saskatchewan Court of Appeal decision against Latimer (1995):

> She could sit up in a wheel chair. During the last five years of her life she could not roll over as a normal baby of two or three months old can. The muscles of her body simply

> could not be controlled by her brain. They tightened when they should not. As a result, her body became "twisted up." To relieve the tension of certain muscles and the pain the tension produced, Tracy underwent a number of serious operations to have muscles cut: the muscles at the top of her legs (so her hips would not dislocate), her toes, her heel chords, knee muscles and so on. During one surgery, stainless steel rods were put on either side of her spine to straighten her body sufficiently to relieve the cramping of her stomach and her lungs.

The Latimers cared for Tracy at home. During the summer of 1993, because Laura Latimer was pregnant with her fourth child, delivered in August, Tracy was sent to a group home for three months. When she came home, at age thirteen, she weighed just eighteen kilograms (forty pounds). Her attending physician told the Latimers, on October 12, 1993, that another surgery was required in order to break Tracy's right hip, and that recuperation from the surgery would be extremely painful and could take one year. The surgery was scheduled for November 4. Also on October 12, the Latimers were contacted by a group home that offered residency for Tracy. As Chief Justice Bayda noted, "The social worker who worked on Tracy's case offered, in effect, to place Tracy in a nursing home. The appellant obviously reasoned that while it may relieve him and the family from having to care for Tracy in the family home, the placement in the nursing home would not relieve her pain. The appellant therefore declined the offer of a placement."

Robert Latimer would later say that it was on this day that he decided to end the life of his daughter, which he did on October 24. Latimer tried to make it look as if Tracy had died in her sleep, but an autopsy revealed that her blood was "saturated" with carbon monoxide. On November 4, Robert Latimer was taken in for questioning and subsequently charged with first-degree murder.

> Everyone has the right to life, liberty and security of the person and the right not to be deprived thereof except in accordance with the principles of fundamental justice.
>
> —Section 7, *Charter of Rights and Freedoms*, 1982

The death of Tracy Latimer was bookended by the very public latter stages of the life and death of Sue Rodriguez. Sue Rodriguez suffered from amyotrophic lateral sclerosis (ALS), a debilitating, terminal disease, and at age forty-two, with a life expectancy of between two and fourteen months, Rodriguez wanted to decide the time and method of her death, with the help of a physician. "Whose body is this?" she famously said. While suicide is not a crime in Canada, section 241(b) of the *Criminal Code* makes it a criminal offence to assist a person to commit suicide. Rodriguez argued that a terminally ill and hence severely disabled person, whose life had become unbearable and who was in a weakened state, would be unable to commit suicide. After the Supreme Court of British Columbia dismissed her application to declare s.241(b) invalid under the *Canadian Charter of Rights and Freedoms*, and after the B.C. Court of Appeal agreed, Ms. Rodriguez appealed to the SCC.

The SCC was very much divided on the Rodriguez appeal; it was a 5 to 4 decision to uphold the law prohibiting assisted death, with several justices writing separate dissenting opinions. The decision was delivered on September 30, 1993. Tracy Latimer was killed by her father on October 24, 1993. On February 12, 1994, Sue Rodriguez died, with the help of a doctor and a friend.

There were many differences between the cases of Robert Latimer and Sue Rodriguez—Rodriguez was terminally ill, Tracy Latimer was severely disabled; Rodriguez was applying for the right to an assisted death; the decisions concerning Tracy Latimer's life and death were made by her father. But they both circled around the issue of the rights of the disabled, and they both engaged the feelings of Canadians, on one side or the other of the euthanasia/assisted suicide discussion, a debate that returns to the SCC in the near future—the SCC announced in January 2014 that it would hear appeals relating to the cases of Gloria Taylor and Lee Carter.

The *Rodriguez* decision raised the spectre of possible dangers if any changes were made to the absolute prohibition of assisted suicide in the *Criminal Code*—"the concerns about abuse and the great difficulty in creating appropriate safeguards." And the death of Tracy Latimer at the hand of her father was seen by many activists for the rights of the disabled as proof that such fears were well-founded.

On November 16, 1994, in Battleford, Saskatchewan, a jury found Robert Latimer guilty of second-degree murder. When asked if he had anything to say on hearing the verdict, Latimer said, "I still feel that what I did was right." Presiding Justice C.R. Wimmer replied:

> There is no joy in this for anyone. I know you believe you did the right thing and many people will agree with it; however, the criminal law is unremitting when it comes to the taking of human life for whatever reason. Life was not kind to Tracy but it was a life that was hers to make of what she could. I am left with no option but to order that you be sentenced to imprisonment for life without eligibility for parole until you have served ten years of the sentence.

Immediately there were calls from across the country for leniency, editorials and op-eds, a petition to Parliament.

> November 18, 1994
> His Excellency, the Governor General,
> The Honourable Ray Hnatyshyn
> Rideau Hall
> 1 Sussex Drive
> Ottawa, Ontario
> K1A 0A1
>
> Your Excellency
>
> We, the undersigned, minister and members of Saint James United Church, Antigonish, Nova Scotia, earnestly petition you to grant speedily a conditional pardon to Mister Robert Latimer, of Wilkie, Saskatchewan.

We fully affirm the sanctity of human life, and recognize the gravity of taking a life. Nevertheless, we believe that the verdict and the sentence given to Mister Latimer are entirely unjust. When one compares the punishment meted out to Mister Latimer with that usually given to the perpetrators of such truly horrible crimes as multiple child abuse, multiple rapes, wife battering, kidnapping and extortion, criminal manslaughter while under the influence of alcohol or drugs, and any number of so-called "white collar crimes," it is immediately and inescapably apparent that Mister Latimer has not received justice from Her Majesty's government in Canada.

We therefore petition you, acting through the Cabinet of Her Majesty's government in Canada, to grant a conditional pardon to Mister Latimer as swiftly as it may be possible.

Yours sincerely,

The Reverend Glenn Ashford, Minister,...

Members [of the congregation]

30 November 1994
BY FAX
The Honourable Allan Rock
Attorney General for Canada

Dear Sir:

The Canadian Civil Liberties Association urges you to take the necessary steps immediately to commute the life sentence imposed upon Robert Latimer for the compassionate killing of his severely disabled 12-year-old daughter Tracy.

To do what we ask would injure no legitimate public interest. No matter what the outcome of the current euthanasia debate, such mercy for Mr. Latimer would not require—and should not precipitate—the legalization of what he did.

Thus, the risk of heavy criminal sanctions would continue to threaten those who contemplate any future homicide.

But our community must be sufficiently humane to recognize extenuating circumstances when they arise. *This is not to treat disabled people as other than human; it is to treat Robert Latimer as other than criminal.*

We ask also that you move to abolish these mandatory and minimum sentences that do not even allow for exceptional circumstances. They are not needed. The overwhelming number of murderers and perpetrators of serious violence will receive substantial punishment, in any event. But these mandatory and minimum sentences deprive society of the flexibility it needs to deal appropriately with exceptional cases such as this one.

Please act at once. Do not let this family endure another moment of needless suffering.

Sincerely,
A. Alan Borovoy
General Counsel

Over the next twenty years, with reference to Robert Latimer and others, CCLA would repeatedly make the argument for the abolishment of mandatory and minimum sentences.

The case of Robert Latimer was heard in the Saskatchewan Court of Appeal in 1995; that court upheld the sentence and found that the judge had made no errors in allowing Latimer's November 4th statement (at which time he repeatedly declined the suggestion that he might want to call a lawyer). The majority opinion stressed the significance of Latimer's "intention" to kill Tracy, and did not accept the argument of Latimer's counsel that a "constitutional exemption" on sentencing might apply.

A permanent marker on the play was laid down in a sustained dissenting opinion, from the Saskatchewan chief justice at the time, Edward Bayda, who wrote at length about the benign character of Robert Latimer and the "gentle, painless and compassionate

way" in which he killed his daughter. Bayda catalogued cases in which mercy had been granted, and included in the judgment examples of what he described as "widespread public outrage in the nation." He noted the recommendations of a recent Senate Special Committee on Assisted Suicide and Euthanasia (prompted by the death of Rodriguez) for a "third category" of murder, one that would not command a mandatory sentence, or something that might be labelled "compassionate homicide."

Chief Justice Bayda strongly endorsed the notion of a constitutional exemption in this circumstance that he describes as "cruel and unusual punishment," an argument also made by dissenting justices in the Rodriguez case. He also addressed the question of the respective roles of Parliament, the executive (Cabinet), and the judiciary, and made the following comment about the Charter:

> It is said that if the law does not reflect the public's thinking in the sphere of compassionate killings it is Parliament's role to do what is necessary to determine that thinking and

translate it into law. The Court should not meddle in that role. I do not disagree. But that is not what granting a constitutional exemption in this case is about. In that respect I echo the sentiments of McLachlin J. in Rodriguez at 628–9.

The underlying purpose for enacting the Charter of Rights was to grant to an individual offended by the excesses of either the legislative or executive branches of government relief from those excesses. Cast in the role of "grantor of relief" is the third branch of government, the judiciary.

Latimer's first trip to the SCC was brief. There were no interveners. The court unanimously upheld the decisions of the trial judge and the Saskatchewan Court of Appeal. However, it was revealed that there had been jury tampering in the original trial, and a second trial was ordered. The second jury also found Latimer guilty of second-degree murder, but Justice Ted Noble chose to make several radical departures in determining the sentence, perhaps choosing to be deliberately provocative.

First, Justice Noble declared, with reference to the Charter, that a sentence of life imprisonment without the prospect of parole for ten years would constitute "cruel and unusual punishment" in these circumstances. He decided to grant a constitutional exemption, over the objections of Crown counsel, who stated that he was not entitled to do so, as that option had already been determined inappropriate by the Saskatchewan Court of Appeal in 1995. He argued that that decision did not apply, because of the differences between the two trials—what he identified as new evidence concerning Mr. Latimer's motives: he had acted out of compassion, because of Tracy's extreme pain, not because she was disabled.

Justice Noble also took into account the jury's recommendation concerning parole and sentenced Latimer to one year in prison, followed by one year on parole.

The Saskatchewan Court of Appeal in 1998 (a different panel of judges) made short shrift of both Justice Noble's actions (appealed by the Saskatchewan Attorney General) and Latimer's appeal (on grounds similar to his first appeal) in a unanimous decision (the tone of which is notably disdainful): "At the outset, we may say that in our respectful opinion the learned trial judge took

KRIEGER © 2001
The Province
SUPREME COURT
OF CANADA
MERCY

too much upon himself in bypassing the judgment of this Court, the direction of Parliament, and the executive power of clemency referred to in section 748 of the *Criminal Code*."

The defence of necessity was not relevant, because of the facts that "Latimer's life was not in peril, he had not acted involuntarily and that he had the option of placing Tracy in a group home if he could no longer stand to care for her." They reiterated the decision of the first court of appeal, that "Mr. Latimer is answerable for the inexcusable murder of Tracy Latimer, a murder that has been classified by Parliament, for sentencing purposes, as second-degree," and reaffirmed that the sentence was not cruel and unusual punishment.

"THREE QUARTERS (73 PER CENT) OF CANADIANS BELIEVE ROBERT LATIMER ENDED HIS DAUGHTER'S LIFE OUT OF COMPASSION AND SHOULD RECEIVE A MORE LENIENT SENTENCE" (IPSOS REID POLL, JANUARY 1999)

In 2001, Latimer's case was once again before the Supreme Court of Canada, this time with ten interveners, including several advocates for the disabled, religious organizations (Catholic and Evangelical), the Christian Medical and Dental Society, the Canadian AIDS Society, and CCLA.

CCLA's brief, presented to the court by Kent Roach (who discusses it in Chapter Two of this book), focused on the question of constitutional exemption, and the issue of cruel and unusual punishment. CCLA argued, with reference to section 12 of the Charter (which protects the right not to be subjected to cruel and unusual punishment), for "an individualized analysis of the effects of punishment on Mr. Latimer given the gravity and particular circumstances of his offence and his personal characteristics." Not only must there be "societal justifications" for imposing such punishment, but the penalty must be examined "from the perspective of the person actually subjected to it." Factors include "the degree of the offender's responsibility.... Canada has never embraced a simplistic and punitive notion of just deserts that ties punishment automatically to the offence committed."

Furthermore, while motive is not a factor in determining

whether or not a crime has been committed, it is relevant to sentencing: "The irrelevance of motive is an accepted principle of criminal liability. It is not, however, an accepted principle of sentencing which is an inherently individualized process tied to the particular circumstances of crimes and offenders."

CCLA referred to the dissenting opinion of Chief Justice Bayda in 1995 to comment on the "gross disproportionality" of mandatory sentences and "the fact that others who have killed to end the pain of a loved one have been convicted but received no imprisonment. The disparity outlined in Chief Justice Bayda's dissent in the first appeal is gross and shocking. . . ." On the question of precedent and example, CCLA quoted its own general counsel, Alan Borovoy: "[There] is simply no basis to believe that leniency shown here will open the floodgates."

The recommendation of CCLA was that the mandatory sentence of life imprisonment be struck down or, alternatively, that a constitutional exemption be allowed.

The SCC (seven justices, five of whom were on both the *Rodriguez* and the first *Latimer* decisions) in its 2001 decision stood firmly with the Saskatchewan Court of Appeal. They described Latimer's actions as "an error in judgment":

> Tracy's proposed surgery did not pose an imminent threat to her life, nor did her medical condition. In fact, Tracy's health might have improved had the Latimers not rejected the option of relying on a feeding tube. Tracy's situation was not an emergency. The appellant can be reasonably expected to have understood that reality. There was no evidence of a legitimate psychological condition that rendered him unable to perceive that there was no imminent peril. The appellant argued that, for him, further surgery *did* amount to imminent peril. It was not reasonable for the appellant to form this belief, particularly when better pain management was available.

With reference to the trial judge's deference to the opinion of the jury concerning sentencing, the SCC stood equally strongly against the practice of "jury nullification," which was used repeatedly when Henry Morgentaler faced juries, in several jurisdictions—in spite of compelling evidence that someone has broken existing laws, the jury exercises the option to return a verdict of not guilty. While admitting that "this Court" had elsewhere described jury nullification as a safety valve—"the citizen's ultimate protection against oppressive laws and the oppressive enforcement of the law"—the court rejected this strategy as an actual right: "How could there be any such 'right'? As a matter of logic and principle, the law cannot encourage jury nullification."

Nor did the court find the mitigating circumstances sufficiently compelling—"Considered together we cannot find that the personal characteristics and particular circumstances of this case displace the serious gravity of this offence"—or that it was the court's role to dispense mercy, the "royal prerogative":

> But the prerogative is a matter for the executive, not the courts. The executive will undoubtedly, if it chooses to consider the matter, examine all of the underlying circumstances surrounding the tragedy of Tracy Latimer that took place on October 24, 1993, some seven years ago. Since that time Mr. Latimer has undergone two trials and two appeals to the Court of Appeal for Saskatchewan and this Court, with attendant publicity and consequential agony for him and his family.

Robert Latimer served his sentence of ten years, and when he first became eligible for day parole, in 2007, he was turned down by the parole board because he showed no signs of remorse. That decision was appealed; Alan Borovoy said, "The board appears to require that he engage in a ritual of contrition...its role is not to brainwash the prisoners but rather to assess whether they would pose a risk to the safety of society." In 2010, Latimer was granted full parole, with conditions that are gradually becoming less stringent. He has refused to consider an appeal for clemency, because to do so would be to admit that he had done wrong, and Latimer still does not believe that he was wrong to kill his child.

CCLA argued for clemency for Latimer, despite his own disinclination to apply. In 2005, CCLA sent a delegation to then Minister of Justice Irwin Cotler, to argue for the abolishment of mandatory and minimum sentences, citing in its brief Latimer's case as "the most poignant example of the evil in minimum sentences":

> It is not necessary to excuse mercy killings in general or Robert Latimer in particular to be outraged by the punishment he is currently suffering. The greatest number of second-degree murders are motivated by hate, greed, or at least selfishness. It is palpably unfair for a compassionate father who misbehaves out of love to receive the same penalty as, for example, a malevolent robber who misbehaves out of greed. Significantly, a nation-wide poll found that support for clemency was more than 70 percent and more than 60,000 Canadians have signed a CCLA petition urging both a substantially reduced penalty for Mr. Latimer and the repeal of all mandatory minimum sentences.

The subject of mandatory minimums has returned to public discourse recently because of the Conservative government's "tough on crime" agenda, and its 2012 Omnibus Bill C-10, the *Safe Streets and Communities Act,* which introduced a number of measures including new and increased mandatory minimum sentences, increased pretrial detention measures, and new criminal offences. (Other aspects of the omnibus bill affect immigrants, refugees, and Canadians detained outside Canada.) CCLA described this bill as "unwise, unjust, and unconstitutional" and has detailed not only the specific clauses of the bill that are unconstitutional, but also the ways in which the "tough on crime" agenda will have a damaging impact on what are already perilous conditions in Canada's prisons.

CCLA presented a comprehensive brief in October 2011 to the House of Commons Standing Committee on Justice and Human Rights in its consultations concerning Bill C-10, and also intervened in two Ontario Court of Appeal cases dealing with the mandatory minimum sentence for possession of prohibited firearms. CCLA made the arguments in an op-ed: Not only are minimum mandatory sentences objectionable because they are ineffective, expensive, and take authority and judgment away from judges, they are also wrong on "moral and philosophical grounds." The op-ed continued:

> Minimum sentences disembody the crime: They make the offender, his or her context, personality, upbringing, intellect, morality or addiction, irrelevant. It matters not that the person was coerced by family members into participating in a grow-op operation, it matters not that she did not understand the implications of her actions, that he was addicted, that she was desperate to provide food for her children, that he has since changed his life around. Minimum sentences impose punishment in a vacuum, mechanically, as though offences and crimes were committed by automatons. Minimum sentences also sideline victims, placing the focus squarely on the act, rather than the circumstances of the individuals—both victim and offender—that are involved.... The whole enterprise of stripping the justice system of its capacity to individualize sentencing is fundamentally flawed: it undermines our sense of fairness and morality, taking us back to the alluring but barbarous simplicity of "an eye for an eye." It is just plain wrong.

CHARTER RIGHTS OF CANADIANS ABROAD #1—MAHER ARAR

> [The] CSIS security liaison officer in Washington spoke of a trend they had noted lately that when the CIA or FBI cannot legally hold a terrorist subject, or wish a target questioned in a firm manner, they have them rendered to countries willing to fulfil that role. He said Mr. Arar was a case in point. On October 10, 2002, Mr. Hooper stated in a memorandum: "I think the US would like to get Arar to Jordan where they can have their way with him."
>
> —From an Initially Redacted Paragraph in the *Report of the Events Relating to Maher Arar*, 2006

> [The cell] was three feet wide. It was six feet deep. It was seven feet high. It had a metal door, with a small opening in the door, which did not let in light because there was a piece of metal on the outside for sliding things into the cell.
>
> There was a small opening in the ceiling.... There were cats and rats up there, and from time to time the cats peed through the opening into the cell. There were two blankets, two dishes and two bottles. One bottle was for water and the other one was used for urinating during the night. Nothing else. No light.
>
> I spent 10 months, and 10 days inside that grave....
>
> The beating started that day and was very intense for a week, and then less intense for another week. That second and the third days were the worst.
>
> The cable is a black electrical cable, about two inches thick. They hit me with it everywhere on my body. They mostly aimed for my palms, but sometimes missed and hit my wrists—they were sore and red for three weeks. They also struck me on my hips, and lower back. Interrogators constantly threatened me with the metal chair, tire and electric shocks.
>
> —From *This is What They Did to Me*, Maher Arar, November 5, 2003, Counterpunch.org

> Mr. Arar strikes me as a person with what one might describe as moral courage.
>
> —Professor Stephen Toope, Fact-Finder, Arar Commission[176]

Maher Arar is a Syrian-born Canadian citizen, educated at McGill University and the Université du Québec, a telecommunications engineer, one of at least ten individuals caught in the web of intensified scrutiny of Muslim Canadians since September 2001. Immediately following the shocking, tragic events in the United States on 9/11, many countries enacted aggressive anti-terror legislation. Law enforcement agencies, like CSIS and the RCMP in Canada, stepped up both their investigations of individuals deemed suspicious and their co-operation with American counterparts. Canada's vigilance began with the RCMP's Project O Canada, in Toronto, an investigation into Ahmed Khadr, the father of Omar Khadr, who was believed to be financing terrorist organizations in Afghanistan. But the RCMP investigation team eventually embraced other Canadian law enforcement agencies, including the Ontario Provincial Police (OPP), CSIS, and Canadian Border Services Agency, and regularly and freely shared information with the FBI and CIA, with no constraints. One of the outcomes was a Canada Customs "terrorist outlook list." Because of meetings with suspected individuals, Maher Arar had been a "person of interest" to the RCMP since October 2001.[177]

In September 2002, RCMP officers faxed a memo to the FBI concerning Arar, stating that Arar and his wife, Dr. Monia Mazigh, were "Islamic Extremist individuals suspected of being linked to the Al Qaeda terrorist movement." Arar had been in Tunisia visiting family for three months, and when he landed at John F. Kennedy International Airport in New York in transit on his way home on September 26, 2002, he was apprehended by American immigration officials and held, without access to family or a lawyer. (He did meet with a Canadian consular official on October 2, who assured him it was "very unlikely" that he would be sent to Syria.)

It has also been reported in investigations of convicted terrorist Omar Khadr that on October 7, 2002, while Khadr was being interrogated in detention in Afghanistan, he identified a photograph of Arar and said that he had seen him in Afghanistan. Arar has never been to Afghanistan, and the American official who testified concerning Khadr's statement later admitted that he may have exaggerated Khadr's words. But on that day, the American officer interrogating Khadr gave this information to those holding Arar in New York. The next day, Arar was flown first to Jordan, and then to Syria.

For the first two weeks of his detention, Arar was interrogated, beaten, and humiliated. He was then kept in solitary confinement for ten months, visited a number of times by Canadian officials. In

August 2003, he was moved to a "better" prison, and he returned to Canada in October 2003.

When Arar revealed what had happened to him in Syria, the outrage of Canadians led to the creation, in January 2004, of a commission of inquiry, led by the Honourable Dennis O'Connor, who previously had carried out the Walkerton Inquiry into water safety, and who recently has been asked to review the use of force by the Toronto Police Service. The Maher Arar Commission of Inquiry reviewed the events, offered conclusions on what had happened and who was responsible, and in a second phase, considered recommendations from individuals and organizations like CCLA. (No American or Syrian officials agreed to participate in the commission of inquiry, and Commissioner O'Connor determined that it was "not deemed appropriate" for Arar to testify before the report was released.)

CCLA has a very long history of criticism of the RCMP, and advocacy for oversight. To the Arar Inquiry, CCLA recommended a separate oversight function, a means to "audit" the RCMP, suggesting that the following questions be asked:

> as a matter of policy and/or practice, is the RCMP adopting a reasonable approach to the statutory definition of "terrorist activity"? To what extent, if at all, is the Force stretching the definition beyond genuine terrorism? To what extent, if at all, are legitimate dissenters and *non*-terrorist law-breakers being targeted? What kind of treatment are racial, religious, and ethnic minorities receiving? Are the RCMP's information sharing practices—with foreign and other domestic agencies—within acceptable limits? How far, if at all, are the methods of investigating and countering ethically appropriate?

In his very detailed report, issued in September 2006, five volumes in total, Commissioner O'Connor systematically unpicked the details of Arar's detention in New York, his year of incarceration in Syria, the egregious staining of his reputation by government officials—who issued strategic leaks to media before and after Arar returned to Canada—and the efforts undertaken by the RCMP to protect its own reputation.[178]

The findings were particularly damning for the RCMP: "It is very likely that, in making the decisions to detain and remove Mr. Arar, American authorities relied on information about Mr. Arar provided by the RCMP." O'Connor found no evidence that the RCMP participated in the decision to send Arar to Syria, but that in addition to providing American authorities with the "entire database" of its terrorism investigation, the RCMP in particular "provided American authorities with information about Mr. Arar that was inaccurate, portrayed him in an unfairly negative fashion and overstated his importance in the RCMP investigation...." And, because they neglected to provide "written caveats," which their own policy required, they actually increased "the risk that the information would be used for purposes of which the RCMP would not approve, such as sending Mr. Arar to Syria."

During Arar's year in Syria, the combined actions of the RCMP, CSIS, and the Department of Foreign Affairs, Trade and Development (DFAIT) conspired to indicate to Syrian authorities that Canada did not have a problem with the likelihood that Canadians (Arar and also Abdullah Almalki) were being tortured while in Syrian custody; they also delayed Arar's release. And, in reference to lengthy diplomatic efforts to facilitate the release of Arar, "the RCMP and CSIS were not supportive of a DFAIT initiative to send the Syrians a letter conveying that Canada spoke with one voice in seeking Mr. Arar's release."

O'Connor elaborated on this incident in his report. The minister of foreign affairs at the time, Bill Graham, wanted to send a "one voice" letter to Syrian officials co-signed with the solicitor general, but CSIS and the RCMP resisted, offering only weak and ambiguous language, even though, according to O'Connor, "it was clear, or should have been clear, to everyone that Mr. Arar's human rights had been and likely continued to be seriously abused. Syria's reputation for mistreating prisoners was well-known and the likelihood of Mr. Arar receiving a fair trial in Syria was remote. By this time, it was also clear that the US authorities had relied on information from Canada in removing Mr. Arar to Syria using their questionable practice of extraordinary rendition. In addition, the official Canadian position was that Canada should seek Mr. Arar's release.... It was well-known that the SMI [Syrian military intelligence service], which was holding Mr. Arar, would be more influenced by the views of a security intelligence agency (CSIS) than those of a politician (Minister Graham)."

Instead, three-and-a-half months later, too late to have any impact, Prime Minister Paul Martin wrote a letter to the president of Syria.

Furthermore, following Arar's return to Canada, "reports were prepared within government that had the effect of downplaying the mistreatment or torture to which Mr. Arar had been subjected.... Canadian officials leaked confidential and sometimes inaccurate information about the case to the media for the purpose of damaging Mr. Arar's reputation or protecting their self-interests or government interests." And again, the actions of the RCMP were shameful: "When briefing the Privy Council Office and senior government officials about the investigation regarding Mr. Arar, the RCMP omitted certain key facts that could have reflected adversely on the Force."

Commissioner O'Connor went to extraordinary lengths to clear the name of one Canadian citizen. He wrote:

> What is most troubling is that, had a public inquiry not been held in this case, some of the written record within government and, certainly, the views of many government officials, would have been incorrect. There would have been a widespread perception that Mr. Arar had not been tortured and that he had lied when describing what had happened to him after returning to Canada. Unquestionably, that perception would have spread to the public domain. That would have been most unfair to Mr. Arar.

And elsewhere, O'Connor noted: "While most leaks likely involve a breach of some form of confidentiality, using confidential information to manipulate public opinion in favour of the Canadian government's interests or the interests of the leak or of the information is obviously more egregious."

The commission of inquiry, in the words of Alan Borovoy, left the government of Canada with "egg on its collective face."

Maher Arar sued the government of Canada and received both an apology, from Prime Minister Stephen Harper in 2008, and a settlement of $10.5 million with an additional $1 million for legal costs. He attempted to sue the governments of the United States, Syria, and Jordan, but was denied the opportunity to press those suits.

As recently as March 2014, in an appearance before the Senate Committee on National Security and Defense, CCLA's General Counsel Sukanya Pillay noted the absolute failure by the government to act on the recommendations made by the Arar Inquiry:

> Justice O'Connor recommended in his second report pursuant to the auspices of the Arar Commission, that there should be an independent review, including complaints investigation and self-initiated review, to review the RCMP's national security activities [Independent Complaints and National Security Review Agency "ICRA"]. He recommended that this independent review mechanism should also review the activities of the CBSA (law enforcement powers, arrest, detention, removal, intelligence, etc.). CCLA strongly recommends that Justice O'Connor's recommendations be implemented without delay—we have been arguing for this for years and are very concerned that eight years after these recommendations were made—there has been no movement on these issues. CCLA cannot underscore enough the importance in a free and democratic society, of the principles of accountability and transparency, secured through independent review, of power—or more to the point, the dangers posed to human rights and dignity—including to life, to liberty, to security of the person—by unchecked power.

Maher Arar was not the only Canadian affected by the zeal of Canadian law enforcement agencies to enact a War on Terror; a separate inquiry dealt with the cases of three other young Muslim Canadian men (an issue dealt with in Chapter Six of this book).[179] There has been tension in the public mind since 9/11 on anything related to terrorism—aggressive anti-terror legislation, participation by Canadian forces in the military interventions led primarily by the United States, the implications of surveillance, and the treatment of prisoners of war in places like Baghdad's Abu Ghraib and Guantánamo Bay, Cuba, a situation rendered relevant to Canadians in the person of Omar Khadr.

CHARTER RIGHTS OF CANADIANS ABROAD #2—OMAR KHADR

Get Khadr—The Dogged Pursuit of a Canadian Child Soldier by the American Military Establishment, Assisted by the Government of Canada

> The Khadr case dramatically exposes the inconsistencies of our politics: we sign international agreements such as the Convention against Torture or the Convention on the Rights of the Child and ignore their application in concrete cases. We claim to want impartial justice, free from politics, but when the courts rule in the Khadr case, the Minister refuses to comply or to acknowledge the implications of the judicial pronouncements. Detention conditions at Guantánamo violate international conventions of human rights, and Canada still does not care.
>
> —Nathalie Des Rosiers,
> CCLA General Counsel, August 2012

> Then they tortured. They tortured men at military bases and detention facilities in Afghanistan and Iraq, in Guantánamo...they tortured men in secret CIA prisons set up across the globe specifically to terrorize and torture prisoners.... They tortured the innocent and the likely-guilty alike when the torture had nothing to do with imminent threats.... They tortured to break people, pure and simple.
>
> —Larry Siems, *The Torture Report: What the Documents Say About America's Post-9/11 Torture Program*, 2011[180]

> In an effort to make him more amenable and willing to talk, [blank] has placed Umar on the "frequent flyer program." [F]or the three weeks before [the] visit, Umar has not been permitted more than three hours in any one location. At three hours intervals he is moved to another cell block, thus denying him uninterrupted sleep and [ensuring] a continued change of neighbours. He will soon be placed in isolation for up to three weeks and then he will be interviewed again.... Certainly Umar did not appear to have been affected by three weeks on the "frequent flyer" program. He did not yawn or indicate in any way that he was tired throughout the two hour interview. It seems likely that the natural resilience of a well-fed and healthy seventeen-year-old are keeping him going.
>
> —From a DFAIT Official's March 2004 Visit to Omar Khadr (Referring to Mr. Khadr as "Umar")

The case of Omar Khadr has been simmering in the public imagination for more than a decade. As in the case of Maher Arar, the exotic locations (Syria, Afghanistan, Cuba), the tangle of geopolitical interests, specifically the role of American players (security and military), and the insidious forces of racism, religion, and anti-terror zealotry obscure the facts of an assault on fundamental rights and freedoms of a Canadian citizen, in this case, a boy of fifteen. Khadr's own case is further complicated by the enormity of the charges against him and the incendiary actions of his family—his mother and sister have made public statements declaring support of Islamist terrorists.[181]

Omar Khadr was born in Canada in 1986. His parents were immigrants from Egypt and Pakistan, who married in Canada, and in the 1980s and 1990s spent a great deal of time with their family in Pakistan and Afghanistan, purportedly working with Osama bin Laden. Omar and his brothers were trained in al-Qaeda camps, and in 2002, Omar Khadr, aged fifteen, allegedly killed an American soldier with a grenade during combat, and was himself wounded and captured. His father, Ahmed Said Khadr, was killed in 2003 in Pakistan; the family returned to Canada.

Khadr was sent by the American military to the Guantánamo Bay detention facility in Cuba in 2002, where he remained for ten years. Within months of his arrival, he was interrogated by Canadian officials (CSIS), who gave their findings to American authorities. (Khadr was interrogated six times in 2003–04 by Canadians; the Federal Court of Canada issued an interim injunction to stop Canadian officials from conducting further interrogations, in 2005.) Khadr was repeatedly interrogated using methods that violated international law; he was deprived of sleep over extended periods of time (the "frequent flyer" program), beaten, subjected to extreme cold and solitary confinement, shackled for hours at a time in painful positions, and threatened with rendition to foreign countries for purposes of torture.

Unlike other minors at Guantánamo, Khadr was always treated like an adult inmate. He was not charged for two years, and then, as an "enemy combatant," charged with "murder by an unprivileged belligerent, attempted murder by an unprivileged belligerent, conspiracy, and aiding the enemy."

When the US Supreme Court declared the military tribunals illegal, the United States Congress, in 2006, created a new mechanism for trying enemy combatants, denying them access to federal courts. Khadr was the only Western foreign national in Guantánamo whose detention was not aggressively and successfully protested by his home country; Australian, British, French, and German detainees were repatriated, and often served shorter sentences than had they been convicted by the US military. Furthermore, only non-US nationals could be tried by the military commission, and Khadr could not be represented by Canadian counsel. The charges against Khadr were dropped twice, and appealed and reinstated by US military, until he finally was tried in a military court in October 2010.

The government of Canada (variously the Prime Minister, Attorney General, minister of foreign affairs, Department of Justice, with CSIS and the RCMP) resisted at every turn in countless ways the principle of fair treatment of Omar Khadr as a Canadian citizen and as a child soldier. Until 2006, the Liberals formed the government; subsequently, the Conservatives have done so; the

Liberal government sent a number of diplomatic notes protesting Khadr's treatment and declaring his transfer to Guantánamo "inappropriate" for him, but the Liberal government did instigate the interrogations and made no move towards repatriation. Evidence has recently surfaced to indicate that the Americans permitted access by Canadian officials to Khadr in Guantánamo only if they would give up evidence to them. The Conservative government resisted repatriation repeatedly.

Between 2005 and 2010, the case of Omar Khadr was twice before the Federal Court, twice before the Federal Court of Appeal, and twice before the Supreme Court of Canada. There were two separate strands of court cases, both ending at the Supreme Court. (A third strand, Khadr's application for damages, instigated in 2004, remains unresolved.) The first chain of legal skirmishes began with the interrogations of Khadr by Canadian officials, the questionable purpose of those interviews, and how they might have been used, and subsequently, Khadr's rights concerning interrogation records, as defined in section 7 of the Charter: "Everyone has the right to life, liberty and security of the person and the right not to be deprived thereof except in accordance with the principles of fundamental justice."

Canadian government officials made their arguments in the name of national security and irrelevance—Khadr was being held and would be tried outside Canadian jurisdiction. They argued this successfully before the Federal Court in 2006, but Khadr won at the subsequent Federal Court of Appeal hearing, in part because new information had been discovered concerning the interrogations. The government appealed then to the SCC, trying to limit, in advance, the nature of the material to be considered relevant, and also to deny the status of several interveners. Both applications were denied.

In May 2008, the SCC unanimously upheld Khadr's section 7 rights and ordered that, after scrutiny by a judge, the interrogation documents be released. Their reasoning was as follows: the principles of international law and comity of nations, which normally require that Canadian officials operating abroad comply with local law, do not extend to participation in processes that violate Canada's international human rights obligations.

The SCC ruling noted that the interrogation methods used at Guantánamo (when Canadian officials "passed the fruits" of their meetings with Khadr to US officials) were found "by the United States Supreme Court to violate US domestic law and international human rights obligations to which Canada is party." Consequently, the usual jurisdictional rules "that would normally justify deference to foreign law do not apply in this case." Khadr was entitled to section 7 rights.

This decision reinforced calls for Khadr to be repatriated to Canada for trial.

A letter from CCLA to Prime Minister Harper that spring noted that while Khadr's age and the nature of the charges against him should have guaranteed him special treatment under international law, instead he'd been held for five years without charge, and had "apparently suffered psychological and physical deterioration" as a result.

In June 2008, a report by the human rights sub-committee of the Parliamentary Foreign and International Affairs Committee (majority held by a combination of Liberals and New Democrats) called for the repatriation of Khadr and prosecution in Canada if appropriate, but also for rehabilitation and re-integration programs. The reason why the government of Canada would *not* rush to demand repatriation was articulated in that report in a dissenting statement from the Conservative Party of Canada:

> We are of the belief that the allegations against Mr. Khadr are serious and should be treated as such. This is not a simple question that ends with whether or not we should repatriate Mr. Khadr, as the Report indicates. Instead, this is a question that has far-reaching implications for our country's stance on terrorism.... Mr. Khadr could become a litmus test on Canada's commitment to impeding global terrorism....

Khadr then applied to the Federal Court of Canada for repatriation. Once again the narrative of the interrogation of Khadr by Canadian officials was examined, and in a decision written by Justice James O'Reilly, the court found Canada's actions illegal, contrary to United Nations and Geneva Conventions on torture:

> By the spring of 2004, then, Canadian officials were knowingly implicated in the imposition of sleep deprivation techniques on Mr. Khadr as a means of making him more willing to provide intelligence. Mr. Khadr was then a 17-year-old minor, who was being detained without legal representation, with no access to his family, and with no Canadian consular assistance....

Justice O'Reilly noted that not only was Khadr's treatment illegal, so too was his detention, under both US and international laws governing torture and the treatment of children: "Mr. Khadr, being a child, was vulnerable to being caught up in armed conflict as a result of his personal and social circumstances in 2002 and before. [Canada] cannot resile from its recognition of the need to protect minors, like Mr. Khadr, who are drawn into hostilities before they can apply mature judgment to the choices they face."

Justice O'Reilly reaffirmed Khadr's section 7 Charter rights and ordered his repatriation for reason of "his youth; his need for medical attention; his lack of education, access to consular assistance, and legal counsel; his inability to challenge his detention or conditions of confinement in a court of law; and his presence in an unfamiliar, remote and isolated prison, with no family contact."

The government of Canada appealed this decision to the Federal Court of Appeal, arguing that repatriation was not an effective remedy "because there was only a remote possibility that the United States would comply"—"one chance in a million" according to government lawyers. In the summer of 2009, the government's appeal was denied in a 2 to 1 decision that again ordered the repatriation of Omar Khadr.

A strong dissenting opinion was written by Justice Marc Nadon (whose subsequent appointment to the SCC by Prime Minister Harper was then deemed unconstitutional by the SCC):

> I agree entirely with Canada that the Judge erred.... Nowhere in his Reasons does the Judge consider the steps taken by Canada, nor does he, in my respectful opinion, consider the context of Mr. Khadr's detention and the extent to which Canada's ability to protect him was limited.... How

> could Canada prevent Mr. Khadr from being unlawfully detained by the US military in Guantánamo Bay? Also, how could Canada prevent the US from detaining Mr. Khadr "for a duration exceeding the shortest appropriate period of time"? And how could Canada remove Mr. Khadr from "an extended period of unlawful detention among adult prisoners"?

The government then appealed to the SCC, which heard the case in 2009–10, and permitted a cast of ten interveners, including CCLA, which made the following statement in its brief:

> Canadian government officials went to Guantánamo to interrogate Mr. Khadr knowing that the United States had "prepared" him for our questioning with weeks of grave mistreatment. Our government has a duty to protect Mr. Khadr, and obligation under the Constitution to treat him fairly—no matter how politically unpopular his family may be.... It is important to note that the issue is not whether the US Government will agree, but rather, whether the Canadian government has done what it should to ensure the protection of Mr. Khadr's constitutional rights.

The SCC unanimously agreed in February 2010 that Khadr's Charter rights, as a child, and other legal rights had been violated. It condemned "Canadian participation in state conduct that violates the principles of fundamental justice." But it did not accept the Federal Court's opinion that repatriation was the only remedy, determining that the remedy had to be determined by the government of Canada, because of the government's "common law royal prerogative" over foreign affairs. "The appropriate remedy in this case is to declare that Khadr's Charter rights were violated, leaving it to the government to decide how best to respond in light of current information, its responsibility over foreign affairs, and the Charter."

The government of Canada did nothing for eight months. When it became evident that Canada would not seek his repatriation to Canada to stand trial, and that he was to be denied a trial with full due process in American civil courts, and would be tried

Omar Khadr's brother Karim (in wheelchair) joins about 300 people protesting the violation of human rights under international standards outside of the US consulate in Toronto in 2008.

before a US military commission, probably facing a forty-year sentence, Omar Khadr pleaded guilty to all charges—despite considerable evidence that many aspects of the US case were unproven. In exchange for his guilty plea, Khadr was sentenced to eight years imprisonment, one of which he would have to serve at the Guantánamo Bay detention centre. After one year, he would be eligible for transfer to Canada.

The government of Canada then simply refused to make the request for repatriation for more than a year.

Nathalie Des Rosiers, then general counsel of CCLA, wrote in the summer of 2012:

> Minister Vic Toews still refuses to accept the transfer request and weighs the political costs of such a decision. The *National Post* invites people to vote on the question: who wants the return of Omar Khadr? People express themselves:

they do not like the Khadr family, are afraid of terrorists, want murderers punished more severely. A decision that should be taken on the basis of legislative criteria is converted into a popular plebiscite.

All Canadians should be concerned about the way this case has been handled. The Khadr case dramatically exposes the inconsistencies of our politics: we sign international agreements such as the Convention against Torture or the Convention on the Rights of the Child and ignore their application in concrete cases. We claim to want impartial justice, free from politics, but when the courts rule in the Khadr case, the Minister refuses to comply or to acknowledge the implications of the judicial pronouncements. Detention conditions at Guantánamo violate international conventions of human rights, and Canada still does not care.

The rights of all Canadians are weakened by indifference and intransigence of the Minister in the Khadr case. The Minister is dragging his feet and refuses to promptly approve a transfer in the case of a prisoner in a context of multiple violations of human rights recognized by Canadian courts. When there are rights violations or abusive conditions of detention, the Minister should act promptly. Approving a transfer is not a "favour" to Mr. Khadr, it is the application of the same law for all Canadians. The process is designed to ensure that the Canadian correctional service is involved in the rehabilitation of persons who, in any case, will be returning to Canada when they finish their sentences.

Public safety is best served by this involvement of the correctional service. The obstinacy of the Minister does not help anyone here: Canadians are not better protected by Khadr's detention in Guantánamo instead of in Canada, the Americans who may want to do other plea bargains with other prisoners do want Canada to honour the deal. What the obstinacy of the Minister is doing is weakening the rule of law and every Canadian's right to believe that he or she will be treated according to law at all times.

In the fall of 2012, Khadr was repatriated to Canada; he served time in both Millhaven Institution and in Edmonton Institution in maximum security until his classification was challenged. He is currently in a medium-security unit and eligible for release in 2018 at the end of his sentence; he has not—to date—applied for parole. In December 2013, Khadr's revised civil case was presented to the Federal Court, which has asked for revisions. The claim is currently for $20 million in damages for the violations of his rights. In July 2014, the Alberta Court of Appeal unanimously found that Khadr should not be serving his sentence in a federal institution. The government of Canada again balked, because Khadr has "pleaded guilty to heinous crimes." Public Safety Minister Steven Blaney stated that the government of Canada will "appeal this decision and seek a stay to ensure that he stays in federal prison—where he belongs." Also in July 2014, several media outlets appealed to the Federal Court to be allowed to speak with Khadr, who has agreed to be interviewed and has the constitutional right to speak with media, a right repeatedly and consistently being denied by CSC.

RIGHTS OF PRISONERS—ASHLEY SMITH

> Everyone Has the Right Not to be Subjected to any Cruel and Unusual Treatment or Punishment.
>
> —Section 12, *Canadian Charter of Rights and Freedoms*

> As recommended by the United Nations Special Rapporteur on Torture and Other Cruel and Inhuman Treatment in 2011, there should be an immediate and absolute prohibition on the placement of individuals with mental health disabilities in segregation.
>
> —CCLA Recommendation to Coroner's Inquest into the Death of Ashley Smith, December 2013

June 2007, Joliette Institution for Women: "She completely destroyed a cell that had been specially prepared for her. In 10 years, never has any inmate caused as much damage. The desk in the cell had to be removed to stop her from gaining access to the cell camera, which had been destroyed and obscured several times. The wall coverings for cables, lights and electrical current had to be sealed. She ripped up a piece of Velcro that held her window curtain in place and used it to choke herself. Even while menstruating, we couldn't give her tampons because she would wrap the fibres around her neck. She would have to show us a used tampon in order to get another one. She succeeded in removing security screws from the cell furniture with her fingers, and used the screws to self-harm."

—*A Rush to Judgment*, Union of
Canadian Correctional Officers Report, 2008

Ashley Smith spent the last four years of her brief life in prison, first in youth detention facilities in New Brunswick, and from the time she turned eighteen, in the federal prisons for women. She was almost always in solitary confinement. As video evidence shown at the coroner's inquest indicated, Smith was treated inhumanely, even illegally, wherever she happened to be, which included maximum security units at three prisons and several psychiatric facilities. She was, as statements like those in the Union of Canadian Corrections Officers Report indicate, an extremely difficult prisoner, who required extraordinary measures wherever she was held. One of her recurring behaviours was choking herself with pieces of cloth she had torn from any available material and fashioned into a ligature. There were different theories on why Smith did this—to attract attention, because she was always alone; to stimulate a form of erotic pleasure; to commit, or threaten to commit, suicide.

Correctional Service Canada had no formal management plan for Ashley Smith, only sporadic and inconsistent recognition of mental health concerns; the only consistency in the treatment of an emotionally vulnerable teenager was to place her in solitary confinement. In the final months of her life, the instructions from management included one consistent element: do not enter her cell unless she has stopped breathing. But no training was ever given to staff to determine if Ashley Smith had indeed stopped breathing.

On October 19, 2007, Smith did stop breathing, watched by prison staff, her final moments dutifully recorded on videotape. Despite the fact that prison suicides are regularly identified by Canada's Corrections Ombudsman as symptomatic of deep institutional problems, it seems clear that CSC would have preferred that Smith's death be labelled a suicide. That would have been a manageable verdict.

Once the Ontario coroner's inquest into the death of Ashley Smith was finally underway, in January 2013, the process of hearing testimony from about a hundred witnesses, reviewing videotape (over the objections of CSC), and reading more than 8,000 pages of documents proceeded smoothly for almost one year, with the decision of the five-person jury rendered in December 2013. CCLA was a party with standing at the inquest, made an oral submission, and, with a number of other organizations, submitted recommendations to be considered by the jury.

CCLA's primary concerns were that solitary confinement for inmates with mental health disabilities should be absolutely prohibited, and that extended solitary confinement (more than fifteen consecutive days) should be acknowledged as a form of torture and absolutely prohibited: "If CSC does not adhere to this prohibition, and continues the use of prolonged segregation...CSC must apply to a court for a determination that continued segregation is necessary and appropriate. The burden at such a hearing shall be on CSC to justify the ongoing use of segregation...."

CCLA made a number of other recommendations concerning oversight, monitoring, and internal and external audits, and specific recommendations concerning body cavity searches and security classifications, especially in the case of inmates with mental health disabilities.

The jury of five young women declared Smith's death a homicide. A coroner's inquest jury is not permitted to assign blame, but the verdict of homicide left open the possibility of further criminal proceedings. The jury also tabled 104 recommendations, which also are simply recommendations, without any enforceable power. They cover every aspect of Smith's brief life in prison and her death, and are both far-reaching and minutely detailed in their condemnation of Canada's correctional services:

> This case study can demonstrate how the correctional system and federal/provincial health care can collectively fail to provide an identified mentally ill, high risk, high needs inmate with the appropriate care, treatment and support. This case study can also demonstrate the lack of communication, cohesiveness, and accountability of a large organization such as Corrections Canada.

Public response to the coroner's jury's "bold and courageous" verdict was compassionate outrage, as expressed in this op-ed by doctors Stuart J. Murray and Dave Holmes in the *Ottawa Citizen,* December 28, 2013:

> [If] we look at our federal correctional system, it appears that we are at war with those who are most vulnerable among us—those who have a mental illness, our youth, the poor, Aboriginal peoples. And while we can expect high rhetoric from government officials, much hollow talk of "victims' rights," Ashley Smith is not and cannot be a victim in their eyes: she is collateral damage in a war being waged in our correctional facilities and in our communities.

Since Smith's death, the federal Conservatives have passed omnibus bills that have imposed harsher sentences on young offenders and the unconstitutional use of mandatory minimums, which have increased our prison population to an all-time high, disproportionately affecting Aboriginal peoples and persons requiring mental health care. Concerning the use of force, physical and/or chemical restraints, and solitary confinement, Bill C-10 changed the wording of the law from the use of "least restrictive measures" to what is deemed "necessary and proportionate...."

• • •

The stories of Ashley Smith, Omar Khadr, Maher Arar, Robert Latimer, and others reveal the vulnerabilities in Canada's system of justice, a system that in recent years has become increasingly punitive, even merciless. The *Charter of Rights and Freedoms* holds us as a society to the highest possible standards of fair trials, fair sentences, and fair treatment in prisons, but the Charter does not operate in a vacuum and is really only invoked in the breach. And it seems that no matter how often a matter such as capital punishment is firmly dealt with by parliamentarians, it is never fully and finally resolved. This constant interplay of competing forces is, after all, the stuff of a democracy.

Were it not for organizations such as CCLA, many egregious violations of the rights of Canadians would go unnoticed, would slip past, buried in classified documents, redacted out of sight and out of mind.

When CCLA came into existence fifty years ago it was described as "a new watchdog" that would monitor "Canadian smugness." The watchdog image is an anachronism; we speak a different language now, and the work and strategies of advocacy organizations such as CCLA are modern, electronic, and professional. Advocacy is conducted on a variety of platforms that intersect and enhance one another—in the courtroom, the media, the parliamentary committee room, the classroom, online.[182]

But the CCLA pamphlet for schools—*Fundamental Freedoms*—which poses fifty-one impossibly hard civil liberties dilemmas for schoolchildren, and notes cheerfully that there are no "right answers," indicates that CCLA is still keeping an eye on Canadian smugness:

> There is no substitute for a committed, intelligent and vigilant *citizenry*. The enlightened conscience of the people remains the most effective safeguard of liberty. Conversely, the greatest peril to liberty is a people with a blunted conscience. History has demonstrated, time and again, how tyranny feeds on apathy. Few of us, of course, are apathetic about ourselves and our own immediate self-interests. But the crucial test is how responsive we will be to the plight of *other* people. Will we insist on civil liberties for others as

well as for ourselves, for our rivals as well as for our allies, for those who think differently as well as for those who think similarly?

The impulse that caused a handful of Canadians to come together in 1964, and start a conversation about a single piece of provincial legislation—they knew Bill 99 was careless, contemptuous of the rights of citizens, and dangerous as a precedent—remains constant. Fifty years later, CCLA is still driven by curiosity, by outrage, by compassion, and overall, by a sense of fairness.

EPILOGUE
2014 and Beyond—
Looking Ahead to the Next Fifty Years

Sukanya Pillay

Fifty years of fighting for rights and freedoms has taught us one thing: we can never be too vigilant.

CCLA has fought many battles over the years, each with the clear intention of protecting the civil liberties and human rights of individuals in Canada—rights that are essential to democracy. This book has detailed many of our great victories—including CCLA's fight for freedom of expression and speech no matter how distasteful, our fights for fair trial and due process rights, and our fights for equality and freedom from discrimination—as well as some of our losses.

Both the wins and the losses have given the organization, its national membership, and its board and staff the impetus to keep fighting for justice, for fairness, and to uphold the rule of law. CCLA has been a historic participant in the Canadian story of rights recognition and protection. Our starting point has always been that any erosion of rights and freedoms is a threat to justice and to democracy. And we have held firm to these principles knowing that they are not mere rhetoric, but rather, are essential pre-requisites to a strong and free nation. When I joined the organization, I noted that one of its mottos was "The freedom of no one is safe unless the freedom of everyone is safe," and I believe this runs through every aspect of our work to this day. The organization has also distinguished itself by arguing for legal safeguards that ensure public safety and effective outcomes while protecting rights—an essential formula in the post 9/11 world where rights themselves are questioned. CCLA has been consistent in the position that a strong and secure Canada can sacrifice neither public safety nor democratic principles.

I was asked to write down my thoughts on where the organization should go next. This is no small task, and I can say that the mandate we have held for fifty years—to fight to protect and uphold civil liberties and human rights—informs every decision we make each day.

Since its inception, CCLA has been at the forefront of recognizing that there is a fluidity that must be respected in understanding how to protect rights and freedoms. That is, rights keep evolving as our understanding of human dignity deepens and evolves. This is particularly true in considering what it really means when speaking about equality and non-discrimination. In CCLA's early days, we demanded racial and ethnic equality, and we continue this fight even today. We realize that many vulnerable groups require vigilant protection of their rights. In the fight for true equality for all persons, we are vigilant in working to ensure that the rights of women, of LGBTQ people, of racial and ethnic minorities, and of individuals with mental or physical vulnerabilities are protected. We believe in true equality for every person. Through our work in public outreach and education—in classrooms or courtrooms—we know that while important gains have been made in our society, many individuals continue to experience discrimination because of their gender, race, ethnicity, sexual orientation, or disabilities. And we have come to recognize how all rights intersect with one another, and that repercussions ensue when any one right is affected.

Accountability of the State has also been an ongoing priority for the organization, and in the post 9/11 era, this has been particularly highlighted as national security agencies and law enforcement gained increasing powers without commensurate accountability mechanisms. The area of privacy and surveillance has been, and will continue to be, a priority for us. It is an area that is complex, given the lack of transparency and the plethora of players, both domestic and international, that can affect the privacy rights of Canadians. Further, a realm of private thought and action is essential to enable individuals to exercise their moral autonomy. As such we have continued to fight for privacy with every new challenge, not content to accept arguments that terror threats or even new technologies and uses such as social media justify dilution of the right. At the time of writing, CCLA, along with privacy advocates across the country, are celebrating a decision of the Supreme Court of Canada confirming that police must obtain warrants before having access to subscriber information from telecom companies. CCLA had intervened in this case and made this very argument before the honourable Court. Indeed, there are several cases in 2014 in which CCLA intervened, and the courts adopted our arguments in deciding to protect the civil liberties in question. And while this is most encouraging, we recognize that there is far too much for us to do to rest.

The hard-won victories of yesterday are facing new threats today. The narrative that 9/11 was a game-changer that justified dispensing with critical legal safeguards has permeated our domestic practices: we have learned from Edward Snowden and other Canadian disclosures that State agencies, in addition to the police, have demanded warrantless access to subscriber information from telecom companies, and have received such information. Information that can be gleaned from subscriber information is highly personal, and, as we have argued before the Supreme Court of Canada, it can form a profile of an individual that may or may not be accurate, and as such, requires a judicial warrant prior to access.

Privacy, as discussed in this book, is a critical issue for our times. The individual's right to privacy—to be free from unlawful search and seizure and unwarranted intrusion by the State—must be protected. The Snowden revelations have disclosed just how easy and pervasive the collection of personal and identifying information can be in the digital age. The Maher Arar case, among others, has illustrated the real and tragic dangers of faulty information processing among domestic agencies, as well as the dangers of improperly sharing such information with foreign agencies. The advancing plans for a Canada-US Security Perimeter and other international agreements increase the possibilities for surveillance and collection and dissemination of personal information in a manner that CCLA argues must be justified and subjected to rigorous scrutiny.

Privacy is not only an issue on the Internet. Genetic privacy is also an area of concern for CCLA—not only in random DNA searches by police, but also with respect to the collection and use of DNA information in the public and private sectors.

The increasing impact of corporations on civil liberties and human rights is a distinct area of concern for CCLA. From genetic testing to closed-circuit surveillance, to marketing studies that collect online patterns or real-world radio-frequency identification (RFID) that monitors movements and purchases, the individual is in danger of becoming a specimen whose private information is used in research, intelligence, and as evidence for those who collect it. CCLA has argued, and will continue to do so, that the individual is entitled to a sphere of privacy within which the State or third parties cannot unjustifiably intrude. This baseline of privacy is crucial in a democratic society that allows individuals to develop and actualize, to reflect and create, and to publicly or anonymously express themselves, or to remain silent.

Another area in which we are concerned about constraint of civil liberties by private corporations is in the area of SLAPP suits. A SLAPP (strategic lawsuit against public participation) involves private actors using the civil justice system as a means of shutting down public expression and participation on matters of public interest. Individuals have a basic right to express themselves and engage publicly on matters of public interest. When private actors use SLAPPs to curb this expression, civil liberties are threatened. We are also concerned about inequities in which private corporations may have deeper pockets than private citizens. CCLA has taken a lead in Canada in challenging the use of SLAPP and we continue to fight for freedom of expression and opinion.

Discrimination and the undermining or denial of equality

rights continues to be an area of serious concern for CCLA. For example, CCLA continues to address experiences of racialized youth in police interactions across the country, particularly with respect to the practice known as "carding." In 1984, Justice Rosalie Abella, in a Royal Commission Report on employment equity, noted the "pervasiveness and subtlety of discrimination," as she wrote of the need to protect substantive equality. The fight for substantive equality for all persons is one CCLA will wage for as long as it takes. Over the years, in my many enjoyable conversations with Alan Borovoy, it has been heartening to learn how CCLA, in the late 1960s, pioneered efforts to uncover racial and religious discrimination and fought for equality. This is a fight that CCLA never stopped waging wherever it took us—to schools, universities, legislatures, municipal councils, workplaces, public services, or to the private sector—and the fight for equality continues to this day.

CCLA has been a staunch supporter of the full range of equality and non-discrimination rights over the years, and we continue to be today. Some of our recent work includes cases where we fought against discrimination in the workplace on the basis of country of origin; for freedom of religion; for LGBTQ rights; for the equality of youths from vulnerable populations; and for racial equality. Equality rights also intersect with many other rights including due process rights. CCLA is committed to protecting the rights of individuals from vulnerable or marginalized populations. We are seriously concerned by the disproportionately high rates of violence against Aboriginal women and the government's inadequate response to the missing, disappeared, and murdered Aboriginal women. In our view, this is a national crisis that demands a response. As well, we are very concerned by the disproportionately high rates of Aboriginal women and men and other visible minorities, in particular Blacks and African-Canadians, who are incarcerated in Canada. We have raised our concerns domestically and internationally, and have identified these as key areas of work moving forward.

But these issues do not exist as discrete problems in a vacuum. They raise broader questions relating to the functioning and intersectionality of our criminal justice system, police accountability and due process, fair trial and equality, and non-discrimination rights protected by the *Canadian Charter of Rights and Freedoms*.

Disability rights is an area of concern for CCLA. We recognize that this area includes the need for a broader and deeper understanding of the rights at stake, as well as meaningful enforcement mechanisms for the implementation of these rights. For example, if we want to go beyond lip-service to having real accessibility, provincial laws prescribing accessibility must not only be passed, they must be monitored and enforced. Recognizing the particular vulnerabilities of individuals with disabilities is a priority area for CCLA. Following several deaths of mentally ill individuals or individuals in crisis, who came into contact with police in Ontario, CCLA made submissions to an independent provincial inquiry examining the use of lethal force by Toronto police against individuals with mental health concerns. The report, written by former Supreme Court Justice, Frank Iacobucci was released in the summer of 2014, and reflects the many recommendations made by CCLA. We will continue to work to ensure these recommendations are implemented, particularly as they concern de-escalation in the use of force, and promote the recognition of all individuals as equal and deserving of protection in the greater goal of public safety.

We also remain committed to ensuring that Canada upholds its humanitarian commitments to refugees. Refugee legislation that creates impediments to the asylum-seeking process undermines the rights of child and family unification; prolongs the time before which a refugee can apply for permanent residency or citizenship; or that seeks to cut health care is incompatible with the basic commitment to assess individuals on a case-by-case basis in order to determine whether a person has legitimately fled persecution and is a *bona fide* refugee deserving of asylum in Canada. To the contrary, the conflation of refugees—individuals who have fled persecution and have the protection of no country—with human smugglers and "queue-jumpers" has contributed to a deliberate amnesia regarding why it is that we stretch out an arm of compassion to protect the lives of our fellow human beings who have fled danger. Nor does it recognize the nation-building contribution of refugees and immigrants to Canada—a country that has flourished from such contributions. And when considering contributions, we cannot fail to acknowledge that as a country we must continue to work very hard to continually recognize, cherish, and foster the incalculable contributions of Aboriginal communities to our history and to our future.

Looking ahead, we are also alert to trends that may challenge civil society work, through constraints to the right to freedom of association. For example, laws that create new registration or licensing requirements or, in the name of public safety, clamp down on protests can have the effect of limiting fundamental freedoms. CCLA will continue to work to uphold fundamental freedoms including expression, the right to protest and to associate, and the duty of the police to protect and facilitate these rights.

CCLA is also concerned by threats to bargaining rights, and will continue to fight for the right to collectively bargain in the workplace. We staunchly believe it is a key component of the dignity of employees to negotiate the terms on which they will sell their labour, and that management must preserve and participate in this process. In looking ahead CCLA will remain committed to public education and engagement. The Canadian Civil Liberties Education Trust (CCLET), CCLA's education arm, was established in 1968 for just this purpose. Teaching Civil Liberties, Civil Liberties in the Schools, and other programs that engage and activate the next generation, are crucial to ensuring that there will always be citizens who care about their rights and freedoms. Each year, through its workshops and seminars held in schools and faculties of education; at conferences for young people; with contests, animated videos, lesson plans, and games, CCLET engages thousands of children and their teachers in thinking critically about the important choices that must be made by those living in a democracy. These thoughtful and energetic young people have a great deal to say about fairness. They are the very people we will always need to ensure that our rights continue to be respected and protected.

As our understanding of rights evolves and deepens, so too does our understanding of the interconnection between collective and individual rights. Poverty, homelessness and housing shortages, food scarcity and food sovereignty, as well as trade rules that affect Canada's independence—all of these will all have an impact upon the enjoyment and realization of the rights and freedoms guaranteed in our Charter. Going forward, these will be issues that command attention.

And finally, in what is undeniably the post 9/11 era, CCLA will continue to work tirelessly to ensure that hard-won legal safeguards are not overlooked but upheld, and that accountability, oversight, transparency, and a commitment to the rule of law go hand in hand with power. Our work has always focused on, and clearly will continue to focus on fair trial rights, due process, the presumption of innocence, the right to know the case against you and to make full answer and defence, and to ensure that the rights to life, liberty, and security of person are upheld, and that any denials of these rights are done only in accordance with the principles of fundamental justice and rule of law.

To work at CCLA at this time in history is a great honour and an even greater responsibility. To follow in the footsteps of Alan Borovoy and Nathalie Des Rosiers is a daily reminder of how their individual courage, dedication, and wisdom has made an enormous impact on ensuring that justice, freedom, and equality are protected for every person. Alan continues to be a source of inspiration for me and for many Canadians, and I daresay he always will be. Working directly with Nathalie for several years, I was not only fortunate to learn from and observe her brilliant intellect and phenomenal energy, I witnessed firsthand her unswerving commitment to justice and truth, her compassion for people in vulnerable situations, her response in seeking just legal solutions—there are countless examples, but one publicly known is her work during the G20—and her continuous action to ensure that every person is afforded the full protection and benefit of the *Canadian Charter of Rights and Freedoms*. Nathalie, building on Alan's forty years of successes, took the work and message of CCLA to newer constituencies and generations within Canada while the country was facing new challenges, and as such she has made a mark with CCLA in broadening the culture of rights awareness in our country.

My incredible colleagues at CCLA each in their special and particular ways, work tirelessly to ensure that every person in

Canada has the chance to enjoy the dignity and opportunity that is their birthright, and to contribute to a society that believes in rule of law and democratic principles. We are also very indebted to our outstanding roster of pro bono lawyers across the country, our dedicated articling students over the years, and our volunteers who enable CCLA each year to punch above its weight. John McCamus has been an amazing and dedicated Chair of CCLA for over twenty years and is an anchor and guide for the organization, and I am extremely grateful for the knowledge he imparts to me. Although they are too many to name, I can say that in the time I have been General Counsel, I have witnessed that CCLA has an outstanding and dedicated board of directors who each in their own right has contributed to civil liberties in Canada, and collectively have been invaluable to CCLA and will continue to play key roles in shaping the ongoing direction and priorities of the organization.

CCLA is fortunate to have had Marian Botsford Fraser—not only an acclaimed and accomplished writer, but herself an ardent champion of rights and freedoms through the years and evidenced most recently in her position as Chair, Writers in Prison Committee, International PEN—to take on this vast history of civil liberties in Canada. Ms. Botsford Fraser has produced an important work of history written with depth and clarity, saliently weaving in the role and impact of CCLA at each turn, and we are extremely grateful to her. We also owe a great debt to Margie Wolfe at Second Story Press and her team of dedicated editors including Kathryn Cole for their vision and commitment to the project.

For fifty years CCLA has fought for freedom, liberty, and democracy in Canada. In the years ahead we are committed to doing the same, so that the rights of all people in Canada are protected and upheld. We will also continue to focus on Canada's international co-operation to ensure we maintain our legal commitments and our sovereignty and that we uphold the cherished values that are legally protected in the *Canadian Charter of Rights and Freedoms*. We know these goals are attainable and vital for a strong and free Canada, and we will accept nothing less.

CANADIAN CHARTER OF RIGHTS AND FREEDOMS
THIS HAS TO COME DOWN!
OCCUPY
POLICE
ROSEN

ENDNOTES

[1] An excellent introduction to the history of civil liberties in Canada: Dominique Clément, *Canada's Rights Revolution: Social Movements and Social Change, 1937–82*, Vancouver: University of British Columbia Press, 2008.

[2] Clément suggests that the fear of communism was not deep-seated in Canadian society, but was exploited by governments and others as "a paper tiger." Since 9/11, fear of terrorism has been exploited in the same way.

[3] Frank R. Scott, *Essays on the Constitution: Aspects of Canadian Law and Politics*, Toronto: University of Toronto Press, 1977.

[4] Thomas Berger, *Fragile Freedoms: Human Rights and Dissent in Canada,* Toronto: Clarke, Irwin & Co., 1982.

[5] These details quoted in an article by William A. Schabas, *Canada and the Adoption of the Universal Declaration of Human Rights*, McGill Law Journal, 1998.

[6] Two useful books on Canada in the 1960s: Bryan D. Palmer, *Canada's 1960s: The Ironies of Identity in a Rebellious Era*, Toronto: University of Toronto Press, 2009, and Myrna Kostash, *Long Way from Home: The Story of the Sixties Generation in Canada,* Toronto: James Lorimer and Company, 1980.

[7] CCLA documents referred to throughout this book are found in several places; many original documents are in the Library and Archives Canada collection, R9833. There are also copies of most CCLA newsletters, correspondence, etc., available through CCLA offices and website.

[8] A list of the books by A. Alan Borovoy can be found in Further Reading. Of particular use, *When Freedoms Collide, A Case for Our Civil Liberties,* Toronto: Lester & Orpen Dennys, 1988.

[9] This website has an excellent collection of primary documents on civil liberties issues in Canada: *Canada's Rights Revolution: A History* at *www.historyofrights.com.* And the website www.mcgill.ca/maritimelaw/crisis contains numerous links to background documents referred to by Prof. William Tetley in his book *The October Crisis, 1970: An Insider's View*, Montreal: McGill-Queen's University Press, 2006. An article by Dominique Clément on Human Rights Abuses during the October Crisis can be found here: https://muse.jhu.edu/login?auth=0&type=summary&url=/journals/journal_of_canadian_studies/v042/42.2.clement.html.

[10] The McDonald Commission Report is quoted in *Secret Service: Political Policing in Canada from the Fenians to Fortress America,* Reg Whitaker, Gregory S. Kealey, and Andrew Parnaby, Toronto: University of Toronto Press, 2012. Clément is also useful on this issue in *Rights Revolution.*

[11] See, for example, A. Alan Borovoy, *When Freedoms Collide: The Case for Our Civil Liberties* (Toronto: Lester & Orpen Dennys, 1988).

[12] Thomas Berger, *Fragile Freedoms: Human Rights and Dissent in Canada*, Toronto: Clarke, Irwin & Co., 1982.

[13] A. Alan Borovoy, *At the Barricades* (Toronto: Irwin Law, 2014) at 305.

[14] Dominique Clément has concluded that CCLA "had a greater impact on the Charter than did any other rights association in the country." Dominique Clément, *Canada's Rights Revolution: Social Movements and Social Change 1937–1982* (Vancouver: University of British Columbia Press, 2008) at 158.

[15] F.L. Morton and Rainer Knopff, *The Charter Revolution and the Court Party*, Peterborough: Broadview Press, 2000.

[16] Kent Roach, *The Supreme Court on Trial: Judicial Activism or Democratic Dialogue* (Toronto: Irwin Law, 2001) ch.5.

[17] Comments of Past CCLA President Syd Midanik to the Joint Committee on the Constitution as quoted in A. Alan Borovoy, *At the Barricades* (Toronto: Irwin Law, 2014) at 305.

[18] CCLA Submissions to the Special Joint Parliamentary Committee on the Constitution Nov. 18, 1980 at para 1.

[19] The drafting of the *Canadian Charter of Rights and Freedoms* is described in greater detail in Kent Roach, *Due Process and Victims' Rights: The New Law and Politics of Criminal Justice* (Toronto: University of Toronto Press, 1999) at pp 42–48.

[20] *R. v. Hogan* [1975] 2 S.C.R. 575.

[21] Kent Roach, *The Supreme Court on Trial: Judicial Activism or Democratic Dialogue* (Toronto: Irwin Law, 2001) ch.5.

[22] CCLA Submissions to the Special Joint Parliamentary Committee on the Constitution Nov. 18, 1980 at 4.

[23] CCLA Submissions to the Special Joint Parliamentary Committee on the Constitution Nov. 18, 1980 at 5.

[24] Ibid at 2.

[25] Ibid at 5.

[26] Ibid at 6.

[27] Ibid at 4.

[28] F.L. Morton and Rainer Knopff, *The Charter Revolution and the Court Party*, Peterborough: Broadview Press, 2000.

[29] CCLA Submissions to the Special Joint Parliamentary Committee on the Constitution Nov. 18, 1980 at 11.

[30] CCLA Submissions to the Special Joint Parliamentary Committee on the Constitution Nov. 18, 1980 at 11.

[31] *R. v. Therens* [1985] 1 S.C.R. 613.

[32] *R. v. Bartle* [1994] 3 S.C.R. 173.

[33] *R. v. Mannien* [1987] 1 S.C.R. 1233.

[34] *R. v. Strachan* [1988] 2 S.C.R. 980; *R. v. Suberu* [2009] 2 S.C.R. 460.

[35] CCLA Submissions to the Special Joint Parliamentary Committee on the Constitution Nov. 18, 1980 at 11.

[36] *R. v. Sinclair* [2010] 2 S.C.R. 310.

[37] CCLA factum in *R. v. Sinclair* (2010) at para 29.

[38] Dominique Clément, *Canada's Rights Revolution: Social Movements and Social Change 1937–1982,* Vancouver: University of British Columbia Press, 2008.

[39] A. Alan Borovoy, *When Freedoms Collide: The Case for Our Civil Liberties*, Toronto: Lester & Orpen Dennys, 1988.

[40] Hon John Pringle, The Royal Commission on the Conduct of the Police Forces at Fort Erie on the 11th of May 1974 (January, 1975) at 64–69.

[41] CCLA Submissions to the Special Joint Parliamentary Committee on the Constitution, Nov. 18, 1980 at 10.

[42] CCLA to the Board Nov. 19, 1998, at ccla.org/wordpress/wp-content/uploads/2008/09/1998-11-19-police-strip-searches.shtml.

[43] A. Alan Borovoy, *At the Barricades* (Toronto: Irwin Law, 2014) at 189–191.

[44] [2001] 3 S.C.R. 679. I acted as counsel for Aboriginal Legal Services of Toronto, which intervened to oppose the strip search in this case.

[45] Ibid at paras. 81–103.

[46] CCLA factum *in R. v. Golden* (2001) at para 6.

[47] "Strip searches likely to stay, despite unrest," *Toronto Star,* Feb. 14, 2014, GT4.

[48] CCLA Submissions to the Special Joint Parliamentary Committee on the Constitution, Nov. 18, 1980, at 7.

[49] CCLA Submissions to the Special Joint Parliamentary Committee on the Constitution Nov. 18, 1980, at 6.

[50] CCLA Submissions to the Special Joint Parliamentary Committee on the Constitution Nov. 18, 1980, at 7.

[51] Christopher Manfredi, *Judicial Power and the Charter* 2nd ed., Toronto: Oxford University Press, 2001.

[52] *Ward v. Vancouver* [2010] 2 S.C.R. 28. The CCLA factum argued that damages may be appropriate "to deter other Charter breaches from occurring in the future. They may also provide a mechanism for registering disapproval of a particular breach or emphasizing the importance of the right that has been breached." CCLA factum in *Ward v. Vancouver*, at para 11. The author represented the British Columbia Civil Liberties Association in this case, which also intervened in support of damages for the unconstitutional strip search. In that case the Canadian Association of Police Chiefs and three Attorneys

General intervened to oppose damage awards, again belying claims that the Court was captured by a Court Party without hearing plenty of arguments from the other side.

[53] *Doucet-Boudreau v. Nova Scotia* [2003] 3 S.C.R. 3.

[54] CCLA Submissions to the Special Joint Parliamentary Committee on the Constitution Nov. 18, 1980 at 7.

[55] Ibid at 7.

[56] F.L. Morton and Rainer Knopff, *The Charter Revolution and the Court Party* (Peterborough: Broadview Press, 2000) at 149.

[57] "Victim bill of rights would compel spouses to testify," CBC News April 3, 2014, www.cbc.ca/news/politics/victims-bill-of-rights-would-compel-spouses-to-testify-1.2596307.

[58] CCLA Submissions to the Special Joint Parliamentary Committee on the Constitution Nov. 18, 1980 at 7.

[59] Joint Committee on the Constitution, 1980–1981, Proceedings Issue 7 at 15, 27.

[60] Ibid Issue 48: 124.

[61] Joint Committee Issue 41: 101.

[62] Joint Committee Issue 48: 124.

[63] On the Dickson Court's interpretation of the Charter between 1984 and 1990 see Robert J. Sharpe and Kent Roach, *Brian Dickson: A Judge's Journey,* Toronto: University of Toronto Press, 2003.

[64] *R. v. Therens* [1985] S.C.R. at para 11.

[65] *R. v. Collins* [1987] 1 S.C.R. 265.

[66] CCLA factum in *R. v. Grant* (2009) at para 3.

[67] CCLA factum in *R. v. Stillman* (1997) at para 9.

[68] Ibid at para 11.

[69] Ibid at paras 22–23.

[70] Ibid at para 14.

[71] Ibid.

[72] *R. v. Stillman* [1997] 1 S.C.R. 607.

[73] CCLA factum in *R. v. Grant* (2009) at para 3.

[74] Ibid at para 15.

[75] Ibid at para 18.

[76] Ibid at para 17.

[77] *R. v. Grant* [2009] 2 S.C.R. 353 at para 75.

[78] Ibid at para 80.

[79] *R. v. Nasogaluak* [2010] 1 S.C.R. 206.

[80] *Ward v. Vancouver* [2010] 2 S.C.R. 28.

[81] CCLA argued not only that officers and the Chief of Police should be liable for not co-operating with an SIU investigation, but that the police board and the province also should be liable. The Supreme Court rejected the last two arguments, but allowed the civil lawsuit for intentional torts to proceed against the police officers and the Police Chief. See *Odhavji Estate v. Woodhouse* [2003] 3 S.C.R. 263.

[82] In *Hill v. Hamilton Wentworth Regional Police Service Board* [2007] 3 S.C.R. 129, CCLA successfully rebutted the idea that individual police officers could be over-deterred by the threat of damage awards by pointing out formal and informal arrangements that allowed police officers to be reimbursed by their employer of damages awarded against them and the fact that the officer could face disciplinary hearings in any event. CCLA factum in *Hill v. Hamilton Wentworth Regional Police Services Board* factum (2007) at paras 26–27.

[83] *Wood v. Schaeffer* [2013] SCC 71.

[84] F.L. Morton and Rainer Knopff, *The Charter Revolution and the Court Party* (Peterborough: Broadview Press, 2000) at 25.

[85] "Victim bill of rights would compel spouses to testify," CBC News, April 3, 2014, at www.cbc.ca/news/politics/victims-bill-of-rights-would-compel-spouses-to-testify-1.2596307.

[86] CCLA Submissions to the Special Joint Parliamentary Committee on the Constitution Nov. 18, 1980 at 14.

[87] *Bliss v. Attorney General of Canada* [1979] 1 S.C.R. 183.

[88] CCLA Submissions to the Special Joint Parliamentary Committee on the Constitution Nov. 18, 1980 at 13.

[89] CCLA factum in *Little Sister's v. Canada* (2001).

[90] CCLA Submissions to the Special Joint Parliamentary Committee on the Constitution Nov. 18, 1980 at 14.

[91] A. Alan Borovoy, *When Freedoms Collide: The Case for Our Civil Liberties* (Toronto: Lester & Orpen Dennys, 1988) at 213.

[92] The leading Left critiques of judicial activism are Michael Mandel, *The Charter of Rights and Freedoms and the Legalization of Politics in Canada* rev'ed ed., Toronto: Thomson, 1994; and Andrew Petter, *The*

Politics of the Charter: The Illusive Promise of Constitutional Rights, Toronto: University of Toronto Press, 2010.

[93] *Andrews v. Law Society of British Columbia* [1989] 1 S.C.R. 143.

[94] A. Alan Borovoy, *At the Barricades* (Toronto: Irwin Law, 2014) at 306.

[95] CCLA Submissions to the Special Joint Parliamentary Committee on the Constitution Nov. 18, 1980 at 2.

[96] A. Alan Borovoy, *At the Barricades* (Toronto: Irwin Law, 2014) at 306.

[97] At the same time, however, CCLA's arguments about the procedural inequities of the abortion law would win the support of four of seven judges in *R. v. Morgentaler* [1988] 1 S.C.R. 30. For further discussion see Robert J. Sharpe and Kent Roach, *Brian Dickson: A Judge's Journey* (Toronto: University of Toronto Press, 2003) ch.1; A. Alan Borovoy, *At the Barricades,* supra at 275; F.L. Morton, *Morgentaler v. Borowski* (Toronto: McClelland and Stewart, 1992) at 74, 222.

[98] *R. v. Miller* [1977] 2 S.C.R. 680.

[99] For arguments that popular support and legislative action was necessary to make real many controversial decisions under the American Bill of Rights see Gerald Rosenberg, *The Hollow Hope* 2nd ed., Chicago: University of Chicago Press, 2008.

[100] CCLA factum in *Miller v. The Queen* (1976) at para 43.

[101] *United States of America v. Burns and Rafay* [2001] 1 S.C.R. 283.

[102] F.L. Morton, "Dialogue or Monologue?" in Peter Russell and Paul Howe eds. *Judicial Power in Canadian Democracy*, Montreal: McGill-Queen's University Press, 2001.

[103] CCLA Submissions to the Special Joint Parliamentary Committee on the Constitution Nov. 18, 1980.

[104] CCLA Submissions to the Special Joint Parliamentary Committee on the Constitution Nov. 18, 1980 at 12.

[105] Ibid at 12.

[106] *Re B.C. Motor Vehicle Reference* [1985] 2 S.C.R. 486.

[107] *Tremblay v. Daigle* [1989] 2 S.C.R. 253.

[108] *R. v. Seaboyer* [1991] 2 S.C.R. 577.

[109] CCLA factum in *Malmo Levine v. Canada* (2003) at para 26.

[110] *Malmo Levine v. Canada* [2003] 3 S.C.R. 571.

[111] *Chaoulli v. Quebec* [2005] 1 S.C.R. 791 at para 167.

[112] CCLA factum in *PHS Community Services v. Canada (the Insite Case)* (2011) at para 27.

[113] *PHS Community Services v. Canada* [2011] 3 S.C.R. 134.

[114] The literature on dialogue between courts and legislatures is vast. See "Symposium" (2007) 45 Osgoode Hall LJ 1. For some of the author's own work, see Kent Roach, "Constitutional and Common Law Dialogues Between the Supreme Court and Canadian Legislatures" (2001) 80 *Can Bar Rev* 481 and Kent Roach, *The Supreme Court on Trial: Judicial Activism or Democratic Dialogue?* (Toronto: Irwin Law, 2001).

[115] F.L. Morton and Rainer Knopff, *The Charter Revolution and the Court Party* (Peterborough: Broadview Press, 2000) at 81.

[116] Ibid at 25.

[117] Ibid at 147.

[118] Ibid at 149.

[119] Ibid at 157.

[120] Ibid at 166.

[121] Robert Bork, *Coercing Virtue The Worldwide Rule of Judges* (Toronto: Vintage Canada, 2002) at 68.

[122] Prime Minister Harper's Chief of Staff at the time, Ian Brodie, was a former student of Morton and Knopff and he had written a book critical of the Court Challenges program; see Ian Brodie *Friends of the Court: The Privileging of Public Interest Litigation*, New York: SUNY Press, 2002.

[123] Dominique Clément, *Canada's Rights Revolution* supra at 205.

[124] A. Alan Borovoy, *At the Barricades* (Toronto: Irwin Law, 2014) at 312.

[125] A. Alan Borovoy *The New Anti-Liberals* (Toronto: Canadian Scholars Press, 1999) at x.

[126] CCLA factum in *R. v. Keegstra* (1990) para 26–27.

[127] A. Alan Borovoy, *The New Anti-Liberals* (Toronto: Canadian Scholars Press, 1999) at 42.

[128] CCLA factum in *R. Keegstra* (1990) at para 31.

[129] *R. v. Zündel* [1992] 2 S.C.R. 731.

[130] A. Alan Borovoy, *At the Barricades* (Toronto: Irwin Law, 2014) at 129.

[131] Ibid at 133.

[132] CCLA factum in *Adler v. Ontario* (1996) at para 16.

[133] A. Alan Borovoy, *The New Anti-Liberals* (Toronto: Canadian Scholars Press, 1999) at 55–56.

[134] A. Alan Borovoy, *When Freedoms Collide: The Case for Our Civil Liberties* (Toronto: Lester & Orpen Dennys, 1988) at 168.

[135] CCLA factum in *R. v. Butler* (1992) at paras 27–28.

[136] *R. v. Butler* [1992] 1 S.C.R. 452.

[137]A. Alan Borovoy, *The New Anti-Liberals* (Toronto: Canadian Scholars Press, 1999) at 9.

[138] CCLA factum in *Little Sister's v. Canada* (2001) at paras 22–23.

[139] *Little Sister's v. Canada* [2000] 2 S.C.R. 1120.

[140] *Little Sister's v. Canada* [2007] 1 S.C.R. 38.

[141] CCLA factum in *Little Sister's v. Canada* (2000) at para 34.

[142] CCLA factum in *R. v. Sharpe* factum (2001) at para 69.

[143] *R. v. Sharpe* [2001] 1 S.C.R. 45.

[144]A. Alan Borovoy, *The New Anti-Liberals* (Toronto: Canadian Scholars Press, 1999) at 17.

[145] CCLA factum in *R. v. Mills* (1999) at para 24.

[146] *R. v. Mills* [1999] 3 S.C.R. 668.

[147] Kent Roach, *Due Process and Victims' Rights: The New Law and Politics of Criminal Justice*,Toronto: University of Toronto Press, 1999.

[148] CCLA factum in *R. v. Latimer* (2001) at para 3.

[149] A. Alan Borovoy, *The New Anti-Liberals* (Toronto: Canadian Scholars Press, 1999) at 69–70.

[150] *R. v. Latimer* [2001] 1 S.C.R. 3.

[151] A. Alan Borovoy, *At the Barricades* (Toronto: Irwin Law, 2014) at 197.

[152] Two useful books on abortion in Canada are by Anne Collins, *The big evasion: Abortion, the issue that won't go away*, Toronto: Lester & Orpen Dennys, 1985; and a biography of Henry Morgentaler by Catherine Dunphy, *Morgentaler, A Difficult Hero,* Toronto: Wiley, 2003.

[153] Useful Government of Canada document on history of abortion in Canada: publications.gc.ca/Collection-R/LoPBdP/CIR/8910-e.htm#D.%20The%20Badgley.

[154] The two key SCC Morgentaler cases can be confused with one another. The first, heard by the SCC from 1974, with the decision published in 1976, is known as *Morgentaler v. the Queen*. The second, 1988, is known as *R. v. Morgentaler*. There is also *R. v. Morgentaler* (1993).

[155] The Morgentaler/Borowski battles from the perspective of Borowski: F.L. Morton, *Morgentaler v. Borowski: Abortion, The Charter, and The Courts,* Toronto: McClelland & Stewart, 1992.

[156] A useful summary of Canadian obscenity/pornography law: The Evolution of Pornography Law in Canada: www.parl.gc.ca/Content/LOP/researchpublications/843-e.htm.

[157] Brenda Cossman, "Censor, Resist, Repeat: A History of Censorship of Gay and Lesbian Sexual Representation in Canada," *Duke Journal Of Gender Law & Policy* Volume 21:45 2013.

[158] Varda Burstyn, ed., *Women Against Censorship,* Vancouver: Douglas & McIntyre, 1985.

[159] Fraser Report: *Pornography and Prostitution In Canada: Report of the Special Committee on Pornography and Prostitution* (1985). For commentary on Fraser Report: Michael, Kanter, *Prohibit Or Regulate? The Fraser Report And New Approaches To Pornography And Prostitution*, digitalcommons.osgoode.yorku.ca/cgi/viewcontent.cgi?article=1910&context=ohlj.

[160] For two opposing feminist positions: ed. Brenda Cossman at al., *Bad Attitude/s On Trial: Pornography, Feminism, and the* Butler *Decision,* University of Toronto Press, 1997 and Karen Busby, *LEAF and Pornography: Litigating on Equality and Sexual Representations*: heinonline.org/HOL/LandingPage?handle=hein.journals/cjls9&div=13&id=&page=.

[161] A lively account of the first trial, in Vancouver: Janine Fuller and Stuart Blackley, *Restricted Entry: Censorship on Trial*, Vancouver: Press Gang Publishers, 1996.

[162] Report to the Minister of Justice. Special Committee on Hate Propaganda in Canada, 1966.

[163] *Equality now: Report of the Special Committee on Visible Minorities in Canadian Society*. Canada. Parliament. House of Commons. Special Committee on Participation of Visible Minorities in Canadian Society, 1984.

[164] Women's Legal Education and Action Fund, *Equality and the Charter: Ten Years of Feminist Advocacy Before the Supreme Court of Canada,* Toronto: Emond Montgomery Publications, 1996.

[165] Report to the Canadian Human Rights Commission Concerning Section 13 of the *Canadian Human Rights Act* and the Regulation of Hate Speech on the Internet, Richard Moon, 2008.

[166] The *ATA* amended the *Criminal Code*, the *Official Secrets Act* (which was renamed the *Security of Information Act*), the *Canada Evidence Act*, and the *Proceeds of Crime (Money Laundering) Act* (renamed the *Proceeds of Crime (Money Laundering and Terrorist Financing Act)*, the *National Defence Act* with respect to the CSEC, and enacted the *Charities Registration (Security Information) Act.*

[167] Even as early as 2002, CCLA's general counsel at the time, Alan Borovoy, penned an op-ed in the *Calgary Herald* in which he described the *ATA* as being as "horrific as its targets" in the extent to which it threatened civil liberties.

[168] Indeed, CCLA would make this argument in 2012 before the SCC in the *Khawaja* case, that the motive clause was overbroad.

[169] For example, see the 2003 report of IPC Anne Cavourkian about hostilities against Muslims, and in cases of mistaken assumptions, against Hindus and Sikhs in Canada by individuals "retaliating" for the 9/11 attacks.

[170] This section is largely adapted from a blog post I wrote on the CCLA website entitled "Hassan Almrei: Case Spotlights Fundamental Justice Concerns of the Security Certificate Process," on March 24, 2011.

[171] Mahjoub 2010 (Federal Court) para 18.

[172] "It must be so inherently repugnant that it could never be an appropriate punishment, however egregious the offence. Torture falls into this category. The prospect of torture induces fear and its consequences may be devastating, irreversible, indeed, fatal." See, generally, E. Scarry, *The Body in Pain: The Making and Unmaking of the World* (1985), at pp. 27–59. "Torture is an instrument of terror and not of justice." *Suresh* at para. 51.

[173] *Suresh v. Canada*, supra, at para 123.

[174] Including but not limited to, in our submissions to the Office Privacy Commissioner of Canada (2014), the Universal Periodic Review

considering Canada (2012) and before the UN Committee Against Torture (2012).

[175] A version of the description of this video appeared in my piece for *The Walrus*, March, 2010. The coroner's jury recommendations can be found on CSC website: www.csc-scc.gc.ca/publications/005007-9009-eng.shtml.

[176] Curiously, the Arar Report, which once had its own website on Government of Canada website, has disappeared. Here is the redacted piece: www.pch.gc.ca/cs-kc/arar/Arar_e.pdf.

[177] Monia Mazigh's book: *Hope & Despair: My Struggle to Free My Husband, Maher Arar,* Toronto: McClelland & Stewart, 2008.

[178] The Security Intelligence Review Committee's (SIRC's) report on Arar can be found here: www.sirc-csars.gc.ca/pdfs/cm_arar_bgv1-eng.pdf.

[179] Kerry Pither, *Dark Days: The Story of Four Canadians Tortured in the Name of Fighting Terror,* Toronto: Penguin, 2008.

[180] A fascinating account of Guantanamo records: Larry Siems, *The Torture Report: What the Documents Say About America's Post-9/11 Torture Program*, New York: OR Books, 2011.

[181] Michele Shepherd, *Guantanamo's Child, The Untold Story of Omar Khadr,* Toronto: Wiley, 2008.

[182] Fundamental Freedoms is a core program for CCLA. One of the first things Alan Borovoy wrote on joining CCLA was a pamphlet called "Fundamental Freedoms," which has been revised over time. The most recent version can be found here: ccla.org/wordpress/wp-content/uploads/2010/01/fooff_e.pdf.

FURTHER READING

This is not a comprehensive reading list or bibliography. It is intended as a guide to further reading. Many of these books contain excellent bibliographies. The websites are those that were essential to the writing of this book.

Margaret Beare and Tonita Murray, eds. *Police & Government Relations: Who's Calling the Shots?*, Toronto: University of Toronto Press, 2007.

Thomas Berger, *Fragile Freedoms, Human Rights and Dissent in Canada,* Toronto: Clarke, Irwin & Co., 1982.

A. Alan Borovoy, *At the Barricades,* Toronto: Irwin Law, 2014.

_____. *The New Anti-Liberals,* Toronto: Canadian Scholars' Press, 1999.

_____. *Categorically Incorrect: Ethical Fallacies in Canada's War on Terror*, Toronto: Dundurn Press, 2008.

_____. *Uncivil Obedience: The Tactics and Tales of a Democratic Agitator,* Toronto: Lester Publishing, 1991.

_____. *When Freedoms Collide, A Case for Our Civil Liberties,* Toronto: Lester & Orpen Dennys, 1988.

Varda Burstyn, ed., *Women Against Censorship,* Vancouver: Douglas & McIntyre, 1985.

Lara Campbell, Dominique Clément, Gregory S. Kealey, eds., *Debating Dissent: Canada and the 1960s,* Toronto: University of Toronto Press, 2012.

Dominique Clément, *Canada's Rights Revolution: Social Movements and Social Change, 1937–82,* Vancouver: UBC Press, 2008.

Anne Collins, *The Big Evasion: Abortion, The Issue That Won't Go Away*, Toronto: Lester & Orpen Dennys, 1985.

Brenda Cossman at al., eds., *Bad Attitude/s On Trial: Pornography, Feminism, and the Butler Decision,* Toronto: University of Toronto Press, 1997.

Catherine Dunphy, *Morgentaler, A Difficult Hero,* Toronto: John Wiley & Sons, 2003.

Janine Fuller and Stuart Blackley, *Restricted Entry: Censorship on Trial,* Vancouver: Raincoast Books/Press Gang Publishers, 1996.

Warren Kinsella, *Web of Hate: Inside Canada's Far Right Network,* Toronto: HarperCollins, 1996.

Myrna Kostash, *Long Way from Home: The Story of the Sixties Generation in Canada,* Toronto: James Lorimer & Company, 1980.

Monia Mazigh, *Hope & Despair: My Struggle to Free My Husband, Maher Arar,* Toronto: McClelland & Stewart, 2008.

Emmett MacFarlane, *Governing from the Bench: The Supreme Court of Canada and the Judicial Role*, Vancouver: UBC Press, 2012.

F.L. Morton, *Morgentaler v. Borowski: Abortion, the Charter, and the Courts,* Toronto: McClelland & Stewart, 1992.

F.L. Morton and Rainer Knopff, *The Charter Revolution and the Court Party,* Peterborough: Broadview Press, 2000.

Bryan D. Palmer, *Canada's 1960s: The Ironies of Identity in a Rebellious Era*, Toronto: University of Toronto Press, 2008.

Andrew Petter, *The Politics of the Charter: The Illusive Promise of Constitutional Rights,* Toronto: University of Toronto Press, 2010.

Kerry Pither, *Dark Days: The Story of Four Canadians Tortured in the Name of Fighting Terror,* Toronto: Viking Canada/Penguin, 2008.

Kent Roach, *Due Process and Victims' Rights: The New Law and Politics of Criminal Justice,* Toronto: University of Toronto Press, 1999.

_____. *The Supreme Court on Trial: Judicial Activism or Democratic Dialogue,* Toronto: Irwin Law, 2001.

Frank R. Scott, *Essays on the Constitution: Aspects of Canadian Law and Politics,* Toronto: University of Toronto Press, 1977.

Michelle Shepherd, *Guantanamo's Child, The Untold Story of Omar Khadr,* Toronto: Wiley, 2008.

Larry Siems, *The Torture Report: What the Documents Say about America's Post-9/11 Torture Program,* OR Books, 2011.

Reg Whitaker, Gregory S. Kealey, and Andrew Parnaby, *Secret Service: Political Policing in Canada from the Fenians to Fortress America,* Toronto: University of Toronto Press, 2012.

Canadian Civil Liberties Association (CCLA): ccla.org

Canada's Rights Revolution: A History: www.historyofrights.com

Women's Legal Aid and Action Fund (LEAF): leaf.ca

For online research, newspapers, etc.: www.proquest.com

Supreme Court of Canada decisions are all available here:
scc-csc.lexum.com/scc-csc/en/nav.do

And here: www.canlii.org/en/ca/scc/index.html

ACKNOWLEDGEMENTS

In early 2012, I sat down with Nathalie Des Rosiers, then the CCLA general counsel, and Danielle McLaughlin, CCLA's director of education, and discussed a simple question: What kind of book would be a fitting way to celebrate the founding of CCLA in 1964? We agreed that we would like a book that was not intended only for CCLA's loyal supporters, the legal scholars and lawyers who have represented CCLA in courtrooms, and the many Canadians who have served as board members and staff and volunteers over the past fifty years. We wanted a book that could address a larger audience of readers—students of Canadian history, people young and old engaged in social and political activism (now or in recent decades), anyone who might be curious about the freedoms we have worked for and need to protect. Older readers will remember clearly galvanizing issues such as the imposition of the *War Measures Act* and abolition of the death penalty; younger Canadians may have no idea what the letters CCLA stand for, but they will identify personally with the image from the G20 2010 meeting in Toronto on the cover of this book.

I have never been a member of CCLA, but I have a longtime interest and engagement in civil liberties and social justice issues through my writing and because of my association with the writers' organization PEN—first as a president of PEN Canada (1994–95) and since 2009, as the chair of the Writers in Prison Committee of PEN International. So I brought to the book the outsider's perspective, a risky combination of curiosity, commitment, and ignorance.

The first thing I discovered was how complex and diverse the civil liberties story in Canada over the past fifty years has been, and how impossible it would be to reveal every facet of that narrative in this book. So we agreed on a selection of major stories that have been signature issues for CCLA and that have resonated with the community at large. A second volume could be made from other key themes—religion in schools, freedom of the press, and emerging concerns about immigration and citizenship. I can only apologize for errors and omissions for which I am responsible.

The second thing I learned was how essential to this story the *Charter of Rights and Freedoms* and the Supreme Court of Canada are. Quite simply, with the introduction of the Charter in 1982, everything changes. I love the Charter as a document; it is lively, demanding, and tricky; it sets up difficult dilemmas and like an especially demanding manifesto, or bible, makes those who must abide by it, meaning all of us, ask and answer difficult questions. The first two clauses, the Guarantee of Rights and Freedoms and the deceptively simple list of four Fundamental Freedoms, are the source of an endless cycle of dramas about competing and balancing rights. And then, lurking at the very end, Clause 33, the ever-threatening *deus ex machina,* the Notwithstanding Clause. My thanks to Charter expert Kent Roach for discussing the history and role of the Charter, for this book, with wisdom, energy, and dedication.

The other key player, often absent from non-legal-expert discussions on civil liberties, is the Supreme Court of Canada. Most SCC decisions get, at best, a single day's attention in the media, and then they disappear, even if they have irrevocably altered the course of a single life, or many lives, or forced politicians to confront an issue they would much prefer to sidestep. For civil liberties challenges of all kinds, it is often a very long, winding trail over time through several layers of judicial intervention, but sooner or later (usually later), the road stops at the SCC. Reading SCC decisions is a challenge for the ordinary reader, but infinitely rewarding. I felt it was essential to look closely at those decisions, which have such a profound effect on our lives, and to bring them into our consciousness. Justices talk about, research, and write tomes on single phrases such as "community standards" and as the community is truly all of us, in one decade or another, we need to pay attention to how we are defined. If there are errors of interpretation in my discussion of judicial words and decisions, they are mine alone, and I would be grateful for correction as long as it does not take the form of an SCC challenge.

During the period that I was researching this book, the issues of digital freedom, surveillance and privacy, and national security exploded worldwide. This subject also required knowledge and expertise that as a writer I do not have, and I am grateful to CCLA's general counsel, Sukanya Pillay, for writing the chapter on those issues.

I was very grateful for the support of CCLA staff and volunteers as I made my way through their history, their filing cabinets and bookcases, and the massive CCLA archive housed at Library and Archives Canada (where the staff was also admirably proactive and efficient both online and in person). I especially thank Danielle McLaughlin for her rich memory of the work and people of CCLA, Cara Zwibel, Abby Deshman, and Noa Mendelsohn Aviv for the knowledge they held at their fingertips, and Jackie Strandberg for excellent preliminary research. Alan Borovoy, Nathalie Des Rosiers, and Sukanya Pillay extended their devotion to the organization and the issues to engagement with this book. Former CCLA board members Louise Arbour, Anthony Doob, and Julian Porter and staff member Erika Abner were generous with their time and reflections. Historian Dominique Clément, a specialist in Canadian civil liberties activism, kindly read sections of the manuscript and provided sound advice.

Another invaluable source, not only for information and facts, but for revelations concerning the temper, feel, language, and passion of Canadians over fifty years was the public library and archive system, especially the online archives of *The Globe and Mail*, to which I returned constantly to get at the heart of a story. Even read digitally, a newspaper clipping—a headline, an editorial, an op-ed, a letter to the editor—rings with authenticity.

A book is no more than a complex thought bubble that expands and explodes into a lot of words in a computer file, until it is physically made into a book. In an exceptionally short time frame, Margie Wolfe and her team at Second Story Press have turned CCLA's idea for a 50th birthday project into a lively, substantial artifact; heartfelt thanks to Kathryn Cole, Kathryn White, and

Kelly Jones for editorial diligence, Melissa Kaita for imaginative design and production, and Allie Chenoweth for hours of photo research and obtaining permissions.

For support of the project through the donation of images and cartoons, CCLA and I both thank the *Toronto Star*, Canadian Lesbian and Gay Archives, Dave Rosen, Guy Badeaux, Charles Dobie, Peter Zorzi, and Terry Mosher (Aislin) for his encouragement and introduction to the McCord Museum.

For moral and intellectual support while writing this book—a writer cannot have too much of either—I thank Katherine Govier, Tony Dawson, Gail Singer, and my family, Sara Botsford and Katherine Fraser.

Marian Botsford Fraser
Toronto, ON
September 2014

INDEX

PHOTO CREDITS

Cover: Steve Russell/
GetStock.com
Page 47: The Canadian Press/
Peter Bregg
Page 50: © Peter Zorzi
Page 51 top: Frank Prazak/Frank
Prazak fonds/e010900421
Page 51: bottom: © Charles
Dobie
Page 82: Robert Cooper/
National Archives of Canada
fonds/a141503
Page 136/137: Lucas Oleniuk/
GetStock.com
Page 144: York University's
Clara Thomas Archives &
Special Collections/1974-002/
ASC06160
Page 146: York University's
Clara Thomas Archives &
Special Collections/1974-002/
ASC06159
Page 152: Library and Archives
Canada/PA-132339/Allan R.
Leishman
Page 160: © Bob Englehart
Page 170: McCord Museum
M988.176.83
Page 195: McCord Museum
M987.217.55
Page 200: © Peter Zorzi
Page 201: Dave Cooper/
GetStock.com
Page 207: Harold Barkley/
GetStock.com
Page 243: © Guy Badeaux
(Bado)
Page 252: McCord Museum
M986.283.27
Page 260: The Canadian Press
Page 261: The Canadian Press/
Barrie Davis
Page 297: Tony Bock/
GetStock.com
Page 300: © Adrian Raeside
Page 306: © Adrian Raeside
Page 314: Toronto Star/
GetStock.com
Page 321: Jessica Doria-Brown/
CBC Licensing
Page 324/325: Barry Philp/
Toronto Star
Page 346: © Ingrid Rice
Page 348: Simon Fraser
University Special Collections
MsC.KRI.2.11
Page 367: Toronto Star/
GetStock.com
Page 384: © Dave Rosen

ABOUT THE AUTHORS

MARIAN BOTSFORD FRASER is an award-winning freelance writer, broadcaster, and critic whose work has appeared in *Granta*, *The Walrus*, *The Globe and Mail*, *Literary Review of Canada*, and *Toronto Life*. She is the author of three nonfiction books—*Requiem for My Brother*; *Solitaire: The Intimate Lives of Single Women*; and *Walking the Line: Travels Along the Canadian/American Border*. Marian has won "Gold" in the National Magazine Awards and in 2009 won the CBC Literary Prize for Creative Nonfiction. She is a long-time contributor to CBC Radio's "Ideas" program, served as guest host for various CBC Radio programs and was Books Editor for Canadian *MORE* Magazine for five years. Marian is a past president of PEN Canada and currently chairs the Writers in Prison Committee of PEN International, the oldest freedom of expression advocacy organization in the world. Marian lives in Toronto. Website: www.marianbotsfordfraser.ca

SUKANYA PILLAY is General Counsel and Executive Director of the Canadian Civil Liberties Association. Previously, she has served as CCLA National Security Director, a Canadian law professor and academic, head of the witness program at Human Rights First New York, and other international positions including in-house counsel in Asia. She has written extensively on human rights, corporate social responsibility, and redress for victims; and has won research, writing and teaching awards, including the President's Award from the South Asian Bar Association and Holmes Cardozo Award for Outstanding Conference Paper from the American Institute for Legal Studies in Business. She has made documentary films broadcast on BBC World, and shown in festivals including the Human Rights Watch Film Festival New York.

KENT ROACH is Professor of Law and Prichard-Wilson Chair of Law and Public Policy at the University of Toronto. He is the author of twelve books, including *Constitutional Remedies in Canada* (winner of the Owen Prize); *Due Process and Victims' Rights* (shortlisted for the Donner Prize), *The Supreme Court on Trial* (same); (with Robert J. Sharpe) *Brian Dickson: A Judge's Journey* (winner of the Dafoe Prize) and *The 9/11 Effect: Comparative Counter-Terrorism* (winner of the Mundell Medal) as well as the Criminal Law and Charter volumes in Irwin Law's Essentials series. Elected a Fellow of the Royal Society of Canada in 2002, he was one of four academics awarded a Trudeau Fellowship in 2013. He worked on the Maher Arar and Air India Commissions. Professor Roach has represented Aboriginal and civil liberties groups in over a dozen cases at the Supreme Court of Canada and is a board member of CCLA.